MICHAEL WITTMANN

AND THE WAFFEN SS
TIGER COMMANDERS OF THE
LEIBSTANDARTE IN WORLD WAR II

VOLUME ONE

0 11557 03334 2

Other titles in the Stackpole Military History Series

MICHAEL WITTMANN

AND THE WAFFEN SS TIGER COMMANDERS OF THE LEIBSTANDARTE IN WORLD WAR II

VOLUME ONE

Patrick Agte

STACKPOLE
BOOKS

Published in 2006 by
STACKPOLE BOOKS
5067 Ritter Road
Mechanicsburg, PA 17055
www.stackpolebooks.com

www.jjfpub.mb.ca

Printed in the United States of America

10 9 8 7 6 5 4 3 2 1

FIRST EDITION

Library of Congress Cataloging-in-Publication Data

Agte, Patrick.
  [Michael Wittmann, erfolgreichster Panzerkommandant im Zweiten Weltkrieg
und die Tiger der Leibstandarte SS Adolf Hitler. English]
  Michael Wittmann and the Waffen SS Tiger commanders of the Leibstandarte
in World War II / Patrick Agte.— 1st ed.
      p. cm. — (Stackpole Military history series)
  Originally published in English under the title: Michael Wittmann and the
Tiger commanders of the Leibstandarte. 1996.
  Includes index.
  ISBN-13: 978-0-8117-3334-2
  ISBN-10: 0-8117-3334-3
  1. Waffen-SS. SS-Panzer-Division Leibstandarte SS "Adolf Hitler," 1. Tigerkom-
panie. 2. World War, 1939–1945—Regimental histories—Germany. 3. World
War, 1939–1945—Campaigns—Eastern Front. 4. World War, 1939–1945—Cam-
paigns—France. 5. Wittmann, Michael, 1914–1944. I. Agte, Patrick. Michael
Wittmann and the Tiger commanders of the Leibstandarte. II. Title. III. Series.

  D757.85.A3413 2006
  940.54'1343—dc22
                              2006008125

In dedication to Michael Wittmann,
to his comrades of the Waffen-SS,
to the fallen and the missing,
and to all those who lost their lives in
imprisonment and internment,
in honor and with gratitude.

Wanderer, who can still see the sun,
greet the homeland,
which we loved more than life itself.

—ABOVE THE ENTRANCE GATE TO A
GERMAN HONORARY CEMETERY IN FRANCE.

Table of Contents

Preface

In this book the history of a panzer company of the 1st SS Panzer Division Leibstandarte SS Adolf Hitler and the later heavy panzer battalion of the Ist SS Panzer Corps will be traced for the first time. The organizational and operational history of the Tiger Company and the Tiger Battalion is the focal point of this work of military history. The units that fought together with and alongside the Tigers were predominantly those of the 1st SS Panzer Division Leibstandarte SS Adolf Hitler and of the 12th SS Panzer Division Hitlerjugend. It is inevitable that within the realm of tank operations the outstanding feats and successes of the Tiger tanks cannot be described alone; the actions of the units that participated with them in the offensive and defensive actions must be depicted as well.

From the beginning of its formation in December 1942, the reader will relive each day with the 4th, later redesignated 13th (Heavy), Company, 1st SS Panzer Regiment and follow it on all its paths. From the winter action at Kharkov in February 1943, and the great Zitadelle offensive in July 1943, its path led into crisis-rocked Italy in the summer of 1943. As a result of the increasingly serious situation, in November 1943 the 13th Company was sent back to the Eastern Front with the units of the Leibstandarte. Here the reader will observe the endless battles in the area of Kiev, Zhitomir, Berdichev and Korosten and experience the unique successes achieved by the company. Michael Wittmann continued his impressive run of success there and within a few days in 1944 was decorated with the Knights Cross and then with the Oak Leaves.

The shrunken company's battles at the Cherkassy Pocket and with the remnant units in the Hube Pocket in April 1944 are described. This is followed by a detailed description of the establishment of the 101st SS Panzer Battalion in Germany, Italy, France and Belgium, including biographies of all officers and those who held positions of responsibility in the battalion. The reader subsequently takes part in the invasion battle in Normandy, experiencing all the highs and lows, sees the reorganization in Germany in autumn 1944, and goes with the 501st SS Panzer Battalion into the

Ardennes offensive in December 1944. In February 1945 he is a witness to the actions in the Gran bridgehead and the Lake Balaton offensive in Hungary, and from March to May 1945 the fighting withdrawal back to Reich territory and the final battles in Austria.

Detailed descriptions are provided of all wearers of the Knight's Cross, the German Cross in Gold and the Honor Roll Clasp with the justification for each decoration. The photographic material, the vast majority of which has never before been published, is drawn largely from private sources. The command structure lists, which were prepared with great care, may be unique in their completeness and organization. The command structure of the 13th Panzer Company is listed for three fixed dates, 1 February 1943, 5 July 1943 and 1 November 1943. A similar table of organization was produced for the 501st SS Panzer Battalion for the fixed dates 6 June 1944 and 16 December 1944. As well, a command structure list covering the entire period of their existence with all changes is included. The chronicle is rounded out with detailed descriptions and technical data on the Tiger I and II.

This work is bound together with the story of the most successful tank commander of the Second World War. SS-Hauptsturmführer Michael Wittmann. The environment in which Michael Wittmann achieved his legendary successes will be revealed to the reader and in the end he will come to see the man Wittmann, who stood behind everything but who in all previous treatments has been depicted too superficially. Named in addition to Wittmann are many unknown tank men who first made possible the unit's success. With its five winners of the Knight's Cross—Staudegger, Wittmann, Woll, Wendorff and Kling, Wittmann receiving the Oak Leaves within two weeks—the 13th Company, 1st SS Panzer Regiment Leibstandarte was not only the company with the most high-ranking decorations for bravery in the Leibstandarte, but within the entire Waffen-SS. Kling also received the German Cross in Gold. While serving with the 501st SS Panzer Battalion Wittmann was awarded the Knight's Cross with Oak Leaves and Swords. Dr. Wolfgang Rabe, Jürgen Brandt and Thomas Amselgruber received the German Cross in Gold, while Hannes Philipsen was awarded the Honor Roll Clasp. It is hoped that this book will help preserve the memories of those men who did not have the inestimable luck to be allowed to return home from this war.

Michael Wittmann is one of the best known and most popular German soldiers outside of Germany. What distinguished him, apart from the masterly precision with which he achieved his combat successes, his meticulousness, his sophisticated tactics, his courage and skill, was the humanity and comradeship he practiced, which were valued by all. Receiving the Knight's Cross with Oak Leaves and Swords did not change him. He remained the quiet, ever deliberate, tactically-sound tank commander who was the acknowledged role model of every man in all situations, radiating security and trust. He was loved and respected by his soldiers and he took the men under his command into his heart and with them formed a close-knit fighting team equal to any demand placed upon it. Michael Wittmann is dead, fallen on 8 August 1944 in a field in Normandy. In the Tiger Battalion this is considered the blackest day in its history.

The reader can judge for himself what lies behind the myth of the Tiger Company and the Tiger Battalion of the Leibstandarte. The men had the best tank of their day and were exceptionally well trained on it. The members of the Tiger Battalion never considered themselves as something better, although they knew that their high command placed special hopes in them. There were no extra privileges. As a corps Tiger battalion they were constantly thrown into the hot spots of the Normandy battle, often they had to lead the way through concentrated defensive fire and were the backbone of the defense as well. In this book the men who manned the Tigers of the Leibstandarte are raised up from their anonymity, they are described as they gave their best, often their young lives, in their tanks over the years. The reader sees the men of this elite unit over two years of their hopeful lives, their laughs, battles and victories, their suffering and dying. That's how they were, the men of the Leibstandarte Tigers.

The information contained in this book was carefully researched and all available original documents were evaluated accordingly. As well, there were diary entries and recollections by former members of the Tiger Company and the Tiger Battalion. Letters, casualty and award lists and other archival material helped complete the effort. The statements by survivors were also made use of. The effort required to have each account confirmed by at least one other participant and thus achieve the maximum balance, was worthwhile. The existing literature was studied critically. Several previous publications were contradicted. The author employed the primary sources in all accounts relating to the actions of the Tiger Company or the Tiger Battalion. If these could not be established with certainty or the accounts did not agree with the information I had already compiled, they were dispensed with. All accounts in this book are verifiable and are of great military-historical significance in this documentation.

I owe special thanks to Frau Hildegard Helmke, Rolf Schamp, Walter Lau and Werner Wendt. I was able to evaluate diary notes by Rolf Schamp and Bobby Warmbrunn, both of whom I thank. For their help I also wish to thank Leopold Aumüller, Ernst Kufner, Alfred Lünser, Alfred Lasar, Waldemar Schütz, Waldemar Warnecke, Hubert Heil, Kurt Fickert, Franz Staudegger, Willi Schenk, Matthias Philipsen, Kurt Stamm, Gustav Reimers, Elisabeth von Westernhagen and Mathilde Kalinowsky.

Patrick Agte

Publisher's Acknowledgments

We wish to thank the following individuals who have contributed to the publishing of this book: David Johnston—Translation; George Bradford—Graphics and Organigrams; and Brian Molloy—Signing Box.

We also wish to thank you the reader for purchasing this book, and all those of you who have purchased our other books, and have written us with your kind words of praise and encouragement. It gives us impetus to continue to publish translations of the best German books and specially commissioned books, as you can see by the additional books which are in preparation for publication in the near future. Other titles are either being negotiated or seriously contemplated, many as a result of your helpful proposals.

John Fedorowicz & Michael Olive

Introduction

In the literature concerning the war, differing source material has produced varying histories of the thirteen German heavy panzer battalions which saw front-line duty wherever the action was the most intense. No operational accounts of the 501st SS Panzer Battalion have been handed down. This was sufficient cause for the author to establish contact with the few surviving former members of the Tiger unit and to use all available archives to chronicle their history. His efforts received vital support from the personal recollections of the former tank commanders, gunners, loaders, tank drivers and radio operators of the heavy tanks. They were there: in the winter of 1943 at Kharkov, in the summer of 1943 in the Kursk offensive, known as Operation Zitadelle, after November 1943 at Kiev and Zhitomir, at the Cherkassy and Hube Pockets; in the summer of 1944 between Caen and Falaise, in December 1944 in the Ardennes, in 1945 in Hungary and Austria. Complementing these accounts of wartime events and the personal recollections of the tank crews are numerous photographs, the majority of which come from the personal collections of the former tank crews of this unit. Charts and battle maps depict the unit's organization, its movements and operations.

Special attention will be paid to the career of Michael Wittmann, his exemplary personality and his outstanding achievements—and justifiably so, for he was the most successful tank commander of the second World War. He is recognized as such in German as well as in international histories of the war. Wittmann was a member of the Tiger unit from the day of its birth until his soldier's death in Normandy on 8 August 1944 while commander of the 101st SS Heavy Panzer Battalion. It will be appreciated that his qualities as a human and a military leader receive an exhaustive examination and that his feats of daring—free from inaccurate descriptions—are retold the way they actually happened by comrades who were at his side. Michael Wittmann and the four Knight's Cross wearers who came from the Tiger company of the Leibstandarte, together with the young tank crews, undoubtedly placed their stamp on the spirit and conduct of this unit: fulfillment of duty to the Fatherland to the end.

But who were these young tank crews, who fought, suffered and—many of them—died? They were predominantly young men from the 1923–25 age class, though later in the war they were joined by members of the class of 1926–27. Their grandfathers had fought at Sedan and Mars-la-Tour in 1870–71, and their fathers at Verdun, the Argonne Forest and in Flanders in 1914–18. These young men were familiar with the story of Tannenburg from their history lessons. Therefore to many of them the soldierly fulfillment of duty was already a familiar traditional concept.

When Germany was placed in great danger in the Second World War, it was a matter of course for the nation's youth to volunteer to defend their homeland. Full of idealism, the young men rallied to the flag. With the utmost willingness and devotion they fought and suffered through the pitiless struggle and cruel weather conditions in the east and endured the crushing material superiority of the enemy in the west. And—provided they managed to escape with their lives, the statistics on birth years 1923 to 1926 tell the story—they sacrificed, including while being held as prisoners of war, the best years of their lives.

These young men were led and magnificently trained by officers and non-commissioned officers who had proved themselves while serving with the Leibstandarte in the years before the formation of the Tiger Company. Their leaders and acknowledged role models were men such as Standartenführer Peiper, Obersturmführer Wendorff, Sturmbanführer Kling, Obersturmführer Philipsen and the incomparable Michael Wittmann. With their military skill and their human and moral qualities, they and the veteran NCOs—men such as Hauptscharführer Hartel, Hauptscharführer Höflinger, Hauptscharführer Lötzsch, Oberscharführer Woll and Sowa, and Standartenjunker Staudegger, for example—made a quite significant contribution to the success of these young men, whose mastery of military technology, exemplary willingness and bravery enabled them to prove themselves wherever they saw action. The tank crews developed a feeling of combat superiority, undoubtedly created and enhanced by the awareness that they were capable of operating the best and most potent tanks in the world. Countless times they had been forced to match themselves against the KV I and II, the T 34, the Sherman and Cromwell, and the enemy's other tanks and self-propelled guns and they knew the quality of their Tiger. It was an acknowledgement of this fact when a senior British officer once said that in Normandy they had to send five Shermans into battle in order to be able to effectively combat a single Tiger.

Truly, German youth from every district in Germany was represented in the Leibstandarte Tiger Battalion. Every dialect was to be heard. Berliners and Rhinelanders, many from Ostmark (Austria), Silesia, East Prussia,

Pomerania and Holstein, as well as men from Alsace and the Sudetenland were there—no German countryman lacked a representative—and ethnic Germans from the Baltic States and the Balkans. And so during the infrequent quiet hours in the Ukraine, in Italy, and in Normandy, the songs of home, from Tirol to the Waterkant, from Silesia to the Saar, were played on accordions and harmonicas. To the young men of today it may seem unbelievable that those young tank soldiers, who faced death every day, indeed every hour, nevertheless found time for humor, fun and games, as is revealed in the accounts contained in this chronicle. On the one hand this is surely attributable to their youth, but on the other hand one must imagine what it meant to a man's state of mind when, after days and nights of tank battles, fighter-bomber attacks and carpet bombing, artillery and naval bombardments, and anti-tank fire, to suddenly have to go to the workshop for three or four days due to mechanical trouble or battle damage. That meant bivouacking in a tent for three or four days in the magnificent summer landscape of Normandy a few kilometers behind the front. One was able to wash, shave, put on clean clothes, write letters, enjoy extra food for a few days, do whatever he liked. Then youthful high spirits rose up, finding expression in a harmonica or a game of soccer. Such hours spent in one's circle of comrades, with whom one had in the truest sense of the word gone through fire and death, do not wither in one's memory.

Common to them all was the readiness to give their best in action, even their young lives if it came to that. When the order "come to battle readiness" was given, when the gun was unlocked and the pistols were cocked, every man knew that it might be his turn, that when the panzers came back to refuel and rearm he might be hanging from the tank in a tent square, to be buried in foreign soil by his comrades. Even this last honor could not be paid to every man who fell, if the knocked-out tank burned or was left stranded in the enemy lines. That is what happened to Unterscharführer Langner, who shot himself in the Sabolot area in December 1943 when Red Army soldiers climbed onto his tank. His comrades were able to observe his fate through a scissors telescope but could not prevent it. Or the fate of Knight's Cross wearer Obersturmführer Wendorff and his radio operator and loader. The notation in the casualty list read "believed fatally wounded." Or Sturmmann Erlander, the short, blonde tank driver from Alsace, whose tank was immobilized by a hit in the running gear. Though his commander, Untersturmführer Hantusch, forbade him to leave the tank, he climbed out to repair the damage under enemy fire. The tank was struck by another shell; no trace of Erlander was ever found. Or loader Paul Sümnich, who had both legs blown off by an anti-tank round while attempting to attach tow cables to Obersturmführer

Wendorff's disabled tank near Grimbosq on the River Orne. And another veteran loader, Günter Boldt, only nineteen years old but in service since 1942, who, at Hill 112, managed to jump from his burning tank in spite of the loss of both his feet and stumble several meters across a Norman field. He is buried at the La Cambe military cemetery. There were many such soldiers' fates in our Tiger Battalion. To them loyalty to the Fatherland was more than empty words. Those who were there will never forget the fallen and missing and wish to take care to see that future generations, too, will honor the memory of the fallen and their devotion to Germany.

Walter Lau
SS-Rottenführer and gunner
in the 13th (Heavy) Company,
1st SS Panzer Regiment Leibstandarte SS Adolf Hitler and the 2nd
Company, 501st SS Panzer Battalion

Development of
the German Panzer Arm

CALLS FROM THE FRONT FOR A GERMAN HEAVY TANK

German Military Superiority in the campaigns against Poland in 1939, Belgium and France in 1940, and in the Balkans in 1941, was based on the revolutionary operational tactics of the panzer divisions. Instead of employing tanks as infantry support weapons, as was the rule in other armies at that time, the German Army used them as weapons of breakthrough, striking deep into enemy territory and taking their opponents by surprise. Together with the Luftwaffe and fast-moving infantry, the flexibly-led German panzer arm was the guarantor of success.

When they invaded the Soviet Union in 1941 the German armed forces encountered Soviet battle tanks, the KV I and especially the T 34, which were superior to German tanks in many ways. The Soviet tanks were more heavily armored, had longer-ranging guns and more robust engines. The inability of the Panzer IV's short-barrelled 75 mm gun to penetrate the frontal armor of the KV I and KV II came as a great surprise. Moreover, the 76.2 mm gun of the T 34 was superior to German tank cannon, not only in range, but in penetrative power as well. Only the superior tactics and training of the German tank crews allowed them to succeed against this technically superior opponent.

German reaction was immediate. The short-barrelled 75 mm gun of the Panzer IV was replaced by a long-barrelled 75 mm weapon, which offered a flatter trajectory and improved accuracy as well as increased penetrative power. Nevertheless, the front was calling for a heavy tank with an even more powerful gun, better armor and improved off-road mobility.

THE BIRTH OF THE TIGER TANK

Efforts to build a heavy tank began in Germany in 1937 and were intensified in early 1941. Development of a heavy battle tank was assigned to the firm of Henschel and Son in the years before the war; prototypes were

1

built but these were not up to requirements. In early 1941 Henschel, MAN, Daimler-Benz and Porsche were instructed to design a thirty-tonne tank, which was to be armed with the 75 mm Kampfwagenkanone L/24, the 75 mm Kampfwagenkanone L/48 (long-barrelled), or the 105 mm Kampfwagenkanone L/28. At a conference at the Berghof on the Obersalzburg in Berchtesgaden Hitler declared to a circle of officers and representatives of the armaments industry that the new development must combine heavier armor and an improved gun with better penetrative ability: "We must create vehicles that first have better penetrative ability against enemy tanks, second are more heavily armored and third have a speed of not less than 40 kph!"

The frontal armor of the future tank was to be ten centimeters thick and the side armor six; drive and idler wheels were to be armored as well. The Henschel Company attempted to install the Kampfwagen-kanone 0725 in the turret of its prototype, while Porsche turned to the well-proven 88 mm gun. The VK 3001 project, which was designated the same for all participating firms, was renamed VK 4501. The name "Tiger" began to be used internally soon afterward.

The naming of German battle tanks after predatory cats continues to this day. The Tiger, Panther and Marder (marten) of the Second World War have been succeeded in Bundeswehr service by the Gepard (cheetah), Luchs (lynx) and the famous Leopard, the best battle tank in service today.

TECHNICAL DEVELOPMENT OF THE TIGER

At the Henschel-Werk in Kassel development of the Tiger was carried out under the highest priority. Under the direction of von Heyking, whom Oskar Henschel named "Commissar for Tiger Production", the first prototype was completed by 20 April 1942.

The Tiger surpassed all the previous norms. 4.93 meters long and weighing 1,310 kilograms, the mighty 88 mm main gun, which had a servicing radius of 1.82 meters, was installed in the fighting compartment after the upper hull had been widened to a point over the tracks. The addition of a third roadwheel and further weight increases made it necessary to increase the width of the tracks from 52 to 72.5 centimeters. Consequently the Tiger could not be transported on standard rail cars. The Reichsbahn (state railroad) acquired 270 Ssyms special flatcars, which were designed for loads of up to 82 tonnes. As well, for transport by train the Tiger had to use special, narrower tracks, which were removed when the tank was unloaded. The Tiger was also equipped with a completely new hydraulic steering system and a semi-automatic transmission. On 20 April 1942,

Hitler's birthday, the Henschel and Porsche prototypes were demonstrated to the Führer at his Wolfsschanze Headquarters.

The testing of both tanks progressed satisfactorily in spite of some minor problems. Although the Porsche Tiger seemed to have the more serious shortcomings, Hitler appeared to favor it initially. A definitive decision as to which company should build the Tiger was postponed. Reichsminister Speer instructed the liaison officer between the Commander of the Replacement Army and himself, Knight's Cross wearer Oberst Thomale, to ascertain which of the prototypes was the more promising. Beginning in May 1942, several Porsche and Henschel Tigers were sent to the Berka Troop Training Grounds for service trials. A committee of experts was formed under the leadership of Oberst Thomale and Professor Ing. von Eberan. Thomale evaluated the Tiger from the point of view of a front-line soldier, while Professor von Eberan, an experienced member of the Dresden Technical Institute, scrutinized the panzers' technical efficiency.

After extensive checks and endurance tests the Henschel Tiger was the unanimous choice. One of the deciding factors in its favor was its greater ease of maintenance; the Porsche Tiger employed a novel type of electric drive that would be difficult for the front-line repair services to maintain. Oberst Thomale reported the evaluation committee's findings to Hitler. Henschel subsequently received the contract to produce the Tiger. The Tiger represented the apex of German technology and went from the drawing board to production in a very short time. Its complete designation was Tiger I, Ausführungl E, VK 4501 (H), Sd.Kfz. 181.

The Tiger weighed 56.9 tonnes. Frontal armor was 10 centimeters thick, the side armor 8 centimeters, turret and rear armor 10 centimeters. The gun mantlet was 12 centimeters thick. A total of 92 rounds of ammunition for the 88mm Kampfwagenkanone 36/L 56 could be stowed in the turret. The tank was also armed with two MG 34 machine-guns. Four tanks held a combined total of 534 liters of fuel. The Tiger's engine burned 900 to 935 liters of fuel per 100 kilometers off-road, 500 to 534 liters per 100 kilometers on-road. Cruising speed in medium terrain was approximately 15 kph, on the road 20 kph. Maximum speed was 35 kph.

The first 495 Tigers possessed a fording ability of four meters. The prototype 0725 gun had a conical barrel which tapered toward the muzzle. As it used only tungsten solid-shot projectiles and tungsten was not available in sufficient quantities, Henschel called off the experiments. In the meantime Professor Porsche had Krupp convert its 88 mm Flak into a tank gun and at the same time design a turret to accommodate it. The 88 mm weapon was the first German tank cannon to incorporate a double-action muzzle brake.

The result was the 88 mm Kampfwagenkanone (Kwk) 36 L/56. It was Hitler's intention that Henschel and Porsche should develop the VK 4501 project independently. Design work at Porsche was headed by Professor Dr. Ferdinand Porsche, while at Henschel Dr. habil. Ernst Aders was responsible for designing the Tiger.

On 6 February 1945 Aders described his work: "There was great consternation in July 1941 when it was discovered that the Russian Army was equipped with the T 34 and even heavier tanks which were superior to anything the Wehrmacht could field against them. The 36-tonne VK 3601, for which no turret had yet been developed, was still in the experimental stage. However, it was possible to borrow important components from it and apply them to the Tiger E, at that time still the VK 4501, whose design was finalized in mid-year. The components in question were the steering mechanism, reduction gear (final drive) units, and running gear with idler and drive wheels. Three weeks after design work began, the steel works were given the program for the sheet steel for the hull. Two months later the steel works received factory drawings of the most important armor plates. The project was complicated by several special requests from the HWA (Heereswaffenamt, or Army Ordnance Office). These included the ability to ford bodies of water up to 4.5 meters deep. As well, the tracks were supposed to be protected by armored skirts which could be raised and lowered when the tank was driving on level ground. Once the entire vehicle had been worked out in detail a total weight of 58 tonnes was calculated and it was determined that the new solid rubber tires for the roadwheels would not be equal to this load over the long run. It was thus necessary to increase the number of rubber tires per wheel from two to three. A design solution had to be found for this too.

In mid-1941 the initial production series was fixed at 60 vehicles and materials for 100 were procured (at the insistence of Henschel on account of minimum procurement levels), however in the course of the month the size of the order grew to 100. Orders were placed for materials and funds for the ultimate construction of 1,300 tanks, including spares, without even one vehicle being available for test purposes.

The following components had to be developed specially for the Tiger E:

- The cooling system outside the engine compartment: two radiators with four cooling fans—in an untried new arrangement—and armored grates, as well as watertight engine compartment cover plates;

- Cooling system for the exhaust headers, which also served to cool the transmission;
- Turret drive from the main cardan shaft;
- The fuel system, consisting of four tanks, two of which had to be equipped for fording to a depth of 4.5 meters;
- The air intake for use while submerged, which had to be capable of being disassembled;
- The arrangement of shock absorbers and mounts for the front and rear roadwheel cranks;
- Stowage of 92 rounds of 88 mm ammunition (this had to be redesigned, as the first solution was based on inaccurate data);
- Internal and external mounts for accessories and items of equipment;
- The radio installation with antenna arrangement (a special antenna was later developed for command tanks);
- Optional dust filters for desert operations;
- Close-combat grenades on the roof (an electrically-ignited launcher for three grenades or smoke candles was in fact later fitted on each side of the turret);
- Hydraulically-operated armored skirts, raising and lowering mechanism with control unit and high-pressure oil pump system;
- A bilge pump system for use while submerged;
- Supplemental drive for the cooling fan system (beginning with the 250th vehicle, in order to match that of the Panther's engine).

The following equipment and components were developed by other firms:

Engine:	Maybach Motorenbau
Transmission OG 4 G 1216:	Maybach Motorenbau
Tracks:	Ritscher-Moorburg
Brakes:	Süddeutsche Argus-Werke
Armored turret and gun:	Friedrich Krupp AG
Machine-gun ball mount:	Daimler-Benz AG
Driver's visor:	Alkett, Berlin

By supplementing the available designing engineers and draftsmen with personnel from other departments of H&S (Locomotive and Auto Manufacture), and through the use of conscripted labor, it was possible to accelerate the work so that the first new-production vehicle could be demonstrated to Hitler at Führer Headquarters on 20 April 1942. The efforts made by the materials procurement offices and workshops, from the pattern makers and metal workers to the machining departments, and the personal sacrifices of the engineers and workers could provide the material for a small book. The final days and nights leading up to loading day were spent in nonstop work, during which the fitters, foremen and engineers went without sleep. This achievement and the cooperation of design, procurement and manufacturing is unique and unlikely to be repeated or surpassed. It is no surprise given the rushed mode of operation that production did not immediately proceed in a satisfactory manner, and at first there could be no consideration of economical production. Nevertheless, since series production was achieved right off the bat after relatively insignificant interruptions for modifications, it may be said that this was due to the reasonable cooperation among the participating offices. Of course, it remains to be said that in this respect many requests went unfulfilled. To have geared up for the type of mass production the Americans, as well as the Russians, appeared to be pursuing, would have meant recommending a radical revision of production plans which, instead of the actual nine months, would have required about twenty-four to thirty months."

There were three versions of the Tiger E, most easily identified by changes to the commander's cupola. The cupola of the initial version was bolted on and was very tall, that of the second was welded on and was lower. The twin headlights of the initial version were replaced by a single headlight in the center of the hull. The ultimate version had thirty-two steel roadwheels in place of the forty-eight rubber-capped roadwheels of the two earlier versions. The 1st SS-Panzer Regiment's 13th (Heavy) Company used both early versions operationally, while the 101st SS Heavy Panzer Battalion was equipped with the second and third versions. Henschel built a total of 1,355 Tiger I tanks from April 1942 to August 1944. The first Tiger bore the chassis number 250001. In the beginning three smoke candle dischargers were fitted on the left side of the turret. Ignited electrically from inside the tank, they enabled the tank to pull back from the enemy under cover of smoke. Internal communications were by way of an intercom system linking all members of the crew. Each crewman wore a throat-type microphone. Tigers were employed in independent heavy panzer battalions; few divisions included a Tiger company in their panzer regiments. The Tiger battalions were assigned to armies or corps, which instructed them to support or attached them to the units under their command. Sent wherever the fighting was heaviest, the Tigers fought on every front, including North Africa.

Generaloberst Heinz Guderian, creator and molder of the German panzer arm.

SS-Oberstgruppenführer Generaloberst der Waffen-SS Josef (Sepp) Dietrich, founder and father figure of the Leibstandarte SS Adolf Hitler.

SS-Hauptsturmführer Michael Wittmann. Most successful tank commander of the Second World War.

Tigers of the 101st SS Heavy Panzer Battalion on the training grounds, spring 1944.

Tiger on the training grounds.

A Tiger of the 2nd Company, 101st SS Panzer Battalion in a wooded area offering excellent cover.

SS-Hauptsturmführer Heinz Kling, from December 1942 commander of the 4th (Heavy) Company, SS Panzer Regiment Leibstandarte SS Adolf Hitler.

SS-Obersturmführer Waldemar Schütz, commander of the Ist Platoon and deputy to the company commander.

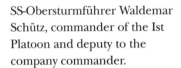

SS-Untersturmführer Helmut Wendorff, commander of the IInd Platoon.

SS-Untersturmführer Hannes
Philipsen, commander of
the IIIrd Platoon.

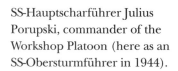

SS-Untersturmführer Michael
Wittmann, commander of
the Light Platoon.

SS-Hauptscharführer Julius
Porupski, commander of the
Workshop Platoon (here as an
SS-Obersturmführer in 1944).

TECHNICAL DATA:
PANZERKAMPFWAGEN VI—TIGER I AND II

DESIGNATION	Tiger I, Ausf. E	Tiger II, Ausf. B
	Sd. Kfz. 181	Sd. Kfz. 182
MANUFACTURER	Henschel & Sohn	Henschel & Sohn
		(Final Assembly)
Combat Weight:	56.9 t	67.7 t
Crew:	5 men	5 men
Armament (Gun, caliber, caliber length, ammunition):	1—88 mm KwK 36 L/56	1—88 mm KwK 43 L/71
Turret Machine-gun:	1 MG 34, 7.92 mm	1 MG 34, 7.92 mm
Bow (radio operator) machine-gun:	1 MG 34, 7.92 mm	1 MG 34, 7.92 mm
Submachine-guns:	1 MP 40, 9 mm	1 MP 40, 9 mm
Ammunition Capacities:		
AP and HE Shells:	92	72–84
MG Ammunition:	3920–4500	5850
SMG Ammunition:	192	192
Firepower-Penetrative Ability:		
AP Shell: Weight	10 kg	10.4 kg
Muzzle Velocity	810 m/sec	ca. 1000 m/sec
Armor Penetration at		
500 meters range:	140 mm	205 mm
1000 meters range:	122 mm	186 mm
1500 meters range:	108 mm	170 mm
2000 meters range:	92 mm	154 mm
2500 meters range:	82 mm	140 mm
Armor Protection—Hull (mm/degrees of slope):		
Bow:	100/66	100/40
Glacis:	100/80	150/40
Side, Lower:	60/90	80/90
Side, Upper:	80/90	80/65
Rear:	82/82	80/60
Hull Roof:	26 mm	40 mm
Hull Floor:	26 mm	25–40 mm
Armor Protection—Turret:		
Mantlet:	110/90	80 mm conical
Turret Side:	80/90	80/69
Turret Rear:	80/90	80/70
Turret Roof:	26/0-9	44/0–10
Maximum Speed:	38–45 kph	38 kph
Cruising Speed:		
Roads:	ca. 20 kph	15–20 kph
Medium Terrain:	ca. 15 kph	ca. 15 kph
Radius of Action:		
Roads:	ca. 100–110 km	ca. 130–140 km
Medium Terrain:	ca. 60 km	ca. 85-90 km

TECHNICAL DATA:
PANZERKAMPFWAGEN VI—TIGER I AND II

DESIGNATION	Tiger I, Ausf. E	Tiger II, Ausf. B
	Sd. Kfz. 181	Sd. Kfz. 182
MANUFACTURER	Henschel & Sohn	Henschel & Sohn
		(Final Assembly)
Fuel Capacity:	534 1	860 1
Fuel Consumption:		
per 100 km on roads:	ca. 500–534 1	ca. 600–650 1
per 100 km off roads:	ca. 900–935 1	ca. 1000 1
Performance:		
Ground Pressure:	1.088 kg/cm2	1.037 kg/cm2
Power-to-Weight Ratio (based on		
engine model and rpm):	12.3 HP/t (10.5)	10.1 HP/t (8.6)
Ground Clearance:	47 cm	49 cm
Trench Clearing Ability:	2.30 m	2.50 m
Climbing Ability:	0.80 m	0.85 m
Fording Ability (4 m with submersible		
equipment):	1.20 m	1.60 m
Dimensions, Length:		
Overall, barrel forward:	8.241 m	10.286 m
Overall, barrel to rear:	8.350 m	9.966 m
Overall, no barrel overhang:	6.200 m	7.734 m
Barrel overhang forward:	2.040 m	2.912 m
Length of Track in Contact with		
Ground:	3.605 m	4.300 m
Dimensions, Width:		
Overall:	3.705 m	3.755 m
Over the Tracks:	3.560 m	3.590 m
Wheelbase:	2.822 m	2.790 m
Battle Tracks:	0.725 m	0.800 m
Transport Tracks:	0.520 m	0.600 m
Interior Hull Width:	1.800 m	1.760 m
Working Area in Turret:	1.790 m	1.850 m
Dimensions, height:		
Overall:	2.880 m (3.00 m)	3.075 m
Axis Height of Gun:	2.195 m	2.250 m
Engine and Transmission:	Tiger I	Tiger II
Engine (Gasoline)	Maybach HL 230 P 45	Maybach HL 230 P 30
	(1st 250 with Maybach HL 210 P 435)	
Engine Output at:	600 HP at 2500 rpm	700 HP at 2500 rpm
Engine Output at:	700 HP at 3000 rpm	700 HP at 3000 rpm
Number of Cylinders/Arrangement:	12/V	12/V
Piston Displacement cm3/Cooling	23.880 (21.353) water	23.880 water
Transmission Type:	Preselector	Preselector
	Olvar 40 12 16	Olvar 40 12 16 B

TECHNICAL DATA:
PANZERKAMPFWAGEN VI—TIGER I AND II

	Tiger I, Ausf. E	Tiger II, Ausf. B
DESIGNATION	Sd. Kfz. 181	Sd. Kfz. 182
MANUFACTURER	Henschel & Sohn	Henschel & Sohn (Final Assembly)
Number of Gears:	8 forward, 4 reverse	8 forward, 4 reverse

Hull and Revolving Turret:

Independent armored hull, armored superstructure with revolving turret, powered by vehicle engine.

Running Gear, Steering and Brakes:
Tiger I

2 tracks each with 96 links (spacing 130mm) Drive sprocket forward idler wheel aft. 8 large triple road-wheels each side in an interleaved arrangement: total of 48 roadwheels. Hydraulic, double-radius steering, controlled by steering wheel. Drive sprocket with hydraulically-activated Argus disc brakes.

Running Gear, Steering and Brakes:
Tiger II

2 tracks each with 96 links (spacing 130 mm) Drive sprocket forward idler wheel aft. 9 large double road-wheels each side in an overlapping arrangement: Hydraulic, double-radius steering, controlled by steering wheel. Drive sprocket with hydraulically-activated Argus disc brakes.

Telescopic Sight:	TZF 9 b	T Z F 9 b/1, later 1/d
Directional Guidance:	1 directional gyro	1 directional gyro
Internal Communications:	1 intercom	1 intercom
Radio equipment:	Ultra short wave transmitter and receiver	Ultra short wave transmitter and receiver

(Some command tanks specially equipped: turret MG deleted, loader served as second radio operator.)

Sources:
Wa Prüf 6, 1943, Die Tigerfibel D 656/27 (crew operations manual)
Wa Prüf 6, 1944, technische Daten von Panzerkampfwagen. Bundesarchiv
von Senger und Etterlin: Die deutschen Panzer 1926–1945
von Senger und Etterlin: Kampfpanzer 1916–1966

Tiger Units of the Waffen SS

Formation of a heavy panzer battalion for the SS Panzer Corps was planned for 1942. This plan was overturned in December 1942 and instead the divisions of the panzer corps—the Leibstandarte SS Adolf Hitler, Das Reich and Totenkopf—each received their own Tiger company. Organization of the companies differed, however. Initially each of the Tiger companies included a light platoon, which, equipped with Panzer IIIs, was supposed to protect the heavy tanks against close range threats.

Following the formation of further SS-Panzer Corps, the Tigers of the Waffen-SS were also concentrated into independent battalions which were permanent components of the corps. The Tiger companies of the Leibstandarte and Das Reich were removed from their respective panzer regiments and assigned to the panzer battalions of the Ist and IInd SS Panzer Corps as they were formed. The Ist, IInd and IIIrd SS Panzer Corps received Tiger battalions, but the IVth SS Panzer Corps, which included the Totenkopf and Wiking Divisions, could not be so equipped before the war ended. A Tiger company fought as part of the Totenkopf Division's panzer regiment until the end of the war.

The 4th Company of the Leibstandarte Division's panzer regiment was equipped with the Tiger in January 1943. The other two division's of Hausser's SS Panzer Corps, Totenkopf and Das Reich, also received their first Tigers at this time.

FORMATION OF THE TIGER COMPANY OF THE LEIBSTANDARTE SS ADOLF HITLER

The senior unit of the Waffen-SS, the Leibstandarte SS Adolf Hitler, had participated in the campaigns in Poland, Holland, Belgium, France, the Balkans and the Soviet Union; however, until the summer of 1942 it was no more than a reinforced regiment or brigade.

Not until after the campaign in France was the LAH expanded to include its own anti-tank, flak and pioneer units, an assault gun battery, a further artillery battalion and a reconnaissance battalion. A fourth infantry battalion was added to the Leibstandarte prior to the invasion of the Soviet Union; when Barbarossa began SS-Obergruppenführer Sepp Dietrich had under his command four infantry battalions, a heavy battalion with light and heavy infantry gun companies, and an anti-tank battalion with 50mm guns. As well there was the Schönberger Battalion, a company of self-propelled 47mm anti-tank guns and the assault gun battery, the light flak battalion and the artillery regiment, which was only two battalions strong. In June 1941the Leibstandarte was equivalent to a reinforced regiment.

The Leibstandarte already enjoyed a legendary reputation and was acclaimed, though never by itself, as the premier military unit of the German Reich. Consequently, the corps in command of the Leibstandarte tended to assign it tasks that would normally have been given to division-size units. The myth that had been woven about the unit brought no advantages—on the contrary, it was required to prove its reputation over and over again in difficult actions. There is no doubt that the Leibstandarte stood the test, but losses among the companies were correspondingly high.

As the only armored formation, the assault gun battery was employed in penny packets, usually in platoon strength but sometimes as single guns, in support of every unit of the Leibstandarte and fought with outstanding success. This battery produced many outstanding and highly-decorated officers and NCOs. The unit commanders would have been all too glad to see more assault guns with their front-line units.

REORGANIZATION OF THE LEIBSTANDARTE
Plans for a strengthening of the Leibstandarte were already taking shape. On the Eastern Front the unit had occupied the Sambek position for the winter; meanwhile, formation of a panzer battalion for the Leibstandarte began in Wildflecken in February 1942. Personnel came from the Leibstandarte as well as from the various replacement and training units. Three panzer companies and a headquarters company were formed, initially under the command of SS-Sturmbannführer Mohnke. However, after Mohnke fell ill, on February 20 SS-Sturmbannführer Schönberger assumed command of the battalion. The panzer companies were issued Panzer IVs armed with the short 75 mm KwK.

Formation of the battalion concluded in Sennelager, Haustenbeck in June 1942, and the SS Panzer Battalion Leibstandarte was transported by train to Russia to join the field unit. Detraining took place in the Stalino area, where formation of the two infantry regiments had already begun. Two more battalions, the Vth, from the Leningrad Front, and the VIth, newly formed from the replacement battalion, had arrived in the meantime. In June 1942 the entire Leibstandarte was loaded aboard trains and transported to France, where reorganization as the Leibstandarte Panzer-Grenadier Division was to be completed. All units were increased in size, the anti-tank and assault gun battalions were established, the flak battalion was enlarged to six batteries and the artillery to four battalions. Special units were formed within both infantry regiments, such as flak, infantry gun, anti-tank and, at a later date, reconnaissance and pioneer companies. Both Leibstandarte panzer-grenadier regiments reached their highest complement of companies after the Battle of Kharkov, when the 1st Regiment had twenty and the 2nd Regiment nineteen.

In autumn 1942 the 2nd Regiment's IIIrd Battalion was reorganized as an armored rifle battalion and completely equipped with armored troop carriers. Formation of a second panzer battalion began at the same time in Evreux. The existing battalion now became the IInd Battalion of the SS Panzer Regiment Leibstandarte with a corresponding change in the numbering of the companies; the 1st, 2nd and 3rd Companies became the 5th, 6th and 7th Companies. The Ist Battalion was commanded by SS-Sturmbannführer Max Wünsche, the IInd Battalion by SS-Hauptsturmführer Martin Groß; SS-Sturmbannführer Schönberger became regimental commander. Each battalion consisted of three panzer companies and a headquarters company.

At the same time, plans called for the three senior units of the Waffen-SS—the panzer-grenadier divisions Leibstandarte SS Adolf Hitler, Das Reich and Totenkopf—to be brought together in an SS Panzer Corps under the command of SS-Obergruppenführer Paul Hausser.

Formation of a heavy panzer battalion for the new corps began in Fallingbostel in autumn 1942. It was to be equipped with the newest and heaviest German battle tank, the Tiger. All three divisions provided personnel. SS-Hauptsturmführer Herbert Kuhlmann was chosen to command the 2nd Company. However, formation of the corps battalion was delayed and the divisions each received a Tiger company of their own. The Leibstandarte's association with the Tiger thus began in November 1942.

THE BIRTH OF THE HEAVY PANZER COMPANY

The SS-Führungshauptamt (Operational Headquarters SS) issued the order for the "formation of a heavy panzer company for the SS Panzer Regiment of the SS Division Leibstandarte SS Adolf Hitler" retroactive to 15 October 1942. Originally intended as the 1st Company of the Corps Panzer Battalion and assigned army postal number 03828, the unit was now renamed "Heavy Company, SS Panzer Regiment Leibstandarte SS Adolf Hitler" and received the army postal number 48165.

The above-mentioned order named Evreux, Normandy as the formation site; the Leibstandarte's panzer regiment was stationed there. However, the Tiger company and all its elements were located exclusively in

Fallingbostel and were thus far separated from the panzer regiment and the division. The division was responsible for providing command personnel for the company, which existed largely on paper at that time, while the SS-Führungshauptamt provided replacements as requested. The division was also supposed to supply NCOs and men; replacements were to be requested. The majority of the personnel came from the division's panzer regiment, but some came from the division's assault gun battalion and the SS Panzer Training and Replacement Battalion.

OFFICERS—NON-COMMISSIONED OFFICERS—MEN OF THE COMPANY

SS-Hauptsturmführer Kling was transferred to the company on Christmas Day 1942. Heinz Kling was born in Kassel on 10 September 1913. He joined the armed forces on 27 August 1935, becoming a member of the 7th Company of the SS Regiment Germania in Arolsen. Kling attended the Junkerschule at Bad Tölz; on 9 November 1938, following the Sudeten action, he was promoted to Untersturmführer and made a platoon leader in the Germania Regiment's 10th Company. Kling served with the 9th Company during the Polish Campaign and shortly afterward was posted to the 12th SS Totenkopf-Standarte, where he took over the 6th Company. Promoted to the rank of Obersturmführer, he subsequently led the 3rd Company, and on 20 August 1940 was awarded the Iron Cross, Second Class. After the regiment was disbanded in the summer of 1940, he joined the 15th SS Totenkopf-Standarte, taking command of the 10th Company. From December 1940 he was the company commander of the 1st Company of the 5th SS Totenkopf Infantry Regiment. Virtually the entire company was sent from Rastenburg to Wischau, near Brunn, in July 1941; there it became the 18th Company, IVth Battalion of the Leibstandarte. Kling was twice wounded in the campaign against the Soviet Union which began in June. On 16 July 1941 he was awarded the Iron Cross, First Class and on 9 November was promoted to the rank of SS-Hauptsturmführer. After being wounded again and spending time in hospital, in June 1942 he was assigned to the SS Panzer Replacement Battalion and subsequently to a training course for panzer company commanders. In November 1942 Kling was transferred to the IInd Battalion of the SS Panzer Regiment Leibstandarte SS Adolf Hitler. He arrived in Fallingbostel on 24 December 1942; from that day on he commanded the Leibstandarte's Tiger company.

The company was unique in its equipment and personnel complement. It soon consisted of a total of 306 officers, NCOs and men, with a vehicle pool of 119 vehicles, including the tanks. In commanding this over strength company Kling's duties were closer to those of a battalion commander. Next in command was Obersturmführer Waldemar Schütz; officially a platoon leader, on account of the company's personnel strength his duties were actually those of a company commander. The type of command structure that existed in the Leibstandarte Tiger Company in the beginning was unique. When the company began entraining for the Eastern Front Schütz assumed command of the 1st Platoon.

Waldemar Schütz was born on 9 October 1913 in Dausenau in the Unterlahn District. In 1937 he became an Ordensjunker in the Ordensburgen. Following the campaign in Poland the Leibstandarte moved through Prague into the lower Lahn Valley. Headquarters and several of the companies took up quarters in Bad Ems. On 7 December 1939 the Bürgermeister invited SS-Obergruppenführer Sepp Dietrich, together with several members of his staff and his friend Waldemar Schütz, to a reception. In the course of the evening Schütz asked if it might be possible for him to join the Leibstandarte. Sepp Dietrich turned to his 1st General Staff Officer: "Keilhaus, can we do that?" The officer replied, "We can't, but you can do anything!" The matter was decided; Schütz joined the 13th Light Infantry Gun Company. On 8 December 1939 he took off the uniform of the Ordensburgen and put on the grey uniform of the Waffen-SS. In March 1940 Sepp Dietrich sent Schütz to the Junkerschule at Bad Tölz to attend an officer candidate training course. On 9 November 1940 he was promoted to the rank of SS-Untersturmführer. During the Balkans Campaign and subsequently in Russia he served with his old company (by then the 1st Company, Heavy Battalion); in 1941 he was awarded the Infantry Assault Badge and the Iron Cross, Second Class. After a period of detached service, in early 1942 Schütz joined the 1st Company of the SS Panzer Battalion Leibstandarte SS Adolf Hitler in Wildflecken. In Evreux he was placed in command of the 7th Panzer Company and in November 1942 joined the 7th Tiger Company in Fallingbostel as an SS-Obersturmführer.

Commander of the IInd Platoon was SS-Untersturmführer Hannes Philipsen. Johannes Philipsen was born on 16 December 1921 in Dollerup in the Flensburg District. In September 1939 the seventeen-year-old agricultural student and Jungstammführer in the Deutschen Jungvolk volunteered for military service and joined the 2nd Motorcycle Company of the Germania Regiment in Ellwangen. After basic training, on 5 May 1940 he was assigned to the Leibstandarte's recently-formed assault gun battery. There Philipsen was trained as a gunner. He was placed on leave of absence from October 1940 until March 1941, during which period he commanded Hitlerjugend-Bann 715 in Bolchen, Lothringen (Lorraine).

After returning to active service on 4 March 1941, Philipsen served as a dispatch rider with the assault gun battery. On 14 March he became the first member of the battery to receive the Iron Cross, Second Class and soon afterward the General Assault Badge. After proving himself further in the fighting on the Eastern Front, in November 1941 Philipsen was sent to the Junkerschule Bad Tölz, where he took part in Reserve Officer Candidate Course No 5. After successfully completing the course, which ended on 1 March 1942, Philipsen, now an SS-Oberscharführer and a reserve officer candidate, joined the Leibstandarte Panzer Battalion, where he took command of a Panzer IV platoon. On 9 November 1942 he was promoted to SS-Untersturmführer and on 15 December went to Fallingbostel as a platoon commander.

Philipsen was a highly idealistic, extremely positive officer whose correctness and comradeship soon earned him the unqualified respect of his men. He was a classical officer, one who provided an example in every situation and stood by his men. The youngest officers were SS-Untersturmführer Gustav Mühlhausen and Ortwin Rohl, both twenty-one years old.

Commanding the 3rd Platoon was SS-Untersturmführer Wendorff. Helmut Max Ernst Wendorff was born on 20 October 1920 in Grauwinkel in the Schweidnitz District. In 1931 he moved with his parents and sisters to Damme, in the Uckermark, where his father had leased a farm. In the autumn of 1939 Wendorff graduated from the Naumburg National-Political School. When war broke out he volunteered for military service and on 4 September 1939 joined the Leibstandarte. On 6 November Wendorff joined up with the field regiment in Prague, where it had temporarily taken up quarters after the Polish Campaign. He was subsequently assigned to the 11th Company, but in February 1940 was transferred to the assault gun battery. Wendorff took part in the fighting in the Balkans and the Soviet Union with this unit. On 14 September 1941, SS-Sturmmann Wendorff was decorated with the Iron Cross, Second Class and the Tank Battle Badge. On 1 November 1941, now an SS-Oberscharführer, he was sent to the Junkerschule in Bad Tölz; in April 1942 Wendorff returned to the assault gun battalion as an SS-Untersturmführer. Christmas Day 1942 saw him transferred to the Tiger Company in Fallingbostel. Helmut Wendorff, who was given the nickname "Bubi" by his men, was a popular and capable young officer who was accepted by everyone. His education, his manner and his military ability were undoubtedly superior and he trained his men to a similar high standard.

The Light Platoon, which consisted of five Panzer IIIs, was led by SS-Untersturmführer Wittmann. Michael Wittmann was born on 22 April 1914 in Vogelthal, near Beilngries in the Upper Pfalz, the son of a farmer. After completing his military service with the 19th Infantry Regiment's 10th Company (from 30 October 1934 to 30 September 1936), on 5 April 1937 Wittmann joined the 17th Company of the Leibstandarte. The armored scout company was reduced in size to platoon strength in the summer of 1939. Wittmann entered the war in 1939 as an SS-Unterscharführer and commander of an eight-wheeled armored car. In February 1940 he was transferred to the assault gun battery. Wittmann was one of the NCOs who, at that time, had a scant three years experience in a branch of the service which was at least similar to the armored forces.

Wittmann was placed in command of one of the battery's six assault guns. It was at this time that he met Hannes Philipsen, Helmut Wendorff, Alfred Günther and many others; these men became friends and enjoyed an outstanding relationship. Wittmann fought in Greece and the Soviet Union in 1941 and received the Iron Cross, Second Class on 12 July. He was later wounded but remained with his unit; after further successes he was awarded the Iron Cross, First Class on 8 September 1941 and the Tank Battle Badge on 21 November 1941, after the fighting for Rostov. As an assault gun commander Wittmann was cool and did his job without attracting a great deal of attention; he was promoted to SS-Oberscharführer and attended an officer candidate course at the Junkerschule in Bad Tölz from 4 June to 5 September 1942. Now an SS-Oberscharführer and a reserve officer candidate, he was subsequently assigned to the SS Panzer Training and Replacement Battalion. On 21 December 1942 he was promoted to SS-Untersturmführer and on 24 December joined the Leibstandarte's Tiger company.

Michael Wittmann soon became a well-liked member of the company on account of his correct, exemplary and reserved manner. There was nothing to suggest the success that would come later, which would make him one of the most fascinating soldiers of the Wehrmacht. The primary role of Wittmann's light platoon was to protect the Tigers against close-range attack; offensive operations were secondary. The platoon was essentially a defensive screen for the Tigers. The Panzer IIIs were armed with the long-barrelled 50 mm gun and had additional armor plates bolted on to the bow and turret front. One of the platoon's Panzer IIIs was commanded by the then nineteen-year-old SS-Rottenführer Franz Staudegger. The origins of the company's non-commissioned officers varied. In Russia SS-Unterscharführer Jürgen Brandt served as the ordnance and equipment administrator in the assault gun battalion and from autumn 1941 as gunner. He was transferred to the Leibstandarte's panzer regiment in autumn 1942 and took part in a tank commander training course given by the army's 4th Panzer Training Battalion in Vienna-Mödling before being assigned to the Tiger company.

SS-Rottenführer Karl Wagner became an infantryman with the 2nd Company of the Der Führer Replacement Battalion in June 1940. Later he was assigned to the 10th Battery of the SS Artillery Replacement and Training Regiment in Munich, where he was trained on the Light Field Howitzer 18 (IFH 18). In June 1942 he was transferred to the Leibstandarte artillery regiment's 150 mm rocket battery. Wagner then joined the 3rd Company of the Leibstandarte's panzer regiment on 28 October 1942 and was trained as a gunner. On 1 December 1942 he was promoted to SS-Rottenführer and on 8 December was transferred to the Tiger Company. Wagner was assigned the personnel roster number 206, an indication of the company's over strength situation even at that date.

Unlike the other panzer companies of the Leibstandarte, the Tiger company had its own maintenance platoon, which consisted of highly-qualified personnel who were familiar with the complicated technology of the Tiger and able to maintain and repair the heavy vehicle. The platoon, which also included the recovery and ordnance sections, was commanded by SS-Hauptscharführer Julius Porupski. The thirty-year-old Carinthian, who had previously served in the old 1st Company of the Leibstandarte, was commonly known within the company as "Bimbo."

The maintenance section was led by SS-Unterscharführer Erich Koreinke. From the very beginning SS-Hauptscharführer Kurt Habermann made a reputation for himself as a ubiquitous Senior NCO. The role of the fuel and supply transport columns was to keep the combat echelon supplied. Soon after receiving its new field postal number the Tiger company was officially designated the 4th (Heavy) Company, SS Panzer Regiment Leibstandarte SS Adolf Hitler. As the fourth panzer company it should normally have belonged to the panzer regiment's Ist Battalion, however as a Tiger company it was designated a regimental unit.

Where did the young men of the company come from? Alfred Lünser, an SS-Panzerschütze, described how he came to the Tiger company and his initial experiences there: "Born on 2 July 1925, volunteered at the age of sixteen; only 7 out of 42 volunteers were accepted, I was one of them. On 19 June 1942 I joined the LSSAH in Berlin-Lichterfelde at the age of seventeen years and seventeen days. It was the infantry, on my identity disk was '8./E-LSSAH.' The training was demanding and after three or four months the training company had been reduced from 270 to 180 men. This brief period played a decisive role in the rest of my life. Those who did not go through it were lost later.

In October 1942 the entire 'society' and I travelled to Evreux, France. About three companies of infantry landed in a former French barracks. They made a panzer unit out of us like this: 'Everyone fall in! All those with drivers licenses step forward. You're going to become drivers! All high-school graduates step forward. You're going to become radio operators! (because of their intelligence?) All those who have trained on the heavy machine-gun step forward. You're going to become gunners!' I was one of the latter. We had learned indirect aiming on the machine-gun. We still wore our grey infantry uniforms and three tanks were available for training the three companies. In the beginning we had only a few instructors who knew anything about the technical aspects of tanks. Most of the instruction was theory. It was not unusual for platoon leaders to show and explain something using illustrations and then say, "We have never seen this ourselves".

TRAINING AND ORGANIZATION OF THE COMPANY

"In November 1942 several dozen of us were sent to Fallingbostel (Lower Saxony, Lüneburg Heath). There we retrained infantrymen began calling ourselves Panzerschützen (private in an armored unit). But there were also medics from Stettin, radio operators from Nuremberg, tank drivers from Weimar-Buchenwald, artillerymen from Munich and others who had come directly from the field units of the Leibstandarte SS Adolf Hitler.

The company commander was Kling, and at his side were Schütz, Philipsen, Wendorff and Wittmann. No crews had yet been assigned, the whole scene was one of wild confusion. On 25 December 1942, Christmas Day, fifteen Panzerschützen, one Sturmmann, one Rottenführer and a platoon leader were called out for special duty; then, early in the morning, right after breakfast:

'Report in one hour with kit bags only, meaning for a few days, to collect tanks from the army ordnance depot.' That afternoon we left by train and travelled via Hanover to the army ordnance depot in Magdeburg-Königsborn. The Panzer IIIs were waiting at the ordnance depot but they refused to release them to us because the brake fluid for the guns—50mm Kampfwagenkanone long—was not available. We were put up in the hall of an old inn, about one hundred men or more, with a pot-bellied stove in the middle. In the morning we washed with water from a pump in the courtyard that had not frozen over. We were given ration cards. Each morning we were given a lecture on motor vehicles in winter, which was held in the clubroom of the bar. In the afternoons we were free to drive into Magdeburg. It was there that I met my former wife; we exchanged letters until January 1948, through six years as a soldier and later as a prisoner of war of the Americans and the English. It is hard to understand today, but having someone at home to hold on to meant a great deal to us! I recall handwritten letters from Kharkov that were twenty-four pages long.

For me the end came at the end of 1947 when I was released by the English. I wrote to Magdeburg saying that as a member of the SS I would never go to the Soviet zone (in England we were able to read all the papers, because as a member of the SS I was once again in a special camp, in Cambridge, where they spoon-fed us democracy). But by then she had met another man. There was no need for me to go to Magdeburg.

Each of us had to pick up a Panzer III in Magdeburg-Königsborn. The tanks were driven onto the rail cars and lashed down for us by the local professionals. Then a list of accessories was read out. Whatever we indicated as missing was ticked off without being checked. So in the end I ended up with a double set of tools for my tank.

We arrived in Fallingbostel with the Panzer IIIs. In the meantime tank crews had been put together; it was the beginning of January 1943. By then the Panzer VI Tigers had also arrived. We trained and did other duty until midnight. In Fallingbostel we learned on the Panzer III and VI, in Evreux we had practiced on the Panzer IV, and we had to learn quickly. Crews were formed in January 1943. I was gunner in the Staudegger crew. The driver was Focke, Graf was the loader and I can't remember the name of the radio operator. We stayed together until mid-March, until the recapture of Kharkov."

SS-Sturmmann Rolf Schamp came to Fallingbostel from the 2nd Company of the SS Panzer Training and Replacement Battalion. His platoon commander there was SS-Oberscharführer and reserve officer candidate Michael Wittmann. In telegram style he noted in his diary: "28/12/1942: arrival Fallingbostel—29/12: Wittmann, light platoon—30/12: company parade, gunner with the platoon commander (Wittmann, the author)—31/12: classes, singing, Christmas Eve in bed—1/01/1943: fall in—2.01: clean the area." Singing was the exception in those cold winter days, however; the training was hard and soon the crews were intimately familiar with their Tigers and in full command of the most modern German tank.

The Gauleiter of Hanover, Hartmann Lautebacher, inspected the company in those cold January days. SS-Untersturmführer Wittmann drove out to meet him at the entrance to the town of Fallingbostel and took him to the company. Lautebacher, who until he suffered an accident had trained in the Leibstandarte's replacement and training battalion, used the occasion to adopt the Tiger Company. The company reached full strength in January 1943, following the arrival of a total of fifteen Tigers and five Panzer IIIs at the beginning of the month. The tank training at Fallingbostel was directed by an army Oberleutnant; several commanders and drivers were sent to the Henschel works in Kassel for three weeks of technical training. Training continued at a rapid pace. There was simulated combat by single tanks and platoons, and firing practice with machine-guns and tank cannon. Once individual training ended, company attacks were practiced in vee and inverted wedge formations with flanking cover provided by Wittmann's light platoon. The training period was soon over. Preparations for entraining began in the final days of January. The Tigers and Panzer IIIs were given a coat of white camouflage paint. Now everyone knew where they were going.

ORDER OF BATTLE:
4th (Heavy) Company, SS Panzer Regiment Leibstandarte SS Adolf Hitler on 1/2/1943

Company Commander

405
Hstuf. Heinz Kling

Reserve Tank

403
Ustuf. Gustav Mühlhausen

Company HQ Squad Leader

404
Ustuf. Ortwin Rohl

Light Platoon

4L1
Ustuf. Michael Wittmann

4L2
Oscha. Max Marten

4L3
Uscha. Franz Staudegger

4L4
Schaf. Georg Lötzsch

4L5
Uscha. Schwerin

Ist Platoon

415
Ostuf. Waldemar Schütz

416
Uscha. Aus der Wieschen

417

418
Hscha. Fritz Hartel

IInd Platoon

425
Ustuf. Hans Philipsen

426
Hscha. Benno Poetschlak

427
Oscha. Heinz Mengele

428
Uscha. Modes

IIIrd Platoon

435
Ustuf. Helmut Wendorff

436
Uscha. Jürgen Brandt

437

438
Uscha. Ewald Mölly

GUNNERS:
Strm. Rolf Schamp
Pz.Sshtz. Fritz Siedelberg
Strm. Balthasar Woll
Pz.Schtz. Karl-Heinz Warmbrunn
Rttf. Werner Wendt
Pz.Schtz. Alfred Lünser
Strm. Klaus Schön v. Wildenegg
Rttf. Karl Wagner
Pz.Schtz. Siegfried Jung
Pz.Schtz. Siegfried Hummel
Pz.Schtz. Leopold Aumüller
Strm. Willems
Pz.Schtz. Heinz Buchner
Strm. Friedrich Aumann
Rttf. Helmut Gräser
Pz.Schtz. Gerhard Knocke
Pz.Schtz. Heinz Schindhelm

LOADERS:
Pz.Schtz. Ewald Graf
Pz.Schtz. Rudi Lechner
Strm. Iwanitz
Pz.Schtz. Gustav Grüner
Strm. Hirsch
Pz.Schtz. Reinhard Wenzel

RADIO OPERATORS:
Pz.Schtz. Herbert Werner
Strm. Wohlgehuth
Pz.Schtz. Werner Irrgang
Strm. Justus Kühn
Pz.Schtz. Lorenz Mähner
Ps.Schtz. Kaminski
Strm. Heinz Stuss
Pz.Schtz. Gerhard Waltersdorf

DRIVERS:
Pz.Schtz. Heinrich Reimers
Strm. Walter Bingert
Strm. Willi Röpstorff
Pz.Schtz. Werner Hepe
Rttf. Kurt Sowa
Rttf. Focke
Strm. Franz Ellmer
Usch. Otto Augst
Pz.Schtz. Piper
Pz.Schtz. Eugen Schmidt
Strm. Hein Rüttgers
Pz.Schtz. Siegfried Fuß
Strm. Walter Poewe
Pz.Schtz. Kurt Kämmer
Strm. Arthur Sommer

LEGEND:
Pz.Schtz. = SS-Panzerschütze
Strm. = SS-Sturmmann
Rttf. - SS-Rottenführer
Uscha. = SS-Unterscharführer

On the Eastern Front

The entraining of the Tiger company with its many vehicles was a difficult and most of all time-consuming task which required a high level of concentration on the part of the drivers. Great hopes rested on the new Tigers and their arrival on the Eastern Front was not supposed to be announced in advance. The tanks were therefore covered with tarpaulins while on the transport trains and kept out of sight.

SS-Sturmmann Rolf Schamp, now the gunner in the Tiger of SS-Unterscharführer Aus der Wieschen, wrote of the rail journey: "01/02/1943: 2330 hours, begin entraining Fallingbostel—02/02: Berlin—03/02: 0412 hours, cross Reich border—04/02: Vilna, Kovno—05/02: Minsk, Gomel—07/02: detrain Kharkov; go for coffee, which freezes in the icy cold."

The company entrained on three transport trains on 1 February 1943; they arrived one after another in Kharkov on 9 February.

Werner Wendt, then an SS-Rottenführer, described the rail journey: "During the journey to Russia by train in early February 1943, our driver laid an important service manual on our tank and carelessly forgot about it. SS-Untersturmführer Wittmann found the manual. He summoned the driver and gave him a stern warning but did not report the matter to the company. This measure on Wittmann's part achieved more than any punishment might have done. That one ability, of being able to put himself in the position of his subordinates and understand their thoughts and feelings, set him apart as an officer."

A fire broke out on one of the trains, however no losses resulted. During transport the batteries were removed from the tanks in order to prevent the release of poisonous vapors. SS-Panzerschütze Alfred Lünser of Wittmann's Panzer III platoon recalled of the transport: "In Fallingbostel there was much discussion among those of us on the second train to Russia as to who might sit in the Panzer Ins during the trip and keep watch. It was February, not very cold, and the Tigers were covered with tarpaulins. When we rolled through Hanover and Magdeburg the workers waved to us jubilantly from the factory windows. The farther east we went the less jubilation there was, the colder it became, and after we had crossed the Reich

27

border no one wanted to sit in the tanks any more. From then on observers were ordered to sit on the tanks; they were supposed to pay attention to the tie-downs securing the tanks to the rail cars so that the panzers didn't slide off. There were the Soviet partisans as well; however, we were spared any incidents during the seven-day trip to Kharkov. It grew increasingly cold.

During detraining in Kharkov the engine of our Panzer III refused to start. Using straw, we lit a fire under the rear of the tank but nothing helped. Then they simply towed us down from the car, for in the background we could already hear the Russian 'rip-boom' (76.2 mm multi-purpose gun) type artillery. The company's maintenance echelon got the tank's engine running and we set out after the company. In front of the station lay equipment and weapons belonging to many units of the allied armies—Romanians, Hungarians, Slovakians and others—mountains of it! We knew the Soviets would attack and that they had the upper hand at the moment. At the Kharkov rail station we supplied ourselves with extra rations, which fit into the smoke candle racks."

The trains were unloaded in Kharkov. Under Wittmann's command, the last transport was directed to Poltava and detrained there. A total of six Tigers and three Panzer IIIs took up positions near the station. They were to remain there waiting for orders until 6 March.

FIRST ACTION BY THE TIGER COMPANY FROM 1 FEBRUARY TO 1 MARCH 1943: THE SITUATION IN KHARKOV

The troops of the SS Panzer Corps under Commanding General SS-Obergruppenführer Paul Hausser assembled around Kharkov in the first days of February 1943. Initially available to the corps were the Leibstandarte SS Adolf Hitler and Das Reich Divisions; the Totenkopf Division had not yet arrived. To the north was the army's Großdeutschland Panzer-Grenadier Division. The available forces were supposed to halt the Red Army's offensive on Kharkov. Those elements of the Leibstandarte that had arrived built defensive positions east and southeast of Kharkov, in some cases with assistance from the populace. The lines were held against the advancing enemy; counter-attacks eliminated local penetrations. On 8 February 1943 it was apparent that the Soviets were preparing to encircle Kharkov. At the same time the Soviets drove into the Donets Basin from the north, in order to cut off the defensive front at the Mius from its supply bases and destroy it. If this move by the Soviets succeeded, the bulk of Army Group South would also be cut off from its rearward communications. The result would be a serious crisis for the entire German eastern front. A determined SS-Obergruppenführer Hausser ordered delaying resistance.

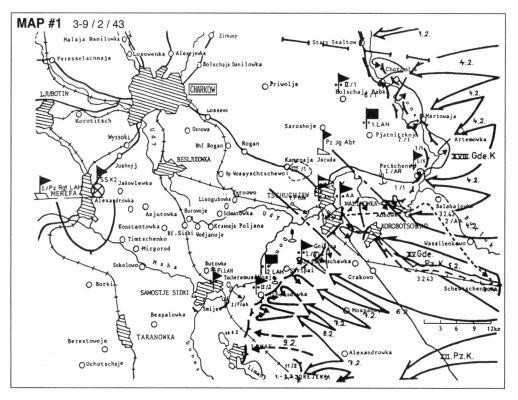

MAP #1 3-9 / 2 / 43

MAP #2 Attack Group Ist SS Panzer Corps

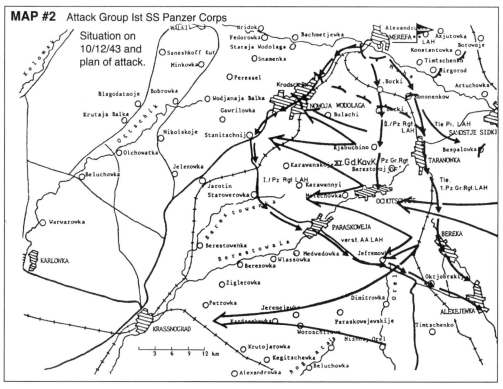

Situation on
10/12/43 and
plan of attack.

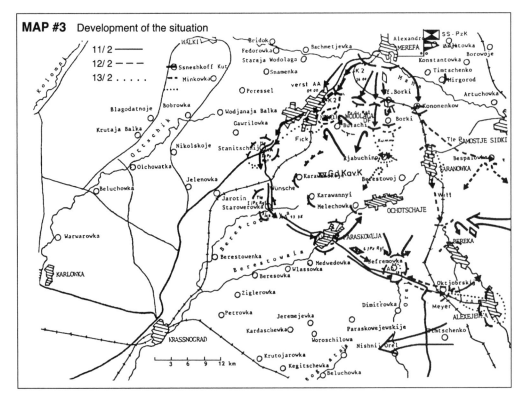

MAP #3   Development of the situation

MAP #4   Situation on

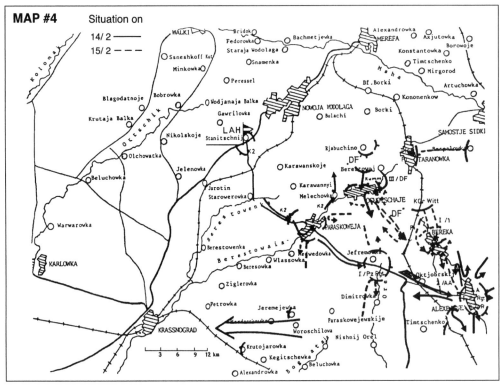

The Leibstandarte was ordered to fall back; the withdrawal began on 10 February 1943 in heavy snow and bitter cold. In some cases the enemy pursued immediately. That day the Leibstandarte formed a potent attack group which was placed under the command of Obersturmbannführer Kumm of the Das Reich Division. The group also included the Leibstandarte's panzer regiment. Some of the serviceable Tigers took part in the withdrawal movements in the wintry landscape; two Tigers were lost due to engine and running gear damage, a third collapsed a bridge and sank in a river. The Tigers engaged enemy forces assaulting the railway station at Rogan, southeast of Kharkov. The fighting there was especially intense as the enemy was attempting to break through at the boundary between the IInd (Hansen) and IIIrd (Weidenhaupt) Battalions of the 1st SS Panzer-Grenadier Regiment. It was at this time that SS-Obergruppenführer Hausser made his decision to ignore the Führer Order and give up Kharkov in order to save his panzer corps from destruction.

For many members of the Tiger company this was their first action. Alfred Lünser, then a seventeen-year-old gunner in a Panzer III, recalled: "We were assigned to Peiper's armored troop carrier battalion. Our tank was commanded by Unterscharführer Staudegger, nineteen years old, the driver was Rottenführer Focke, nineteen years old. He had experience in armored operations, having been the driver of an assault gun the previous winter, and wore the 'order of the frozen flesh'. At seventeen I was the gunner; Graf was the loader and I can't remember the name of the radio operator. With Peiper we were employed in a delaying action in a sector of front eighty kilometers long. Normally a division looked after about twenty kilometers. A dispute developed: in the midst of the action the commander became agitated, nervous, or as we said then 'jumpy'; he didn't agree with Focke's style of driving and berated him over the intercom. Focke, who in our opinion was an experienced driver, simply switched off the engine and said, 'Unterscharführer, if you can drive better than I, then come down!' Staudegger: 'Focke, I'll have you court martialled!' Focke: 'Then go ahead!' Focke started the engine again and drove away. There was no court martial and this only served to confirm the opinion of the commander already held by the crew."

THE EVACUATION OF KHARKOV

The Leibstandarte's situation became increasingly critical. The division's southern offensive group had no contact with Army Group South; a gap of 200 kilometers loomed between them. It was precisely into this gap in the front that Soviet General Popov sent his tank and rifle divisions. They outflanked the bulk of Army Group South at the northern rim of the Donets

Basin and advanced rapidly toward the Dniepr. This advance was covered by the Soviet 6th Army. Its left wing, the VIth Guards Cavalry Corps, engaged elements of the Leibstandarte. While dealing with this southward attack the Leibstandarte had to expect an attack from behind. On 15 February 1943 the enemy drove into the northwest section of Kharkov as well as the west and southeast parts of the city. The Leibstandarte had to defend an eighty-kilometer-wide sector of front. It was then that the evacuation of Kharkov ordered by Hausser began. The same day the Leibstandarte was able to report that it had smashed the VIth Guards Cavalry Corps. Elements of the reconnaissance battalion and the Ist Panzer Battalion under SS-Sturmbannführer Max Wünsche took part in this action.

The Leibstandarte now moved into new defensive positions southwest of Kharkov. Poor surface conditions made the use of tanks extremely difficult. The snow was up to two meters deep in places; however, it was covered with a thick crust that bore up under light vehicles such as Schwimmwagen and in some cases armored troop carriers. Tanks broke through immediately, however, and ended up pushing a growing wall of snow which obscured the driver's view and ultimately stopped the tank. The Tiger company was unable to go into battle as a unit. Individual serviceable tanks fought near Merefa. On 7 February 1943 driver SS-Sturmmann Poewe used his Tiger to recover a Panzer IV of the 7th Company (tank 717) that had slid over the embankment during the drive to Merefa. There are few detailed records from those days, but the Tigers suffered from this and similar problems. SS-Sturmmann Schamp noted in his diary: '8/02/1943: night march, tank caught fire.—9/02: Merefa, breakfast with Russian farmers."

On 12 February 1943 SS-Unterscharführer Aus der Wischen set out from Merefa in his Tiger (gunner Schamp) in the direction of Poltava. As the driver shifted gears he noticed that the tank was burning and at 1100 hours the crew were forced to abandon the vehicle. In the early days the Tiger was prone to catching fire for seemingly inexplicable reasons. As they were not allowed to leave the Tiger, the crew remained nearby. Aus der Wischen and his men camped near the Tiger until 15 February, spending the ice-cold nights inside the tank. The Tiger was blown up at 1115 hours on 16 February. The men reached Novaya Vodolaga on 17 February, where they stood guard at the brickworks the next day. They served as a standing patrol there until 21 February and reached Krasnograd on 25 February 1943. Aus der Wischen was killed on 9 March 1943.

Alfred Lünser, gunner in Staudegger's Panzer III, described his experiences in those days: "We and our tanks were employed to support the delaying action until the Soviets were stopped. For this we were attached to Jochen Peiper's armored troop carrier battalion, which had only half-tracks, Schwimmwagen and motorcycles. I too was 'wounded' in this defensive fighting. It was a brilliant morning in a village between Poltava and Kharkov. Our tank was on the village street behind a house and in front of Peiper's command post. Suddenly a column of Russian trucks appeared on the horizon, driving along blissfully unawares. When informed of their presence, all Peiper said was, 'What cheek, let them have it!'

Our driver was absent, but the tank had to be moved forward to get a free field of fire. Staudegger jumped into the driver's seat: "Lünser, give me directions!' We had all learned how to move the tank, but we weren't tank drivers nor was Staudegger. But he didn't want Peiper to find out that the driver was absent so he drove himself. We had also learned how to direct a tank, but the driver had to pull the correct brake lever. Staudegger did exactly the opposite and pinned me between our tank and an armored troop carrier. He backed up and the tracks of our tank caught my pants and tossed me over the front end of the half-track. All Peiper had to say was, 'What a lucky break!'

To this day I don't know if he was referring to me or Staudegger. They carried me into Peiper's quarters, laid me on a bedstead with nothing on it, just a wire net, and brought the medic. Because of the cold—28 below was the record—we all wore several layers of clothing: I had on long socks, long underwear, dungarees, blue denim pants, black uniform trousers, padded overalls, and the white linen camouflage pants which the oil and grease had turned grey. These numerous pairs of pants saved my right leg. The shinbone became swollen and turned black and blue, and the entire leg went stiff. There was no wound to dress, the war went on. They lifted me onto the tank and into the turret; there was no replacement available, therefore I had to fight! This went on for two or three weeks. With my stiff leg, they heaved me into the tank in the morning and pulled me out in the evening. While the rest of the crew spent the evening cleaning the weapons and pulling through the gun tube, I sat in a Russian hut and cleaned the cannon breech mechanism and the turret machine-gun. They brought me the ammunition boxes and I had to refill the ammo belts, every fifth round a tracer. In short I was ballast, but they couldn't do anything without me as there were no replacements in sight. One day, however, a replacement arrived and I ended up in the hands of Senior NCO Habermann."

The SS Panzer Corps halted three Soviet armies and stabilized the situation; on 19 February 1943 the defense south of Kharkov began assuming an offensive stance. On 17 February the Leibstandarte left the Yefremovka-Ochotschaje-East-Taranovka sector and moved into a new line from Beresovka (inclusive)—Melekhovka—hill east of Ochotschaje—east end of Rjabuchino—hills south of Borki. On 21 February, the daily report gave the Leibstandarte's tank situation as six Tigers and forty-nine Panzer IVs. The panzer regiment was instructed to transfer its headquarters and those elements not in action to Krasnograd on 24 February 1943 for a brief period of rest and refitting. The division command post was also located in Krasnograd from 24 February. Still in Poltava were the Tigers and the Panzer IIIs, which Wittmann had brought to the Eastern Front aboard the last train.

SS-Rottenführer Werner Wendt recalled this period: "In Poltava Untersturmführer Wittmann frequently came into our quarters to speak to old comrades who had transferred to us from the assault guns. Once while he was there I began cleaning my pistol. The pistol went off as a result of my own carelessness. Terrified, I looked at Untersturmführer Wittmann and braced myself for the storm. Wittmann just gave me a long, stern look and then left the room without saying a word. This gesture by the Untersturmführer succeeded in embarrassing an old soldier like me more than a barrage of abuse would have done. I reproached myself for my carelessness. Wittmann's silence and his look had the desired effect."

On 25 February 1943 the elements of the Tiger company in Poltava were sent to join the company's tanks deployed in other sectors. The muddy period began setting in slowly at the end of February 1943, softening the roads. On 1 March 1943 the Leibstandarte was given an offensive mission; it was to destroy the enemy forces between Orel and the Berestoveya River line.

THE SECOND (OFFENSIVE) BATTLE OF KHARKOV,
5–14 MARCH 1943

On 5 March 1943 the Tiger company moved from Poltava into the area about thirty kilometers north of Krasnograd. On the way there the Tiger of SS-Unterscharführer Jürgen Brandt caught fire and completely burned out. The cause was an engine fire, one of the difficulties then being faced by the Tiger. Several other Tigers suffered mechanical breakdowns en route and were left behind to wait for the repair service. Altogether four Tigers arrived in the destination area.

New assignments were contained in a division order which was issued on 5 March 1943. The reinforced 2nd SS Panzer-Grenadier Regiment was to take Belezkowo and then Federovka, the Bridok collective farm, while the reinforced 1st SS Panzer-Grenadier Regiment was to occupy Sukhaya Balka and then Peski and Valki-East. Together with the Ist Battalion, SS Panzer Regiment LAH, the 3rd Battery, SS Artillery Regiment LAH, the 2nd Company, SS Anti-tank Battalion LAH and the Ist Battalion, 55th Rocket Regiment, the Tiger company was placed under the command of the Leibstandarte's reconnaissance battalion. Following preparations in

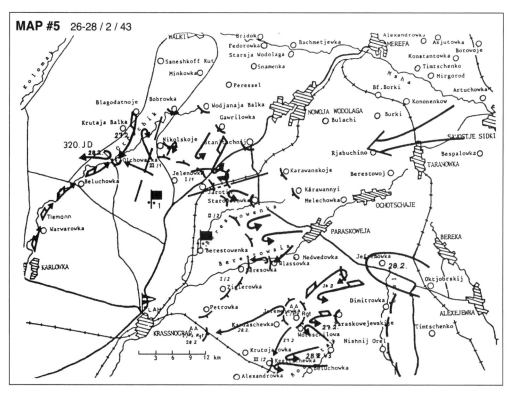

MAP #5 26-28 / 2 / 43

WALKI
Bridok
Fedorowka
Starja Wodolaga
Snamenka
Bachmetjewka
Alexandrowka
MEREFA
Axjutowka
Borowoje
Konstantowka
Timtschenko
Mirgorod
Ssneshkoff Kut
Minkowka
Peressel
Msha
Bf. Borki
Artuchowka
Blagodatnoje
Bobrowka
Wodjanaja Balka
Gawrilowka
NOWOJA WODOLAGA
Bulachi
Borki
Kononenkow
Krutaja Balka
320. JD
Nikolskoje
Stanitschnij
SAMOSTJE SIDKI
Rjabuchino
Bespalowka
Olchowatka
III /1
Jelenowka
I /1
Karawanskoje
Berestowoj
TARANOWKA
Jaroti
Staroje
Karawannyi
Melechowka
OCHOTSCHAJE
Tiemann
Warwarowka
II /2
PARASKOWEJA
BEREKA
Berestowenka
Jefasowka
28.2.
KARLOWKA
Beresowka
Medwedowka
Wlassowka
I /2
Ziglerowka
26.2
Dimitrowka
Oktjobrskij
Petrowka
AA
Jeremejewka
Rgt
ALEXEJEWKA
LAH
Kardaschewka
28.2.
Paraskowejewskije
27.2
Nishnij Orel
Timtschenko
KRASSNOGRAD
Rgt
28.2
Woroschilowa
III /2
Kegi
Krutojarowka
28.2
3
Alexandrowka
Beluchowka

3   6   9   12 km

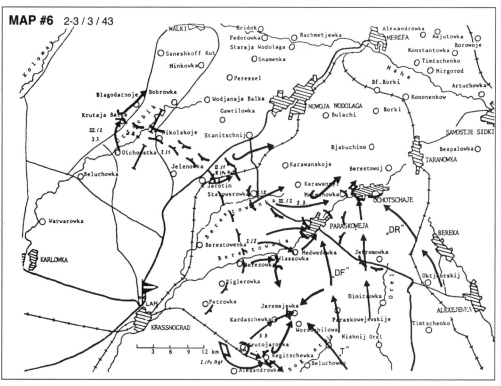

MAP #6 2-3 / 3 / 43

WALKI
Bridok
Fedorowka
Starja Wodolaga
Snamenka
Bachmetjewka
Alexandrowka
MEREFA
Axjutowka
Borowoje
Konstantowka
Timtschenko
Mirgorod
Ssneshkoff Kut
Minkowka
Peressel
Msha
Bf. Borki
Artuchowka
Blagodatnoje
Bobrowka
Wodjanaja Balka
Gawrilowka
NOWOJA WODOLAGA
Bulachi
Borki
Kononenkow
Krutaja Balka
III /2
3.3.
Nikolskoje
Stanitschnij
SAMOSTJE SIDKI
Rjabuchino
Bespalowka
Olchowatka I /1
Jelenowka
II /1
Karawanskoje
Berestowoj
TARANOWKA
Beluchowka
Jarotin
Starowerowka
Karawannyi
Melechowka
OCHOTSCHAJE
Warwarowka
Berestowenka I /2
III /2 2.3.
PARASKOWEJA
"DR"
BEREKA
KARLOWKA
Beresowka
Medwedowka
Wlassowka
Jeremejewka
Oktjobrskij
Ziglerowka
"DF"
Orel
Petrowka
Dimitrowka
ALEXEJEWKA
LAH
Kardaschewka
Jeremejewka
Paraskowejewskije
Timtschenko
KRASSNOGRAD
3.3.
Woroschilowa
Nishnij Orel
Krutojarowka
"T"
I./Pz.Rgt
Kegitschewka
Alexandrowka
Beluchowka

3   6   9   12 km

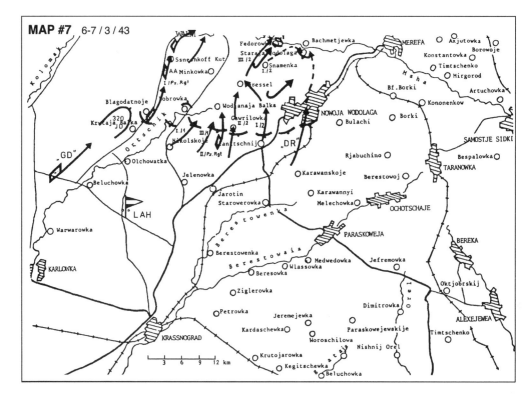

MAP #7 6-7 / 3 / 43

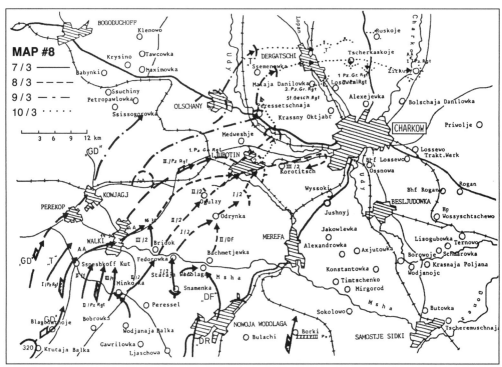

MAP #8

7/3 ———
8/3 – – –
9/3 –·–·–
10/3 ·······

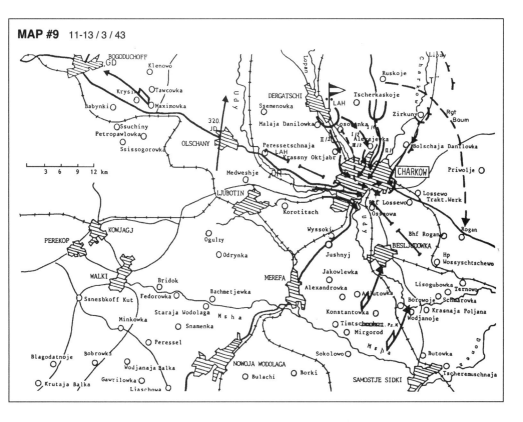

MAP #9 11-13 / 3 / 43

the area southeast of Krutaya Balka it was to attack the villages of Landyschewo and Blagodatnoye and subsequently break through toward Ssneshkoff Kut. The first objective of the day was Landyschewo—Blagodatnoye, the second Valki-West. Once the road conditions had been checked, the Tiger company was to be sent to Wünsche's Ist Panzer Battalion and placed under its command.

Preparations for the attack began during the night of 6 March 1943; the division received the reports confirming preparations completed between 0100 and 0600 hours. At 0700 the reconnaissance battalion reported that only four of the Tiger Company's tanks had so far arrived, the rest were immobilized on the way to the assembly area. The following four Tiger commanders saw action that day: SS-Hauptsturmführer Kling, SS-Untersturmführer Wendorff, SS-Hauptscharführer Poetschlack and Hauptscharführer Hartel. Over catastrophic roads the Tiger company set off at 1100 hours with Meyer's reconnaissance battalion and the Ist Panzer Battalion as well as the I st SS Panzer-Grenadier Regiment. Initial progress was good, but at approximately 1400 the tanks ran into a powerful anti-tank front a few kilometers south of Ssneshkoff Kut.

SS-Obersturmführer Isecke, adjutant of Wünsche's Ist Panzer Battalion, described the battle: "Our battle group was on the division's left wing. For the first time we were to be supported by the Tiger company. Just before we moved off, the CO brought me a war correspondent by the name of Fernau. 'Take him along in your tank, he wants to take part in the attack.' Where to put him? After talking it over with the crew I decided the best place was below and to the side of the cannon. The guns opened fire and we moved off. The breakthrough succeeded. On account of the deep snow the crews of the two motorcycles rode on the tanks, while the reconnaissance battalion's light armored troop carriers were able to keep up fairly well. The amphibious Volkswagens were towed. SS-Sturmbannführer Meyer led the attack from the tank of SS-Obersturmführer Beck (CO of 2nd Panzer Company). SS-Sturmbannführer Wünsche drove in the middle. On the right was the 3rd Company, Panzer Regiment Leibstandarte (SS-Hauptsturmführer Lambrecht); the 1st Panzer Company (SS-Hauptsturmführer Jorgensen) followed about 500 meters back. Two of the Tigers followed behind SS-Sturmbannführer Wünsche. Most of the others had been disabled by components or racks inside the tank falling off and in some cases even injuring members of the crew. We heard the sound of combat behind us to the left where the 320th Infantry Division was. We continued our advance across a snow-covered plain on a broad front. On the horizon we could see a line of roofs at right angles to our direction of attack. That could only be Ssneshkoff Kut. During a brief halt the CO, SS-Sturmbannführer Wünsche, instructed the 1st Company to swing out to the right and attack the extended village from the east, toward us. We would attack in our previous direction. A gentle rise in front of the village, and especially to the left of it, appeared to be occupied by the enemy. There were several flashes there.

The attack proceeded. Our guest Fernau observed that there was a strange crackling in his headset and that it was a bit tight as well, but otherwise he found it pleasantly exciting. Meanwhile we had approached to within two kilometers of the hill position, of which we now had a better view. Now and then the snow whirled up in front of or to the side of us and shells whizzed past. We were eighteen tanks, the two Tigers behind us, the infantry crouched down behind the turrets. Halt, fire! Then there were flashes all along and in front of the gentle rise. Damn! It looked very much like an anti-tank front. The CO called both companies: "Faster, more movement! Forward!' To the left the Beck crew abandoned their tank. What about SS-Sturmbannführer Meyer? The tank did not burn and I could see movement behind it. Our tanks' rapid fire had certainly had an effect on the hill. The leading tanks were still 800 meters from it. To the left and right of us two tanks were in flames. We found ourselves in the phase where most tank attacks become critical. No one was moving at that moment. Moments earlier Jorgensen (CO of the 1st Panzer Company) had called: "Orion to Mercury, village begins two kilometers in front of me, no resistance." The CO's reply: 'Increase speed!' and then: 'CO to everyone, follow me!' In my position as adjutant—fifty meters to the side and behind the command panzer, which was tossing up a spray of snow—I called to my crew, 'Full speed, hang on!' Tensely I peered through the vision blocks to the side and behind but saw nothing out of the ordinary.

We had gone 150 meters when I saw the command panzer turn to the right toward a barn, obviously to stop out of sight behind it and assess the situation. In fractions of a second it registered that the air was abuzz all around us; the muzzle flashes from the now clearly-visible hill were becoming unpleasantly more frequent. Apparently the fire was less effective in the direction of the barn. The other tanks were now in motion as well. As we reached the hill—to my right the CO had traversed the 100 meters to the barn—I saw the first houses two to three-hundred meters away. There was a flash from the first house and something hit us. In the glare of the fire I roared out, 'Back up!' Seconds later there was another crash. I shouted 'Get out!' and we all found ourselves in the snow beside the tank. The cords of the throat microphones dangled at our necks. The flames had resulted in burns. Instinctively we stuck our heads in the snow. All six of us, luckily including Fernau, crawled some distance away from the tank. We couldn't understand why the tank hadn't kept burning after the initial flash.

The tank had rolled back about 20 meters on one track. As we later found out, a T 34 had been hiding in the first house and the first hit wrecked our left drive sprocket. Then as we backed up we drove over a mine. We didn't have long to think about things. Rifle fire meant that the positions were still occupied. Where were the other tanks? The sound of gunfire and impacting shells told us that the tank versus anti-tank gun battle was in full swing. We couldn't make out the command panzer. Then a Tiger approached the hill about 80 meters to one side of us. We wanted to draw its attention to the T 34 but of course they couldn't hear us. What happened next took our feelings low and high. Mesmerized, we peered out through our swollen eyelids to the left, all pain from the burns was forgotten. The Tiger had scarcely reached the top of the hill when there was a crash. We were showered by sparks and fragments. When we looked up we saw a mark on the turret of the Tiger a meter square. But at the same time we saw the 88mm gun turn and point toward the target like a finger. A jet of flame shot from the muzzle—we were now half standing so as to see what would happen next. Half of the house was blown away and we could clearly see a burning tank, now without its turret. We hugged each other for joy.

From then on things happened quickly. At least two dozen T 34s left their hiding places at the edge of the village. Meanwhile, the second Tiger (commander SS-Untersturmführer Wendorff) had arrived; eight enemy tanks were destroyed in front of Ssneshkoff Kut. After driving through the village our tanks were able to knock out four more, while the rest of the T 34s disappeared northeast in the direction of Valki. SS-Sturmbannführer Wünsche had meanwhile directed the efforts of the battalion in front of the anti-tank front. Fifty-six anti-tank guns were counted after the fighting was over. He then organized the mopping up of the village with the commander of the reconnaissance battalion. After receiving medical attention I was able to return to duty with a bandage on my head."

Tiger 426 commanded by Hauptscharführer Poetschlag was hit several times in the commander's cupola and gun mantlet during the fight with the anti-tank front and the T 34s, resulting in its gun being put out of action. The commander received serious head wounds. After the Tiger had been repaired in the workshop it was taken over by SS- Unterscharführer Modes. His gunner was SS-Rottenführer Wendt. For eighteen-year-old gunner SS-Panzerschütze Karl-Heinz "Bobby" Warmbrunn in the company commander's tank this was his first combat. He noted in his diary: "Baptism of fire. One T 34 and five 76.2mm antitank guns knocked out."

The Tiger of SS-Unterscharführer Aus der Wischen was in action about 40 kilometers farther southwest, near Karlovka. That day the crew received its first mail from home. Aus der Wischen was also wounded that day. The Soviets sent reinforcements to Kharkov. But now the Leibstandarte was on the attack and with it the entire SS Panzer Corps. The Leibstandarte's left flank was guarded by the Totenkopf Division, while attacking on the right was the Das Reich Division.

At 1315 hours on 7 March 1943 the Tiger company, together with the 1st SS Panzer-Grenadier Regiment under SS-Standartenführer Fritz Witt and the reinforced reconnaissance battalion, reached Valki. Attacking from the southwest, by 1630 hours the village was taken and contact established with Peiper's armored troop carrier battalion located farther to the north. Another anti-tank front was breached in the course of the attack.

On 8 March 1943 the units resumed their northward advance. The mission given the Leibstandarte: continue the attack toward Ogulzy and the villages west of Lyubotin, in order to close off the road to Kharkov in the northern part of Lyubotin. The Tiger company advanced with the reconnaissance battalion from Valki through Bogar to the rail and road crossing at Schljach, arriving at about noon. Resistance was negligible.

Peresechnaya was taken on 9 March 1943. In the evening the reconnaissance battalion, and with it the Tiger company, was placed under the command of the 1st SS Panzer-Grenadier Regiment under SS-Standarten-führer Witt. It was now in Lyubotin. In Valki SS-Sturmmann Schamp found printed firing tables in a knocked-out T 34 designed to assist Soviet tank commanders in engaging the Tiger, proof that the other side had received timely information concerning the appearance of the new tank and had had sufficient time to react accordingly. On 10 March 1943, the 1st Regiment set out toward Dergaci; prevailing road conditions were poor. Toward evening the reconnaissance battalion and the tanks reached Zirkuny. During the night the 1st Regiment moved toward the airfield at the north end of Kharkov. SS-Untersturmführer Gustav Mühlhausen of the Tiger company was killed.

THE RECAPTURE OF KHARKOV

The commanding officer of the Leibstandarte ordered the recapture of Kharkov for 11 March 1943. During the night SS-Obergruppenführer Sepp Dietrich received a telephone call from Hitler, who was with the high command of Army Group South in Zaporozhye. The Führer inquired about the well-being of the men of the Leibstandarte and expressed concern over their losses. He ended the conversation with the words: "If my Leibstandarte attacks with its usual vigor, then we must succeed in retaking Kharkov from the enemy!"

The Tiger company and the 1st SS Panzer-Grenadier Regiment moved off at 0400 on 11 March 1943. The Leibstandarte's battle groups entered the city from the northeast after heavy fighting. The rocket launchers of the 55th Rocket Regiment gave effective support. In the evening the first units fought their way to the Red Square, the center of the large city. During the fighting at the outskirts of Kharkov SS-Untersturmführer Philipsen was able to destroy a T 34 and two anti-tank guns.

SS-Sturmmann Walter Schüle, a tank driver in the 6th Company of the Leibstandarte Panzer Regiment, recalled of this action: "After churning through swamp, mud and softened morass all night with several tanks under Wünsche's command, we reached the outskirts of Kharkov and the water tower standing in front of us to the left with three Panzer IVs. That was also where the Russian artillery observer was. In the morning, after the following units had caught up, we stood ready on both sides of the road to attack the city center. When we attempted to enter the city several of our Panzer IVs were knocked out—as it later turned out by a KV I sitting behind the corner of a house. In the meantime a Tiger had joined us; it rolled past slowly on its way to SS-Sturmbannführer Wünsche. This was the first time I had seen a Tiger in action. According to rumors most had been lost to mechanical breakdown and things were less than perfect inside the fighting compartment. In any case the Tiger was suddenly there. After the commander had been briefed Wünsche shouted, 'Now let the big fellow pass!' The street was cleared and it approached slowly, the long gun lowered slightly, pointing menacingly toward the street which curved to the left, ready to destroy the assigned target at any time. The street, on which anything passing a certain point had previously been knocked out, was blasted clear by the Tiger. The sound of shells striking home was heard several times; one of them, which hit the sight of the Tiger, must have been from a KV I. Exactly where the shot came from was not determined. It was suspected that the Tiger and the KV I had fired simultaneously. The Tiger backed up slowly, its gun turned to six o'clock, and the attack began. I remember the incident very clearly because we thought the hit on the gunsight was something quite out of the ordinary; later I experienced the same thing in our tank on 12 July 1943."

The Soviet shell, solid armor-piercing shot, had in fact struck the telescopic sight of the Tiger and detonated inside the turret. The gunner, SS-Rottenführer Willems, was killed instantly; SS-Untersturmführer Philipsen sustained serious wounds in his legs. The remaining crew members were SS-Sturmmann Willi Röpstorff (driver), SS-Panzerschützen Rudi Lechner (loader) and Lorenz Mähner (radio operator). The Panzer IV of Obersturmführer Malchow of the 5th Company of the Leibstandarte Panzer Regiment was also knocked out on the outskirts of Kharkov. Malchow's driver Heider recalled that a Tiger destroyed six T 34s and a KV II. Heinz Freiberg of the 7th Panzer Company noted in his diary, "Our Panzer IVs wouldn't have survived these battles as well without the support of the Tigers," confirming the success of which the Tigers were capable when not hampered by mechanical troubles and when employed where they could be most effective and in a tactically correct manner.

Heavy fighting raged in the city; Soviet snipers firing from houses inflicted losses on the attackers. The flak battalion's heavy guns were moved forward and thrown into the battle in the streets. The assault guns and armored troop carriers were also heavily engaged. SS-Oberschütze Edgar Börner of the 11th Company of the 1st SS Panzer-Grenadier Regiment described a patrol sent into Kharkov late on the evening of 11 March: "Our patrol reached the Red Square under cover of darkness; there was no contact with the enemy. The huge square was brightly lit in the moonlight and a deceptive quiet reigned. Our 2nd Regiment was supposedly already at the Red Square, so a short time later we asked several infantrymen, 'Are you from 2nd Regiment?' We received no answer, instead a well-concealed tank fired a shell into the house above us from about 100 meters away. We crawled into a cellar and sent the runner to report to our battalion commander, SS-Sturmbannführer Weidenhaupt. The runner returned with orders for us to remain at the Red Square for the night and observe. We established contact by field telephone. In our cellar we were protected from the night cold. When it became light we couldn't believe our eyes. The entire square was full of Soviet infantry; rifles slung, they were collecting their morning rations. We watched these proceedings until IInd Battalion, 1st Regiment with SS-Sturmbannführer Max Hansen reached us and we were able to crawl out of our mouse hole."

The determined enemy resistance continued on 12 and 13 March 1943. Each block of houses had to be cleared individually. The Soviets fired from the houses with anti-tank guns, machine-guns and anti-tank rifles; tanks lurked in driveways and yards. As the day went on the battalion groups of the Leibstandarte fought their way through to the southeast. By evening two-thirds of the city was under German control. There was more bitter fighting on 14 March. At 1645 hours the Leibstandarte reported to the SS Panzer Corps that the city center had been taken and was firmly in German hands. On the afternoon of 14 March the German state radio network broadcast a special bulletin over all transmitters: "Special Bulletin! From the headquarters of the Führer, 14 March 1943. The Wehrmacht High Command announces: After days of heavy fighting, Army Group South, whose counterattack threw the enemy back across the Donets in a weeks-long battle, has retaken the city of Kharkov in a pincer attack from the north and east by units of the Waffen-SS, effectively supported by the Luftwaffe. The full extent of the enemy's losses in men and material has not yet been ascertained."

SS-Obergruppenführer Sepp Dietrich was decorated with the Knight's Cross with Oak Leaves and Swords. Final mopping up in the city took place on 15 March 1943. The three-hundred-kilometer gap in the front that had resulted from the Battle of Stalingrad and its aftermath had been closed. The surrounding towns were taken in the days that followed; the Leibstandarte was given the new objective of Belgorod, situated north of Kharkov. On 18 March 1943, a sunny day with a clear blue sky, the reinforced 2nd SS Panzer-Grenadier Regiment Leibstandarte moved off with Peiper's armored troop carrier battalion. Two Tigers had been sent to the troop carrier battalion the night before. The attack began at 0640 hours. Stukas attacked the Soviet Krestovo—Kaumovka line at 0700 and ten minutes later Peiper reported that he had breached the blocking line and was advancing on Otradny. In one of the two Tigers taking part in the attack was gunner SS-Rottenführer Werner Wendt. The tank's commander was SS-Unterscharführer Modes, driver SS-Unterscharführer Otto Augst.

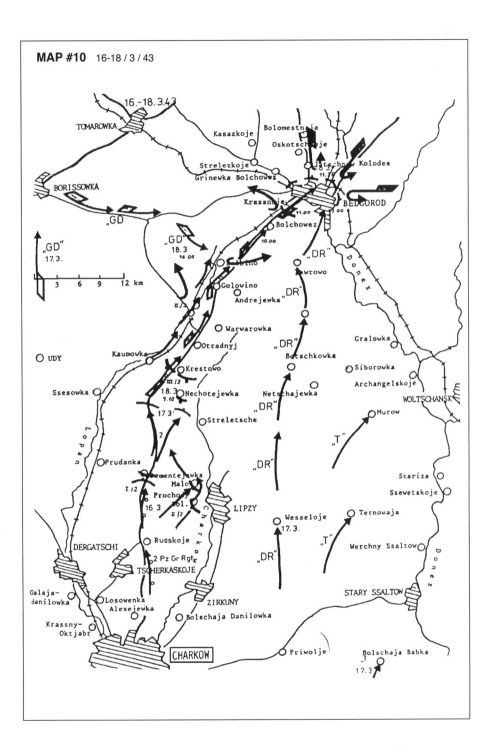

MAP #10   16-18 / 3 / 43

Tiger 411, platoon commander SS-Obersturmführer Schütz's tank during a field exercise in May 1943. Development of a heavy battle tank was essential to improve the fighting strength and maintain the tactical superiority of the German panzer arm. Not only was increased armor with no reduction in mobility called for; the front-line units were also demanding a gun with increased range, accuracy and penetrating ability. All these demands were addressed in the development of the Tiger.

The greatest tank battle of the Second World War began in the Kursk Salient on 5 July 1943. Pictured are a mixture of PzKpfw II and III tanks, also SdKfz 250 and 251 armored personnel carriers.

Inside the Tiger:
From the loader's
position.

Inside the Tiger:
Gunner's position with
binocular telescopic
sight.

Inside the Tiger:
The radio operator's
position.

Inside the Tiger:
The driver's position.

Inside the Tiger:
The gunner's position.

Inside the Tiger:
The driver's position.

Inside the Tiger: The commander's position.

Rail transport arrives in the Kharkov area at the end of January 1943. SdKfz 251 Ausf C armored troop carriers of the 11th (Armored) Company, 2nd SS Panzer-Grenadier Regiment.

The units immediately engaged the attacking Soviets. Panzer IV Ausf G of the 6th Company, SS Panzer Regiment Leibstandarte.

Gunner Heinz Buchner on a Panzer III Ausf J of the Tiger Company's Light Platoon.

A tank which broke through the ice near Lyubotin.

March 1943, in front of Kharkov, final conference before the attack. *Left:* SS-Standartenführer Fritz Witt (commander of the 1st SS Panzer-Grenadier Regiment). *Middle:* SS-Sturmbannführer Max Wünsche (commander Ist Battalion, 1st SS Panzer Regiment). *Right:* SS-Obersturmbannführer Kurt Meyer (commander of the 1st SS Reconnaissance Battalion).

Leibstandarte Tigers in front of Kharkov. The German offensive began on 6 March 1943.

Panzer III Ausf J of the Light Platoon in Poltava, February 1943. Wittmann remained at readiness there until March 1943.

Panzers of the 2nd Company, 1st SS Panzer Regiment Leibstandarte in March 1943. In the foreground is a Panzer IV Ausf G.

SS-Sturmbannführer
Jochen Peiper (left),
the commander of
the Leibstandarte's
armored troop carrier
battalion, and his
regimental commander,
SS-Standartenführer
Teddy Wisch, coordinate
their next move.

A Panzer IV of the
Leibstandarte which
broke through melting
ice.

In Kharkov. *Left:*
SS-Sturmbannführer
Max Hansen issues
instructions to his men
for the battle in the city.

March 1943, street
fighting in Kharkov.
Tank-destroyers and
tanks eliminate enemy
resistance.

18 March 1943. The
capture of Belgorod, in
which the Tigers played
a significant role. On the
right a panzer III of
Wittmann's Light
Platoon.

March 1943, anti-tank
barricade (Spanish
horsemen) in front of
Kharkov. The Russian
tank is a T-35.

A bridge in Kharkov.

SS-Oberstgruppenführer and
Generaloberst der Waffen-SS
Paul Hausser.

Following a Stuka attack,
tanks and panzer-
grenadiers of the
Leibstandarte advance
deeper into Kharkov.

SdKfz 251/1 Ausf C armored troop carriers advance through a suburb of Kharkov.

The attack rolls past a burning Soviet tank into the interior of the city.

Even fiercer resistance had to be broken south of Kharkov.

BELGOROD FALLS TO A SURPRISE ATTACK

Wendt related: "There was still snow everywhere and the road conditions were less than ideal, but a brilliant blue sky lent wings to our plans. In the morning the 2nd SS Panzer-Grenadier Regiment's IIIrd (Armored) Battalion (SS-Sturmbannführer Peiper) broke through the forward Soviet lines at 0710 hours; we started our engines and formed up. March sequence, direction of advance and objective had been laid down in advance. In the lead was a Panzer IV and then our Tigers.

We had scarcely gotten under way and had just crossed the front lines when we spotted two well-camouflaged T 34s in ambush positions. We traversed our turret and opened fire on the T 34s. Our shells were on target and the Soviet tanks subsequently left cover, which was a fatal mistake as they were knocked out for good by us as they tried to flee. They scarcely had a chance to return fire. Our tank engines thundered powerfully and our tracks bit into the Ukrainian earth and propelled us forward. Then a tactical reconnaissance aircraft (Henschel Hs 126) appeared above us. The machine swooped down and dropped a smoke capsule containing a report that there were still several Soviet tanks cruising around in our attack lane. This report heightened our watchfulness.

The Tigers had moved into the point position after the last engagement, which required us to be especially careful. As we burst into the next village the advance road curved slightly to the right. We couldn't believe our eyes; in position in front of us was an enemy 76.2 mm anti-tank gun. It was obvious that our appearance had come as a surprise, for instead of being behind their gun, the Red Army men were sitting on a bench in front of a nearby cottage flirting with several girls from the village.

There was no need for us to fire. Without hesitating we drove over the gun at full speed; it was no threat to us now, having been reduced to scrap. As we continued down the advance road we were challenged by two T 34s which we destroyed easily. To the left of the road there was a vast expanse over which hundreds of Red Army troops were fleeing, driven by fear of being overrun by our rapid advance. Their coats flapped as they ran, as if they were trying to escape an approaching disaster. We paid no attention to what was happening to the left and right. Our full concentration was on our objective, Belgorod, and we increased our pace.

It was 1130, almost noon, when Belgorod appeared before us. We couldn't read the sign, for the cyrillic script was unfamiliar to us, but it could and had to be Belgorod, which we intended to take in a surprise attack. Approaching from the southwest, we cautiously drove over a wooden bridge. The bridge held up under our panzers and we drove north into Belgorod. Two armored troop carriers accompanied us. We were about to exit the city when a call rang out: 'Tanks from behind!' The crews of the half-tracks jumped down from their vehicles and took cover in the ditches. 'Turret six o'clock!' ordered our commander. We began traversing the turret immediately, for the Soviet tanks had already approached to within about 200 meters. The first shot was a direct hit, for the high profile of the General Grant (supplied by the US) made it difficult to miss.

After this combat we received a radio message informing us that enemy tanks were firing on our munitions trucks and the following vehicles on our advance road. We were to attempt to keep the road open at all costs. We turned around at once, our tracks tearing up the softened street. As we approached the wooden bridge we saw a T 34 positioned about 300 meters beyond it, completely blocking the access road. We opened fire at once and scored a hit on the engine compartment of the enemy tank, which began to emit smoke. The T 34 fired back, undaunted by the hit. Our next shot was on target and it silenced the enemy's gun. The road was open again. Another of our company's Tigers had meanwhile arrived and cleared the road. Now all our vehicles could drive to Belgorod in safety. The city was taken and our mission accomplished. By attacking with great elan, we were the first tank to reach Belgorod, after which we drove irresistibly through the city; this gave us fresh impetus, made us proud and fortified our faith in our weapon."

In the other Tiger were Hauptsturmführer Kling and his gunner SS-Panzerschütze "Bobby" Warmbrunn. They knocked out a T 34, an M 2, three 76.2mm anti-tank guns and an armored car and ran over a 150 mm gun. At 1135 hours Peiper radioed: "Belgorod has been seized. Eight tanks destroyed."

On 19 March 1943 the enemy increased his pressure on the armored troop carrier battalion holding the northern part of Belgorod. At 1315 hours the half-tracks, together with the 7th Panzer Company and two Tigers, set off to the northwest. At 1535 hours SS-Sturmbannführer Peiper reported engagements with enemy tanks near Streletskoye, in which seven were destroyed without loss. The bridge in the village was destroyed and the battalion and the tanks withdrew to the eastern section during the night. Kling destroyed a super-heavy KV II, his gunner was Warmbrunn.

At 0615 hours on 20 March 1943, the few Tigers and Kampfgruppe Peiper headed down the road in the direction of Kursk. Stiff resistance was encountered at Skopino and Gonki; the battle group subsequently withdrew toward Jatschew—Kolodes and Oskotschnoje as per previous orders and assumed covering positions there. The battle group was twelve kilometers north of Belgorod. The next day the deployed elements of the Leibstandarte held and secured all of the specified objectives. There was scant contact with the enemy.

Approximately six-hundred NCOs and enlisted men arrived in Kharkov on 22 March 1943 and were immediately distributed among the units, the first replacements to reach the Leibstandarte. In the days that followed, all the elements of the division arrived in their assigned rest areas for a well-deserved break. The unit's accomplishments were lauded in orders of the day issued by the SS Panzer Corps, the army, and the army group. Earlier, on 19 March 1943, Adolf Hitler had issued an order of the day to Army Groups South and Center.

The division's outstanding tactical conduct, first in a defensive role and from 5 March in an offensive one—which resulted in the retaking of Kharkov after heavy street and house-to-house fighting—produced a large number of well-deserved decorations in all the units of the Leibstandarte. The division was featured prominently in the German newspapers and special radio bulletins. The Leibstandarte SS Adolf Hitler had achieved a great victory over a superior enemy and in doing so added further fame to its banner.

The Tigers that had broken down in front of Kharkov arrived in the city and rejoined the company. SS-Sturmmann Schamp hadn't participated in the fighting in Kharkov; he was still in Valki on 11 March 1943. SS-Sturmmann Tacina was killed there while fiddling with Russian ammunition. Schamp and his crew left Valki on 13 March 1943 and reached Lyubotin, arriving in Dergaci on the following day. The onset of the spring thaw had turned the roads into morasses. It took twelve hours to cover 35 kilometers. On 16 March 1943 they finally arrived in Kharkov.

SS-Untersturmführer Ortwin Rohl succumbed to his wounds on 24 March 1943. The Tiger company had suffered twelve killed.

QUARTERS IN KHARKOV-TRAINING,
20 MARCH–29 JUNE 1943

The Tiger company moved into quarters in a workers settlement on the outskirts of Kharkov that had escaped destruction. The men took advantage of the rest to tend to personal grooming—they washed and shaved, had their hair cut and were finally able to change clothes. They had their old clothes washed by local civilians. All members of the Tiger company were housed in private quarters. Relations with the population were good; the language barrier did not prove to be an insurmountable problem. The men were able to improve their rations by bartering with the local farmers; many German soldiers were invited to supper and had no cause to complain about the food. In some cases the soldiers shared their rations with the residents of their quarters and ate with them. They were on very good, almost familiar, terms with the residents. There were pianos in some of the quarters, which those who could play used to provide evening entertainment. There were gramophones too, even German records.

The daily routine was a light one, but the men were not permitted to be become lazy. There was also free time in the evenings and the men went out. SS-Sturmmann Schamp spent much of his time with SS-Rottenführer Gustav Swiezy, a Galician German from Ternopol who was the commander of a Panzer III and who also served as the company commander's interpreter. One day when Schamp went to pick him up, he became engaged in conversation with SS-Hauptsturmführer Kling. Kling, who was most affable toward his fellow Hessian, had Schamp write a paper on the recent action by the Tigers and Panzer IIIs. The paper was finished by 20 March 1943 and Schamp discussed it with Kling. The company commander then invited him to coffee.

The first decorations were awarded the same day. The Tiger Company had not participated in the recapture of Kharkov as a unit; only a few of its tanks saw action there. The Iron Cross, Second Class was presented to SS-Unterscharführer Franz Staudegger, SS-Rottenführer Arthur Sommer and Karl Jauss, the crew of Obersturmführer Philipsen, SS-Sturmmann Willi Ropstörff, and SS-Panzerschützen Lorenz Mähner, Rudolf Lechner, Heinz Willems and Bobby Warmbrunn. The first Tank Battle Badges in Silver were awarded on 1 April 1943. Everyone who had seen combat on at least three days while in a tank received the decoration. SS-Sturmmann Rolf Schamp was made commander of a Tiger, which at that time was very unusual for someone of his rank. On 26 March 1943 he wrote enthusiastically: "Tank commander 418—Hurray, when will I finally see action?"

On 31 March 1943 there was a reorganization of crews within the Tiger Company. Rolf Schamp became commander of Tiger 426. His crew consisted of Panzerschützen Fritz Seidelberg (gunner), Werner Irrgang (loader), Herbert Werner (radio operator) and Piper (driver). When they were off duty the men took in shows at the soldier's hostel, many went to the theater or the cinema; in any case boredom was not a problem.

The Inspector of Armored Forces, Generaloberst Guderian, and General Kempf visited the Leibstandarte in Kharkov. Parked in the middle of the Red Square, which had been renamed Leibstandarte Square, was the company commander's Tiger. Guderian inspected the tank and SS-Untersturmführer Wittmann answered technical questions about this most modern German battle tank. On 5 April 1943 Generaloberst Model visited the company.

Five new Tigers arrived. SS-Untersturmführer Wittmann took command of the IIIrd Platoon and for the first time became a Tiger commander. A group of approximately ten men were transferred to the company from the Leibstandarte's supply troops; all had made repeated requests for combat duty.

Among them were SS-Unterscharführer Heinz Werner and Hans Rosenberger, both of whom later became tank commanders in the light platoon; SS-Oberscharführer Marten, SS-Scharführer Lötzsch and SS-Unterscharführer Staudegger went on to become Tiger commanders. Others in this group included SS-Schützen Walter Lau and Hermann Grosse, both of whom were trained as loaders.

Meanwhile, SS-Panzerschütze Alfred Lünser had been delivered to a Kharkov hospital: "We took over everything, the fleas, the lice, the Russian nurses and the beds with their straw mattresses, often soiled with blood. My leg was looked after, but it was a long time, several weeks, before I was released and even then my leg was not yet fit. I landed back at my unit in April-May. It was at rest north of Kharkov. There I met my new commander,

Unterscharführer Blase. He came from the Luftwaffe. There were no more Panzer IIIs, I moved up to a Tiger. My leg gave me a lot of trouble. When I sat in the sun fluid oozed from my lower leg like sweat. The doctor subsequently sent me to a skin clinic at the field hospital in Kremenchug. They did a lot of experimenting, but there was no improvement! Then one day a senior medical officer—right out of Thomas Mann's Felix Krull—came and said: 'I got this for you from the army medical stores in Kiev.' In a few days my dermatitis was healed."

A trickle of wounded made their way back to "the old gang" while others recuperated in hospitals in Germany. One of the latter was SS-Untersturmführer Hannes Philipsen, who had been wounded in his tank in front of Kharkov on 11 March 1943. While in hospital, on 20 March he received the Iron Cross, First Class, the first member of the Tiger company to receive this decoration. On 20 April he wrote to his parents from the hospital in Meiningen. The letter began with a look back at his time as a Jungvolk leader before the war: "As a Pimpfenführer this day (Hitler's birthday) was always one of the loveliest of the year for me.

Each year on this day a new, young, fresh age class joined our group and the oldest boys left us, and I was proud of them. If you look at them now, those boys of yesterday are the best soldiers on every front and as far as they're concerned there's nothing they can't do. We guessed back then that some day we would take up arms against bolshevism if our beloved homeland willed it. This was made clear to us in many afternoons at home and at school. Therefore, even as boys we steeled and hardened our bodies and love of our nation became our faith. Yesterday I listened with enthusiasm here in the east as the ten-year-old Jungmädel and Pimpfe were enrolled in front of the Marienburg, and to the message from our Reich Youth Leader Axmann and later that night to the congratulations of our Führer. At times such as these I am a Pimpf again as I was several years ago. But the war has taught us to think about many other things, and our idealism is firmer. My thoughts are especially with my company comrades, for this was always a great day for us officers and men of his bodyguard!

My leg was taken out of the support frame yesterday and now it has been placed in a cast so that my knee can heal properly. The day after tomorrow I wIII be allowed to make my first attempt to walk with the cast, so that when Matthias comes I can get up and perhaps sit in the garden or on the balcony. I am looking forward tremendously to Matthias and it will be a lovely Easter holiday for both of us, especially since I no longer have to lie in bed! If you should come in the lovely month of May, dear parents, then I will be completely happy. I estimate that I will be in the cast for about three weeks and then it will be several more weeks before I can walk . . ."

Another member of the Tiger company should be mentioned here, Sepp Hafner. He came directly to the company from the Maybach Works as shop foreman in charge of the Tigers' engines. At first he went around in blue mechanic's overhauls, but soon he was given a uniform with the rank badges of an Oberschurführer. Hafner was a capable specialist who was highly thought of on account of his expert knowledge.

EARLY TECHNICAL EXPERIENCES

The Tiger was not capable of long overland drives; in the long run the running gear suffered from the loads imposed by the fifty-seven tonne vehicle. For example, shock-absorber swing arms broke as a result of worn inner road-wheel tires and the resulting damage to the roadwheels themselves. Repair times for such damage could be as high as thirty-six hours. The engine had to be removed in order to replace the rear shock-absorber swing arms, which in turn called for the removal of the turret. Reduction gear failures were common. The Olvar transmission tended to become very hot under prolonged use, which had the effect of thinning the oil. The result was the loss of individual transmission cylinders and floating, the latter causing damage to entire transmission assemblies. Several Tigers had caught fire for reasons other than enemy action and burned out completely. Initially unexplained, it was found that the cause was the high temperatures reached by the exhaust pipes and ignition of fuel in the engine compartment. Quickly repairing damage wrought by these initial teething troubles called for highly-qualified and well-trained personnel in the maintenance echelon and the workshop platoon.

In addition to Sepp Hafner, the Maybach Firm sent Walter Häring to the Tiger company as an engine and transmission specialist. He wrote: "The so-called Tiger tank, which was equipped with the Maybach engine— at first the Hl 210 but soon afterward the Hl 230—and the Maybach Olvar transmission, went into action with newly-developed weapons and equipment. The transmission was a development of the Variorex and was controlled by means of oil pressure. This development made it absolutely vital to provide the affected units with specially-trained fitters who, by referring to a gearshift diagram, would be able to determine the cause of the inevitable transmission problems immediately and see to the necessary repairs. The fitters were allocated to the respective repair-shop companies with the understanding of the OKH; however, as civilians they could not go into action with the troops. They were therefore issued uniforms and served under the title of Kriegswerkmeister, or military shop foreman. Nevertheless, they remained employees of Maybach as before.

The fitters were controlled and looked after by Maybach's field and service departments. There was a constant exchange of information between the parent company and the fitters. The fitters were obliged to keep the company informed of experience gained with engines and transmissions. These reports were evaluated by the company's field department and then made available to the design and test departments, which initiated necessary corrective measures such as modifications. The fitters were informed of the resulting measures, including from which engine or transmission number this or that change was to be introduced and as of when the necessary replacement parts would be available to the units. Priority was of course given to the introduction of eventual changes into ongoing production.

Personnel serving with the major front-line maintenance facilities were dealt with in the same way. In contrast to the front-line units, which were only capable of handling minor repairs, including engine and transmission changes and less serious problems, the maintenance facilities set up behind the front carried out major repairs, for example general overhauls of engines and transmissions. These facilities included technical personnel from all the firms, fitters, foremen and assembly inspectors. These technical personnel were well looked after by their firms, ensuring a smooth-functioning maintenance service.

I have already described how Maybach organized its field service. Only those units equipped with tanks with Maybach transmissions were assigned special fitters, because in the event of transmission breakdown only these fitters would be able to help by referring to a gearshift diagram. The field service functioned extremely well thanks to the support of the responsible Wehrmacht offices, the OKH and Inspector-General of Armored Forces Guderian. Oil leaks at the crankshaft and the fan drive caused by the high excess pressure in the engine crankcase were the main problem encountered with the engines in the beginning.

The result was vehicle fires. Cases of broken connecting rods became more common as the number of engines in service grew, including those in the Panther tank which also used the H1 230. It took a long time before they succeeded in informing me of the cause in Russia. In a vehicle with full fuel tanks the maximum fuel level was significantly higher than the carburetor or the float gauge. Leaky float needle valves allowed fuel to run into the cylinders (in a 12-cylinder engine, 6 inlet valves are always open). Starting the engine resulted in so-called hydrostatic locks; the weakest part, the connecting rod, buckled and soon broke. The ratio of the starter pinion to the flywheel gear wheel was so great that the starter motor easily turned the engine over. The situation was remedied by inserting an oil pressure activated valve in the fuel line in front of the carburetors (four two-stage double carburetors per engine); consequently, when the engine was off there was no oil pressure and thus no delivery of fuel. Once this problem had been solved, there were no more engine problems apart from normal wear. My impression of the state of development of the Maybach engines compared to those of the enemy was that the Maybach engine was far superior.

Our greatest disadvantage, however, was that we had far too few tanks. This was the main reason why one combat unit collected Russian T 34 tanks, repaired them, and then used them in action. (The Das Reich Panzer Regiment equipped one company with captured T 34 tanks.) All in all, the spares system functioned well, even though the destruction caused by enemy bombing created a number of bottlenecks in production and transport. Everything associated with the production of tanks and its supply was given priority. In spite of the relocation of many important production facilities to lessor non-threatened locations, there was no break in production and a well-organized supply system was maintained."

Obersturmführer Waldemar Schütz oversaw the training and provided most of the company instruction. On 20 April 1943, the Führer's birthday, he gave an obligatory speech to the assembled men, after which they were given some free time and an opportunity to take advantage of a special issue of sales articles.

To the joy of the assembled troops, decorations were presented and promotions announced. Gunner SS-Rottenführer Werner Wendt, a former

Leibstandarte artilleryman, was promoted to the rank of SS-Unterschar-
führer for the six enemy tanks he destroyed during the seizure of Belgo-
rod. SS-Unterscharführer and Tiger commanders Jürgen Brandt and Hans
Hold received the Iron Cross, Second Class, as did Oberscharführer Max
Marten and SS-Unterscharführer Gustav Swietzy, tank commanders in the
light platoon. SS-Sturmmann Hein Reimers, SS-Unterscharführer Otto
Augst, SS-Unterscharführer Friedrich Aumann, SS-Panzeroberschütze Rolf
Heß and SS-Panzerschütze Roland Söffker were also decorated with the
Iron Cross, Second Class. Several days earlier the young tank soldiers witnessed an unusual event. A field court martial had sentenced an SS-Sturm-
mann to death for desertion. The sentence was carried out in front of the
assembled company on 12 April 1943.

THE TIGER COMPANY RESTS AND REFITS
SS-Schütze Walter Lau, then twenty years old, was one of ten men from the
Leibstandarte's supply units to join the Tiger company: "A few days after
the retaking of Kharkov, on 15 March 1943, we—the supply company of
the division supply troops, commanding officer SS-Sturmbannführer
Siebken—moved into a billet near 'Leibstandarte Square.' That was what
the Red Square was called since the capture of Kharkov. I remember the
concrete square very well, because we were soon carrying out our morning
close-order and rifle drill on it.

The supply company with its four platoons (flak, anti-tank and two
rifle platoons) was a smart company. The company commander, Hauptsturmführer Stamp, was a veteran member of the Leibstandarte, and the
NCOs, especially the senior ones, were mostly so-called 'last sons' who had
been withdrawn from combat units and sent to supply or to the replacement and training battalion. All were decorated with the Iron Cross and
the Assault Badge. In the truest sense of the word they made soldiers of us
in France in the period August to December 1942.

Their motto: 'SS men are jewels, they only need polishing.' But we
weren't very happy. It was only supply. We hadn't volunteered to take part
in the war as 'supply soldiers.' Many of us had several times asked, verbally
or in writing, for a transfer to the panzer-grenadiers or better yet to Panzermeyer's reconnaissance battalion. Now, in March 1943, we finally got our
wish; about one hundred men from the division supply troops were transferred to the front-line units to make good the losses suffered in the Battle
of Kharkov.

All were assigned to the panzer regiment. Sturmbannführer Schönberger greeted us in front of the regimental command post at the northern outskirts of Kharkov. Obersturmführer Rudolf von Ribbentrop was

serving as regimental adjutant at the time and it was he who assigned the newcomers. The majority went to the IInd Battalion, some to the workshop company, and about ten men to the Tiger company.

I will insert an incident here, my first experience with the Tiger. It was in February, somewhere in front of Valki. We were in a village on the main road. Sitting beside a Russian cottage was a Tiger tank. It had broken down and we marvelled at this colossus which was seeing action with the Leibstandarte for the first time. We were even more amazed by the young, blond tank commander, an Untersturmführer with the Iron Cross, Second Class, who pitched in and helped with the repairs. Not three weeks later I found out that it had been SS-Untersturmführer Helmut Wendorff. I had no idea at the time what I would later go through with him.

But back to the Tiger company's billet at the northern outskirts of Kharkov. For about two or three weeks we ten of the supply company received combat-related training on the Panzer III from Rottenführer Swiezy and Sturmmann Schamp, and then on the Panzer VI, or Tiger, from Unterscharführer Staudegger and Unterscharführer Sowa. The usual routine looked like this: 0600 wake up, 0700 morning roll call by Senior NCO Habermann, followed by one to two hours of drill directed by Obersturmführer Schütz, and finally tank training in the platoons under the direction of Untersturmführer Wendorff and Wittmann. The two had built a sand table in the front garden and they kept us busy there playing the roles of individual tanks and platoons. As well there was live firing, weapons theory and maintenance duties. We were soon able to change track links and road wheels in our sleep."

In the meantime the Leibstandarte received a large number of replacements from the Luftwaffe. The Tiger company also received some of these men, who in soldier's jargon were referred to as "donations from Hermann Göring." These soldiers, NCOs and enlisted men, had been thoroughly trained in the use of infantry weapons. They were willing and worked hard to prove themselves as tank soldiers. A training platoon was set up for these soldiers and the new replacements from Germany. In contrast to many other units, the Tiger company did not receive any long-service NCOs. Among the NCOs were some who had been passed over for pilot training. A number of them were now trained as tank commanders. Among this group were Unterscharführer Erich Langner, Otto Blase, Arthur Bernhard, Kurt Hühnerbein and Franz Enderl.

On 29 April 1943 the Tiger company moved north, in order to occupy quarters outside Kharkov; however, on 5 May the company returned to the city. On 2 May the Tiger of SS-Sturmmann Schamp suffered a broken pump spindle and had to go into the repair shop. It returned to the company on 15 May. His notes: "0400 hours, departure for Kharkov. Rest in forester's house, fried eggs, bee's honey.—1800 hours, back at the company—21/05: sand table—25/05: cross-country drive—26/05: in the field with the training platoon."

This was the typical routine of those days, which also included technical instruction on the tanks. The training of the newcomers was in the hands of SS-Untersturmführer Wittmann and Wendorff, who demonstrated tactics on the sand table set up in the company area behind the munitions storage area. The newly-arrived, young soldiers were impressed by Wittmann; the lessons he gave at the sand table demonstrated his skill as a tactician; as well his obvious grasp of terrain conditions, range, attack speed, field of fire, firing position, and the element of surprise made a lasting impression on the men. Wittmann did not simply offer dry lectures; his classes were lively and graphic.

SS-Sturmmann Schamp found an elderly Austrian who had moved to Kharkov years before who could carve miniature tanks from wood; these were used for tactical instruction on the sand table. Payment was in the form of bread and fuel. The Austrian also had beehives, and from time to time Schamp was able to procure honey for company commander Hauptsturm-führer Kling, Swiezy and himself.

The following minor episode concerns Gustav Swiezy, the company commander's batman and interpreter. He had been awarded the Iron Cross, Second Class and promoted to SS-Unterscharführer for his actions as commander of a Panzer III. One day while talking with his friend Rudolf Schamp, he mused that he had been in battle with T 34s several times in the Panzer III and that after all this counted for more than the actions of those who had fought in the Tiger. Swiezy reached the conclusion that he should actually have received the Iron Cross, First Class. Schamp advised him to speak to the company commander about it. Firmly convinced that he was right, the good Swiezy did just that. He returned soon afterward, quite disappointed, because Hauptsturmführer Kling had been unwilling to endorse his line of reasoning. Michael Wittmann and Helmut Wendorff—always just "Axel" to Wittmann—were often visited by Knight's Cross wearer SS-Hauptscharführer Alfred Günther of the assault gun battalion. Freddi Günther had been friends with the pair since 1940, when they were founding members of the Assault Gun Battery. Günther had served as gunner in Wittmann's assault gun in Russia in 1941.

The new men rarely saw the company commander. In some ways Kling was unable to completely free himself from the customs of the pre-war period. Disciplined, hard training was his number one priority. He concerned himself with the officers and NCOs and was interested in the overall training of the company. Kling's authority was based on respect and he had a firm grip on the company. However, he could react badly to slackness, treating the entire company to a highly explosive dressing-down. The daily routine was determined by the platoon commanders, while duties within the company were under the direction of Obersturmführer Schütz.

Toward the end of May another group of Luftwaffe personnel—several NCOs and thirty enlisted men—joined the company. It included Kurt Kleber, Herbert Stief, Kurt Diefenbach, Gehrke and Cap—all of whom held the rank of SS-Unterscharführer—and the single long-service non-commissioned officer, SS-Oberscharführer Behrens. This new influx of former Luftwaffe personnel blended harmoniously into the close-knit fighting team of the company. Where did these Luftwaffe soldiers come from? Many had originally been slated for pilot training, others came from air bases, some came to the Tiger company direct from basic training. Only one had any combat experience. From Langenrohr in Austria, SS-Unterscharführer Eduard Stadler had joined the Luftwaffe in February 1941 and had won the Luftwaffe Ground Combat Badge on the Eastern Front while serving with a Luftwaffe Field Division.

The completely different environment of a panzer company demanded a rapid readjustment by the former Luftwaffe soldiers. It remains to be said that nearly all of them made the transition and found their feet in their new positions. Contributing to this was the good atmosphere that existed in the company and the awareness that they were now members of the Leibstandarte, one of the most famous divisions in the German Reich.

One example may be seen as representative of all the recruits: Rudi Hirschel was just nineteen when he was called up by the 71st Flying Regiment. On 29 March 1943 he was released by the Luftwaffe and on 2 April 1943 he arrived at the Tiger company in Kharkov, where he was retrained and saw action as a radio operator. "I was called up by the Luftwaffe on 20 January 1943. After two and a half months of infantry training in France I am now with a heavy tank unit of the Leibstandarte SS Adolf Hitler, of which I am proud to be a member."

The men were issued new garrison caps made of light and dark green spotted camouflage cloth. As well, one-piece tank coveralls of the same camouflage material were issued to the combat echelon. Unlike the black panzer uniforms, they were less sensitive to dirt and were less likely to become caught on an interior fixture of the tank. Wittmann and Wendorff often wore their grey assault gun uniforms during training, as these were less susceptible to dirt than the black uniform. The men of the train converted their 3-tonne Opel Blitz trucks and equipped them with fixed superstructures. The conversions produced one each of orderly room, radio maintenance, ordnance shop and rations trucks, as well as two mess trucks. The maintenance echelon carried out a similar conversion on one of its 5-tonne MAN trucks to produce a spare-parts vehicle.

One day the regimental commander, SS-Obersturmbannführer Schünberger, visited the company during an exercise to check on the progress of the training. When he noticed that Schamp was a tank commander although only a Sturmmann, he engaged him in conversation and asked what he was doing there. At that point SS-Hauptsturmführer Kling appeared and answered for Schamp; he justified his decision to employ a Sturmmann as a tank commander on the basis of his performance.

In the weeks that followed, training focused on battle tactics. The great German summer offensive was imminent, although the starting date had to be pushed back several times. The Leibstandarte released a number of officers, NCOs and enlisted men to serve as a cadre for the Hitlerjugend Division then being raised. New officers and NCOs had to take their places, representing a great organizational feat by all those responsible in those weeks. The new commanding officers took over their units on 13 May 1943; they were all members of the division and had served in lower positions. Great responsibility rested upon their shoulders.

The Ist Battalion of the Leibstandarte Panzer Regiment under SS-Sturmbannführer Max Wünsche was transferred as a body to form the basis of the Hitlerjugend Division's panzer regiment. A new Ist Battalion was raised in Germany and was equipped with the Panther, but it was not yet available to the division. On 4 June 1943 SS-Standartenführer 'Teddy' Wisch officially replaced Sepp Dietrich as division commander. Dietrich had been selected to command another new formation, the Ist SS Panzer Corps Leibstandarte.

The Tiger company was renamed at the end of May. Instead of the 4th Company, it became the 13th (Heavy) Company, SS Panzer Regiment Leibstandarte SS Adolf Hitler. Why the number 13 was chosen is unknown. The intent was probably to demonstrate that the Tiger company was a regimental unit and did not belong to either of the two battalions. A fourth company had been formed for the new Ist Battalion, and for this reason alone the previous designation could no longer be used. The number 13 was painted on the turrets of all of the company's tanks, including those of the light platoon; the other numbers denoting the platoon and the tank were applied after the 13 in slightly smaller characters. The Tigers received a multi-color camouflage finish for the first time; the chosen color scheme blended well with the Ukrainian landscape.

On 18 June 1943 the company held another exercise. Former Luftwaffe members—now SS-Unterscharführer—Enderl, Bernhard, Langner
and Hühnerbein served as tank commanders. In the midst of the exercise,
the Tiger driven by SS-Sturmmann Franz Elmer slipped out of gear and
skidded down a slope. Of course this resulted in a great fuss. Training continued at a high tempo.

A human atmosphere nevertheless prevailed in the company in spite
of the necessary strictness of the training. During one exercise SS-
Untersturmführer Helmut Wendorff ordered the Tigers camouflaged.
"Camouflage the tanks even better this time!" The regiment's CO, SS-
Obersturmbannführer Schönberger, cautioned him. "You're an Untersturmführer not a Sturmmann!" he said, referring to Wendorff's tone of
voice. When Wendorff determined that his men had followed his instructions to the letter, had mastered all the practice attacks, and that the training objective had been achieved, he gave an order that was typical of him:
"Attention! To the horizon, march—march—lie down, you may smoke."

SS-Untersturmführer Wittmann also received "advice" from the CO, as
SS-Panzerschütze 1 Lau recalled: "A company exercise took place outside
Kharkov sometime in May. It included driving, security on the march,
deploying into inverted wedge formation and firing at a large, stationary
metal target. I remember a conference with SS-Obersturmbannführer
Schönberger as he evaluated the exercise. The crews were assembled
around him in a semicircle. He directed one of his questions to the junior-
ranking platoon commander, SS-Untersturmführer Wittmann: 'About
thirty T 34s are attacking from a range of 1,500 meters, what do you do?'
Wittmann's answer: 'Give it the gas and have at them!' Schönberger smiled
and corrected him, pointing out that he should drive into cover and wait
for reinforcements."

Normally 92 rounds of ammunition could be accommodated inside
the Tiger. Modifications to the ammunition racks allowed approximately
120 rounds to be carried. The member of the 13th Company who came up
with the idea, whose name is unfortunately unknown, received a promotion
to Unterscharführer. The most recent Luftwaffe arrivals did not take part in
the planned offensive. On 30 June 1943 the 13th Panzer Company headed
north. The company commander's tank broke down with a reduction gear
failure and was taken under tow by Sturmmann Schamp on 1 July. On
4 July Tiger 1321 received a new engine near Tomarovka. The company
would soon be going into action; the radio code had already been changed.
The men knew that they were going on the offensive.

SS-Hauptsturmführer Kling (kneeling) explains the Tiger to Guderian.

In April 1943 Generaloberst Guderian visited the Leibstandarte's Tiger Company in Kharkov.

GUDERIAN BEI DEN ⚡⚡-PANZERN

Das Innere des „Tigers" ist sehr geräumig

Der deutschen Rüstungsindustrie ist es gelungen, den „Tiger" in überraschend kurzer Zeit zu entwickeln und fertigzustellen. Die Sowjets, die die außerordentliche Kampfkraft dieser neuen Waffe schon in früheren Kämpfen kennenlernen mußten, haben ihn die deutsche „Geheimwaffe" genannt.

SS-Hauptsturmführer Kling describes to Guderian the combat lessons learned with the Tiger during the Kharkov action. Left is SS-Standartenführer Fritz Witt, right SS-Standartenführer Werner Ostendorff, Ia of the SS Panzer Corps.

SS-Untersturmführer Michael Wittmann in the turret of Tiger 405 (company commander's tank) during the explanation of technical details. On the right Generaloberst Guderian, in the foreground SS-Hauptsturmführer Kling.

Guderian in conversation with General Dollmann. *From the left:* SS-Standartenführer Ostendorff, General Dollmann, Generaloberst Guderian, SS-Sturmbannführer Lehmann (1a of the Leibstandarte), SS-Hauptsturmführer Kling,
SS-Oberführer Staudinger (CO of the SS Artillery Regiment Leibstandarte).

From left: SS-Untersturmführer van Ribbentrop, an officer of Guderian's staff,
SS-Obersturmbannführer Ewert (partially hidden Ib of the Leibstandarte), SS-
Standartenführer Ostendorff, Guderian, Dollmann, SS-Hauptsturmführer Kling
and SS-Sturmbannführer Schönberger (commanding officer of the SS Panzer
Regiment Leibstandarte).

Generaloberst Guderian
shows great interest in
the latest German battle
tank and the lessons
learned from its use
in combat to date.

SS-Hauptscharführer Hartel (with peaked cap) and a group of men en route to Magdeburg to pick up new Tigers in April 1943.

Kharkov, Spring 1943. A Tiger of the 4th (Heavy) Company wearing the new camouflage scheme.

A Tiger in the Workshop Platoon's quarters.

A "Strength through Joy" group poses on one of the company's Tigers.

Kharkov, 20 April 1943. From left: SS-Untersturmführer Wendorff, SS-Obersturmführer Schütz, SS-Untersturmführer Wittmann.

SS-Panzerschütze
Werner Hepe, tank
driver.

SS-Sturmann
Wohlgemuth in front
of his Tiger; note the
ten kill rings on the
gun tube.

Inspection of the Tiger Company in Kharkov's Red Square, which was renamed "Leibstandarte Square" after the city was retaken. *From left:* SS-Unterscharführer Höld (tank commander), SS-Panzerschützen Warmbrunn and Bürvenich (gunner and loader), and SS-Sturmmänner Wohlgemuth and Reimers (radio operator and driver).

Tiger 411 in the field.

SS-Panzerschütze Bürvenich, SS-Sturmmann Wohlgemuth and SS-Sturmmann Reimers.

May 1943 near Kharkov.
SS-Obersturmführer
Waldemar Schütz
instructing the company.

SS-Obersturmführer Schütz in front of his quarters with his Ukranian hosts, with whom the men of the Leibstandarte had a good relationship.

SS-Obersturmführer Schütz with the Senior NCO, SS-Hauptscharführer Habermann.

SS-Unterscharführer Werner Wendt, SS-Obersturmführer Schütz's gunner.

SS-Obersturmführer Schütz in the turret of his Tiger 411 during a test drive.

Schütz presents the Tank Battle Badge in Silver to, *from left:* SS-Unterschar-führer Wendt, SS-Sturmmann Reimers, SS-Panzerschütz Bürvenich and SS-Sturmmann Wohlgemuth.

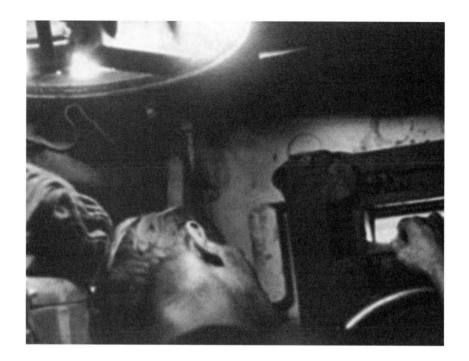

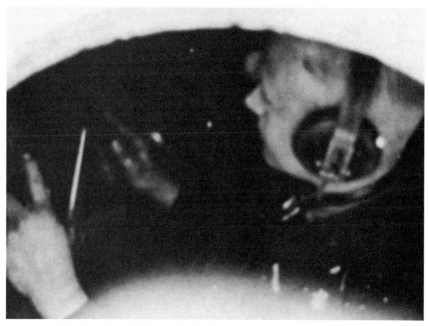

The interior of Tiger 411. Driver Hein Reimers at the wheel.

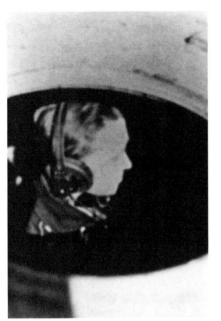

Radio operator SS-Sturmmann Wohlgemuth.

Loader Klaus Bürvenich with an
88mm round.

Driver Hein Reimers.

Tiger crew cleaning the tank's main gun.

SS-Obersturmführer Schütz discusses the duty roster for the next day. *From left:* Bürvenich, Reimers, Wendt, Schütz and Wohlgemuth.

2000 hours. Now off duty, the same men are busy cleaning and mending. Reimers, Wohlgemuth and Wendt.

SS-Obersturmführer Schütz in a game of skat.

The Battle in the Kursk Salient

OPERATION ZITADELLE, 5–17 JULY 1943

The recapture of Kharkov created a large westward-facing salient in the front; approximately 200 kilometers wide, it was centered on Kursk. The salient separated Army Group Center from Army Group South. Operation Zitadelle, which had been planned for some time, was directed against this salient. Its objective was to cut off the bulge in the front lines and destroy the powerful Soviet forces inside; this would seize the strategic initiative from the Soviets in that sector and considerably shorten the German front line. This was to be achieved by launching assaults from the north and south, resulting in a large-scale encirclement of the Soviets. The Leibstandarte would attack north from its positions, together with the IInd SS Panzer Corps, the Totenkopf and Das Reich Divisions.

The Fourth Panzer Army (XXXXVIIIth Panzer Corps, LIInd Army Corps) received the following order: "Headquarters, Fourth Panzer Army will set out to encircle and destroy the enemy in the Kursk salient as part of the Zitadelle attack. On X-Day the panzer army will break through the first position in the hill sector northwest of Belgorod—Korovino in planned attacks, following the capture of the hills on both sides of Butovo and south of Gerzowka by the XXXXVIIIth Panzer Corps on X-Day-1.

After quickly breaking all resistance in the second position and smashing opposing armored forces, it will then drive toward Kursk and east, bypassing Oboyan to the east. The operation will be screened offensively to the east by Army Detachment Kempf. The left wing of the army detachment (6th Panzer Division) will attack from Belgorod through Sabynino in the direction of Prokhorovka.

Following intensive artillery preparation, on X-Day the IInd SS Panzer Corps will break through the forward enemy defense zone in the Berezov—Sadelnoje sector in a planned attack with tank support by the Panzer-Grenadier Divisions LAH, Das Reich and Totenkopf and one third of the 167th Infantry Division. Echeloned to the right rear, one division will initially attack as far as the vicinity of Zhuravliny and open the Belgorod-Yakovlevo road. The corps is to proceed with the attack on the second

85

ORDER OF BATTLE: at the beginning of Operation "Zitadelle" on 5 July, 1943.
13th (Heavy) Company, 1st SS Panzer Regiment

1301
Company Commander
Hstuf. Heinz Kling

1302
Company HQ Squad Leader

1310
Uscha. Heinz Werner

1320
Uscha. Schwerin

Light Platoon

1300
Uscha. Gustav Swiezy

1330
Uscha. Hans Rosenberger

1340
Uscha. Kurt Hühnerbein

Ist Platoon

1311
Ostuf. Waldemar Schütz

1312
Uscha. Arthur Bernhard

1313
Uscha. Otto Augst

1314
Hscha. Fritz Hertel

1315
Uschä. Franz Enderl

IInd Platoon

1321
Ustuf. Helmut Wendorff

1322
Uscha. Ewald Mölly

1323
Schaf. Georg Lötzsch

1324
Strm. Rolf Schamp

1325
Uscha. Franz Staudegger

IIIrd Platoon

1331
Ustuf. Michael Wittmann

1332
Oscha. Max Marten

1333
Uscha. Hans Höld

1334
Uscha. Jürgen Brandt

1335
Uscha. Kurt Sowa

GUNNERS:
Pz.Schtz. Heinz Buchner
Strm. Balthasar Woll
Strm. Karl-Heinz Warmbrunn
Pz.Schtz. Fritz Seidelberg
Uscha. Werner Wendt
Strm. Siegfried Jung
Rttf. Helmut Gräser
Strm. Heinrich Knöss
Strm. Roland Söffker
Uscha. Karl Wagner
Strm. Rolf Schamp
Strm. Siegfried Hummel
Strm. Leopold Aumuller
Pz.Schtz. Alfred Lünser
Rttf. Friedrich Aumann
Strm. Ewald König
Pz.Schtz. Gerhard Knocke
Strm. Alfred Faltlhauser
Pz.Schtz. Heinz Schindhelm

LOADERS:
Pz.Schtz. Walter Lau
Pz.Schtz. Rudi Lechner
Pz.Schtz. Walter Henke
Strm. Johann Schütz
Pz.Schtz. Paul Sümnich
Pz. Schtz. Erich Tille
Pz.Schtz. Iwanitz
Pz.Schtz. Josef Rößner
Pz.Schtz. Max Gaube
Pz.Schtz. Ewald Graf
Pz.Schtz. Hermann Grosse
Strm. Alfred Bernhard
Pz.Schtz. Gustav Grüner
Strm. Mantow
Strm. Günther Braubach
Strm. Hirsch
Strm. Reinhard Wenzel

RADIO OPERATORS:
Pz.Schtz. Werner Irrgang
Pz.Schtz. Gerhard Waltersdorf
Strm. Justus Kühn
Strm. Wohlgemuth
Strm. Peter Winkler
Strm. Herbert Werner
Pz.Schtz. Rudolf Hirschel
Strm. Lorenz Mähner
Pz.Schtz. Kaminski
Strm. Heinz Stuss
Strm. Wunderlich

DRIVERS:
Strm. Franz Elmer
Strm. Ludwig Hoffmann
Strm. Werner Hepe
Strm. Eugen Schmidt
Strm. Heinrich Reimers
Rttf. Willi Röpstorff
Strm. Piper
Uscha. Kurt Sowa
Uscha. Pollak
Strm. Walter Bingert
Rttf. Focke
Strm. Herbert Stellmacher
Strm. Hein Rüttgers
Strm. Siegfried Fuss
Rttf. Jupp Selzer
Strm. Walter Poewe
Pz.Schtz. Kurt Kämmer
Rttf. Arthur Sommer

enemy position between Lutschki and Yakovlevo without delay after it has fought its way through the forward defense zone. The left flank is to be guarded by the 167th Infantry Division at the Vorskla. After breaking through the second position, the corps is to ready itself so that, echeloned to the right rear, it can advance northeast with its main force south of the Psel River line, with its right wing through Prokhorovka."

The mission given the Panzer-Grenadier Division LAH in Corps Order No 17 read: "LSSAH, reinforced by the 315th Grenadier Regiment and IInd Battalion, 238th Artillery Regiment, will attack the enemy positions along the Tomarovka-Bykovka road, drive north—screening the left flank near Kamenij Log—Sadelnoye, which are to be taken, and advancing rapidly, force a breakthrough east of Yakovlevo.

It will be the division's subsequent mission to break through to the northeast without delay and initially secure a crossing over the Psel in the Mikhailovka—Klyuchki sector. After conclusion of the preparatory barrage the 55th Rocket Regiment and the 861st Light Artillery Battalion will be placed under the command of the LAH.

The bulk of the VIIIth Fliegerkorps will support the attack by the IInd SS Panzer Corps. Initial attack targets positions in Berezov and area northeast of Berezov in front of SS.Pz.Gren.Div. DR excluding bridges; last bomb Y + 50, in front of LAH on positions on both sides of 220.5 and north of it; last bomb Y + 65. Close-support units will accompany attack spearheads of Das Reich and Leibstandarte Adolf Hitler from the beginning of the attack."

THE SOVIET PREPARATIONS

Solovyov's book *Battle at Kursk* describes the Red Army's preparations: "The Soviet command paid great attention to the creation of a strong and in-depth defense with the maximum use of combat engineers in the entire operational area. Special attention was given to the anti-tank and anti-aircraft defenses. When the German offensive began there were eight defense zones and lines with a total depth of 300 kilometers. At the same time the troops of the Central and Voronezh Fronts dug a total of 9,240 kilometers of rifle and communications trenches.

Hundreds of thousands of workers from the Oryol, Kursk, Voronezh and Kharkov areas helped the Red Army prepare for the Battle of Kursk. In the Kursk salient alone 105,000 residents of the Kursk region took part in defensive work in April and 300,000 in June. As part of the preparations for the battles near Kursk the soldiers and officers of the Soviet Army increased their military skills. Extensive party-political work was carried out among the troops. Thousands of officers and soldiers joined the Communist Party in the course of preparations for the Kursk battle. At the beginning of the battle there were 120,000 communists in the troops of the Central Front and more than 93,000 in the troops of the Voronezh Front. There were more than 7,000 ground-level party organizations in these two fronts."

Never before had an area of terrain been so organized for defense; the salient bristled with trenches, bunkers, field positions, dug-in anti-tank guns, entire anti-tank fronts and observation posts. "Firing positions were prepared for every tank, every gun and machine-gun, firing sectors and orientation points were laid down, initial firing values were prepared, and main, reserve and dummy positions were con-structed," wrote Lieutenant-General Dragunski, commander of the 1st Mechanized Brigade. The Soviets paid special attention to a massed anti-tank defense, in par-ticular to deal with the expected Tigers and Panthers.

Army General Rokossovski: "As we expected the enemy to commit his heavy Tiger with its 88mm gun, soldiers and com-manders familiarized themselves with tactical and technical data and the methods of engaging this tank." In every platoon of the Red rifle companies, tank-killing squads equipped with molotov cocktails, anti-tank mines and hand grenades waited for the German tanks.

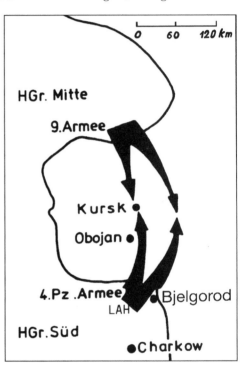

Planned German pincer movement.

In addition to new types of anti-tank rifle, the 57 mm "game-killer" anti-tank gun was incorporated into the defense. As well as anti-tank guns and anti-tank rifles, tanks and assault guns—frequently dug in up to their turrets—were installed in the anti-tank strongpoints, which also included anti-aircraft guns and Stalin Organs. Approximately 1,500 anti-tank mines per kilometer were laid in the Kursk salient; 2,133 anti-tank and 2,126 anti-personnel mines were laid in the area of the 81st Rifle Division alone.

The Soviets prepared to meet the attack in fortress-like positions bris-tling with dug-in tanks, anti-tank guns and flamethrowers. The Leibstandarte was once again up to strength in equipment and personnel, but it had available only the IInd Panzer Battalion as the new Ist (Panther) Battalion was still being raised in Germany. Eleven Tigers, 72 Panzer IVs, 16 Panzer IIs and IIIs and 31 assault guns were serviceable on 2 July 1943. Moving by night, all units reached their departure positions by 2 July 1943.

The armored group, consisting of the 1st SS Panzer Regiment, the IIIrd (Armored) Battalion, 2nd SS Panzer-Grenadier Regiment, the Reconnaissance Battalion and the bulk of the Anti-tank Battalion, was moved forward into the assembly area during the night of 4 July 1943. At 2300 hours on 4 July the forward enemy outposts were taken out and the German forces moved forward into their jump-off positions.

ADOLF HITLER'S ORDER

When darkness fell the company commanders read aloud an order from Adolf Hitler. The order was destroyed as soon as it had been read.

"Soldiers! Today you set out on a great offensive whose result can decisively affect the outcome of the war. Your victory must reinforce the conviction throughout the entire world, even more so than in the past, that all resistance against the German armed forces is ultimately futile. Moreover, a new Russian defeat will further destroy the belief in a possible bolshevik success, which is already waning in many units of the Soviet armed forces. In spite of everything, one day they will fall just as in the last great war.

For whatever success the Russian has been able to achieve has been on account of his tanks. My soldiers! But now, finally, you have better tanks than he. His apparently inexhaustible mass of men has been so weakened in two years of war that he was forced to call up his youngest age classes and old men. Our infantry is superior to them, just as our gunners, our anti-tank forces, our tank drivers, our combat engineers and above all our air force have always been.

The tremendous blow that will strike the Soviet armies this morning must therefore shake them to the core. And you should know that everything may depend on the success of this battle. As a soldier myself, I know exactly what I am asking of you, nevertheless we must achieve victory in the end, no matter how bitter and difficult the individual battles may be. The German homeland, which—women, boys and girls included—is fending off the enemy air attacks with great bravery while, my soldiers, working tirelessly for victory, looks to you with ardent confidence. Adolf Hitler."

THE LEIBSTANDARTE'S MISSION

The following missions were contained in the division order for the Leibstandarte: "6. II. Penetration and breakthrough on X-Day (5 July 1943)—

Approach during darkness under cover of the forward line of security. The depth of the enemy defense zone and the limited width of the attack lanes call for extremely forceful battles. The penetration itself will be made assault team fashion, immediately following the preparatory bombardment by artillery and Stukas. Covering fire from Tigers and assault guns.

Preparatory artillery fire from Y + 15 to Y + 65 (0315–0405 hours). Intensification of artillery fire from Y + 60 to Y + 65 (0400–0405 hours). Stuka attack on 220.5 from Y + 50. Last bomb falls at Y + 65.

In detail:

(a) Reinforced 1st Panzer-Grenadier Regiment LAH (one company of the Anti-tank Battalion LAH, 4th (Medium) Battery, Flak Battalion LAH) will work its way along the gorge northwest of Jachontoff toward the assault jump-off position during the artillery barrage and break into the enemy positions as soon as the last Stuka bombs have fallen. Then continuation of the attack with main force toward the second position east of Yakovlevo, with elements toward the eastern outskirts of Bykovka. 1st day's objective: Yakovlevo.

(b) Reinforced 1st Panzer-Grenadier regiment LAH (without IIIrd Armored Battalion, with Assault Gun Battalion LAH, 13th (Tiger) Company, Panzer Regiment LAH, one company of the Pioneer Battalion LAH, 5th (Medium) Battery, Flak Battalion LAH) will work its way to the assault jump-off position during the artillery barrage from Y + 15 to Y + 65 and immediately after the last bomb has fallen on 220.5 will break into the enemy position with supporting fire from the assault gun battalion and the Tiger company. Then continuation of the attack both sides of the road toward Bykovka, clear the line of villages along the Vorskla and eliminate flanking threats from the west bank. 1st day's objective: Bykovka.

After the successful penetration of the first position one battery of the assault gun battalion is to be sent to the 315th Grenadier Regiment and placed under its command. Following break-in the 627th Pioneer Company and Pioneer Battalion LAH to be committed to erect crossings over the anti-tank ditches.

(c) Empty transport columns of both panzer-grenadier regiments are to deploy themselves so that their forward elements, widely spaced, are at road fork 185.7 (1 kilometer southeast of Tomarovka) at 0800 hours on 5 July.

(d) The reinforced 315th Grenadier Regiment (II Battalion, 318th Artillery Regiment, 1st Company, 238th Pioneer Battalion, one battery of the 55th Rocket Regiment, later one battery of the Assault Gun Battalion LAH) will advance behind the last attacking elements of the reinforced 2nd Panzer-Grenadier Regiment LAH, roll up the enemy positions to the

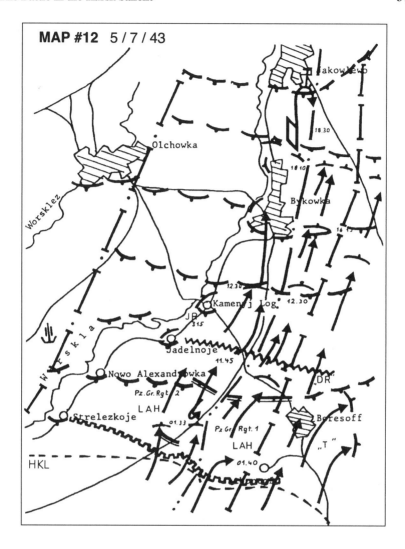

MAP #12   5 / 7 / 43

northwest exploiting this regiment's break-in point, attack Kamenij Log and Sadelnoye, and take and hold these towns including a bridgehead on the west bank of the Vorskla. 1st day's objective: Kamenij Log—Sadelnoje.

(e) The LAH Armored Group (probable composition: Panzer Regiment LAH—less 13th (Tiger) Company and Ist Battalion, IIIrd (Armored) Battalion, 2nd Panzer-Grenadier Regiment LAH, one company from the Anti-tank Battalion LAH, IInd (Armored) Battalion, Artillery Regiment LAH, 6th (Light) Battery, Flak Battalion LAH) will stand ready to break through east of Yakovlevo to the northeast after the anti-tank strong-points have been taken, skirting east of Bykovka, in order to capture a bridgehead over the Psel.

(f) The Reconnaissance Battalion LAH and the rest of the Anti-tank Battalion LAH will make preparations for action with the armored group or to take on reconnaissance or security duties depending on how the situation develops. Technically they will remain under the command of the armored group until the latter is called away.

(g) As per the artillery order the reinforced Artillery Regiment LAH (without ranging battery and 100mm cannon battery, with the 861st Artillery Battalion) is instructed to cooperate as follows after the preparatory bombardment:

1st Battalion, Artillery Regiment LAH and 861st Artillery Battalion with the 1st Panzer-Grenadier Regiment LAH—IInd Battalion, Artillery Regiment LAH with the 2nd Panzer-Grenadier Regiment LAH and the 315th Grenadier Regiment—IIIrd Battalion, Artillery Regiment LAH to send forward observers to both panzer-grenadier regiments—after carrying out its mission the Range-finding Battery LAH to be sent to the artillery regiment.

The primary task of the Artillery Regiment LAH will be to combat the enemy anti-tank strongpoints with smoke and concentrated fire. The Artillery Regiment LAH will make preparations to execute change of position by battalions in support of the attack toward Yakovlevo. Position area east of Bykovka.

(h) The 55th Rocket Regiment (less one battery from IInd Battalion) directed to cooperate with the 2nd Panzer-Grenadier Regiment LAH, support the break-in as per artillery order, and make preparations to eliminate flanking threats from the west bank of the Vorskla and support the break-in into Bykovka.

(i) On arriving in the assembly area on the night of 5 July, the Assault Gun Battalion and the 13th (Tiger) Company, Panzer Regiment LAH will be placed under the command of the 2nd Panzer-Grenadier Regiment LAH and pass through it into the marshalling area south of 228.6 along the road."

The night of 5 July 1943 found the eleven serviceable Tigers south of the road from Tomarovka to Bykovka near Reference Point 222.3. They moved forward at 0315 hours. Together with the assault guns, the Tigers were to advance down the Tomarovka—Bykovka road to Point 228.6 as quickly as possible. Informed of the precise starting time of the attack, the enemy blanketed the assembly areas with artillery fire. B. Solovyov wrote from the Soviet viewpoint: "Soviet reconnaissance discovered the enemy plans in spite of the efforts of the fascist German command to mask its offensive preparations and guarantee the element of surprise."

SS-Panzerschütze Lau described the drive to the assembly area by the Tigers and the final hours before the attack: "The Zitadelle operation was of great significance to me, as it was my baptism of fire in the Tiger tank. Shortly before the attack I was assigned to the tank of my friend SS-Unterscharführer Staudegger as loader. 'Bubi' Wendorff was our platoon commander in the IInd Platoon. We departed for the assembly area on 30 June 1943. At this point I would like to mention the friendly farewell given us by the local civilian population in our quartering area. We had developed an excellent relationship with our hosts in those weeks. This was also the case with panzer crews everywhere. I recall that we made three stops during the drive to the assembly area. The first time we halted it was raining, and we crawled under the tank: our platoon commander Untersturmführer Wendorff, Heinz Buchner, Franz Staudegger and several others. Wendorff and Buchner talked about their Napola experiences.

The next evening we bivouacked in a flattened wheat field and as was Wendorff's practice he had the entire platoon lay in rest positions in a semicircle on their bellies with heads facing the center. As expected, Wendorff called for a song. We spent that evening singing. We halted again in an elongated village. There the platoon commanders told us what was coming. They gave us the Führer order—I don't know if they read it out or conveyed the general sense of it—and explained the operation to us in general outlines. We were to attack from the south while troops from another army group came toward us from the north.

We were therefore generally informed about the sense of the operation and knew from the words of our Führer and Supreme Commander that it was supposed to be a decisive battle. Expectations and emotions were naturally at a high point and I already had a slightly uneasy feeling in my stomach, especially as this was to be my first time in action. Then we set out for the jump-off position during the night of 5 July 1943."

The first units of the 2nd SS Panzer-Grenadier Regiment set off at 2315 hours to capture the enemy's combat outposts on the hills west of Jachontoff and on Hill 228.6. At 0133 hours on 5 July 1943, Hill 228.6 fell to Obersturmführer Karck (9th Company, 2nd SS Panzer-Grenadier Regiment) after fierce close-quarters fighting and soon afterward the northern part of Streletskoye was occupied. An enemy counterattack on Hill 228.6 was repulsed at 0215. After the artillery barrage both regiments moved forward at 0300, at 0315 the Tigers were moved up to Hill 228.6.

Both panzer-grenadier regiments went to the attack at 0405 hours, in each case with two battalions in the lead. The objective was Hill 220.5. The enemy had fortified, mined and wired the battlefield lying in front of the men to a depth of up to twenty kilometers. Dug-in T 34s and concealed anti-tank guns made the going difficult for the Tigers and assault guns. The grenadiers came upon a fortified anti-tank ditch in front of Hill 220.5.

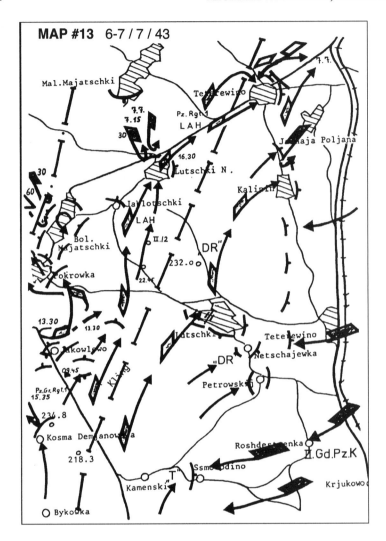

The Tiger company was instructed to break through the system of positions south and southeast of Bykovka.

SS-Hauptsturmführer Kling radioed the order to attack to all the panzer crews: "Panzers forward!" The eleven Tigers drove north at high speed. Before long the crews spotted muzzle flashes from enemy anti-tank guns. The Tigers wouldn't have been able to spot these dangerous weapons in their camouflaged hides if it they hadn't opened fire. Never before had the German panzers encountered such a massing of anti-tank guns and dug-in tanks.

The enemy had blended his anti-tanks perfectly into the structure of the terrain and camouflaged them masterfully in field bunkers and positions. The concealed anti-tank guns were extremely dangerous opponents, but the commanders and gunners in the Tigers located their positions as soon as the anti-tank guns opened fire. The Tigers had to halt briefly to fire. SS-Sturmmann Woll, SS-Untersturmführer Wittmann's gunner, traversed the turret to the left; an enemy anti-tank gun loomed large in his telescopic sight. He destroyed it with his first shot. Then he saw another muzzle flash father to the left. Reacting quickly, the little Saarlander targeted and destroyed this target too. The other commanders silenced further anti-tank guns in their open field bunkers with accurate fire. The advance continued and the first T 34s appeared, about twelve of them. Hauptsturmführer Kling was in a favorable position and hisgunner, Sturmmann Warmbrunn, knocked out two T 34s in a matter of minutes. The other Tigers also scored hits and the surviving T 34s turned tail and fled.

Fresh surprises lurked in the extremely deep system of positions. Bright red, meter-long lances of fire suddenly darted across the battlefield and transformed large areas into seas of flame. To the grenadiers these emplaced automatic flamethrowers were fearsome weapons which were difficult to approach. Kling guided his Tiger toward one of the squat earth bunkers containing a flamethrower and destroyed it with high-explosive shells. In the course of the day Kling's gunner Warmbrunn destroyed nine more flamethrowers, took out seven bunkers and knocked out four T 34s and nineteen 76.2 mm anti-tank guns.

The Tigers resumed their advance as soon as the pioneers had cleared lanes through the minefields and erected crossings over the anti-tank ditches. Soon they found themselves in front of a heavily-fortified hill position bristling with anti-tank guns. There were also T 34s, dug in with only their turrets showing; they showered the Tigers with fire. Several were immobilized with track damage, but they fired on the enemy and scored hits. The first dug-in T 34 soon exploded in a pillar of fire. "When the attack by the grenadiers bogged down in front of the positions, Hauptsturmführer Kling decided to commit his company in an attempt to break through, in spite of the heavily-mined terrain and the massed anti-tank and artillery defense.

Attacking with eleven tanks, he fought his way up to the hill position step by step; four times he was forced to transfer to another tank and breached the enemy system of positions with the last remaining tanks." (From the recommendation for the German Cross in Gold for Kling.) Concealed anti-tank guns allowed the Tigers to approach to within twenty meters. The fighting was extremely tough.

After receiving supporting artillery and rocket fire, at 1145 hours the Tigers and the assault guns, together with the 2nd SS Panzer-Grenadier

Regiment, took Hill 220.5 after almost five hours of unbroken fighting. The Tigers destroyed a number of tanks and anti-tank guns. At 1230 hours the bulk of the 2nd SS Panzer-Grenadier Regiment under SS-Obersturmbannführer Hugo Kraas reached Hill 215.4, placing it 2.5 kilometers south of Bykovka, the first day's objective. By afternoon both of the Leibstandarte Panzer-Grenadier Regiments were in Bykovka. Elements of the 2nd Regiment pursued the fleeing enemy through the town.

The Soviet Colonel I.I. Markin wrote in the book *The Battle of Kursk*: "The courage and determination of the Soviet soldiers enabled the 28th Anti-tank Artillery Brigade and combat engineer units to transfer into the sector where the SS Panzer-Grenadier Divisions Leibstandarte and Totenkopf (actually Das Reich) made their main thrust. The 1008th Anti-tank Regiment went into position from on the move five kilometers south of Bykovka.

The enemy deployed eighteen Tigers as cover for his medium tanks (it was eleven, the author). The Soviet artillerymen set four Tigers on fire in a matter of minutes, two of which were immobilized. (Two Tigers sustained track damage, none was a total loss, the author.) Together with elements of the 52nd Guards Rifle Division, the 1008th Anti-tank Regiment fought off four attacks in one hour and destroyed eighteen tanks. In order to expedite the advance, the high command of the German Army Group South committed all of its air forces in this sector, concentrated almost three-hundred tanks in a narrow sector of the front, and attacked along the bank of the Vorskla in an attempt to outflank the center of Soviet resistance south of Bykovka.

Toward evening German troops drove a narrow wedge into the towns of Bykovka and Kosimo Demyanovka. On orders of the corps commander, the 52nd Guards Rifle Division sent two regiments into position on the west bank of the Vorskla southwest of Bykovka, while the division's 3rd Regiment took up defensive positions north of Kosimo Demyanovka, where it halted the enemy attack together with the 96th Tank Brigade. As well, the commander in chief of the 6th Guards Army committed elements of the 51st Guards Rifle Division, which had been transferred there from the second echelon. The enemy's advance to the north was stopped."

The units of the Leibstandarte destroyed a large number of tanks on the first day of the attack. By evening the division was in front of Yakovlevo and the Das Reich Division had caught up on the right. SS-Sturmmänner Georg Gentsch and Heinz Owczarek of the Tiger company had been killed in action and SS-Untersturmführer Wendorff wounded. Untersturmführer Wittmann knocked out eight tanks and seven guns that day. Other commanders also had good success. A company rations truck with a

German driver and two Russian auxiliaries strayed into the enemy lines; all three occupants lost their lives. The men of the Tiger company's supply service were in constant action.

SS-Panzerschütze Walter Lau recalled that first day: "When the first artillery fire began, our Tigers had to cross a small stream, a demanding affair for the driver; however the Tiger made it easy. It was still dawn. The Tigers readied themselves on a broad plain. Most impressive in those final minutes before the start of the attack were the rocket salvoes and the Stuka attacks. It was the first time I had seen the wall of smoke and heard the frightful noise made by the rocket batteries, and when the rocket salvoes and the smoke subsided the Stuka squadrons appeared. But at the same moment the tanks moved off. After a few hundred meters in the attack lane came the first halt at the anti-tank ditch; the Frey Regiment (1st SS Panzer-Grenadier Regiment) had seized the ditch and the pioneers were preparing a crossing.

The first tank to drive across the ditch belonged to the commander of the IIIrd Platoon, Untersturmführer Wittmann; it was followed by Untersturmführer Wendorff's Tiger. Unterscharführer Staudegger was still our commander during the advance. For some reason—Wendorff's tank probably had mechanical problems—he got into our tank and Staudegger got out. (Gunner Buchner, loader Lau, driver Stellmacher, radio operator Waltersdorf.) The crossing was quite complicated. We had to wait awhile, for the pioneers had maneuvered a T 34 into the ditch and were working hard to create a crossing for the tanks. They finally succeeded and the company deployed into inverted wedge formation for the resumption of the attack. The defenders opened up with heavy fire. My state was not exactly the best; I don't know if it was fear, but in any case I had a damned queer feeling in my belly. At the same moment we were hit for the first time.

I had no experience from which to tell what sort of hit it might be. We were hit by an anti-tank rifle simultaneously in the commander's cupola and the running gear. My condition worsened noticeably when we saw that Untersturmführer Wendorff was covered with blood and had apparently been badly wounded. Thank God, it soon turned out that he had only been scratched in the face by a splinter from the vision block and was not seriously wounded. From somewhere there came the order to bail out and I opened the emergency escape hatch in the turret. When the minor nature of Wendorff's wound and of the hits became apparent the order was cancelled, but we were unable to close the hatch from inside.

At this point a conversation sprang up between Wendorff and a company commander of the pioneer battalion. I remember this well because, silly ass that I was, I didn't use enough force when I tried to close the emergency escape hatch and the hatch cover fell back down onto the pioneer company commander's hand. Once again my nervous state approached the nadir. We were sitting motionless in the main line of resistance; beside us was the panzer of Obersturmführer Schütz. It had taken a hit from an anti-tank gun in the loader's vision slit and Schütz's loader Klaus Bürvenich, a young, blonde Panzerschütze, had been badly wounded.

I now received orders to move over to Obersturmführer Schütz's tank. This upset my nerves even more, for he was the deputy company commander. His gunner was SS-Unterscharführer Werner Wendt, an older, experienced gunner. I had little time to think it over as the attack continued in inverted wedge formation under Hauptsturmführer Kling. We attacked the hill behind the anti-tank ditch several times and expended our ammunition in no time. As I recall, from that morning to the afternoon we pulled back three times to rearm. One can easily figure out how many shells the loaders in the tanks had to load and how many casings were ejected. On top of this there was the considerable July heat. The queer feeling in my stomach was now completely gone, but I was becoming physically exhausted from the hard work with the 88 mm shells and the tremendous heat inside the tank. By evening all the Tiger loaders were visibly physically exhausted. We slept in the open that night, behind the tanks."

On the evening of that nerve-wracking first day of the attack, the panzer crews sat down together and talked over their experiences. Night soon fell, bringing some relief after a very hot day. A young soldier, an officer candidate, went on night watch. Exhausted from the trials of the previous day, he fell asleep. Wittmann found him while making his rounds. He badly needed sleep himself, but he took over the young soldier's watch. Wittmann didn't say much about such things, to him it was part of his sense of responsibility for his young soldiers. The soldier involved in this incident may have been Sturmmann Roland Söffker. But not all the panzer crews were able to rest.

SS-Unterscharführer Franz Staudegger set out alone after darkness fell to rejoin the company. Slowly his Tiger drove down a narrow road through a wood; Staudegger stood in the open turret hatch to find the way in the eerie darkness. The tank had been rolling through the wood for some time; the warm July night was quiet apart from the rumble of the engine.

Suddenly Staudegger noticed tiny sparks glimmering directly in front of him. He quickly ordered his driver to come to a halt. Now he could make out the outline of a tank; the sparks from its exhausts had alerted him just in time to avoid a collision. Staudegger jumped from the turret to bawl out the commander of the tank in front of him and to ask why he was sitting there in the dead of night blocking the road.

The commander of the other tank was standing in the turret smoking a cigarette, Staudegger could see the glowing stub. He must have been shocked as well, for with the engine running he couldn't hear the Tiger's approach. Then he asked Staudegger if he was crazy—but in Russian! Staudegger winced, he was standing all alone in front of a Soviet tank! Controlling his fear, he reached down to his belt, armed a hand grenade, lobbed it into the open hatch of the Soviet tank, and then leapt for cover. As he did so, Staudegger saw that there was a second enemy tank a few meters behind the first one. A muffled explosion shook the colossus. Staudegger shouted a warning to his crew, there was no time to do more. Acting quickly, he ran toward the second tank and jumped up on to it.

At the same moment the turret hatch opened, for the crew had heard the explosion and wanted to see what had happened. Staudegger had correctly guessed what would happen and tossed a second hand grenade into the open hatch. The second tank, too, was put out of action. Staudegger had destroyed two Soviet tanks in a matter of minutes. Instinctively reaching for the hand grenade had won him decisive seconds, for the Red tank commander would inevitably have recognized him as the enemy. As a former infantryman, Staudegger always kept hand grenades with him and knew how to use them. He climbed back into his tank and he and his crew resumed their drive back to the company. The very next day Franz Staudegger was awarded the Iron Cross, First Class for his quick and courageous action.

In the course of the night the enemy withdrew from his position east of Yakovlevo and took up new defensive positions, especially on Hill 243.2. The assignment given the Leibstandarte and Das Reich1 Divisions on 6 July 1943 was to break through the fortified enemy positions southeast of Yakovlevo. The Tiger company was to take the mined, wired and heavily fortified position on Hill 243.2. The attack by the Tigers began in the morning. The enemy on Hill 243.2 put upstubborn resistance. The Tigers had to fight their way through heavily-mined terrain. Aboard the tank of the commander of the Ist Platoon Obersturmführer Schütz was war correspondent Joachim Fernau. During the attack the tank took a hit which dislodged the vision block; it struck Schütz in the stomach with full force. At first Schütz thought that both his legs had been torn off, but fortunately he was wrong. While in action some of the young tank crews also had to battle their own nerves. While moving up to attack driver Johann Graf sang Viennese songs over the Tiger's intercom. In command of Tiger 1324 was SS-Sturmmann Rolf Schamp. His crew consisted of SS-Sturmmann Siegfried Jung (gunner), SS-Panzerschütze Iwanitz (radio operator), SS-Panzerschütze Reinhard Wenzel (loader) and SS-Sturmmann Franz Elmer (driver). During the attack Schamp's Tiger drove over a mine and was disabled. The right reduction gear was destroyed. The Russians had laid numerous wooden-case mines, which disabled a large number of German vehicles.

SS-Hauptsturmführer Kling took the enemy positions with his three remaining Tigers and by midday had captured Hill 243.2. The Tigers had created the necessary conditions for the successful pursuit of the enemy. At 1315 hours the Soviets launched an attack against the 1st SS Panzer-Grenadier Regiment from Yakovlevo supported by thirty-eight tanks. The Tiger company was with the Leibstandarte's armored group and together with it was able to repulse the attack while destroying eight enemy tanks.

Kling now weighed his chances and with his few Tigers ". . . he immediately set out in pursuit of the enemy and, leading the armored group without regard to his own safety, captured the hill terrain west of Prokhorovka. Our spearheads had now penetrated about sixty to seventy kilometers into enemy territory. In these two days his company destroyed fifty T 34s, one KV I and one KV II, as well as forty-three anti-tank guns. SS-Hauptsturmführer Kling himself contributed to this success with nine tanks destroyed." (Excerpt from the recommendation for the German Cross in Gold for Kling.)

Wittmann led his platoon against the enemy and destroyed several tanks. Then he had the bad luck to drive over a mine and his Tiger was immobilized with a wrecked right track. Under fire, the tank was hit in the front several times, destroying the radio operator's machine-gun and blowing off a hatch cover. Loader Walter Koch was hit in the head by splinters. In this critical situation Wittmann displayed his coolness under fire and strength of nerve, which had a reassuring effect on his men. In fact help was already on the way. SS-Unterscharführer Brandt took the crippled Tiger under tow and pulled it out of the line of fire. SS-Panzerschütze Max Gaube took over as Wittmann's loader.

The other commanders, Wittmann, Brandt, Höld, Lötzsch, and several others, also scored well. Bitter combats were fought above the battlefield; the sky was full of fighters, bombers and Stukas. Hauptmann Rudel achieved great success in his experimental "cannon bird," a Ju 87 armed with two 37 mm cannon beneath the wings.

The commander of a Red Army regiment, Yakubovski, wrote: "The attacks by the Leibstandarte Division lasted all day, the Tigers in front and the light tanks and armored troop carriers behind them." So far the Tiger had convincingly demonstrated its superiority over both Soviet tanks and anti-tank guns. In spite of determined resistance from dug-in T 34s and anti-tank guns the Tigers were repeatedly able to break through and smash gaps in the enemy fortifications for the panzer-grenadiers.

The Russians fought back with every weapon at their disposal, which included emplaced flamethrowers. On the other hand, T 34s camouflaged as haystacks no longer came as a surprise. A constant watch had to be kept for mines and the pioneers were kept busy. The Tigers of SS-Unterscharführer Staudegger, and shortly afterward SS-Sturmmann Schamp, were also disabled by mines. That evening Sepp Dietrich appeared and asked both commanders if there was anything they needed. He promised to personally see to the finding of replacements for the reduction gears of both Tigers. Several crewmen were relieved on account of the summer heat—temperatures were much higher inside the tanks—and the great strain the attack placed on the men.

Staudegger's loader wrote: "The first and second days of the 'Zitadelle' attack were terribly arduous for the loaders. It was extremely hot and we had to rearm three to four times. This meant repeating the process of taking on forty to fifty shells, throwing out the empty casings and reloading three to four times. I recall that loaders had to be relieved. I was one of them."

Soon night fell. The Tiger crews spent the warm nights in the open or in tents. Most Russian houses were bug-ridden or full of lice, so camping beside the tanks was preferred as long as the weather was suitable. Before the crews turned in the Tigers were made fully combat-ready again, 88 mm shells were stowed away, ammo belts for the machine-guns were filled, fuel tanks were filled, water levels topped up and so on.

Then one member of the crew, usually the radio operator, went to find something to eat, as the field kitchens did not always find the tanks far to the front. They preferred not to wait and so they helped themselves. While they waited the men took time to wash. It wasn't always possible to sit together. The fierce battles under the hot sun during Zitadelle took their toll. Men often fell asleep as soon as there was even a brief pause in the fighting.

During the night of 7 July 1943 three enemy tanks carrying mounted infantry drove through Teterevino, where the armored group had stopped for the night. A Tiger guarding the road there destroyed all three tanks in a brief firefight. The enemy attacked again the next morning and broke into Teterevino with thirty tanks. The IInd Battalion, 2nd SS Panzer-Grenadier Regiment drove the enemy out again. By 1000 the 1st SS Panzer-Grenadier Regiment had completely occupied Pokrovka and Yakovlevo. Following air strikes by Stukas, the Leibstandarte armored group and that of the Das Reich struck out along the Teterevino-Prokhorovka road. At

0710 hours the group was attacked from the north by twenty T 34s; however, by noon the entire enemy force had been wiped out in a series of fierce tank-versus-tank duels.

During the advance several Tigers were mistakenly bombed by Stukas. Wittmann opened the turret hatch while the bombs were falling and spread out the air identification panel on the back of the tank, thus preventing other Stukas from dropping their bombs too short.

In the evening radio operator SS-Panzerschütze Bender, had to be replaced on account of an abscessed jaw and fever. Joining Wittmann's crew as driver was SS-Panzerschütze Siegfried Fuss. Together with "Bobby" Woll (gunner), SS-Sturmmann Karl Lieber (radio operator) and SS-Panzerschütze Max Gaube (driver), Fuss remained a member of Wittmann's crew until January 1944.

The Fourth Panzer Army was now threatened by the 2nd Guards Tank Corps and two further tank corps of the Soviet 1st Army. The flanks of the IInd SS Panzer Corps were in acute danger. The Totenkopf Division was subsequently moved into position on the left of the Leibstandarte in order to strengthen the IInd SS Panzer Corps's spearhead. The 167th Infantry Division, previously deployed at the southern edge of the west flank, relieved the Totenkopf Division in the east.

That day the Soviet information bureau announced that: ". . . The backbone of the German offensive thrust, the Tiger units, was singled out for special attention by our anti-tank units. They suffered heavy losses. At least 250 of these large tanks went up in flames on the battlefield on the first day." Furthermore, the Soviets claimed to have destroyed 70 Tigers and 450 other German tanks on 7 July 1943 alone. It is manifestly obvious that these numbers bear no relation to the actual losses. The Soviet claim of 320 Tigers destroyed exceeded the total number deployed in that entire area of the front.

At 0710 hours on 8 July 1943 the 1st SS Panzer-Grenadier Regiment took Bolshaya Majatschki to the southwest. At 0800 the armored groups of the Leibstandarte and Das Reich attacked to the northwest. Southeast of Vesely the Leibstandarte armored group encountered eighty enemy tanks. The ensuing battle lasted until 1030 hours, then the enemy veered south and attacked the Ist Battalion of the 2nd SS Panzer-Grenadier Regiment in Jablotschki. After regrouping, the Leibstandarte armored group advanced farther to the west. At 1205 fighting began for Vesely, which had been heavily fortified.

The following was recorded of the Tigers' battle at Vesely and Rylskij: "After the attack by the IInd Battalion of the 1st SS Panzer Regiment was stopped by a strong front of anti-tank guns and dug-in tanks, SS-Hauptsturmführer Kling and four tanks worked their way in from the Russian flank and picked off several dug-in enemy tanks. As the battle developed, Kling, once again at the head of his mixed unit, charged ahead recklessly and drove into the Soviet rear with elements of the armored battalion. This caused the enemy, who that day lost forty-two T 34s and three General Lees to Kling's company alone, to flee in panic." (From the submission for the German Cross in Gold for Kling.)

SS-Sturmmann Warmbrunn destroyed three T 34s in the melee. The starting point for the attack by the armored group, which at the beginning of the day included the Tigers, was Teterevino. Early that morning the Ist Battalion of the SS Panzer-Grenadier Regiment Deutschland (Das Reich Division) went into position there.

The front line ran east of Teterevino. The railway line from Prokhorovka formed the boundary and farther north the main line of resistance ran in a westerly direction. SS-Unterscharführer Franz Staudegger of Wendorff's IInd Platoon was unable to take part in the attack by his company on the morning of that 8 July as his Tiger had suffered a mechanical breakdown. He therefore stayed behind in Teterevino. A few hours later Staudegger was told that a group of about fifty to sixty Soviet T 34s was approaching from the northeast.

TWENTY-TWO ENEMY TANKS DESTROYED

"I'm not driving to the company, I'm going to go hunting for them," he said to Rolf Schamp, whose Tiger was also broken down. Without hesitating for a second, Staudegger used all the means at his disposal to make his Tiger drivable again, then set out alone in the direction of the reported enemy tanks. His crew consisted of driver SS-Sturmmann Herbert Stellmacher, radio operator SS-Panzerschütze Gerhard Waltersdorf, gunner SS-Panzerschütze Heinz Buchner and loader SS-Panzerschütze Walter Henke.

On the way a grenadier advised him that five Soviet tanks had already broken into the German positions. Shortly thereafter Staudegger saw the infantry knock out two of the T 34s. He was able to dispatch the remaining three in short order. Then, suddenly, two T 34s appeared on the railway embankment. Direct hits destroyed both in a matter of seconds. Staudegger drove through the infantry positions into no-man's-land, completely on his own, one man against sixty enemy tanks. Then he saw them. Five more tanks emerged from a wood beyond the railway embankment. Staudegger issued his instructions. Immediately Heinz Buchner took aim at the first and put a round into its turret, whereupon it exploded. The other T 34s now opened fire on the Tiger. Staudegger fired repeatedly and destroyed all five Soviet tanks in this incredibly difficult fire-fight.

Then more T 34s poured out of the wood and Staudegger immediately took up the fight. He directed a stream of orders at his gunner: aim, fire, hit! The hardest work was done by loader Walter Henke as he heaved shell after shell into the breech of the eighty-eight. Herbert Stellmacher kept the Tiger constantly in motion, skillfully changing positions in front of the mass of enemy tanks so that they were unable to zero in on the lone Tiger. The green T 34s with the red star were not far away. The Tiger's solo battle lasted for two hours, by which time Staudegger had destroyed a total of seventeen tanks.

The Tiger had taken hits but they had inflicted no damage. The enemy finally realized that there was no getting through there and withdrew. However, Staudegger wasn't ready to just pull back to the Deutschland Regiment's line of security. He wanted more. Throwing caution to the wind, he set his Tiger in motion to track down the enemy tanks. It was a daring decision whose chances of success were limited, for the danger of walking into a Soviet trap was great. But Staudegger had other intentions.

The big Tiger rolled forward slowly; its commander's attention was focused on the terrain. An armor-piercing shell lay in the breech and Buchner sat at the telescopic sight, senses taut. Then, suddenly, he saw them; the enemy tanks had regrouped in a gully. The Tiger's engine raced as it approached, then it halted abruptly and the first shell left the long barrel and struck its target. The Tiger fired shell after shell and Staudegger picked off five more T 34s from the middle of the mass of tanks. With its armor-piercing ammunition expended, the Tiger began firing HE rounds. Four additional T 34s were seen to be hit.

The Soviets were completely dismayed, the Tiger seemed invincible. The survivors took to flight in panic in the hope of avoiding total destruction. Staudegger backed his heavy tank away from the enemy, never letting them out of his sight in order to guard against surprises. With all his ammunition gone and the engine beginning to sputter, it was high time to disengage. The grenadiers of the Deutschland Regiment waved to Staudegger and his crew enthusiastically. They knew what they had to thank them for.

The daring action by the twenty-year-old Carinthian had prevented a breakthrough by enemy tanks whose objective was to open the main road for their units to the southwest whose lines of supply had been cut. In doing so Staudegger destroyed twenty-two tanks. A patrol dispatched by the Germania Regiment's 2nd Company later confirmed Staudegger's kills. The next day commanding officer SS-Obersturmbannführer Schönberger submitted a recommendation for the Knight's Cross. Only one day later, on 10 July 1943, SS-Unterscharführer Franz Staudegger was awarded the coveted decoration.

The award of the Knight's Cross to Staudegger took the company by surprise at first, for it had been in action elsewhere on 8 July and no one knew about his lone action that day. He was the first member of the Tiger company and also the first Austrian member of the Leibstandarte to receive the Knight's Cross. The following is his Knight's Cross Submission:

Justification and Endorsement of Immediate Superiors

On 8/7/1943 the SS.Panz.Rgt. 1/LSSAH launched an attack west from Teterevino. The regiment had been relieved by elements of the "Deutschland" Rgt. on the morning of the same day. Several hours after the regiment's departure an armored formation of 50-60 T 34s was sighted attacking from the northeast.

As commander of an unserviceable tank, SS-Unterscharführer Staudegger was unable to take part in the attack and therefore remained in Teterevino. After he learned of the tank attack he employed all available means to make his Pz.Kfw. VI drivable. He set out alone against the attacking enemy tanks and destroyed 17 T 34s in a two-hour tank battle.

The enemy armored formation subsequently broke off and withdrew into a gully. Without waiting for orders, SS-Uscha. Staudegger now decided to attack the enemy unit, which had meanwhile regrouped. Driving far beyond his own lines and without support, he knocked out 5 more T 34s. The rest fled.

SS-Uscha. Staudegger carried out this exceptional act on his own initiative, giving his all and without loss. In so doing he prevented an otherwise unavoidable penetration by tanks into our covering positions, decisively weakened the enemy tank formation and thus frustrated the enemy's tactical objective, the opening of the main road for his units in the southwest, which were virtually cut off from their supplies.

Staudegger was decorated with the E.K. II for bravery during the winter fighting in the Battle of Kharkov while serving as the driver of a Pz.Kfw. III.

He received the E.K. I for especially courageous conduct with his tank during the breaching of the enemy defensive position northeast of Tomarovka.

He is worthy of receiving the highest decoration, the "Knight's Cross of the Iron Cross."

SS-Obersturmbannführer and Rgt. CO.

Endorsement of the Division Commander:
Approved and endorsed.

SS-Oberführer

Spring 1943, Kharkov. SS-Obersturmführer Waldemar Schütz in the quartering area of the Tiger Company's Workshop Platoon.

Men of the Workshop Platoon, Ganz and Neisige.

Repair Platoon
of 4 Pz. Komp.,
March 1943.

Bürvenich,
Hein Reimers
and Wohlgemuth
during lunch break.

SS-Obersturmführer
Schütz still has
questions.

Alois Pumberger on
sentry duty in front of
the Tiger Company's
orderly room in
Kharkov.

SS-Obersturmführer
Schütz visits the
tank crews.

SS-Obersturmführer Schutz visits the Tiger Company's Light Platoon, which was equipped with the Panzer III.

4 July 1943. The Leibstandarte's panzer regiment moves up to its line of departure in preparation for the offensive on Kursk.

Observing the battlefield in the Leibstandarte's attack sector.

Concentrated observation prior to the attack.

5 July 1943, the first day of the German Offensive, Operation "Zitadelle".

Heavy Soviet artillery fire falls in front of the German armor.

Tigers of the 13th (Heavy) Company, 1st SS Panzer Regiment Leibstandarte roll forward. They were in the heat of the action from the outset of the offensive on Kursk.

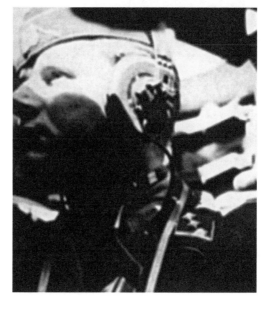

SS-Obersturmführer Schütz in the turret of his Tiger.

Leibstandarte tank-destroyer. 7.5cm PaK40/3 on PzKpfw 38(t) chassis.

Grenadiers have just taken a Soviet trench; in the background the Tigers set out after the enemy.

Propaganda Company drawing of the Tiger's attack near Kursk.

Two Tigers seen shortly before the attack, left 1311 and right 1332, with mounted grenadiers. Visible on the rear of the nearest tank is the Feifel filter system, which was supposed to protect the Tiger's engine from dust and dirt.

Tiger 1313. The crew has placed a swastika flag on the rear of the tank as an identification signal for the Luftwaffe. Standing in the turret is gunner Heinrich Knöß.

A Panzer III of the IInd Battalion, 1st SS Panzer Regiment Leibstandarte advances across a Soviet trench while the panzergrenadiers take a short break.

A young soldier of the
Leibstandarte brings
fresh eggs to supplement
his comrades' rations.

Grenadiers take cover
from Soviet artillery fire.

Panzer-grenadiers go to the attack from a trench.

The advance continues in the burning heat of the Kursk offensive.

Panzer-grenadiers repel an enemy counterattack.

Attack on Soviet positions. The stress of combat is evident in the faces of the young soldiers.

The following are three newspaper articles on Staudegger:

22 "T 34s" Destroyed with the Tiger

From the headquarters of the Führer. On 10 July 1943 the Führer awarded the Knight's Cross of the Iron Cross to SS Unterscharführer Franz Staudegger, tank commander in a panzer regiment of the Panzer-Grenadier Division Leibstandarte SS Adolf Hitler. Staudegger, who for technical reasons could not take part in an attack by his regiment, received news that a Soviet armored force consisting of 50-60 "T 34s" was attempting to reach the rear of our forces. In spite of the enemy's vast superiority, Staudegger decided on his own initiative to attack the enemy armored formation. In the initial two-hour firefight he destoryed 17 "T 34s" with his "Tiger" tank from a favorable firing position. When the enemy unit subsequently broke off and withdrew, Staudegger followed it far beyond his own lines and, with no support, knocked out another five enemy tanks of the "T 34" type. The rest of the bolsheviks fled. Through his courageous decision Staudegger frustrated an otherwise unavoidable penetration and decisively weakened the enemy armored formation.

The Black Corps

SS-Unterscharführer Staudegger

SS-Propaganda Company. A powerful Soviet armored formation is reported. Unterscharführer Franz Staudegger, a tall, husky Carinthian, climbs into the turret of his Tiger and roars off in the direction of the front. On the way a grenadier tells him that five Soviet tanks have already broken through, then he sees two of them, attacked by lone men with close-range weapons, blow apart. In minutes his panzer's cannon has destroyed the remaining three T 34s. Staudegger now heads his panzer into no-man's-land.

Two further T 34s appear over a railway embankment. Within a minute they are reduced to pIIIars of smoke. Five more emerge from a wood beyond the embankment. They too are destroyed following a fierce firefight. Continuing to advance, Staudegger sees the reported tank unit in a gully. Quick as lightning, from a favorable position, the gunner takes aim and shot after shot leaves the barrel. After 22 tanks have been destroyed the armor-piercing ammunition is gone. The remaining tanks are fired on with high-explosive shells, which inflict serious damage on a large number of them. Then Staudegger withdraws, his Tiger in reverse gear, always keeping the enemy in sight. But it is high time too, for his ammunition is all but gone, the engine sputters, fuel is running low. Already grenadiers wave to him enthusiastically from their positions in the distance. The regimental commander spontaneously pins the Iron Cross, First Class on the daring tank commander.

For his exceptional bravery and devotion to duty the Führer has awarded him the Knight's Cross of the Iron Cross. SS War Correspondent Wondratsch."

SS-Unterscharführer Franz Staudegger

Franz Staudegger was born on 12 February 1923 in Unterloibach, near Bleiburg in Carinthia. He was the son of an innkeeper and one of three brothers. After attending a secondary school in Klagenfurt and the Spanheim National Political Borstel in St. Paul in the Lavant Valley, in 1940 he graduated from the Wiener Theresianum. At the age of seventeen he volunteered for military service and on 8 July 1940 joined the replacement and training battalion of the Leibstandarte SS Adolf Hitler. He saw action with the 1st Company of the Leibstandarte in 1941 and was soon wounded. Staudegger received the Wound Badge in Black and in March 1942 was promoted to SS-Sturmmann.

After recovering from his wounds he retrained for service in the panzer arm and at the end of 1942 he joined the Tiger company in Fallingbostel. There he was placed in command of a Panzer III in Wittmann's light platoon. Promotion to SS-Unterscharführer followed on 30 January 1943. His first tour of duty as a tank commander began a few days later, in the desert of snow in front of Kharkov. On 20 March 1943, following the recapture of Kharkov, he received the Iron Cross, Second Class and on 1 April 1943 the Tank Battle Badge in Silver. By then he was commanding a Tiger. Staudegger destroyed two Soviet tanks in close combat on 5 July 1943 and the next day was awarded the Iron Cross, First Class. On 8 July 1943 he seized the opportunity presented him, and he is now rightly a celebrated hero.

The twenty-year-old Franz Staudegger is a fine figure of barely 1.9 meters, he has dark hair and blue eyes. The men of his crew respect him, but otherwise he does not enjoy wide popularity. His somewhat refined manner makes him appear excessively stiff and formal. The young Carinthian is very self-assured in his manner, and in spite of his tendency towards arrogance he is generally well-accepted in the company.

July 9, 1943 was a day of rest for the Tigers in Teterevino. Repair work on the broken-down panzers was in high gear. The crews took advantage of the brief rest to recover from the recent battles. SS-Untersturmführer Wittmann took over Tiger 1324 from SS-Sturmmann Schamp. The light platoon and its Panzer IIIs was not employed in the front rank with the Tigers during Operation Zitadelle, instead it was used mostly on security and guard duties. SS-Untersturmführer Wendorff had returned to the company after treatment at the main dressing station and was with the combat train. The 1st SS Panzer-Grenadier Regiment had reached Rylskij unopposed by 1210 hours on 9 July 1943 and was now in Ssuch. Ssolotino, which was cleared of weak enemy forces. Tiger commander SS-Unterscharführer Franz Enderl was killed in action that day.

For 10 July 1943 the Tiger company—which together with the assault gun battalion, the 5th Battery of the 1st SS Flak Battalion and a pioneer company was again placed under the command of the 2nd SS Panzer-Grenadier Regiment (Kraas)—was ordered to break through the enemy position on the heels of an artillery and rocket barrage and then advance

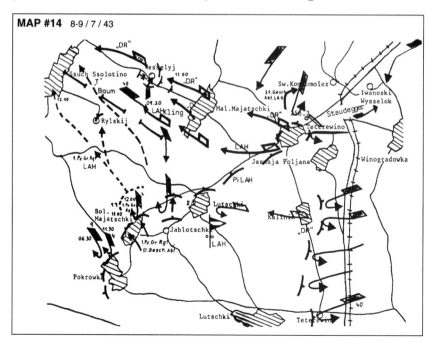

MAP #14 8-9 / 7 / 43

on Prokhorovka. Artillery support was promised by the entire Leibstandarte Artillery Regiment and the 55th Rocket Regiment, as well as air support. The Leibstandarte Panzer Regiment initially stood ready behind the 2nd SS Panzer-Grenadier Regiment, south of the Teterevino-Lutschki road. As minefields were expected, the 2nd Regiment was assigned a pioneer company, which stood by east of Lutschki ready to expand the lanes through the minefields.

That day four T 34s broke through the positions of the 10th (Heavy) Company, 2nd SS Panzer-Grenadier Regiment in Lutschki-North. SS-Unterscharführer Fürst's anti-tank gun was quickly moved forward through a garden but one wheel became hung up in a hole. By then the first T 34 was only meters away and trained its gun on the lone anti-tank gun. Then SS-Sturmmann Rudi Nadler leapt onto the tank, placed a hollow charge on its sloped side over the tracks and took cover. The blast disabled the T 34. The second T 34 had stout planks on its sloped surfaces as protection against such an attack but Nadler was undaunted. He jumped on to the enemy tank and affixed his charge to the turret. Soon afterward the young SS-Sturmmann destroyed a third T 34. Nadler's courageous actions foiled this threatening breakthrough attempt. He was one of many panzer-grenadiers to perform such feats in those days. Even the company medic of the 2nd SS Panzer-Grenadier Regiment's 7th Company destroyed a T 34 with a hollow charge.

The rocket launchers and artillery opened up with adjustment fire at daybreak on 10 July 1943. Together with the 2nd Regiment and attached elements, the Tigers had begun moving into the assembly area southwest of Teterevino during the night, beginning at 0000. By 0300 the battle group was ready. Because the Totenkopf Division had failed to take the commanding Hill 226.6 north of the bend in the Psel during the night, one of the important conditions for the IInd SS Panzer Corps' attack to the northwest was missing. The battalions of the Leibstandarte's 2nd SS Panzer-Grenadier Regiment attacked at 1045. The Ist and IInd Battalions were blanketed by artillery fire directed from the Psel hills, where the Totenkopf Division was engaged in fierce fighting. At 1300 both battalions successfully stormed the southwest tip of the Sloyevoye District Forest, Reference Point 241.6. Late in the morning it began to rain heavily. In the afternoon Sturmbannführer Sandig's IInd Battalion, 2nd SS Panzer-Grenadier Regiment advanced on Hill 241.6; resistance was fierce, but the Tigers and assault guns provided outstanding support. The attack was rolling and a breakthrough appeared imminent. The Soviets had dug in numerous tanks in front of the hill, some of which the attackers were able to destroy. The Tigers fired H.E. rounds at the bunkers from which the Soviets were firing on the panzer-grenadiers with machine-guns and light automatic weapons. Once again several well-concealed anti-tank guns were spotted at the last minute and knocked out with point-blank fire. During a conference with other Tiger commanders, SS-Obersturmführer Schütz was wounded by fragments from an exploding shell. His gunner, SS-Unterscharführer Wendt, assumed command of his Tiger 1311.

With support from the reconnaissance battalion and Ist Battalion of the 2nd SS Panzer-Grenadier Regiment, by 1630 hours the enemy position was rolled up and the hill taken. SS-Sturmmann Warmbrunn, gunner in the company commander's tank, destroyed nine T 34s and three 76.2 mm anti-tank guns. SS-Unterscharführer Bernhardt, a Tiger commander, was killed. Approximately twenty members of the company were on hand to celebrate the awarding of the Knight's Cross to Franz Staudegger. SS-Oberführer Wisch presented the decoration at about noon. Naturally the company's first Knight's Cross was cause for a hastily-improvised party to celebrate the great event. There was plenty to drink and the raucous celebration attracted a number of men from outside the company. Staudegger could scarcely believe his luck. Informed of this feat by a lone Tiger, Adolf Hitler summoned Staudegger to see him at Führer Headquarters. Staudegger turned up in his field uniform, the one-piece camouflage outfit, and gave the Führer a detailed account of his experiences in tank-versus-tank combat in the Tiger. Afterward, Staudegger went on leave; his home town of Bleiburg laid on a big reception for the local hero. In front of the assembled townsfolk he received the gift of a voucher for a Volkswagen car. While at home Staudegger gave several speeches on the Tiger and his experiences on the Eastern Front. He also sent several packages to his company at the front.

The attack on Prokhorovka took place on 11 July 1943. When the attack began the Leibstandarte came under fire from both flanks. The 2nd Regiment was attacked by Soviet tanks near Jamki and soon afterward came upon a previously unknown anti-tank ditch southwest of Swch. Oktjabrskij. At 0900 Stukas attacked targets in front of the 2nd Regiment, after which the reconnaissance battalion and the 2nd Regiment, supported by the Tigers, stormed the northern part of Hill 252.2. The fighting was fierce and the hill was taken trench by trench in a textbook attack.

Hauptsturmführer Becker (Ist Battalion) occupied part of the anti-tank ditch and the 1st Company of the Ist SS Pioneer Battalion cleared lanes through the mines so that the Tigers could follow quickly. Shortly afterward, Peiper and his group also moved forward through the anti-tank ditch and attacked the southern part of Hill 252.2 with the armored group. The hill was taken by the tanks and panzer-grenadiers at 1310 hours following a seesaw battle, and Peiper continued on to Swch. Oktjabrskij with support from Stukas. At 1330 hours the enemy attacked the 2nd Regiment's Ist Battalion south of Reference Point 252.2 with tanks, however the panzer-grenadiers fought back fiercely and forced the enemy to withdraw to his point of departure.

The following was recorded of the Tiger company's efforts on 10 and 11 July 1943: "After the withdrawal of the unit to Teterevino and the advance against the high ground 1.5 kilometers west of Prokhorovka, four panzers of the Kling Company again took part in the successful defense against several Russian attacks on our positions. Kling and his three serviceable tanks rushed tirelessly to meet the tank units attacking from all sides and on 10 and 11 July 1943 destroyed a further twenty-four T 34s. He made a decisive contribution to our own attack on the hill 1.5 kilometers west of Prokhorovka by destroying twenty-eight anti-tank guns and six artillery pieces and was himself severely wounded during this attack."

Bobby Warmbrunn, normally Kling's gunner, knocked out a T 34 and five anti-tank guns that day. As Kling's deputy Schütz was likewise out of action, SS-Untersturmführer Wittmann assumed command of the company. A frontal assault on Prokhorovka was postponed until the following day on account of a strong concentration of anti-tank guns and artillery on Hill 252.4, northwest of the Psel. On 12 July 1943, after the Totenkopf Division had eliminated the flanking threat at the Psel, the 2nd SS Panzer-Grenadier Regiment, with the Leibstandarte's armored group and the reconnaissance battalion, was to take Prokhorovka in a joint attack with the Totenkopf Division.

THE TANK BATTLE OF PROKHOROVKA

The 12th of July 1943 was to go down in history as the day of the greatest tank battle in military history. That day the Soviets threw two tank corps against the IInd SS Panzer Corps, whose three divisions had set out together. In the morning the armored group of the Leibstandarte was attacked by fifty enemy tanks across the line Prokhorovka-Petrovka soon after it moved off. The 1st SS Panzer-Grenadier Regiment was also attacked by forty tanks from Jamki. SS-Oberscharführer Kurt Sametreiter of the 3rd Company of the Leibstandarte Anti-tank Battalion knocked out twenty-four enemy tanks in this action and was later decorated with the Knight's Cross.

At 0920 hours 150 enemy tanks, carrying infantry and moving at high speed, attacked from Prokhorovka with strong artillery support. The 2nd SS Panzer-Grenadier Regiment's lines were broken and four of seven Panzer IVs under the command of Obersturmführer von Ribbentrop standing guard at Swch. Oktjabrskij were destroyed. Von Ribbentrop's three surviving tanks joined the wave of Soviet tanks and destroyed fourteen from close range. The T 34s came upon the assembly area of the IInd Battalion of the SS Panzer Regiment Leibstandarte under SS-Sturmbannführer Martin Gross. Also there were the Tigers under Wittmann's command. The armored troop carrier battalion was struck by the full force of the massed Soviet armored assault.

SS-Rottenführer Johannes Bräuer, driver of an armored troop carrier in the 11th (Armored) Company, described the event from the point of view of the troops: "After crossing an anti-tank ditch, we drove into an assembly area during the night of 11 July 1943. It wasn't until dawn on 11 July that one could properly see the surrounding area and the mass of vehicles and troops drawn up around us. One could only guess that something big was in the offing. In any case we enlisted men had no idea of what was soon to happen to us. I had taken part in everything since the beginning of the eastern campaign, from Zhitomir to Rostov and in the winter position, but I had never experienced such a surprise attack and inferno. Everything happened in such a surprisingly short time that one didn't know what to do . . ."

Bräuer was subsequently wounded in the eye and the lung by shell fragments. SS-Unterscharführer Erhard Knöfel of the same company added to Bräuer's account: "We drove into readiness positions with the armored troop carrier battalion on 11 July 1943, positioned on the reverse slope between our division's tanks and assault guns like men on a chessboard. We scooped out a shallow depression beneath our half-track in order to get a few hours sleep, so-called 'night rest.' Our tanks moved off at dawn and we thought that we could get another half hour of sleep, but things turned out quite different. The Red tanks andours arrived on the hill simultaneously. Our tanks came back mingled with the Soviet ones carrying infantry. We were singled out by a T 34, which rammed us. We put our hollow charges to use, some of which failed in the tumult. SS-Untersturmführer Wolff knocked out a tank in the melee. He lay shoulder to shoulder with us but the day was long yet. Then we became involved with the Soviet mounted infantry. In the meantime our Grille (Crickets) and self-propelled guns began 'reaping' with direct fire from the anti-tank ditch. The Soviet attack began to falter. All hell now broke loose; jets of flame and tank turrets flew through the air. But we took losses too. I myself stayed in the company headquarters squad vehicle with Guhl; as a medic, I had more than enough to do that day. I was shot in the thigh while in the kneeling position tending to a wounded man. I removed my pistol belt and applied a dressing to the wound then looked for cover. I found a hole nearby and was about to jump in, but what did I see? Two pairs of fear-filled eyes staring at me, the crew of a knocked-out enemy tank, unarmed like me."

SS-Untersturmführer Erhard Guhrs, commander of the tank gun platoon of the 14th (Heavy Armored) Company: "They attacked in the morning. They were around us, above us and among us. We fought man against
man, leapt from our holes, grabbed the hollow charges from our half-
tracks and placed them on the enemy tanks, then jumped into our vehicle
and took on every enemy. It was hell! By 0900 the battlefield was again
firmly in our hands. Fortunately our tanks had helped us tremendously.
My company alone destroyed fifteen Soviet tanks in the battle."

It was the hour of the lone tank killer. In the midst of the inferno
Peiper's adjutant, SS-Untersturmführer Werner Wolff, took command of a
leaderless company and took on the Soviet tanks. Wolff, who had a reputation as a daredevil and who was known for his courage in close combat,
destroyed a T 34 and stood his ground; he and his company refused to
yield a single meter. For his steadfastness that day he was awarded the
Knight's Cross. Jochen Peiper, too, destroyed an enemy tank at close range
in the front lines. The panzers of IInd Battalion, 1st SS Panzer Regiment
under SS-Sturmbannführer Martin Gross were also heavily engaged. Morning found the battalion about 2.5 kilometers southeast of Prokhorovka, in
the area of Reference Point 252.2.

The panzer regiment's war diary recorded: "At approximately 0815
about 150 enemy tanks, predominantly type T 34, broke through our
infantry lines of security and stormed into our tank assembly area on a narrow front, making use of their high speed and firing all weapons. SS-
Sturmbannführer Martin Groß hastily organized the defense, so skillfully
that it was possible to engage the enemy tanks from three sides. He himself
stood among his men, fighting to all sides. Groß' courageous example
served as an inspiration to the entire battalion . . ."

Daring in concept, the operation by Groß and his tanks smashed the
attack and destroyed 107 Soviet tanks in a bitter, sustained firefight. The
remaining enemy tanks were destroyed by individuals with close-range
weapons and the artillery. The commander of the Tiger company, SS-
Untersturmführer Wittmann, destroyed several enemy tanks as well. His
outstanding total of enemy tanks destroyed in the past days of fighting was
impressive proof of his personal skill.

A propaganda company reporter wrote: "The war no longer evades
him, now begins the great tank duel, the iron one-on-one battles which
elevate Wittmann to the highest level. When the great battle began on the
day of Belgorod he succeeded in blowing apart eight tanks. Wittmann
showed what he could do in the rapid advance, in driving over fields, in
entering villages, in unpredictable tank duels. He flushed out artillery batteries, picked out even the most cleverly camouflaged anti-tank nests,

drove over them, blew them apart, cautious when he had to be, daring when it paid off. His keen instincts and the luck of the skilled enabled him to survive five grim, fire-filled days unscathed. Again and again enemy tanks went up in flames before him, and when Michael Wittmann washed his sweaty, powder-blackened face on the evening of the fifth day, he knew he had left behind him thirty wrecked T 34s, twenty-eight crushed and blasted Soviet anti-tank guns and two destroyed batteries."

There is no information concerning kills by other Tiger commanders on 12 July, though it is known that gunner Warmbrunn destroyed a T 34. The foundation of Wittmann's successes was his precision and meticulousness. For the first time he showed that his tactics, combined with aggressiveness, could lead to success. He demanded a maximum effort from his crew. Wittmann wasn't one to underline his wishes with army-style shouting or drill, but he refused to stand for sloppiness and demanded meticulousness and mastery of the tank, the gun, the machine-gun and other elements. He responded to lack of attention by having his orders repeated. Wittmann's gunner that day was the recently promoted SS-Untersturmführer Helmut Gräser. Gaube (loader), Fuss (driver) and Lieber (radio operator) made up the rest of his crew.

Commander in Chief of Army Group South Generalfeldmarschall Erich von Manstein expressed his gratitude and appreciation to the divisions of the IInd SS Panzer Corps for their conduct and success in the recent battles.

On 13 July 1943, SS-Sturmmann Schamp delivered a repaired Tiger to Wittmann. At 1000 hours the Leibstandarte armored group set out to attack the hills northwest of Swch. Oktjabrskij, while the reconnaissance battalion advanced toward Michailovka to solidify contact with the Totenkopf Division there. The panzers made rapid progress and reached the foot of the hills in half an hour. There they found themselves facing an anti-tank front installed on the reverse slope. Bolstered by dug-in tanks, the Soviet positions completely commanded the crest of the hill with their firepower. The reinforced reconnaissance battalion entered Mikhailovka, but extremely heavy fire from the hills north of the Psel forced it to withdraw to a line north of Reference Point 241.6. The day was marked by heavy enemy artillery fire. The Soviets attacked with two regiments with air support; however, the attack was halted in front of the main line of resistance. The Soviet artillery fire subsided somewhat in the afternoon, then increased in intensity again after darkness fell. Weak enemy forces probed the German lines, but otherwise the night passed quietly. Tank commander SS-Unterscharführer Arthur Bernhard was killed on 13 July 1943.

That same day the commanders of Army Groups South and Center, Generalfeldmarschälle von Manstein and von Kluge, met with Hitler to decide whether to continue or cancel Operation Zitadelle. Von Manstein wished to continue the offensive under certain conditions, for in his sector his armies were poised on the brink of success. The enemy's operational reserve had been badly battered and he wanted to wear down the Soviets in a battle of attrition. Von Kluge, however, pleaded for an end to the battle. Hitler decided in favor of the latter option, however the Fourth Panzer Army and the Second Army were to smash enemy forces south of Kursk.

The following original entry from the diary of SS-Sturmmann Warmbrunn concerns the final days of the battle:

"On 13 July 1943 Wittmann and I were rummaging through a collective farm. We were caught by a salvo from a Stalin Organ; it was as if the Red Army troops had been informed of our presence. We dropped to the ground and were showered by the remains of a wall. Wittmann said drily, 'We should be praying now.' Then I let slip out, 'To whom?' I don't think anyone ever laughed so hard in such a ticklish situation as Wittmann did then. He often repeated the story when the opportunity arose."

The 13th Panzer Company had fought magnificently in those hot July days of 1943. Michael Wittmann wrote: "The company has meanwhile achieved a series of fine successes. It destroyed 151 enemy tanks, 87 heavy anti-tank guns and four batteries of artillery without a single loss in five days during the offensive and defensive battles in the Belgorod area in July 1943."

Supplementing these impressive totals of knocked-out Soviet tanks and guns were the countless emplaced flamethrowers, bunkers and field positions destroyed by the Tigers. This success is all the more impressive because not a single Tiger tank had to be written off as a total loss. The company had proved to be a keen-edged weapon in the hands of the Leibstandarte, whose success was known throughout the division. The destruction of thirty enemy tanks by SS-Untersturmführer Michael Wittmann had made the rest of the company sit up and take notice. Other tank commanders had also demonstrated their abilities: SS-Unterscharführer Staudegger had destroyed twenty-four tanks, two of them in close combat. SS-Unterscharführer Brandt and Höld achieved outstanding results and together with SS-Scharführer Lötzsch, the "panzer general" from Dresden, made names for themselves. However, the fast-reacting gunners, mostly young men barely twenty years of age, also played a part in the astonishing success of the Tiger company. Their number included men such as SS-Sturmmänner Warmbrunn, Woll, Schamp, Helmut Gräser and SS Panzerschütze Büchner. The young crews proved themselves equal to the task in those hot July days.

On 14 July 1943 the Tiger company had five serviceable tanks; the panzer regiment of the Leibstandarte had thirty-two Panzer IVs and ten lighter tanks. The armored group was situated near Reference Point 247.6, northeast of Komsomolets. After the Das Reich Division had taken Pravorot, the Leibstandarte was to advance on Jamki. The Leibstandarte's armored group was placed under the command of the Das Reich Division's armored group for this operation. When reconnaissance revealed a massing of Soviet forces, with more than one hundred tanks in Jamki and Michailovka, it became apparent that the enemy intended to cut off the salient held by the Leibstandarte. Headquarters, IInd SS Panzer Corps therefore decided not to carry out the attack on Jamki. Heavy rain completely softened the roads and paths and rendered them impassable. Referring to the Tiger company's sector that day, SS-Sturmmann Schamp wrote: "Bombs, Stalin Organs, artillery."

Enemy reconnaissance forces probed the German lines on 15 July 1943 and there was heavy activity in the air. A Ic report stated that the division had destroyed 501 Soviet tanks by 14 July 1943. Eight Tigers were serviceable on 15 July. The Tiger company guarded the railway line, there was no combat.

On 16 July 1943, enemy mortars and artillery laid down harassing fire on the German main line of resistance. Soviet patrols probed the lines all day and close-support aircraft were extremely active. The main line of resistance was taken back during the night of 17 July 1943. The Leibstandarte held the line Teterevino-Prokhorovka—east end of Wassylewka. Wittmann had nine Tigers at his disposal in the new area.

The move into the area west of Belgorod began after darkness fell on 17 July. For the Leibstandarte this marked the end of Operation Zitadelle. In spite of the undeniable successes that were achieved against the Soviets' unprecedented defensive system of positions, anti-tank barriers, tanks and artillery, in the end the pincer operation was denied success. The division's losses were 474 killed (21 officers), 2,202 wounded (65 officers) and 77 missing (1 officer). The Tiger company lost five killed.

POSTSCRIPT TO THE ZITADELLE OFFENSIVE

Contrary to claims made by some historians in Germany and abroad, that nearly all the German panzer divisions employed in Operation Zitadelle were equipped with Tigers, it is an established fact that a total of only 146 Tigers saw action. Allan Bullock, for example, claims seventeen panzer divi-

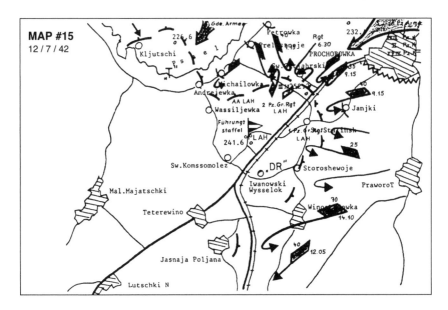

sions whose panzer regiments were supposed to have been equipped with the Tiger. That would have been a total of 2,000 Tigers, 118 per division, a utopian figure, for it exceeds the total number of Tiger Is built during the war. It is understandable on account of their numerical relationship to the total German strength that the Tigers were unable to decide the offensive and carry entire divisions forward. Nevertheless, they did prove to be an outstanding success in classic tank-versus-tank engagements—committed there for the first time under relatively favorable conditions—and clearly exceeded the high expectations placed in them. The number of opposing tanks destroyed was out of all proportion to their own total losses. In the five days of the offensive many of the Leibstandarte Tigers achieved great success. Wittmann and his gunner, Sturmmann Woll, destroyed at least 30 tanks, 28 anti-tank guns and 2 batteries of Soviet artillery. The company commander, Hauptsturmführer Kling, and his gunner, Sturmmann Warm-brunn, knocked out 18 tanks and 27 anti-tank guns. Unterscharführer Staudegger and Panzerschütze Buchner were able to put twenty-two tanks out of action on 8 July 1943 alone.

Altogether, the 13th Panzer Company destroyed 151 tanks, 87 anti-tank guns, four batteries of Soviet artillery and countless other weapons during the five days of the Kursk offensive. The Tiger also proved to be an effective assault weapon against Soviet anti-tank barriers, smashing gaps in the anti-tank fronts for the grenadiers to advance through. The number of anti-tank guns, gun bunkers, automatic flamethrowers and other enemy weapons destroyed was high. Each day the Soviet propaganda reports announced the destruction of dozens of Tigers. The total claimed destroyed by them exceeded the actual number of Tigers that existed on the German side. All told, the Soviets claimed to have destroyed 2,818 German tanks, including 700 Tigers, and 1,392 aircraft. The Tiger had quickly established itself as the Red Army's most dangerous opponent and from then on the Soviets accorded it great respect

WITHDRAWAL FROM THE FRONT AND TRANSFER, 18–28 JULY 1943

On 18 July 1943 the IInd SS Panzer Corps left the Fourth Panzer Army. On the occasion of the corps' departure from his command, the Commander in Chief of the Fourth Panzer Army, Generaloberst Hoth, issued the following order of the day:

"The Commander in Chief of the Fourth Panzer Army, Army H.Q., 18 July 1943, Order of the Day:

The IInd SS Panzer Corps is leaving the area of the Fourth Panzer Army on 18/7.

When the corps with its three panzer-grenadier divisions came under the command of the army in the second half of March, the Russian winter offensive was at its high point and had torn open wide gaps in the German front. Under the most difficult conditions, the corps took up the fight shoulder to shoulder with the units of the army and bore the brunt of the fighting in the great spring battles. The corps repulsed the Soviet shock armies with incomparable offensive drive and by recapturing Kharkov and Belgorod turned the imminent catastrophe into a glorious victory. After weeks of reorganization, which were filled with hard training, on 5 July the corps struck again. The in-depth enemy positions were stormed with the corps' usual offensive spirit, counterattacking Soviet tank corps were beaten back in the most violent tank battles and their attacking strength broken. To the IInd SS Panzer Corps I express my thanks and utmost appreciation for the behavior, toughness and exemplary bravery which it displayed while under the command of the Fourth Panzer Army.

When the corps is assigned new and difficult missions I am certain that it will master them successfully in loyalty to the Führer, for German victory.

The Commander in Chief, signed Hoth, Generaloberst."

Rolf Schamp made this laconic entry in his diary on 18 July 1943: "Night march, sixty kilometers; slept in cornfield." On 19 July the Tigers were loaded aboard trains in Belgorod and transported into the area north of Stalino. On 21 July 1943 the Tiger company arrived in Slavyansk with twelve tanks. On 23 July the men were assembled in an open field.

There the company commander, SS-Untersturmführer Wittmann, handed out the first decorations to the most successful members of the Tiger crews. SS-Panzerschütze Heinz Buchner received both Iron Crosses for his accurate shooting on 8 July 1943, when as Staudegger's gunner he took part in the destruction of twenty-two enemy tanks. Buchner had just turned nineteen and with fifty-one enemy tanks destroyed was one of the best gunners in the company. The other members of Staudegger's crew on 8 July—SS-Panzerschütze Gerhard Waltersdorf (radio operator), SS-Panzerschütze Walter Henke (loader), SS-Sturmmann Herbert Stellmacher (driver)—all received the Iron Cross, Second Class. SS-Panzerschütze Heinz Schindhelm, a gunner, and tank driver SS-Sturmmann Walter Bingert were likewise decorated with the Iron Cross, Second Class, as was Wittmann's driver, SS-Panzerschütze Siegfried Fuß. SS-Unterscharführer "Captain" Jürgen Brandt, one of the more successful tank commanders, received the Iron Cross, First Class. Promotions were also announced that day, to become effective on 1 August 1943.

The Leibstandarte was supposed to launch an attack from the Mius bridgehead on 24 July 1943, however the order to attack was cancelled. All units received transport notifications. On 25 July 1943 the division arrived in Artemovsk as per orders. After leaving Artemovsk, at 2335 hours the Leibstandarte received the following order: "Cease movement. Make preparations for rail transport! Destination unknown." As always happened in such cases, the most fantastic rumors began circulating among the companies. The Tiger company handed all its tanks over to the Totenkopf and Das Reich Divisions. Four Tigers were handed over to Oberscharführer Konrad Schweigert of the Das Reich Panzer-Grenadier Division's Tiger company. He wrote: "We now have eighteen Panzer VIs and thus more tanks than crews. The tank that I delivered attracted attention everywhere on account of the large number of black rings of insulating tape on the barrel of the 88 mm gun used to mark tank kills. I suspect that it might even have been Michael Wittmann's tank."

Departure orders were issued to all units of the Leibstandarte at 0000 hours on 27 July 1943. The panzer regiment's remaining tanks were also handed over en masse. The "Blitz-Pfeil Transport" of the Tiger company began on 29 July. At 0700 the men were taken by truck to Golovka, where they boarded the trains. The tension increased immeasurably, especially since the unit had handed in all its tanks. After the recent heavy fighting the men now enjoyed the chance to rest to the full; morale was excellent.

The Tiger Company in Italy

The "Blitz-Pfeil Transport" (Lightning-Arrow) was the fastest mode of travel by rail, and the units received provisions only during absolutely necessary locomotive changes. Walter Lau, just promoted to SS-Sturmmann, recalled: "We steamed in the direction of Germany at maximum speed, there were no stops, all the trains coming the other way stopped. This was unusual, for normally trains coming from the front stopped and let those coming from the Reich proceed. Something had to be going on. Soon it was obvious that we were headed in the direction of Nuremberg-Munich, but no one knew where it might end. Beyond Munich came Rosenheim and rumors started that our destination was Innsbruck. We detrained in Innsbruck late in the evening. We spent the first night in the open or in the surrounding houses; however, we had to sleep in the halls, for after all we weren't in a hostile country where we were permitted to requisition quarters. The combat echelon was billeted in a school-like building for a time; they were wonderful days with walks, movies and drives into the surrounding countryside."

The transport train with the wheeled elements of the Tiger company arrived in Innsbruck on the afternoon of 1 August 1943. The company detrained in the evening and moved into the surrounding streets for the night. The men slept in their vehicles. Some were billeted in a school. After several days in Innsbruck the 13th Company set out for Brenner. Sitting in their trucks and other vehicles, the men had a marvelous drive through South-Tirol. The soldiers were given a tumultuous reception as they crossed the South-Tirolean border. The local population showered the soldiers with wine, fruit and other delicacies. The jubilation appeared to have no bounds and the drive through South-Tirol turned into a triumphal procession. The South-Tiroleans were beside themselves with joy to finally have German instead of Italian troops in their homeland. The men spent the night near the road on which they were driving. In the following days the trip—for that is how it seemed to the men—continued. The vehicles passed through Sterzing, Bozen, Trient, Verona, Mantua and Parma and arrived in Reggio nell Emilia.

The Tiger company occupied quarters northwest of Reggio on 8 August 1943. The unit's vehicles were dispersed and camouflaged in a large vineyard. Officers, NCOs and men slept in tents. After the hard and deprivation-filled months on the Eastern Front, this time was like a paradise to the soldiers. Some members of the company arrived on a later train and joined the unit in Italy. One of those was our faithful reporter Rolf Schamp: "29/7: 0700 hours departed by truck for Golovka. Shower. Industrial region, limestone pyramids—30/7: cleaning of weapons, general repairs, reading—31/7: delousing—01/8: 0300 departure—02/8: Alexandria, Fastov, Kasatin, Berdichev—03/8: Lvov—04/8: Cracow, Kattowitz. Crossed border into Reich at 1225 hours—05/8: Hirschberg, Görlitz (heavy thunderstorm), Dresden—06/8: Chemnitz, Zeschendorf, Zwickau, Hof—07/8: Regensburg, Landshut, Rosenheim, Innsbruck. Slept in house. Walk in Innsbruck—08/8: Walk in Innsbruck—12/8: Left Innsbruck at 1400 hours. Crossed border into Italy at the Brenner at 1720 hours, Fortagga, Bruneck—13/8: Bozen, Trient, Verona, Mantua to Reggio."

The company had become a second home to the men; they felt happy and safe there in the circle of their comrades. The first wounded from the Kursk action returned to the unit and received a joyous welcome.

SS-Panzerschütze Alfred Lünser, who was released from Kremenchug hospital at the beginning of July 1943, described the odyssey that took him back to the company: "I went to Kharkov by train. Operation "Zitadelle" had begun and I was assigned to a completely foreign unit. Then I ran away. I walked to the Red Square in Kharkov and jumped into a truck bearing the emblem of the Leibstandarte; that's how I got out of the city. I later changed to an armored troop carrier, from it to another truck and then to a Kübelwagen, and then I landed back at my unit. There was singing in broad daylight, when had that happened before? They were celebrating Staudegger's Knight's Cross. It was 10 July 1943. Then we departed for Italy via Innsbruck. We were dropped off in a large vineyard at the beginning of August. We had no tanks and slept in tents."

FORMATION OF THE 101ST SS PANZER BATTALION—THE INITIAL PHASE, 29 JULY–21 OCTOBER 1943

Once in Italy the soldiers were finally able to find time to write long overdue letters to their loved ones at home. Packages were sent and mail arrived from Germany. At the request of a propaganda company SS-Oberscharführer Jürgen Brandt made a recording, probably for a musical request program. The Northern German's clear voice was especially well-suited to this. His prepared text began, "Dear mother . . ." While the troops enjoyed the peace, the sunshine and the other amenities of Italy, plans were already being put into action for the formation of the Ist SS Panzer Corps Leibstandarte. SS Operational Headquarters ordered the formation of a heavy tank battalion for the Ist SS Panzer Corps on 19 July 1943: the Tiger battalion had been born. The battalion received the number 101; a subsequent decree by the SS Operational Headquarters explained the numbering system for corps units. The last number indicated the corps, plus one hundred. The 101st SS Panzer Battalion was to consist of a battalion headquarters plus a headquarters company, three panzer companies and a repair shop company. The Tiger company of the Leibstandarte SS Adolf Hitler (13th Heavy Company, 1st SS Panzer Regiment) was to be transferred lock, stock and barrel to the 101st SS Panzer Battalion, forming the battalion's 3rd Company. The first officers, NCOs and men began arriving in Sennelager in July 1943. Many of the NCOs and men came from the Leibstandarte's assault gun battalion. These personnel were sent to Reggio-Emila in August 1943 after the Tiger company had taken up quarters there.

SS-Hauptsturmführer Kling, who had been wounded during the Kursk offensive rejoined the company in Italy. On 25 August 1943 he was awarded the Wound Badge in Gold for having been wounded five times. The company was unaware that a recommendation for the Knight's Cross for Kling had been turned down.

Twenty-seven new Tigers arrived at the railway station in Reggio from the 10th to the 13th of August. Their number included two command tanks. SS-Sturmmann Schamp recorded some of the serial numbers of his new tank: chassis number 250333, loader's machine-gun number 2160, radio operator's machine-gun number 2631, submachine-gun No 4594, engine number 61202, gun book number 225. The tank had only 202 kilometers on it.

Division of the 13th Company resulted in two companies which were placed under the command of SS-Hauptsturmführer Kling and SS-Untersturmführer Wendorff. Kling was also responsible for the planned formation of the 101st SS Panzer Battalion. The first division of the company took place on 14 August. As of 5 August 1943 SS-Sturmbannführer Heinz von Westernhagen was officially the commanding officer of the 101st SS Panzer Battalion, which was still in the formation process. Von Westernhagen had not yet joined the unit, however. After receiving treatment for the head injury he had suffered in Zitadelle, von Westernhagen attended a course for battalion commanders at the Armored Forces School in Paris. Hauptsturmführer Kling remained the officer responsible for the formation of the battalion pending von Westernhagen's arrival. Crews were selected for the 27 Tigers and training began immediately. Hours were spent in the classroom, which meant boring theory for the old hands of the 13th Company. Fortunately Siegfried Hummel was there to provide comic relief. Effective 30 July 1943, SS-Unterscharführer Eduard Kalinowsky, Walter Hahn, Winfried Lukasius, Wilhelm Iriohn, Sepp Stich and Paul Vogt were transferred to the 101st SS Panzer Battalion after completing reserve officer candidate courses at Junkerschulen and subsequent weapons courses. The daily routine in Reggio-Emila is revealed in the notes kept by SS-Sturmmann Schamp: "31 August 1943: platoon party—1 September: swimming in Modena—2 September: roll call—3 September: training company."

Several members of the company were on very good terms with the Italians and were occasionally invited to dinner. However, their attempts to obtain the favors of the female sex met with very little success. One group laid its hands on a locally-made cheese. The large round cheese was taken in a "night and fog" operation; it was cut into more manageable portions with a bayonet and then divided up. Somehow or other word about this unauthorized supplement to the company's rations got out and there was a huge flap. SS-Untersturmführer Wittmann crawled into every Tiger looking for cheese. Faced with the threat posed by Wittmann, the evil-doers used the opportunity to eat their hoarded portions. In most cases this was sufficient to satisfy the thieves' appetite for parmesan cheese for some time.

On 8 September 1943 came the surprising order to go to the highest state of readiness. The Italians had surrendered to the Allies. No Tigers were required in the subsequent disarming action in the Italian garrisons. On 9 September 1943 La Villa military airfield and San Illono, near Reggio, were occupied by a number of officers, NCOs and men. Their former allies were interned. The soldiers of the Tiger battalion helped themselves to clothing from the Italian stores; the smart black shirts were especially popular. Other items taken from the clothing stores included mountain boots and belts and brown one-piece flight suits, which were later worn in action. The battalion also bolstered its motor pool; the headquarters drove Fiat automobiles, as well as Studebakers. There was also home leave again, for many the first in months.

The Leibstandarte's panzer regiment had been complete again since 10 August 1943, following the arrival of the newly-formed Ist Battalion, which had been equipped with Panthers. On 4 September 1943 SS-Untersturmführer Helmut Wendorff, who had been wounded in Operation Zitadelle, married twenty-year-old Hannelore Michel from Mühlhausen.

Decorations were handed out on 16 September 1943. SS-Untersturmführer "Bubi" Wendorff received the Iron Cross, First Class, as did SS-Unterscharführer Hans Höld. A spit and polish type, tank commander Höld, who
was jokingly called "SS Höld" within the company, was especially proud.
Wittmann's gunner, the twenty-one-year-old SS-Sturmmann Balthasar Woll,
was also decorated with the Iron Cross, First Class. A friendly type, the small,
dark-haired Saarlander was generally well liked and was acknowledged as
one of the best gunners in the company. The Iron Cross, Second Class was
awarded to tank commander SS-Oberscharführer Georg Lötzsch (the
"panzer general") and gunner SS-Unterscharführer Helmut Gräser. SS-
Oberscharführer Sepp Hafner, the engine specialist from Maybach, was
decorated with the War Service Cross First Class with Swords. Loader Ewald
König received the Iron Cross, Second Class and was promoted to the rank
of SS-Unterscharführer. He had joined the company in Kharkov from a
party post in order to take the "Iron Cross course", soldier's jargon for
front-line service. Tank Battle Badges and Wound Badges were also presented. Other members of Ewald König's group were SS-Panzeroberschützen Alfred Schumacher and Walter Rose. Both were already forty years
old and had taken part in Operation Zitadelle as gunners. Both Schumacher and Rose were awarded the Iron Cross, Second Class.

The Iron Cross, Second Class was also awarded to the wounded mem-
bers of Wittmann's and Schutz's crews, SS-Sturmmänner Walter Koch,
Klaus Bürvenich and Karl Lieber and SS-Rottenführer Walter Müller, SS-
Sturmmänner Franz Elmer, Siegfried Jung, Helmut Gruber, Gerhard
Kaschlan, Helmut Lange, Paul Sümnich, Karl-Heinz Grothum and SS-
Panzerschütze Siegfried Schneider.

SS-Untersturmführer Hannes Philipsen, who had been badly wounded
outside Kharkov, rejoined his company comrades in Italy in September
1943 after a six-month stay in hospital. With grim determination, Philipsen
worked to restore full mobility to his injured leg. The following officers
were on strength with the battalion in September 1943: SS-Hauptsturmführer Kling and SS-Untersturmführer Wittmann, Wendorff and Philipsen
(the latter with no official position). On 1 September 1943 SS-Oberscharführer (reserve officer candidates) Walter Hahn, Wilhelm Iriohn, Eduard
Kalinowsky, Winfried Lukasius, Sepp Stich and Paul Vogt were promoted to
SS-Untersturmführer of the Reserve. The battalion's administration officer
was SS-Obersturmführer Alfred Veller, while the battalion adjutant was SS-
Untersturmführer Helmut Dollinger. SS-Untersturmführer Sepp Stich was
transferred to the battalion headquarters staff. Transferred from the Leibstandarte's anti-tank battalion were SS-Untersturmführer Georg Bartel, who

became Technical Director for Motor Engineering (TKF), and SS-Unter-sturmführer Herbert Walther, who began forming the workshop company.

There were training platoons for each of the functions within the panzer crew. SS-Untersturmführer Dollinger was placed in charge of the radio platoon, where the new radio operators were trained. The battalion also received another "Hermann Göring Donation." Some were former flak soldiers, who proved less fit than the Luftwaffe replacements sent to Kharkov earlier in the year. One of the flak gunners was expelled from the unit by Kling in front of the assembled company and sent back to the Luft-waffe. From the Luftwaffe came Unterscharführer Günter Kunze, Willi Sadzio, Schützen Eberhard Schulte, Helmut Jacobi, Kurt Cisarz, Hans D. Sauer and Ewald Zajons. From the Luftwaffe flak came Rottenführer Paul Bockey, Schütze Erich Scheller, Walter Kirchner and Richard Felder (list is incomplete). Naturally, during this period of quiet and training the com-pany was more under the unloved watch of Senior NCO Habermann. A group photo of the 13th Company was taken on 17 September 1943.

As a result of the high consumption of grapes, the men needed only reach outside their tents to pick them, many soldiers developed diarrhoea, as their digestive systems were unaccustomed to fresh fruit. Eventually, this led to a ban on eating grapes. The evening outings were made more diffi-cult by the distance to Reggio but were no less popular for it. The food was excellent, duties bearable. Near the billets there was a small lake with a concrete rim. The Italians often swam there as did the men of the battal-ion. The daytime heat was unbearable. The swimming pool in Modena was another popular destination.

Rolf Schamp made the following entries in those days: "19/9: pistol shooting—20/9: machine-gun shooting—21/9: unit party." The latter char-acterization scarcely told the tale. A roaring company party was held in an Italian Dopo laporo House (similar to the German organization "Strength Through Joy"). It began in the afternoon out of doors, something the men had never seen before, and was then moved inside in the evening. After a show put on by the fiery Italian women there was abundant food and drink of all kinds. The company had raised the money for the party itself. The men of the Tiger company celebrated boisterously, knowing all too well that for some of them it was probably the last such celebration.

All the elements of the battalion were transferred to Correggio, north-east of Reggio, on 23 September 1943. There the men occupied quarters in a school and a party building, while the vehicles were parked and camou-flaged near a sports field. Routine duties were carried out in the morning and in the afternoon the men played sports. The battalion's officers also actively took part. Wendorff was more of a sports enthusiast than Wittmann. In September the Leibstandarte disarmed the soldiers in numerous Italian garrisons. Turin and Milan were occupied without hostilities. The same month several men of the Flak Platoon of the 101st SS Panzer Battalion's Headquarters Company escorted a POW train to Villach, Carinthia.

The battalion was administered independently as of 8 October 1943 and received a steady flow of new personnel. The companies of the Tiger battalion, which had not yet reached full strength, pushed ahead with intensive training. There was separate training for the gunners, loaders and radio operators. On 10 October it was time to pack, load everything and move again. This time the battalion went to Pontecurone, southwest of Voghera. The men were billeted in a school; the tanks and other vehicles were parked on the grounds of a brickworks. The Tigers now wore a letter "S" on their turrets instead of the number "13" (the "S" standing for schwere, or heavy, company), which was followed by two numerals indicating the platoon and tank. Applied on the right front of the tanks was the Dietrich (skeleton key), the division emblem of the Leibstandarte.

The Tigers all wore a camouflage scheme consisting of an ocher-yellow base oversprayed with patches of dark brown and red. The light platoon had been disbanded and its personnel now belonged to the Tiger platoons.

In October 1943 twelve NCOs were transferred to the battalion from the Führer Escort Detachment and the Reich Chancellery Motor Vehicle Detachment as tank commanders and drivers. Among them were SS Hauptscharführer Max Görgens, Hermann Barkhausen, SS-Oberscharführer Grosser and SS-Unterscharführer Heinrich Ernst, Helmut Fritzsche, Hein Bode and Walter Sturhahn. The daily routine continued at a high pace in order to turn the new arrivals into capable tank soldiers. An NCO course gave proven soldiers (at the rank of SS-Sturmmann and SS-Rottenführer) the opportunity to advance to Unterscharführer. SS-Untersturmführer Wendorff directed the course, SS-Untersturmführer Philipsen also taught. Among the other instructors were SS-Unterscharführer Brandt, Höld and Sowa. The course was held in a church building in Correggio.

Tigers and assault guns on the advance.

An enemy trench is taken by the 7th Company. 2nd SS Panzer-Grenadier Regiment.

SS-Sturmmann Rudi
Nadler of the 10th
Company, 2nd Panzer-
Grenadier Regiment.
On 9 July 1943, near
Lushki, he used hollow
charges to destroy
three T-34s that had
broken through.

On 10 July 1943 SS-
Unterscharführer
Franz Staudegger
became the first
member of the Tiger
Company to receive
the Knight's Cross.

German close-support aircraft (in circle) attacks a group of Soviet armor.

Tigers in the undulating terrain south of Prokhorovka.

Inspecting a knocked-out Soviet T-34/76.

The number of enemy tanks destroyed climbed rapidly during the heavy fighting in the Kursk Salient.

An American M3A3 Lee.

StuG III assault guns support the grenadiers.

SS-Sturmmann Rolf Schamp, commander of a Tiger Company Panzer III.

Panzer III commanded
by Heinz Werner (above,
middle). On his right is
Heinrich Knöß, far right
Johann Schütz.

Panzer III. *From left:* Werner Irrgang (radio operator), Schade (gunner), Schamp and far right Johann Schütz.

SS-Sturmmann Rolf Schamp in the turret of his Panzer III.

The wounded loader, SS-Sturmmann Paul Sümnich.

SS-Sturmmann Peter Winkler, radio operator in the Tiger of SS-Unterscharführer Brandt.

SS-Unterscharführer Werner Freytag of the Workshop Platoon.

SS-Sturmmann Walter Koch, Michael Wittmann's loader.

SS-Panzerschütz Heinz Buchner, Staudegger's gunner, received the Iron Cross, First and Second Classes on 23/7/43.

On 19 July 1943 the Tigers entrained in Belgorod and on 21 July arrived in Slavyansk.

A Tiger crew has a meal during transport.

On 29 July 1943 the transport trains of the Leibstandarte departed for Italy.

Transport by rail through Tirol.

SS-Unterscharführer Gustav Swiezy, SS-Sturmmann Rolf Schamp and the well-tried company medic, SS-Unterscharführer Adolf Schmidt, on the train.

Maintenance work on the just-arrived Tigers. In the foregound SS-Sturmmänner Johann Graf, Johann Schütz, right SS-Sturmmann Schamp and SS-Unterscharführer Erich Koreinke, commander of the maintenance Echelon.

Italy, August 1943.
Newly-delivered Tigers
are taken care of by the
company.

Grüner, Hummel and Schindhelm listen to the sound of the gramophone.

The crew of SS-Unterscharführer "Captain" Brandt: Wohlgemuth, Reimers, Warmbrunn, the loader and Brandt.

From left: Heinz Buchner, Bobby Warmbrunn, Gerhard Waltersdorf.

The Workshop Platoon set up its quarters in this vineyard in Reggio. On the left a Tiger, whose turret has been removed in the course of repairs by the gantry crane in front of it. An Italian woman has parked her ice cream cart in front of the crane. Sitting in the B-Krad in the foreground is Michael Wittmann. A charming photo from the summer in Italy.

The 13th Company's orderly office truck. On the right the shaded work area. On the truck is the field post office mail box.

Idyllic summer scene beneath the trees in Reggio; the shade they provided made daytime heat bearable. Here the men are belting ammunition.

The men of the Tiger Company on parade.

The Tiger Company's most successful gunners seen in Innsbruck in August 1943. During Kursk offensive Heinz Buchner accounted for 51 tanks. Bobby Warmbrunn 13 tanks and 38 anti-tank guns, and Bobby Woll approximately 30 tanks.

10 September 1943, SS-Hauptsturmführer Kling's thirtieth birthday. SS-Untersturmführer Wittmann (top, far right) presents the company's gift, a photo album.

The company commander with his officers.

SS-Hauptsturmführer Kling and his crew. *From left:* Bobby Warmbrunn (gunner), Wohlgemuth (radio operator), Heinz Kling, Hein Reimers (driver) and Max Gaube (loader).

Kling and his senior NCO, SS-Hauptscharführer Habermann.

New Plans

Another division of personnel involving both panzer companies took place on 5 October 1943. The first reference to the existence of a 3rd Panzer Company appears the following day. With the company was Knight's Cross wearer SS-Hauptscharführer Alfred Günther, who had transferred from the assault gun battalion. The still-incomplete companies received army postal numbers.

Previously the 13th Company had had the postal number 48165; now, with new designations came new postal numbers: "101st Heavy SS Panzer Battalion—HQ and Headquarters Company 59450 A—1st Company, 101st SS Panzer Battalion 59450 B—2nd Company, 101st SS Panzer Battalion 59450 C—3rd Company, 101st SS Panzer Battalion 59450 D—Workshop Company 59450 E." On 7 October 1943 SS-Rottenführer Herbert Stewig of the 3rd Company was killed in an accident in Reggio-Emilia; his comrades provided an honor guard as he was laid to rest.

More decorations were awarded on 14 October 1943. Several went to men who had been overlooked before, and those who had returned from hospital were honored for their accomplishments during Operation Zitadelle. SS-Sturmmann Schamp received the Tank Battle Badge and the Iron Cross, Second Class. The companies were reorganized on 18 October. SS-Untersturmführer Wendorff continued to lead the 2nd Company and Kling the 1st Company.

More changes and restructuring took place on 24 October. On 21 October it was announced that the division would soon be going into action again. Extensive preparations for rail transport began immediately. The original plan was to issue the Leibstandarte winter equipment in Munich then billet it in St. Pölten. Action against American landing forces in Italy—which had appeared possible—was therefore out of the question. Elements of the division—which had just been renamed 1st SS Panzer Division Leibstandarte SS Adolf Hitler—were to be transported from the various areas of Italy and Istria to St. Pölten, receive winter equipment, and occupy quarters there temporarily. The sequence of subsequent transports to the Eastern Front would be planned by taking into consideration the most favorable tactical organization of the units.

"27 October 1943. Departure for Russia," SS-Sturmmann Rolf Schamp wrote in his diary. The warning order for entraining those elements of the Tiger battalion slated to see action arrived that day. Several tank commanders—SS-Hauptscharführer Leo Spranz and SS-Unterscharführer Werner Wendt among them—and ten tank drivers—Ludwig Hofmann, Willi Röpstorff, Paul Rohweder, Walter Sturhahn, Theo Janekzek and others—drove to the army ordnance depot at Burg bei Madgeburg to pick up ten new Tigers and deliver them to the unit. On 2 November 1943 the tanks arrived in Lvov, where were ordered by SS Operational Headquarters to proceed to Paderborn.

As a result of this order, the Tigers never reached the unit in Italy. Not all of the rump battalion was destined for transport to the Eastern Front. One operational company was assembled from the parts of the three panzer companies. It joined the division under the designation 13th (Heavy) Company, 1st SS Panzer Regiment.

On 29 October 1943, while the panzers were being loaded at the Voghera railway station, SS-Untersturmführer Sepp Stich stood up in the turret of one of the Tigers to direct the men. Suddenly his head touched the overhead wire and he was killed on the spot. The twenty-two-year-old officer from Brand in the Sudetenland was buried in the cemetery in Pavia, south of Milan. A detachment from the company fired the volley at his graveside.

SS-Obersturmführer Michalski had been transferred to the company a short time before. Michalski was born in Berlin-Spandau on 11 January 1920 and he joined the Leibstandarte SS Adolf Hitler's 8th Company before the war. He was later transferred and returned to the Leibstandarte from the 1st SS Infantry Brigade on 1 November 1942. He received the Iron Cross, First Class after the recapture of Kharkov while serving with the headquarters of the IInd Battalion, SS Panzer Regiment Leibstandarte. In the end Michalski saw service there as an operations officer. In those days departure fever reigned in the Tiger Battalion and the entire Leibstandarte; there was hectic activity everywhere.

On 6 November 1943 SS-Untersturmführer Philipsen, who was ill with nephritis, wrote to his family from a hospital in Italy: ". . . Instead this winter will see us in the east again locked in battle with the bolsheviks. Yes, in the fine summer months they let us traipse about Upper Italy as roving occupation troops and reorganize and train, and in the cold winter we must return to the great mixup on the Eastern Front and restore order. It's exactly the same as last winter except that this time we must intervene sooner. Hopefully things will work out as they did last winter in the area of Kharkov and Belgorod. It will be a hard nut again, but we will be harder!

For us it can always mean only one thing: Führer command, we will follow!' Our first elements are already arriving at the front in the east . . ."

The Tigers and wheeled vehicles of the 13th Panzer Company were loaded aboard four transport trains on 1st and 2nd November 1943. The personnel and elements not destined for combat were transferred to Sennelager-South/Augustdorf, where the ten Tigers that had been transported to Lvov also arrived. These elements were now used to form the 3rd Company of the 101st SS Panzer Battalion as well as the headquarters and workshop companies. The 1st and 2nd Companies, which existed in theory, were combined into the 13th Company. The 13th Company was organized into five (!) platoons each with five Tigers. Never before had it possessed such strength. With the company commander's and company headquarters squad leader's tanks, SS-Hauptsturmführer Kling had at his disposal a total of twenty-seven Tigers. Kling once again took over command of the company and the veteran SS-Untersturmführer Wendorff and Wittmann took over the Ist and IInd Platoons. During the detraining in the Soviet Union the Ist Platoon was still under the command of SS-Untersturmführer Michalski.

The IIIrd Platoon was commanded by SS-Untersturmführer Kalinowsky. Eduard Kalinowsky was born in Frankfurt am Main on 3 February 1912 and was a qualified brewmaster by profession. He joined the 2nd Company of the 9th SS Infantry Regiment as a war volunteer and was decorated with the Iron Cross, Second Class for his actions on the Eastern Front. From the Westland Replacement Battalion he came in May 1942 to the 3rd Company of the Das Reich Division's SS Panzer Battalion and from January 1943 to the Headquarters Company of the SS Panzer Regiment Das Reich. After a tank course and a reserve officer course at Bad Tölz, on 30 July 1943 Kalinowsky joined the 101st SS Panzer Battalion as an SS-Unterscharführer of the Reserve and a reserve officer candidate. He was promoted to SS-Untersturmführer of the Reserve in Italy on 1 September 1943.

The IVth Platoon was commanded by SS-Untersturmführer Hahn. Born in Cologne on 9 June 1913, Walter Hahn served as a government advisor before volunteering for military service. He served with the 9th SS Infantry Regiment and later to the Das Reich Division. After completing a tank course, Hahn attended a reserve officer candidate course at Bad Tölz, and on 30 July 1943 he was transferred to the 101st SS Panzer Battalion as an SS-Oberscharführer and a reserve officer candidate. On 1 September 1943 Hahn was promoted to SS-Untersturmführer of the Reserve.

In command of the Vth Platoon was SS-Untersturmführer Hartel. Fritz Hartel was born in Grünhagen, East Prussia on 10 May 1914. After working on his parents' farm, in February 1934 he joined the Volunteer Labor Service, where he became a battalion sport instructor.

On 30 July 1934, Fritz Hartel joined the Leibstandarte SS Adolf Hitler, where he served with the 9th Company. Unterscharführer Hartel took part in all the Leibstandarte's actions and was awarded both Iron Crosses, the Wound Badge in Gold and the Infantry Assault Badge, before he joined the panzer regiment in 1942. Hartel was as a member of the Tiger company from the time of its formation. By then a veteran Hauptscharführer, he saw action in the Kharkov fighting and the Kursk offensive with the 13th Company and on 9 November was promoted to SS-Untersturmführer.

Recent arrivals SS-Unterscharführer Kunze and Sadzio had become tank commanders. From Borken in East Prussia, the twenty-seven-year-old Sadzio came to the unit from the Pütnitz Flying School. Other tank commanders originally from the Luftwaffe were Unterscharführer Kurt Kleber, Herbert Stief, Eduard Stadler, Erich Langner, Cap, and Kurt Hühnerbein, as well as Oberscharführer Behrens. At this point the way began to part; the subsequent development of the 101st SS Panzer Battalion is described elsewhere.

The focus now is on the Tiger company, which was preparing for its new mission. The organization of the 13th Company was highly unusual for a panzer company, for twenty-seven Tigers possessed enormous striking power and represented an imposing force.

ORDER OF BATTLE:
13th (Heavy) Company, 1st SS Panzer Regiment

S 05
Company Commander
Hstuf. Heinz Kling

S 04
Company HQ Squad Leader
Oscha. Krohn

Ist Platoon

IInd Platoon

IIIrd Platoon

S 11
Ustuf. Helmut Wendorff

S 21
Ustuf. Michael Wittmann

S 31
Ustuf. Eduard Kalinowsky

S 12
Uscha. Hans Höld

S 22
Uscha. Ewald Mölly

S 32
Oscha. Eduard Stadler

S 13
Uscha. Hans Rosenberger

S 23
Hscha. Hans Höflinger

S 33
Oscha. Georg Lötzsch

S 14
Oscha. Otto Augst

S 24
Oscha. Jürgen Brandt

S 34
Uscha. Günter Kunze

S 15
Uscha. Kurt Hühnerbein

S 25
Uscha. Kurt Kleber

S 35
Uscha. Willi Sadzio

GUNNERS:
Strm. Balthasar Woll
Strm. Karl-Heinz Warmbrunn
Strm. Leopold Aumüler
Uscha. Karl Wagner
Strm. Siegfried Jung
Strm. Heinrich Knöss
Strm. Söffker
Strm. Rolf Schamp
Strm. Siegfried Hummel
Pz.O.Schtz Werner Knocke
Rttf. Willi Otterbein
Uscha. Helmut Gräser
Rttf. Aumann
Strm. Alfred Falkenhausen
Strm. Reinhard Wenzel
Strm. Heinz Schindhelm

LOADERS:
Pz.Schtz. Rudi Lechner
Pz.Schtz. Walter Henke
Strm. Walter Lau
Strm. Johann Schütz
Strm. Erich Tille
Pz.Schtz. Josef Rößner
Strm. Paul Sümnich
Strm. Max Gaube
Strm. Iwanitz
Strm. Bold
Strm. Grosse
Pz.Schtz. Harald Henn
Strm. Alfred Bernhard
Strm. Güner
Strm. Günther Braubach
Strm. Hirsch

RADIO OPERATORS:
Strm. Wunderlich
Strm. Gerhard Waltersdorf
Strm. Stuss
Pz.O.Schtz. Günter Jonas
Pz.O.Schtz. Johan Graf
Pz.Schtz. Hubert Heil
Pz.Schtz. Fred Zimmermann
Rttf. Wohlgemuth
Pz.Schtz. Karl Daum
Pz.O.Schtz. Werner Irrgang
Strm. Justus Kühn
Strm. Heinz Werner
Strm. Peter Winkler
Pz.Schtz. Ernst Braun
Strm. Kaminski
Strm. Lorenz Mähner
Pz.Schtz. Rudolf Hirschel
Pz.Schtz. Kurt Cisarz

DRIVERS:
Rttf. Heinrich Reimers
Strm. Franz Ellmer
Strm. Werner Hepp
Strm. Eugen Schmidt
Strm. Walter Bingert
Uscha. Jupp Selzer
Pz.O.Schtz. Kurt Kämmerer
Strm. Herbert Stellmacher
Rttf. Walter müller
Uscha. Pollak
Strm. Piper
Strm. Siegfried Fuß
Rttf. Bernhard Ahlte
Rttf. Arthur Sommer

Senior NCO:
Hscha. Habermann
Maintenance Echelon:
Uscha. Erich Koreinke

IVth Platoon

S 41
Ustuf. Walter Hahn

S 42
Uscha. Kurt Sowa

S 43
Uscha. Schwerin

S 44
Hscha. Erich Langner

S 45
Uscha. Herbert Stief

Vth Platoon

S 51
Ustuf. Fritz Hartel

S 52
Uscha. Otto Bard

S 53
Schaf. Behrens

S 54
Uscha. Heinz Werner

S 55
Uscha. Cap

Technical Sergeant (Radio): Oscha. Mengeles
Field Kitchen: Uscha. Jakob Mohrs,
(2nd Cook: Strm. Jankowski,
Drivers: Strm. Fritz Jäger, Strm. Käse)
Clothing Stores: Uscha. Heib
Ordnance & Equipment: Uscha. Tässler
SDG: Uscha. Adolf Schmidt
Quartermaster Sergeant: Uscha. Jarosch

Workshop Platoon: Hscha. Julius Porupski
Fuel & Ammo Column: Uscha. Karl Mollenhauer
Gas Supply: Uscha.Johann Reiter
Motor Transport Sergeant: Oscha Lindermann
Armorer-Artificer: Rttf. ??
Account & Pay NCO: Rttf. ??
Clerk: Strm. Hartwig

Other members of 13. (s.)/SS-Pz. Rgt. 1, whose exact position is not known.

Strm. Wilhelm Bischoff
Pz.Schtz. Horst Schwarzer
Pz.Schtz. Herbert Wastler
Pz.Schtz. Willi Werthmann
Strm. Gerhard Driedrich
Pz.Schtz. Helmut Jacobi
Pz.Schtz. Werner Schilling
Pz.Schtz. Walter Kirchner
Rttf. Willibald Ernst
Pz.O.Schtz. Günter Schade
Pz.O.Schtz. Eberhard Schulte
Pz.O.Schtz. Willi Koppmann
Pz.O.Schtz. Ewald Zajons
Pz.O.Schtz. Horst Grell Schultz

Pz.Schtz.Helmut Pott
Pz.Schtz. Erhard Reeck
Pz.Schtz. Hans-D. Sauer
Pz.Schtz. Helmut Becker
Pz.Schtz. Herbert Jargow
Pz.Schtz. Erich Scheller
Pz.Schtz. Peter Kruth
Pz.Schtz. Richard Fedder
Pz.O.Schtz. Josef Steininger
Rttf. Paul Bockey

Fuel & Ammo Column:
Oscha. Georg Conrad
Pz.Schtz. Harald Ramm
Strm. Hans Schlegel
Strm. Koch

Maintenance Echelon:
Strm. Adolf Frank
Strm. Helmut Heinke
Rttf. Erich Schöller
Rttf. Graber
Strm. Zeger
Strm. Erich Dittl
Strm. Gustav Peter
Strm. Laverwald

Workshop Platoon:
Uscha. Werner Freytag
Strm. Oskar Ganz
Strm. Josef Schmitz
Oscha. Sepp Hafner
Werkm. Walter Häring
Strm. Willi Neisige
Strm. Werner Lampe
Strm. Wagner
Rttf. Erwin Reisch
Rttf. Erich Kleinschmidt
Rttf. Heinrich Roth
Rttf. Heinz Fiebig
Rttf. Rolf Kirstein
Uscha. Pitt Roland
Uscha. Zimmermann

Back on the Eastern Front

The entraining of the over-strength Tiger company with its numerous wheeled vehicles and the twenty-seven tanks proceeded smoothly and without incident. On 30 October 1943 the order reached the Leibstandarte that it was not to detrain in St. Pölten, instead the trains would take it straight into the Ukraine. The division consequently found itself travelling toward its area of operations in a completely unsuitable order which did not fit its tactical organization. This was to prove a great disadvantage to the units.

On 11 November 1943 the four trains carrying the Tiger company arrived in Berdichev. Concerning the rail transport, SS-Sturmmann Schamp noted: "27/10/1943: Departure, Voghera, Cremona, Verona, Mantua, Padua—28/10: Treviso, Pinzano, Genona, Carnia—29/10: Crossed border at 1420 hours, Arnoldstein—30/10: Semmering, St. Veit, Neumarkt, Leoben, Vienna—31/10: Mährisch Ostrau, Oderberg—01/11: Lvov—02/11: Ternopol—03/11: Kasatin—04/11: Fastov—05/11: 0900 hours Krivoy Rog. Night in tank."

THE BATTLES FOR BRUSILOV, 1–25 NOVEMBER 1943

In the months prior to mid-October 1943 the Soviet 2nd Ukrainian Front under General Konev had succeeded in forcing three bridgeheads across the Dniepr east of Kremenchug. The subsequent advance by the enemy was aimed at the industrial region of Krivoy Rog and on 25 October 1943 the Soviets occupied Dniepropetrovsk. Army Group South launched a successful counterattack against Konev's advance with the First Panzer Army. At the same time, in the south the 4th Ukrainian Front continued to advance into the area of Army Group A, captured Melitopol and threatened the Isthmus of Perekop. To make this chaos perfect, on 3 November 1943 the 1st Ukrainian Front under Army General Vatutin launched a major offensive on both sides of Kiev. Vatutin threw thirty infantry divisions, twenty-four tank brigades and ten motorized infantry brigades at Kiev, which fell into his hands on 6 November. Fastov, situated sixty kilometers southwest of Kiev, and whose railway station was important to the detraining of the Leibstandarte, fell the following day. Radomyshl on the

Teterev was lost on 11 November and by the 13th Vatutin's tanks were in Zhitomir. The battered northern wing of Army Group South found itself in an extremely serious situation. It was in danger of being cut off from the rest of the army group and destroyed. Fast action was the dictate of the moment. As a result the Leibstandarte was once again employed in the role of mobile fire-brigade and was sent to wherever the front was ablaze.

Together with the 1st SS Panzer Division Leibstandarte SS Adolf Hitler, the army's 1st Panzer Division, which was assembled at Kirovograd in the center of Army Group South, was also assigned the task of restoring the situation on the northern wing of the army group. The Leibstandarte faced a dangerous situation as soon as it arrived at the detraining stations. Contrary to all tactical logic, the individual parts of the Leibstandarte had to be sent into battle unprepared, in the order in which they arrived. As soon as they detrained the units of the division found themselves engaged in heavy fighting with an enemy advancing west on a broad front.

SS-Hauptsturmführer Kling had eighteen Tigers under his command on 14 November 1943, nine of which were undergoing minor repairs. The company was north of Zydowce, above the railway line leading to Fastov. Concerning the Tigers' route into the assembly area, SS-Sturmmann Schamp wrote: "06/11: Departure 0600 hours—07/11: Maintenance—08/11: Maintenance—09/11 Towing—10/11: Loading—11/11: Snamenka."

On 15 November 1943 the Tiger company was placed under the command of the 2nd SS Panzer-Grenadier Regiment, which was commanded by Obersturmbannführer Hugo Kraas. The 1st Panzer Division and the Leibstandarte were to attack north, the former on the left side of the road from Zhitomir to Kiev, the latter on the right. The right flank of the advance was to be guarded by the 25th Panzer Division and elements of the 2nd SS Panzer Division Das Reich. In the focal point of the attack were the 1st SS Panzer Division Leibstandarte SS Adolf Hitler and the Army's 1st Panzer Division.

The Ist Platoon of the 13th Company under Obersturmführer Michalski took shelter in the stables of a collective farm and in the evening received its movement orders. Michalski, who lacked any experience in combat with the Tiger, having joined the company shortly before it entrained for the Eastern Front, had each tank detail one member of its crew to walk in front of the tank to watch for concealed mines. This seriously hampered the platoon's progress and it was several hours before it came upon units of the 1st SS Panzer-Grenadier Regiment in a village. The panzers subsequently deployed for an attack together with the panzer-grenadiers. One of the Tigers drove into a tank trap, a cleverly-concealed

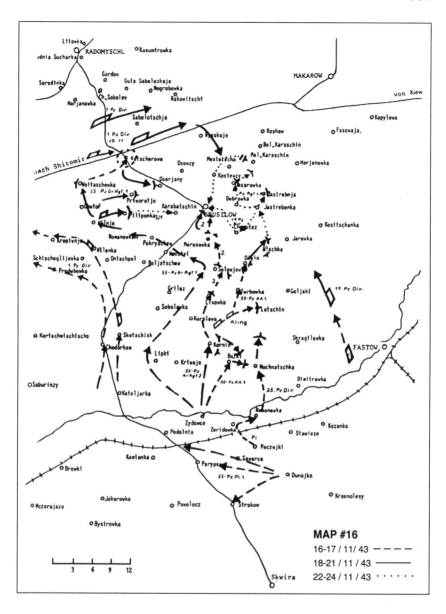

MAP #16

16-17 / 11/ 43 — — — —
18-21 / 11/ 43 ————
22-24 / 11/ 43 · · · · · ·

pit. On Michalski's order, SS-Unterscharführer Kleber coupled the trapped Tiger to his tank and was able to pull it free. When the operation was completed, both Tigers sat on the road coupled to each other by steel cables.

The enemy chose that very moment to attack with powerful forces; the rest of the platoon's Tigers were forced to withdraw several-hundred meters as they lacked covering infantry. When, in the midst of this confused situation, it was found that both tanks had been abandoned by their crews, Michalski gave the order to open fire on the two Tigers in order to prevent them from falling into the hands of the Soviet troops which were closing in. Both tanks were fired on by the platoon's remaining Tigers and went up in flames. Soon afterward the 1st SS Panzer-Grenadier Regiment attacked the enemy in the flank and drove him back. The Tigers rolled forward past the two burnt-out panzers. SS-Obersturmführer Michalski subsequently received a highly-explosive reception from SS-Hauptsturm-führer Kling. The company commander reproached him for the loss of the two Tigers and subsequently had him transferred to the 8th Company.

On 15 November 1943 the Tigers moved into position behind the 2nd SS Panzer-Grenadier Regiment between Kornin and Lisovka. The Tiger in which SS-Sturmmann Schamp was serving as gunner became involved in a night engagement at 2300 hours, but was able to hold its own. The leading attack units of the Leibstandarte were meanwhile gaining ground, as was made clear by a Soviet radio message intercepted at 0840 hours: "Armored spearhead advancing. I am trying to cut it off. Need ammunition, fuel. If this fails I am finished." By evening the attack spearheads reached positions near Turbovka (1st SS Armored Reconnaissance Battalion), Wodotij (1st SS Panzer Regiment) and Brusilov (2nd SS Panzer-Grenadier Regiment). On that day SS-Panzeroberschützen Hans Roos and Eberhard Schulte were seriously wounded by bomb fragments near Solovyevka. The Tigers were committed en masse for the first time on 16 November 1943.

The 11th Company of the 1st SS Panzer-Grenadier Regiment under SS-Obersturmführer Schmid had been at Wodotij since the previous day. SS-Rottenführer Börner described the fighting: "During the hours of darkness our 11th Company drove in its vehicles into the assigned security area under the command of Obersturmführer Rudi Schmid. The Ist Platoon was instructed to stand guard in front of a small village to the right. Digging-in began and the vehicles were sent on with the other two platoons. So far there had been no contact with the enemy. It was after midnight when suddenly small arms fire was heard in the rear of the Ist Platoon and tracer flew over the platoon from behind. The small arms fire intensified and the sound of combat became louder. At dusk we realized what had happened and the order came for Ist Platoon to prepare to attack.

The IInd and IIIrd Platoons, with our company commander, SS-Obersturmführer Schmid, had driven into a Soviet position in the darkness. The vehicles were parked close together, one behind the other. Surprised in their sleep, the grenadiers took cover in the ditches, some without their weapons. When daybreak came the dug-in Red Army soldiers, approximately a company, were about 100 meters from our vehicles and the grenadiers lying in the ditches. The Soviets appeared to be armed with machine-guns and anti-tank rifles. The enemy successfully countered every movement by our grenadiers and the vehicles were set on fire. Our company commander Obersturmführer Schmid was the first to fall, shot through the head.

The attack by our Ist Platoon to rescue the defenseless grenadiers was unsuccessful and bogged down under enemy fire. The saving angel in this situation was SS-Unterscharführer Rudi Renger, who was also in the ditch. Renger tried to leave the long ditch by crawling backwards. He escaped the enemy small-arms fire. Looking for help, Renger came upon a Tiger unit in a village in the rear. The panzers already had their orders, but after describing the situation to the commander of the Tiger unit Renger was able to convince him to intervene to relieve the 11th Company. The Russian infantry had no chance whatever against the Tigers; nevertheless, not one of them gave up and simply let themselves be buried in their foxholes by the tank tracks."

Renger had run into SS-Untersturmführer Kalinowsky in a village about two kilometers from the scene of the action. The latter had come from the workshop with two Tigers and was on his way to the company. After Renger had described the situation, he immediately set out in the direction of Wodotij and freed the 11th Company from its dangerous situation. Rudi Renger was later awarded the Honor Roll Clasp for his selfless and courageous action.

The Soviet 894th Rifle Regiment (211th Rifle Division) carried out an attack on Wodotij from Brusilov and cut the division's advance road. SS-Oberscharführer Jürgen Brandt was sent with two Tigers to restore the situation. Acting on his own initiative, "Captain" Brandt attacked the Soviet battalion in the flank. The enemy force was completely destroyed by the Tigers. Brandt's daring decision prevented a German company that had lost its leader from being cut off and wiped out. Farther south, in Lisovka, several Tigers under the command of SS-Hauptsturmführer Kling engaged enemy tanks.

The following is taken from the recommendation for the German Cross in Gold for Kling: "On 16 November 1943 a reinforced Russian battalion cut the advance road by occupying the village of Lisovka. SS-Hauptsturmführer Kling was placed in command of the battle group tasked with reopening the road, then advanced on the enemy with five Tigers and a weak infantry escort. His circumspect command and ruthless aggressiveness resulted in the recapture of the village; eight heavy anti-tank guns and the bulk of a Russian battalion were destroyed in the subsequent pursuit.

The success of this operation was due to the unbending will and personal bravery of SS-Hauptsturmführer Kling, who, through this success, secured the supply of the elements of the division advancing along the north road."

SS-Sturmmann Schamp carried out two attacks that day, at 1145 and 1600 hours. His Tiger was hit in the reduction gear and the turret. "Night engagement at Fastov, one 76.2 mm anti-tank gun destroyed," noted Bobby Warmbrunn in his diary, describing his first success as a Tiger gunner.

On 17 November 1943 the Tigers, together with the armored troop carriers and Grillen (crickets) of the 14th (Heavy Armored) Company, 2nd SS Panzer-Grenadier Regiment under Obersturmführer Otto Dinse, attacked the village of Lutschin in order to eliminate a threat to the flank. The ten Tigers and the armored troop carriers rolled at maximum speed toward Lutschin. The Soviets had moved a reinforced regiment with tanks and numerous anti-tank guns into position. The Tigers opened fire with their 88 mm guns from long range. Nearly every shot was on target, striking an anti-tank gun, anti-tank rifle or artillery piece. The enemy fought desperately; the anti-tank guns fired until they were destroyed or overrun. SS-Unterscharführer Karl Bartl's Tiger was knocked out. The tank commander was killed, gunner Herbert Jargow was seriously injured, and radio operator SS-Panzerschütze Hubert Heil escaped unhurt.

"0730 hours. Dug-in tanks, anti-tank guns. Hit from in front," read SS-Sturmmann Schamp's notes on this attack. The Tigers knocked out five T 34s and a number of anti-tank guns. After a battle lasting one and a half hours Lutschin was in German hands. The assault on Lutschin was typical of the type of attack practiced successfully by Peiper's armored troop carrier battalion. "The armored troop carrier battalion attacked the Russian villages like a cavalry unit: from several sides while moving at full speed and firing from all barrels," as Jochen Peiper later described it. The panzer crews and their comrades of the armored troop carrier battalion stopped to rest in Lutschin. However, it wasn't long before the enemy moved to retake the village; during the night of 18 November the Soviets attacked Lutschin from Fedorovka. Kampfgruppe Kling was able to repulse the reconnaissance in force, which was made in battalion strength.

The Soviets attacked again during the day, from Goljaki this time, with a stronger force. The fighting was heavy and the enemy was able to force Kling's group back toward the western end of Lutschin. There, however, the Tigers made a successful stand, knocking out several enemy tanks. At 1200 hours an enemy regiment broke into the village. The IInd Battalion of the 2nd SS Panzer- Grenadier Regiment (SS-Sturmbannführer Sandig) was subsequently readied as a reserve farther to the west in Lisovka. Strong enemy forces were then attempting to outflank Lutschin to the north and threaten the division's flank. The continuous enemy attacks were supported by heavy artillery firing from open positions southwest of Goljaki. The enemy also continued to advance southeast of Diwin with his superior forces. Rolf Schamp's Tiger saw action separated from the rest of the company: "0900 hours, attack. Stalin Organs, artillery. Single Tiger." SS-Sturmmann Warmbrunn knocked out two T 34s and two anti-tank guns. The Tigers in Lutschin were able to stand up to every attack, however, repeatedly striking the enemy in the flank and smashing his attacks. In the two days the Tiger company destroyed thirteen T 34s, twenty-five heavy anti-tank guns, one 122 mm artillery piece and large numbers of anti-tank rifles, machine-guns, trucks and artillery tractors.

Obersturmbannführer Albert Frey and his 1st SS Panzer-Grenadier Regiment succeeded in reaching the Zhitomir-Kiev road at Kocherovo the same day, barring it to the enemy. The 1st Panzer Division was assigned the task of taking Zhitomir on 19 November 1943; immediately afterward it was to attack the enemy forces holding northwest of Kocherovo and drive them back. As a result of the XXXXVIIIth Panzer Corps' attack, the situation at Zhitomir had become critical for the Soviets. The enemy hastily attempted to reach a defensive front on the general line south of Fastov-Wel. Goljaki-Brusilov-Priworotje-Wilija River line- Tererev River line-Studenzia. However the Leibstandarte was already in Kocherovo. During the night of 19 November 1943, the 9th Panzer Division, in cooperation with the 1st Panzer Division, succeeded in taking Zhitomir; the 1st Panzer Division then immediately turned north in order to take the pressure off the Leibstandarte at Kocherovo.

The Tigers were relieved in Lutschin on the morning of 19 November 1943 by elements of the 25th Panzer Division. The Tiger company drove to Morosovka and assembled south of the village, ready to attack. The objective on 20 November 1943 was to attack and take Brusilov. SS-Sturtnmann Schamp accompanied an advance by SS-Untersturmführer Wittmann: "1000 hours, attack. Ustuf. Wittmann. Two anti-tank guns, three major hits." Warmbrunn knocked out a T 34 and an anti-tank gun. There were also several Tigers with the reinforced Reconnaissance Battalion under SS-Sturmbannführer Knittel. The next day it was to drive out of the Morosovka area through Krakowschtschina and Chomutez, take both towns and by doing so cover the right flank of the Leibstandarte.

On 20 November 1943 the reinforced 2nd SS Panzer-Grenadier Regiment (without the IIIrd Armored Battalion) launched an attack on both sides of the Wodotij—Brusilov road. At 0315 enemy tanks attacked the Ist Battalion of the 2nd SS Panzer-Grenadier Regiment from the northeast and east and the Ist SS Reconnaissance Battalion in Morosovka. The Tigers immediately fell upon the enemy and destroyed twenty-one T 34s and several anti-tank guns. One Tiger was knocked out by the enemy. By 0415 hours the IInd Battalion, 2nd SS Panzer-Grenadier Regiment under SS-Sturmbannführer Sandig was able to fight its way through two enemy positions to within 1.5 kilometers of Brusilov.

There in the forest was an anti-tank ditch, both ends of which ended in an impassable swamp. At daybreak the attack spearheads were immobilized under artillery and anti-tank fire. Sandig's battalion attacked again at 0430 hours; his men outflanked the anti-tank ditch to the east, but one hour later they were halted again by the swamp and enemy fire. West of Brusilov SS-Sturmbannführer Kuhlmann and his Panther battalion were in Piliponka. At 0545 hours the division called a halt to the attack.

The Tiger company had driven three kilometers into the enemy positions. SS-Oberscharführer Jürgen Brandt stood guard over a Tiger disabled with track damage. The crews of both tanks worked feverishly to complete the repair. Standing in the turret of his Tiger, Brandt sighted a Soviet battalion column. Immediately sensing danger, he summoned his crew and drove toward the Soviet motorized unit. Brandt's Tiger fired shell after shell, which struck the trucks and other vehicles. The HE and armor-piercing shells pounded the entire width of the enemy battalion, which was ultimately wiped out. Although his Tiger had sustained reduction gear damage, Brandt returned unhindered to the German lines, accompanied by the support troops that had joined him in the meantime. SS-Sturmmann Warmbrunn destroyed one T 34 and two anti-tank guns.

That day the commanding officer of the Leibstandarte's panzer regiment, Obersturmbannführer Schönberger, was killed by artillery fire at Solovyevka. SS-Sturmbannführer Jochen Peiper, commanding officer of the armored troop carrier battalion, assumed command of the panzer regiment. Peiper was well known throughout the division as a cool daredevil and a dazzling tactician. He was to emphatically demonstrate his skill in his new position as regimental commander as well.

21 November 1943 witnessed further attacks on Brusilov; the IInd Battalion, 2nd SS Panzer-Grenadier Regiment succeeded in capturing the triangular wood southwest of Brusilov in the face of stubborn resistance. Farther west the 1st SS Panzer-Grenadier Regiment took Priworotje and stood in front of Oserjany. Panzerschützen Erich Scheller and Peter Kruth of the 13th Company were wounded. The day before SS-Untersturmführer Wittmann's tank was disabled by mechanical trouble.

Gunner Bobby Warmbrunn recalled that day: "Wittmann had a fever, but he nevertheless planned to carry out the attack, for he wanted to provide the expected example and inspire everyone with his presence. Our many tank battles had turned us into a well-oiled team. I moved into the gunner's position and he took command. Wittmann informed me of his condition and instructed me to keep it to myself. In spite of his condition he had to try to observe and direct the unit. Working on my own, with no target information from the commander, I knocked out thirteen T 34s and seven anti-tank guns. Wittmann clapped me on the shoulder. For me that was the highest praise, I was very proud."

The 1st Panzer Division was supposed to attack Brusilov on 22 November 1943, and the 19th Panzer Division, which was on the eastern flank, was to advance through Ulschka to Chotumez. The Leibstandarte had orders to set out via Diwin and Ulschka toward Yastrebenka, take the town, then turn and attack Brusilov from the east. The Tiger crews made careful preparations for this important attack. The men sat together on the evening of 21 November and discussed the plan of operations. Michael Wittmann pored over the maps until late into the night, considering the best method of attack. This was typical of him, always on duty; while the others recovered from the trials of the day, he sat quietly, lost in thought, studying the maps and busying himself with the coming day's attack. He was determined to be well-prepared and discussed the most favorable mode of attack with several Tiger commanders. Wittmann had already destroyed a considerable number of enemy tanks in the first days of action in the east; he took part in every attack, and his battle tactics made him an example to the men, beyond the realm of his platoon.

On 22 November the Tigers came to battle readiness. At 0555 hours three of them lent their support to an attack from Ulschka north toward Yastrebenka by the Ist Battalion, 2nd SS Panzer-Grenadier Regiment (SS-Sturmbannführer Hans Becker). The IInd Battalion, 2nd SS Panzer-Grenadier Regiment followed echeloned to the right rear. At 0700 the men of the 2nd SS Panzer-Grenadier Regiment were struck by a heavy attack from Soviet close-support aircraft. The attack group made good progress, in spite of strong anti-tank defenses in front and on the flank. The Tigers kept the flank open and provided the grenadiers with outstanding protection. At 1005 hours the group was halted by enemy fire 1.5 kilometers south of Yastrebenka. SS-Obersturmbannführer Kraas, with twenty-five Panzer IVs of the IInd Battalion, SS Panzer Regiment Leibstandarte under his command, resumed the attack at 1305 hours.

Leading the way were the Tigers. Soon after the attack began the crews observed the muzzle flashes from numerous anti-tank guns. South of Yastrebenka the enemy had established an anti-tank front of unprecedented strength, which now opened up on the attacking panzers with everything it had. The Tigers took countless hits. Often the shells bounced off and

howled away steeply. The Tigers were also fired on by dug-in tanks camouflaged as haystacks. To have stopped then would have inevitably led to
destruction. Before a crisis arose the Tigers smashed the threat to the flank
of the following elements and charged into the anti-tank guns at the southern end of the village, crushing them. The Tigers were in the eye of the
storm and themselves took numerous hits. SS-Untersturmführer Kalinowsky's tank was hit several times by anti-tank gun fire, as a result of which
the barrel of the Tiger's main gun was bent. The attackers broke into Yastrebenka at 1615, thanks to the massed assault by the Tigers. The grenadiers
broke all enemy resistance in house-to-house fighting; by 1800 hours the village was in German hands and had been cleared of the enemy. Two Soviet
assault guns and twenty- four anti-tank guns were destroyed.

The recommendation for the award of the German Cross in Gold to
the company commander also made reference to the Tiger company: "On
22 November 1943 the panzer group attacked the village of Yastrebenka,
which had been heavily fortified by the enemy. Driving in the first wave,
the Kling Company once again had to bear the main burden of the battle
against an unbelievably-strong anti-tank front. In spite of heavy losses and
numerous hits, Kling not only eliminated the flanking threat to the following units, but in his daring and skilled fighting style charged and overran
the anti-tank strongpoints set up at the southern end of the village and
thus made it possible for the battle group to break into the village."

SS-Sturmmann Rolf Schamp, gunner in the Tiger of SS-Unterscharführer Hans Höld, remembered the attack on Yastrebenka: "The sun was
shining, in front of us lay a small grassy slope from which we scanned the
terrain. We saw a level field, I estimate eight-hundred to one-thousand
meters across, and beyond it a long, extended wood. The enemy situation
was unknown. We were supposed to attack in the direction of the wood.
We were several tanks, it was a medium-size operation. We walked back
and climbed into the tank. Wild ordered, 'Panzers forward!' We enjoyed
serving together, he as commander, I as gunner, for we got along well.

We drove up the slope and then, as it reached the crest, the tank
tipped forward. We drove a few meters and then suddenly the wood turned
into a sea of flame. They were firing at us! The flashes looked like a fire-
works display. Then there was a crash up above in the tank, a jolt, and all
was still. It smelled of ozone and the driver shouted, 'My collarbone is broken!' I myself was bleeding from the forehead; I turned around. Höld was
sitting there, bent forward. I asked, 'Unterscharführer, what do we do
now?' There was mucous running from both of his nostrils.

Höld said nothing. Between his eyebrows there was something that
looked like a pin. Then there was another crash and my first reaction was

to turn to the driver and say, 'Reverse, go!' The tank was still able to move. We drove back down the slope and I examined Höld. He was dead."

The Tiger's cupola had been blown off. Loader Paul Sümnich was also wounded. Höld was posthumously promoted to the rank of SS-Oberscharführer. The native of the Black Forest was a proven tank commander, who had received the Iron Cross, First Class for his efforts during Zitadelle. Eighteen-year-old radio operator SS-Panzerschütze Günter Jonas was seriously wounded in the back and head by fragments when his tank was hit. At Ulschka radio operator Ernst Braun was shot through the head and killed.

An attack from Yastrebenka toward the northwest was ordered for 23 November 1943. The 1st Panzer Division was supposed to move through Lasarovka and link up with the Leibstandarte, then advance on Brusilov. The road conditions were extremely difficult and this increasingly delayed the movements of the motorized elements. Heavy rain began falling during the night. By 23 November 1943 the Tiger company had been reduced to four serviceable tanks. At 1230 hours the Tigers and the armored group—consisting of the IInd Battalion, 1st SS Panzer-Grenadier Regiment and the IIIrd (Armored) Battalion, 2nd SS Panzer-Grenadier Regiment—attacked through Dubrovka toward Lasarovka. Bobby Warmbrunn destroyed four T 34s and three anti-tank guns. Afterward the Tigers were refuelled in Mestetschko, somewhat farther north. SS-Panzerschütze Werner Schilling was wounded that day. Enemy tanks, but also growing numbers of anti-tank fronts, demanded the utmost alertness and concentration during every attack. The gunners therefore examined the terrain very closely, in order to pick out anti-tank positions, most of which were very well camouflaged. In a firefight the gunner had to be able to acquire a target quickly, for the small targets offered by enemy anti-tank guns had to be eliminated quickly to prevent being fired on from the flank later.

Loader and gunner SS-Sturmmann Walter Lau wrote of the firing technique: "Many times adjustment fire took place as follows: a call to the loader: 'Machine-gun ready to fire!' Then the target was captured with the right foot on the pedal for the machine-gun and tracing ammunition. The turret was traversed until the tracer was on target. Naturally this method was not used in attacks on tanks, but primarily when the target was a village or a target point in the terrain. The machine-gun quickly ceased firing on targets of this size and it was possible to read off the range. This applied when the enemy was engaged with high-explosive shells. If, for example, the range was determined to be 600 meters using this method, one had to set the high-explosive shells to 600, then the range was correct and the shells fell on the target with increasing effect."

The gunner traversed the turret in the direction specified by the commander by applying pressure to the foot pedal. The amount of pressure applied determined the speed of rotation. Fine aiming adjustments were made using the traversing mechanism handwheel, which the gunner operated with his left hand. Then he set the range on the telescopic sight with his left hand. The trigger for the tank's main gun was coupled with the elevation handwheel. If the electrical system was knocked out, as often happened when the tank was hit, the turret could only be traversed and the elevation of the gun changed by using the hand-wheels. The lost electrical firing system could be restored by an on-the-spot modification to make contact with the battery. This "firing by battery" was used by the crew of SS-Unterscharführer Kleber's Tiger in the winter of 1943–44, whereby Kleber made contact with the battery using two large wrenches. This was in no way standard practice, however. Walter Lau wrote: "Using the battery to shoot was not an official method, it had—and I don't know how—developed out of an emergency situation. The approved method of battery firing (emergency firing) used a small installation to the gunner's left, in which several flashlight batteries had to be inserted."

The tank crews spent most of 24 and 25 November 1943 carrying out maintenance on the Tigers. They used this brief respite from combat to rest, clean themselves up and collect rations. On 24 November the armored group advanced on K. Starizkaja. The following day was quiet, apart from harassing artillery fire. The Leibstandarte set off at 0630 hours on 26 November; advancing northwest, by 1300 it reached the area south of Negrebovka. The Leibstandarte was supposed to stop and destroy the enemy forces advancing south near Radomyshl.

The Tigers' main opponents were not the Soviet tanks, but instead the well-camouflaged anti-tank fronts. Frontal attacks against such positions, which consisted of an extended line of anti-tank guns (76.2 mm all-purpose guns), usually resulted in losses and were to be avoided whenever possible. When an anti-tank front was suspected in an area to be attacked, a single Tiger, usually commanded by an SS-Untersturmführer (platoon commander), drove ahead to scout the situation. Driving to the crest of a rise, behind which the remaining tanks were assembled out of sight, it revealed itself briefly in order to tempt the enemy anti-tank gunners into opening fire and revealing their positions. This method of "scouting," to discover if and where there was an anti-tank front lurking, was of course very dangerous, and the drivers backed up their Tigers as soon as the first muzzle flash was sighted, in order to escape the ensuing hail of fire. The crew's observations revealed the location and strength of the anti-tank front.

SS-Untersturmführer Helmut "Bubi" Wendorff's loader, SS-Sturmmann Lau, recalled one such scouting mission, when they halted to pick out the positions of the anti- tank guns: "We drove ahead in the manner described, in order to bring the Ivans out of their reserve and draw their anti-tank fire. We came under terrific fire. Later, while refuelling, we counted a total of twenty-eight hits on the Tiger. Some of them were smaller, of course, but there were also some big enough to easily put one's fist into. All of the hits were on the frontal armor. At the very moment when the Tiger was being showered with hits, we heard Bubi Wendorff say in his Berlin dialect, 'Man, this is just like being in the middle of a war!' Michael Wittmann, too, detested the well-camouflaged anti-tank guns, which seemed to be hidden everywhere. The Soviet tanks were no source of worry to him. He considered the anti-tank guns which lurked everywhere to be a much greater threat. Therefore the destruction of an anti-tank gun soon came to count more to him than knocking out a T 34.

A PK (propaganda company) account described the threat posed by the anti-tank guns: "In the fall and winter of 1943 armored warfare took on another face in the Kiev-Korosten triangle of highways. Soviet anti-tank regiments scattered the country with hundreds of cannon, anti-tank rifles of all calibers, barricades, and solid anti-tank fronts. And in villages and field positions they lurked behind every field road with their almost invisible guns and put the panzer crews to a severe test. There was a growing hatred, and not just in Michael Wittmann, of the nearly invisible enemy, who had by then fully mastered the handiwork of the man-versus-tank struggle. A tank was no longer a test of nerve, but the devil take the anti-tank guns!"

Added to the many deprivations of that time was a salt shortage that lasted weeks. The kitchens had to prepare the food without that important ingredient. In a Ukrainian village several of the young tankers met an old woman who promised to tell their fortunes. At first purely for fun, then with a slowly-awakening interest, they listened to the old woman's words. Then the men asked the Ukrainian which of them would return home from the war. She predicted a happy homecoming for some, not for others. When asked who would win the war, whether Hitler or Stalin would be victorious, she decided for Hitler.

BATTLES FOR RADOMYSHL, 26 NOVEMBER–16 DECEMBER 1943

On 27 November 1943 the units of the Leibstandarte pushed farther to the west in sustained, difficult fighting. The enemy withdrew to the north and northeast, but the exhausted grenadiers were unable to mount a quick and effective pursuit over the muddy roads.

On 28 November the Tiger Company and the IIIrd (Armored) Battalion of the 2nd SS Panzer-Grenadier Regiment launched an attack toward Radomyshl from north of Sabelotsche. The panzer regiment wrote of the Tiger Company: "In extremely difficult forest terrain, at times without infantry protection, Kling was the first to reach the important highway and took possession of Hill 153.4. In a tireless pursuit, he drove through the fleeing columns—ignoring the enemy infantry lying to the right and left of the road—and turned the planned Soviet retreat into an incoherent flight. Finally, with only his own tank still serviceable, he felt his way forward toward Garboroff—personally clearing a path through the many minefields in the darkness. He knocked out many anti-tank guns and, although in the end he was reduced to fighting with just his machine-gun, played a decisive part in the capture of the village."

SS-Sturmmann Bobby Warmbrunn, who often served as Kling's gunner, destroyed a T 34 and an anti-tank gun that day. The Tigers remained at Gardow, southwest of Radomyshl, as a mobile reserve from 29 November to 1 December, 1943. The men of the workshop platoon worked overtime to restore the many disabled panzers to service. SS-Rottenführer Willibald Ernst and SS-Panzerschütze Walter Kirchner were killed at Jusefowka. SS-Unterscharführer Karl Mollenhauer, the commander of the fuel transport column, and SS-Unterscharführer Johann Reiter, munitions NCO, were wounded.

SS-Sturmmann Schamp recalled of the men of the supply units: "They worked very hard, a lot of sweat flowed, but our comrades of the train also had courage. The boys beamed like welding torches when they found us in spite of snow, mud and the most abominable conditions. But how dangerous was their work, getting through to us laden with fuel and ammunition, toiling endlessly and almost defenseless against an enemy who might appear suddenly. In November-December 1943 they often drove an Italian three-axle vehicle (probably a Fiat) with large tires. They carried a mixed load of ammunition, fuel and rations, because they often had to supply individual tanks."

On 29 November Jochen Peiper took Gardow. Additional enemy forces were smashed in the immediate vicinity. There was little activity on 30 November and the first elements of the Leibstandarte were relieved by the 2nd Parachute Division. There were casualties, however; SS-Panzerschütze Richard Redder was killed that day and SS-Panzerschütze Herbert Wastler was listed as missing.

Up to and including 30 November 1943, the Leibstandarte had sustained casualties of 363 killed, 1,289 wounded and 32 missing. The combat strengths of the panzer-grenadier regiments had fallen shockingly on account of the heavy casualties. The Ist Battalion, 2nd Regiment, for example, had only 103 men left (3 officers, 10 NCOs and 90 men). The other battalions were little better off; the combat strength of the 1st SS Panzer-Grenadier Regiment was down to only 795 men (27 officers, 87 NCOs and 681 men) and that of the 2nd Regiment to 736 men (21 officers, 86 NCOs and 628 men).

The thrust by the XXXXVIIIth Panzer Corps into the flank of the 1st Ukrainian Front, which had advanced as far as Zhitomir, denied the enemy access to the, by Soviet standards, good road system south of the Pripet Marshes. The enemy had not been destroyed, however. He assembled the operational elements of his 60th Army northeast of Zhitomir and threatened to break through north of the city. Faced with this threat, the army group ordered the XXXXVIIIth Panzer Corps to strike the enemy forces gathering between Teterev and the Zhitomir-Korosten road, a move that took the Soviets by surprise. At the same time it enabled the XIIIth Army Corps to veer toward the Teterev and link up with the LIXth Army Corps to the north. The situation between Zhitomir and Korosten, the Leibstandarte's new area of operations, was largely uncertain.

Relief of the Leibstandarte and its transfer into the area north of Zhitomir began on 2 December 1943. The Tiger Company was at Siljanschtschina. On 4 December Kling had four serviceable Tigers; twelve were undergoing short-term repairs and another nine long-term repairs. The company still had a total of twenty-five Tigers, of which barely a fifth were serviceable, however. Four to six Tigers was often the company's combat strength. Tigers coming from the workshop were often sent straight into action, frittered away before they could rejoin the company. This dispersed use of the Tigers caused SS-Hauptsturmführer Kling plenty of headaches.

Rolf Schamp recalled this period in the winter of 1943: "In November 1943 the Tiger Company was quite split up in the Zhitomir area. Often one didn't know where the company was. Kling came by occasionally and was happy to be able to greet a Tiger crew from his company. I only saw Wittmann once and Kling perhaps two or three times in that period, November and December. As we and our Tiger were often deployed alone in other sectors, contact with the company by way of dispatch rider and munitions and supply trucks was tenuous at best."

The potent Tigers were often the backbone of the panzer-grenadiers and their commanders welcomed their help at any time. The company's impressive total of enemy tanks destroyed had quickly become known throughout the division. Wittmann and his crew had once destroyed thirteen T 34s and seven heavy anti-tank guns in a single day. Such feats had long since ceased to be something extraordinary. Wittmann was already the leading figure in the company and everyone trusted him. Simply called Michel by his close friends, Wittmann's greatest claim to fame was his steadily growing total of enemy tanks knocked out. The seemingly rather introverted twenty-nine-year-old from the Upper Pfalz was an absolute expert. A fellow soldier recalled: "He was a brooder, a man who made life difficult. He prepared for every action with extreme thoroughness. But when the die were cast, he acted quickly and as if controlled by an internal clock."

Wittmann always had a scissors telescope installed in his Tiger so that he could scan the battlefield without exposing his upper body. The advantages of the "scissors" were known to him from his time with the Assault Gun Battalion, where each assault gun had one of these useful devices.

By 5 December 1943 the Tiger Company had destroyed a total of 205 tanks and 130 anti-tank guns in the fighting at Kharkov, Operation Zitadelle and the winter battles in the east. These numbers do not include the countless armored vehicles, artillery pieces, armored cars, trucks and other weapons destroyed by the Tiger crews.

The Tiger crews spent the days until 5 December 1943 conducting maintenance. Whatever time was left was used by the men to take care of personal matters or simply to rest from their exertions. The remaining elements of the division also worked to raise their battle readiness. The division formed a march group from train units, which marched through Zhitomir to the southeast to deceive the enemy. The days were filled with extensive preparations for the attack. The 1st and 7th Panzer Divisions and the 1st SS Panzer Division Leibstandarte SS Adolf Hitler assembled north of Chernyakhov. The striking power and success of the Tiger Company had not escaped the attention of the panzer regiment's new commander, SS-Sturmbannführer Jochen Peiper.

On 5 December 1943 he recommended SS-Hauptsturmführer Kling for the German Cross in Gold. "Under his outstanding leadership, and maintained at a constant state of readiness, the Tiger Company has achieved amazing success thanks to his extraordinary energy," Peiper wrote in his submission. Iron Crosses were awarded to a number of NCOs and men of the company that day. SS-Sturmmann Bobby Warmbrunn was decorated with the Iron Cross, First Class. In addition to his other successes, by this time he had destroyed forty-seven enemy tanks as a gunner. Tank commanders SS-Unterscharführer Kurt Sowa and Heinz Werner, as well as SS-Hauptscharführer Habermann, the Senior NCO, were awarded the Iron Cross, Second Class. SS-Panzerschütze Herbert Werner and SS-Sturmmänner Siegfried Hummel and Heinrich Knöß also received the Iron Cross, Second Class. The latter was thirty-five years old and a former government

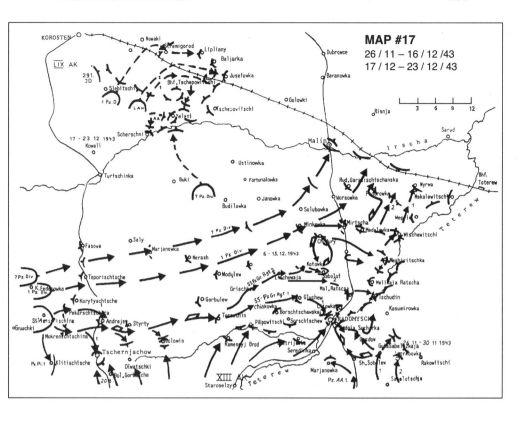

employee at the Beckum Revenue Office who had volunteered for service in the Waffen-SS.

SS-Sturmmann Walter Lau described how the Tiger crews spent the ice-cold nights: "Very often we spent the night on guard duty, about thirty to fifty meters behind the combat outposts of the grenadiers. One man stood watch in the turret and the other four slept as best they could at their places inside the tank, as long as the situation permitted. The cold was terrible, for after two or three hours the fighting compartment became iced up and resembled a stalactite cavern. One's clothing stuck to the steel walls of the tank. When conditions permitted, we ran the engine every hour to get some warmth, but often the enemy situation made this impossible.

Naturally there was plenty of time for telling stories during these quiet hours and especially during double sentry duty. After a while one knew just about everything about one's closest comrades." This intimate knowledge of one another and the feeling of mutual absolute trust was one of the foundations of the unshakable comradeship within the company, a comradeship that was proven again and again in difficult situations and which bound everyone in an invisible but strong bond of loyalty.

The Leibstandarte's armored group—consisting of the Panzer Regiment, the Armored Troop Carrier Battalion, the 2nd Company of the Ist SS Pioneer Battalion and the 5th Flak Battery—was given the following mission for 5 December 1943: depart Chernyakhov, skirt the enemy-occupied town to the west in a night march, and reach the high ground on both sides of Styrty on a broad front via Andreyev. Styrty was the first objective, then Radomyshl. The division's overall mission was to depart the area northwest of Chernyakhov, across the line Mokrenschtschina-Pekarschtschina, and drive into the flank of the enemy forces in front of the XIIIth Army Corps and destroy them. A subsequent advance together with the divisions of the XXXXVIIIth Panzer Corps was supposed to enable the XIIIth Army Corps to veer towards the Teterev and establish contact with the advancing LIXth Army Corps.

The Tigers prepared for battle on 5 December. They moved off with the armored group at 1500 hours. At 2000 the leading elements were in Siljanschtschina. Reconnaissance by the Armored Troop Carrier Battalion revealed that the enemy had prepared Pekarschtschina for all-round defense; heavily-fortified positions had been built to the west. Difficult terrain made it impossible to go around the village, moreover the important bridge, capable of supporting fifty tonnes, had to be taken. Peiper decided on a night assault by the Armored Troop Carrier Battalion.

This daring operation succeeded despite the strong enemy positions; the half-tracks broke through and the panzer-grenadiers took possession of the village and the vital bridge. The armored troop carriers drove toward the enemy at maximum speed, all weapons blazing, ignoring return fire from anti-tank guns, anti-tank rifles and machine-guns. The commander of the battalion, SS-Hauptsturmführer Guhl, was badly wounded when a shell struck the machine-gun's armor shield. He was hit in the face and lost an eye. Peiper held the Tigers in reserve and subsequently led a reconnaissance in force against Andreyev. Peiper's force made ready as dawn was breaking on 6 December 1943. The Tigers took on ammunition and waited for the order to attack. Then the radio operators heard the following transmission: "Rose Leader (Peiper) to Granite Leader (Kling), come in please." Kling's radio operator replied, "Granite Leader reads you, go ahead!"— "Granite, attack with Veilchen (IInd Battalion, 1st Panzer-Grenadier Regiment). Utmost despatch requested!"—"Granite to everyone: start engines, wedge formation, move out!"

The Tigers set themselves in motion at once. They hadn't gone far when they came upon an anti-tank front. The Tigers halted, fired, then moved off again immediately so as not to offer the gunners behind the enemy anti-tank guns a stationary target. Several guns were destroyed by

Wittmann and the anti-tank front was broken. By 0600 hours Peiper was in Andreyev, where he blocked the Zhitomir-Korosten highway. Untersturm-führer Kalinowsky's Tiger was fired on and hit from the flank; the shell struck the side armor. The tank caught fire but the crew—the driver was SS-Sturmmann Bingert—were able to extinguish it. Peiper resumed the advance. East of Andreyev his battle group destroyed several batteries of Soviet artillery; after smashing several anti-tank strongpoints, at approximately 1000 hours Peiper's forces captured the high ground on both sides of Styrty.

The first day's objective had been reached. But Peiper did not stop there; instead he drove further east and his panzers smashed several anti-tank fronts and artillery positions. Wittmann knocked out three T 34s and destroyed an anti-tank front near Tortschin. The command posts of four Red Army rifle divisions were overrun. Sixty-seven anti-tank guns, twenty-two artillery pieces and other materiel had been destroyed. SS-Rottenführer Paul Bockey and SS-Panzerschütze Helmut Pott were severely wounded near Katainovka on 6 December 1943. This daring thrust led by Peiper rocked the entire Soviet front in that sector.

At 1230 on 7 December the Tiger Company set out toward Chaikovka from the south in support of the IInd Battalion of the 2nd SS Panzer-Grenadier Regiment. In the end this attack failed in the face of the extremely powerful Soviet anti-tank defense. Peiper attacked after dark, outflanked Chaikovka to the north and then advanced on Chodory from the northeast. After heavy fighting from house to house, by the morning of 8 December 1943 Sabolot, north of Radomyshl, was in German hands. Tiger commander SS-Unterscharführer Erich Langner was killed in the fighting for Sabolot. His tank was hit and immobilized, and when the Ivans reached his Tiger he shot himself. Langner, from Weißenbach in Steiermark, was buried by the church in Sabolot.

Peiper's daring night attack had smashed a breach in the enemy defense and had prevented the Soviets from establishing a bridgehead over the Teterev. Sixty-two anti-tank guns, eight heavy guns, one T 34 and other war materiel belonging to the enemy had been destroyed. In recognition of this success Peiper was awarded the Knight's Cross with Oak Leaves on 27 January 1944.

Group photo of the 13th (Heavy) Company, 1st SS Panzer Regiment Leibstandarte SS Adolf Hitler.

Company commander SS-Hauptsturmführer Kling before the assembled company.

From left: SS-Hauptscharführer Hartel, Habermann and Poetschlak and SS-Oberscharführer Brandt (hidden), Mengeles and Hafner.

The technical
Sergeant Radio,
SS-Oberscharführer
Mengeles.

Senior NCO Habermann with several of his specialist NCOs.

Tiger S04, the company Headquarters Squad Leader's tank, with SS-Sturmmann Max Gaude.

Tigers in Coreggio.

One of the factory-fresh Tigers that arrived in Reggio on 10 August 1943; the tank still lacks a camouflage finish.

Training radio operators in Italy.

The ubiquitous
Senior NCO,
SS-Hauptscharführer
Habermann.

Above and below: Veteran NCOs and future officers. *Above, standing from left:* Brandt, Lötzsch, Hartel, Habermann, Poetschlak, Krohn. *Above, kneeling:* Mengeles, Lindemann, Augst, Hafner.

SS-Sturmmann Reinhard Wenzel.

SS-Panzerschütz Hubert Heil, radio operator.

Tiger S33 wearing the characteristic camouflage finish. The base color was ochre-yellow, the camouflage scheme consisted of brown, dark red and green tones.

SS-Untersturmführer
Michael Wittmann.

Knight's Cross wearer
SS-Hauptscharführer Alfred
Günther. Günther joined the
101st SS Panzer Battalion in
Italy in summer 1943.

Helmut "Bubi" Wendorff.

At the man-made lake in Reggio, where the men often went swimming in the summer of 1943; on the right SS-Untersturmführer Helmut Wendorff.

Some of the NCOs and men of the Tiger Company in Italy.

Men of the Workshop Platoon at work. *At right:* Oscar Ganz.

Correggio, October 1943. The Senior NCO, SS-Hauptscharführer Habermann, out and about on his bicycle. In the center foreground is SS-Unterscharführer Mollenhauer, while several Tigers may be seen in the background.

S51, the tank of the commander of the Vth Platoon, in the workshop. *From left:* Freytag, Reisch, unidentified, Ganz, Kleinschmidt, Roth.

SS-Rottenführer Erwin Reisch of the Workshop Platoon.

SS-Unterscharführer Brandt's Tiger S34. The tank's snorkel, which enabled it to drive while submerged, is seen here in the extended position. Note the two fairings on the rear of the tank, part of the Feifel dust filter system.

SS-Untersturmführer Walter Hahn.

SS-Hauptscharführer Fritz Hartel.

SS-Unterscharführer Eduard Stadler.

SS-Unterscharführer Karl Wagner.

SS-Sturmmann Rolf Schamp.

SS-Sturmmann
Walter Lau.

SS-Hauptsturmführer
Kling during entraining
of the Tiger Company in
Voghera in October
1943.

The trains carrying the Leibstandarte arrived in the southern sector of the Eastern Front in November 1943.

Tigers of the IVth and Vth Platoons of the 13th (Heavy) Company, 1st SS Panzer Regiment Leibstandarte in camouflaged positions in the Kiev area in November 1943.

Whitewashed Tigers seen shortly before assembling for a counterattack. These appear to be mid-production models with new "Panther type" cupolas and simplified exhausts. Note the anti-magnetic "Zimmerit" paste.

The Battles at Chepovichi and Berdichev

MICHAEL WITTMANN—MODEL FOR THE COMPANY

One Tiger had been lost in the previous battles. Michael Wittmann pushed himself further into the limelight through his constant success in the weeks of uninterrupted fighting. He led his Tiger against the enemy with unshakable calm and an almost eerie certainty. He was successful under the most difficult conditions. Fear of the dark, a not uncommon phenomenon, was foreign to him. Wittmann knew how to transmit the feeling of unconditional safety to his men. Warmbrunn wrote: "When Wittmann was present no mission could produce fear or skepticism. It simply had to succeed and it did succeed!

That sounds like a rather simplistic answer—but why did he always succeed? Even Wittmann was no magician. Not only were his attacks well thought out and prepared, but he was also able to immediately assess a changing situation and quickly take appropriate action. Mentally he was always one hundred percent involved. When he considered it necessary, he carried out a reconnaissance advance before an attack, either in the tank or alone on foot. Often it was on the basis of his own reconnaissance results that he decided how and where to most effectively employ his Tigers. His total mastery of armor tactics, combined with a high degree of natural dynamism, enabled him to achieve his great success. Wittmann was more than just a daredevil. All of his actions were planned, with him nothing was left to chance. This sureness and his methodical approach was passed on to his men. Only by remembering that can one understand Bobby Warmbrunn when he says: "It simply had to succeed and it did succeed."

SS-Sturmmann Walter Lau confirmed that, before an attack, Wittmann ". . . almost always drove forward to the crest of a hill in his tank to reconnoiter the enemy situation, and then gave his orders. When the result was an attack, his was the lead vehicle. It wasn't just his instinct—his good nose—but also his tactical skill and his experience, and his ability to accurately assess the enemy situation and effectively use the terrain and his own

199

assets; all these in harmony led to success. Of course, at the decisive moment his indescribable dauntlessness, courage and nerve also came into play. From this time at the latest, there existed within the company an unconditional trust in him and the irrefutable image of Wittmann the ideal."

Wittmann's total of kills increased at a rapid rate in those weeks. Together with his gunner, SS-Rottenführer Bobby Woll, who used a simplified firing technique, he was successful almost every day. The range setting on his telescopic sight remained set at 800 meters, even when the targets were farther away or closer. This demanded a gunner able to make the necessary adjustments on his own, aiming high or low as required. "Near Brusilov Wittmann ran into a Soviet tank unit as it was preparing for an attack and took the enemy by surprise. He was faster, more skilful and braver and he blew apart ten of the Soviets from the mass of tanks. Three more fell victim to him that same afternoon. He counted every tank, but he valued every anti-tank gun he destroyed, as it were, twice as much. He hated the concealed nests, those hiding places of death; he ferreted them out with special satisfaction and said that enemy tanks were no longer a strain on his nerves, that only the anti-tank guns, lurking in their concealed positions and so much more difficult to make out, were unpleasant.

On 6 December 1943 he overcame a strong anti-tank front. Once again his skill decided the outcome of in his favor. He blasted the enemy with furious barrages of gunfire, crashed through the position and positioned himself astride the enemy's supply road like a wolf in a herd of sheep. He placed his fierymark on the road, smashing long lines of vehicles into junk and causing mass confusion among the Soviets. Michael Wittmann was by now a veteran tank commander. His instinct, or his nose if you will, told him where something was up. It was said that he could see just as well at night as by day, and the story was told that he aimed at targets himself at night, until a pillar of fire unmistakably told the others that a tank must have been there. Wittmann was destroying enemy tanks almost every day now, usually more than one, and the list of his successes grew steadily longer."

These accounts from the pen of a war correspondent show Wittmann in action, but what about the man himself? In his rather unaffected-pleasant way, Michael Wittmann was an example to every member of the company. He never claimed his successes as personal accomplishments, nor did he place himself above others. SS-Sturmmann Rolf Schamp, a gunner in the Tiger Company, served with Wittmann for a year. He wrote of that time: "I joined the Wittmann Platoon in Weimar as a replacement in November 1942. He was then an Oberscharführer (RFA). I still remember well my first meeting with him in the hallway of the barracks building. My first impression: a very likeable man. His pleasant-sounding voice, clear, not too loud, warm-hearted, with a slight Bavarian accent, together with his almost elegant—but not in the least affected—personality, made a united and harmonious impression. His eyes were firmly fixed on the Sturmmann saluting him. He spoke a few friendly words to me and later, when I was assigned to his platoon, I had the—relatively rare—feeling of being well taken care of as a person and a soldier. Nothing happened in months of being with him in training, in the tank or in the platoon, to change this impression. On the contrary, my initial impression was confirmed in every situation and it has stayed alive with me to the present day. Even now Wittmann is to me an unclouded example as a man and as a soldier. It sounds improbable, but on reflection I can think of no 'weaknesses' to tell about Wittmann. He was careful, precise, always humane in his dealings with people—he almost never shouted. Modesty, with no inclination toward alcohol or adventures with women, characterized him. He was often rather shy and reserved with strangers but was conscious of his person.

I can never recall him undertaking anything in an ill-prepared or rash way. He always endeavored to judge fairly, but he refused to tolerate carelessness of any kind. He was tactful and considerate of others, always striving to do his best or bring out the best in others. He also had numerous good qualities which certainly contributed to his great success: caution, good eyes, a 'good nose' for situations, quick reactions, and the ability to go to sleep quickly and deeply when all the necessary things had been done. This enabled him to stay fresh and alert in most situations. As a minor aside, I recall his lovely, straight-line handwriting, with no flashy flourishes or anything else deliberate about it. I'm starting to become too sentimental, but in fact Wittmann is one of the very few men I met in the military or in civilian life who I could without hesitation call a 'model' and who is alive, with me and in me. If it were possible I would still want Wittmann as a friend, I know that this friendship would last."

On 9 December 1943 the 1st SS Panzer-Grenadier Regiment launched an attack on Radomyshl. Two kilometers northwest of the city strong enemy resistance halted the advance. The division called off the attack. On orders from corps, the Leibstandarte regrouped its forces, assembling the units southeast of Medelevka for an assault by the entire division against the enemy bridgehead from the north. First, however, Meshiritschka had to be taken. SS-Hauptsturmführer Kling had four Tigers available, ten each were undergoing long-and short-term repairs. Compared with the panzer regiment his was still a tolerable figure when one considers that theIstBattalion had only six serviceable Panthers and the IInd Battalion eight Panzer IVs. This illustrates to what level the Leibstandarte Panzer Regiment's strength had sunk in a period of uninterrupted action. Despite stubborn opposition, Meshiritschka was taken with tank support at approximately 1930 hours. The next objective was the Teterev. Wittmann was about to surprise a group of Soviet tanks in their assembly area with a force of three Tigers, when twenty Soviet tanks suddenly emerged from hiding and opened fire. Now he was the one surprised. The result was a bitter tank-versus-tank duel at extremely close quarters; the Tigers fired as fast as they could. Bobby Woll needed no target information, he took aim at any T 34 and fired. Michael Wittmann destroyed six enemy tanks. Some of the others were destroyed by the remaining Tigers, the rest took to flight.

During the attack on Meshiritschka, SS-Untersturmführer Kalinowsky's Tiger was hit several times, wounding the commander in the face and right arm. SS-Panzerschütze Ewald Zajons was also wounded. At 2200 the Tigers attacked Mal. Ratscha, west of the Teterev, but they were then recalled on account of the very strong anti-tank defense. The 68th Infantry Division successfully broke into Radomyshl.

SS-Hauptsturmführer Kling's loader recalled an action which was typical of SS-Sturmbannführer Peiper's style of fighting: "After Panzermeyer, Sturmbannführer Jochen Peiper was definitely one of the Leibstandarte's most dashing and audacious commanders. We Tiger people were proud and pleased when Peiper assumed command of the panzer regiment after the death of Obersturmbannführer Schönberger. Even as commander of the 2nd SS Panzer-Grenadier Regiment's IIIrd (Armored) Battalion, he was one of those commanders with whom one could feel safe even while on the most hazardous operations.

In December 1943 in the Radomyshl area an armored group with four or five Tigers, several assault guns and Panzer IVs and a number of armored troop carriers and Schwimmwagen was parked on a highway (Rollbahn). Highway was what we called those roads that had been widened to five to sometimes fifty meters by tracked vehicles. They resembled highways in periods of dry weather, but wet snow and rain turned them into morasses. This was the buildup, or to put it more accurately, the assembly point for an attack under Sturmbannführer Peiper. The point group consisted of two or three Tigers under the command of Untersturmführer Wendorff accompanied by a number of armored troop carriers of the reconnaissance battalion.

We advanced through a wooded area a good twenty kilometers into enemy territory and then executed a horizon crawl—as Peiper referred to it in his memoirs—behind the Russian lines. Toward evening on the second day we returned to the German lines. During this action I was the gunner in the tank commanded by Hauptsturmführer Kling. For me this

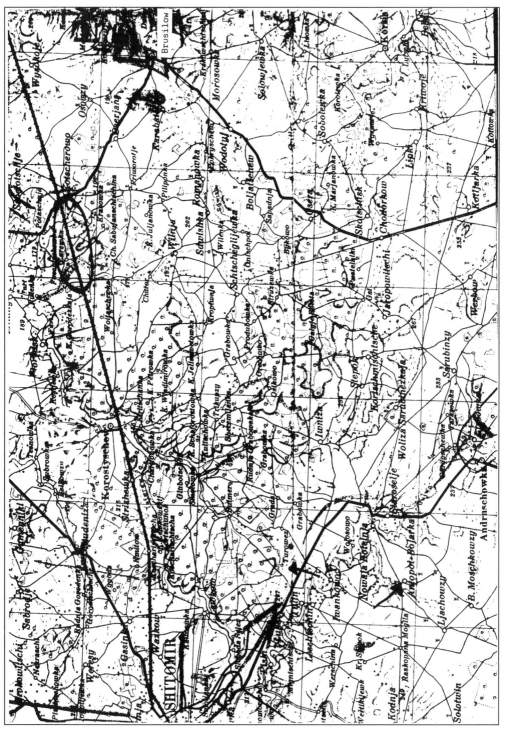

Map illustrating some of the attacks made by Ustuf. Wendorff on 27 and 28/12/1943, in which he destroyed 37 enemy tanks and several times kept open the avenue of retreat for units of the LSSAH.

was interesting and a stroke of luck. It was interesting in that Kling's tank was roughly in the middle of the battle group, which was driving in a dispersed march order, and directly in front of Peiper, who drove in a heavy all-wheel-drive car. I therefore got to see Peiper close up as he sat on the fender of his car with a submachine-gun at the ready. One could pick up many of Peiper's orders. It was also a stroke of luck for me when the forest roads and tracks proved to be heavily mined. The mines, wooden boxes resembling fish crates with yellow explosives, were extremely well hidden. At least three of the Tigers with the point group drove over mines in those two days and sustained serious damage to their running gear. They were left in the woods; an armored troop carrier and five or six panzergrenadiers stayed behind to guard them. It was truly a stroke of luck for me not to belong to those crews stranded approximately twenty kilometers behind enemy lines. We nervously awaited what would happen in the evening when darkness fell. This, too, was typical of Peiper: 'Establish a hedgehog position!' Parked in the center of a clearing was his car and Kling's Tiger, beside them the Tiger of SS-Unterscharführer Mölly, which had run over a mine, and within a one-hundred-meter circle all the elements of the battle group. It was probably one of the most nerve-wracking situations of my time as a soldier, but Kling and Peiper, who were right beside us, exuded a singular confidence, although there were skirmishes with enemy patrols all night. The Soviets were obviously in a position where they no longer knew where front and rear were. Sturmmann Wenzel, loader in one of the Tigers disabled by mines, later related that they went into a Russian cottage to look for something to eat. In the hut they discovered a Russian soldier who was probably there for the same reason. Terrified, the Russian dropped his mess kit, and the people from the Tiger, who were all but unarmed, took advantage of this to decamp.

Toward noon of the second day we had to break through the enemy lines from behind. As I recall, only one of Kling's Tigers was still serviceable. We went into position behind a house in order to engage an anti-tank gun. We were moving toward a position several paces behind the house in order to place the turret and gun in a position to fire at the anti-tank gun, when we were hit. The effect of the hit was to cause the gun to shake inside the tank. I believe the gunner was Bobby Warmbrunn. I had to open the breech. As Kling suspected, we had taken a hit on the gun tube, the effect of which was visible in the interior of the barrel. Had we fired there would have been a terrific explosion when the barrel burst, which would probably have been fatal to us. Peiper, who was standing behind us, ordered an SS-Unterscharführer of the Reconnaissance Battalion to take out the anti-tank gun. We were able to watch as the skilled troops tossed

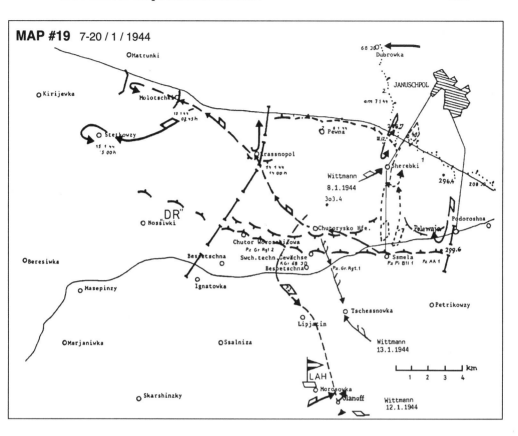

MAP #19 7-20 / 1 / 1944

hand grenades and fell upon the crew of the anti-tank gun. We reached our lines late in the afternoon; exhausted, we took shelter in a Russian cottage. What happened next was typical of Bubi Wendorff: he went from crew to crew, seeking volunteers to help the crews stranded on account of mine damage. We drove to the two stranded Tigers in a 3-tonne prime mover loaded with replacement track links, road wheels and some ammunition and food. With the help of some panzer-grenadiers of the Reconnaissance Battalion, who had meanwhile taken up forward positions, we were able to repair both tanks. Yes, there were many reasons why such officers as Michael Wittmann, who played no part in this action, and Bubi Wendorff enjoyed such esteem and respect in the 13th (Heavy) Company of the 1st SS Panzer Regiment."

On 10 December 1943, the armored group tried to attack farther to the south, but at 0800 hours the Tigers came under heavy fire from anti-tank guns in front of Krasnoborki. The men spent the remainder of the day at rest. The attack on Krasnoborki was scheduled for the following day. Michael Wittmann and several commanders planned the attack carefully and discussed the selected tactics at length. He wanted to leave nothing to chance. The attack had to be made across a broad, open plain, therefore the attack force had to move off as soon as the artillery barrage ended. The heavy weapons were given precise target information; the infantry commanders discussed the joint action with the tanks and assault guns. The artillery drew up its plan of fire.

The Leibstandarte began assembling for the attack in the gullies northwest of Meshiritschka at 0400 hours on 11 December. The Ist and IInd Battalions of the 2nd SS Panzer-Grenadier Regiment formed the front line with the Assault Gun Battalion and the armored group with the Tigers. Following the artillery barrage, the attack west toward the heavily-fortified town of Krasnoborki began at 1200 hours. Supported by the assault guns, the spearhead broke through the east end of Krasnoborki and became involved in house to house fighting, after which it drove southeast toward Velikaya Ratscha. The Tigers drove over Hill 170 toward Ratscha, destroying several anti-tank guns. SS-Untersturmführer Kalinowsky's Tiger was hit and he was wounded in the face and nose by splinters. At 1650 hours the panzers entered Velikaya Ratscha and then halted in front of Chudin, which was strongly defended by the enemy. On 12 December the enemy withdrew further to the west into the forests near Glukhov. Otherwise the day saw little combat. The Tigers saw no action on 12 and 13 December.

The attack north toward the Irsha River line began on 14 December. The enemy launched attacks against the XXXXVIIIth Panzer Corps in the Teterev-Irsha River triangle, in order to protect the Kiev-Korosten railway line and at the same time win time for a larger buildup. The Leibstandarte was sent to counter these with Irsha as the objective. The Tigers moved off at 1130 hours; they spearheaded the advance by the panzer regiment along the Weprin-Federovka road. Soviet anti-tank guns and tanks were waiting at the fork in the road one kilometer south of the east end of Federovka and a firefight developed. The Tigers had advanced through a stream bed and now became engaged in a duel with the Soviet tanks. Three T 34s were destroyed; one of the successful commanders was SS-Untersturmführer Wendorff. The panzer regiment's losses were two tanks. The panzers deployed and advanced further north, however they were halted at a stream in front of Wyrwa as there was no way across. On orders from corps the Leibstandarte disengaged from the enemy and, setting out while it was still dark, marched south. The Tigers reached Ssabolot. The pursuing enemy was driven back in Krasnoborki and Mal. Ratscha by various elements of the division. The latter was positioned in such a way that it could attack immediately in any direction within a short time of being placed on alert. The bulk of the Soviet 16th Army had been crushed and a far-reaching enemy offensive forestalled at the last moment. There was to be no rest for the Leibstandarte and with it the men of the Tiger Company, however.

BATTLE OF CHEPOVICHI, 17–23 DECEMBER 1943

On 17 December 1943, our faithful reporter Rolf Schamp left the Tiger Company. The SS-Sturmmann, who had attended the SS NCO school in Lauenburg some time earlier, was sent on an officer training course. Leaving the company, which had become his second home, was a heavy blow. He had been in action with his comrades too long, had shared with them all the trials and hardships, and some good times as well. SS-Sturmmänner Heinrich Knöß and Roland Söffker, both gunners, felt the same. Veteran Tiger commander SS-Oberscharführer Jürgen "Captain" Brandt and Knight's Cross wearer SS-Unterscharführer Franz Staudegger, who was in Germany, were sent to Fallingbostel to take part in the 2nd SS Panzer-junker Special Course. They were followed later by SS-Sturmmänner Heinz Buchner, Siegfried Hummel, Heinz Schindhelm and Götz—all of whom were gunners—and by Wittmann's driver, SS-Sturmmann Siegfried Fuss.

Moving under cover of darkness, it took the Leibstandarte two nights to reach the area west of Meleni. On 19 December the division was ready to attack. Kling had seven operational Tigers; the panzer regiment had available twelve Panzer Vs and thirty-three Panzer IVs. The tanks set off toward the north at 1005 hours, driving close together. A time-consuming battle took place in heavy brush-covered terrain. The enemy was visibly surprised and at 1320 hours was driven out of his second position at the Meleni collective farm. The Balyarka collective farm was reached in the afternoon and enemy tanks and infantry were forced to withdraw in front of Stremigorod. The Tigers destroyed one T 34 and several anti-tank guns.

The XXXXVIIIth Panzer Corps confirmed that the Soviets had been defeated in the paragraph concerning the enemy situation in its Corps Order No 14: "As a result of the rapid advance by the LAH (Leibstandarte) his forces in the Chepovichi-Melini area are facing encirclement."

The Chief of Staff of the XXXXVIIIth Panzer Corps, General Staff Oberst von Mellenthin, went on to note that: "Such a joint attack from various directions could only be carried out by high quality fighting units. Both of the attacking panzer divisions involved here (1st Panzer Division and 1st SS Panzer Division Leibstandarte SS Adolf Hitler) are undoubtedly among the best German divisions."

The Tigers were moved behind the 2nd SS Panzer-Grenadier Regiment during the night of 20 December 1943. At 1345 hours they attacked Chepovichi's railway station. Together with Oberstleutnant Bradel's battle

group (1st Panzer Division), the armored group succeeded in taking the
extended station. Once again the Tigers played a decisive role in the German success, using their power to get the attack moving and smashing a
path for the battle group. In the course of this action SS-Hauptsturmführer Kling destroyed his 46th enemy tank.

In the evening the panzer-grenadiers of the 2nd Regiment's IInd Battalion stormed each house in the western part of Chepovichi; resistance
was fierce. Three Tigers and the armored group stood guard at the railway
crossing. SS-Panzerschütze Willi Werthmann of the 13th Company was
killed in the fighting in the town; SS-Panzerschütze Helmut Jakobi was
wounded. SS-Obersturmführer Michalski of the 8th Panzer Company, who
had been transferred there from the Tiger Company in November, was
also killed in action that day.

The enemy had lost a total of seventeen T 34s, four assault guns and
forty-four guns. The Leibstandarte had destroyed 1,003 tanks in Russia so
far in 1943. This figure does not take into account other armored vehicles
and armored troop carriers. The 21st of December 1943 saw the Soviets
launch heavy counterattacks toward Ossefowka; the 1st SS Panzer-
Grenadier Regiment held its ground and its six panzers destroyed twenty-
one Soviet tanks. German forces, their front facing south, withstood
further Soviet attacks at the Chepovichi railway station. The enemy's intention was obviously to attack south toward Zhitomir.

Once again attacking enemy tanks fell prey to the Tigers. All told the
enemy lost twenty-three T 34s and two anti-tank guns. At about 1800 hours
there were two Tigers serviceable; together with four Panthers and six
Panzer IVs, this gave Peiper a total of twelve tanks in his regiment. Beginning at 0000 hours on 22 December 1943, units of the 1st Panzer Division
began relieving the elements of the Leibstandarte deployed at Chepovichi
station. An attack on Melini failed to achieve the desired results. This was
followed by an attack by enemy tanks; two T 34s were destroyed by SS-Oberscharführer Georg Lötzsch. The twenty-nine-year-old from Dresden was
known within the company as the "panzer general." Two Tigers remained
in action.

Dirty and tired, several panzer crews took shelter in a Russian cottage
for the night. SS-Sturmmann Walter Lau recalled the evenings and nights
in the Ukrainian winter of 1943:

"In the summer it was customary to sleep outdoors in tents or in the
open, for the Russian houses were full of fleas and lice. We thus were not
plagued by lice in the summer and we could even wash in a stream or at a
well. In the winter, however, the Russian houses were in demand. Whenever the combat situation permitted, several crews crawled into a house to

get warm. Often there were soldiers from other units, including from the army, in the house. I am not exaggerating when I say that, with temperatures as low as minus 25 to 30 degrees and an icy wind, often as many as twenty men sought shelter in a fifteen-square-meter room.

Often we joined two or three other crews from the same platoon in the evening. The routine was as follows: refuel, load ammunition, refill ammo belts, clean the cylinder heads and top up with water or anti-freeze. Afterward we had to turn our attention to supper, usually a chicken and a few potatoes, or some other vegetable. When the front lines were occupied by our grenadiers and were about 500 to 1,000 meters away, we washed thoroughly with hot water and put on clean clothes—if we had any! When a high-numbered army infantry division was up front we didn't take our boots off or unbuckle our belts. Then there was only one thing: sleep, sleep! Story telling or letter writing had to wait until we were five to six kilometers back in the workshop or at 'one-hour' march readiness."

On 23 December 1943, the Leibstandarte formed an armored intervention group consisting of three Tigers, seven Panthers and sixteen Panzer IVs as well as the Reconnaissance Battalion. The division went over to the defensive. In the afternoon the enemy attacked the 291st Infantry Division with tanks. The intervention group was committed against the enemy advance; it destroyed four T 34s and smashed the attack.

In the meantime, Michael Wittmann's reputation had spread outside the company. His advice was sought by commanders before important decisions were made. After a reconnaissance carried out by Wittmann had revealed a strong concentration of enemy tanks, he spoke out against the plan of attack and suggested that it be made from the opposite direction, against the flank and rear of the enemy. The commanders of the other companies involved accepted his suggestion and the operation proved to be a complete success.

TRANSFER SOUTH AND THE DEFENSIVE BATTLE AT BERDICHEV, 24 DECEMBER 1943–21 JANUARY 1944

On 24 December 1943 the serviceable tanks of the Leibstandarte and the 1st Panzer Division were standing by in Sobolovka at the disposal of the corps. At 1000 hours a battle group under the command of General Staff Oberst von Mellenthin, consisting of the Ist (Armored) Battalion, 113th Panzer-Grenadier Regiment and 25 tanks of the 1st SS Panzer Regiment Leibstandarte SS Adolf Hitler under SS-Hauptsturmführer Kling, attacked north toward Schatrischtsche and destroyed numerous enemy elements there. In the evening corps reported that the enemy had gone to the attack on a broad front east of Zhitomir and that his spearheads were northeast of Kocherovo. The XXXXVIIIth Panzer Corps, with the Leib-standarte and the 1st Panzer Division, moved south at once to a position below Zhitomir. Near Chepovichi the 13th Panzer Company was forced to blow up seven Tigers which could not be recovered.

The 24th of December witnessed a hurried, but orderly, move by the two armored units. Once again the Leibstandarte was sent to a hot spot in the front in the role of a mobile fire-brigade. The division had achieved considerable success in recent weeks: it had defeated and wiped out the first of three strong groups of enemy forces sent across the Dniepr at Brusilov, and then smashed the second in the Radomyshl-Zhitomir area. It had then gone on to batter the third group southeast of Korosten. On Christmas Day 1943 SS-Untersturmführer Kalinowsky, who was absent from the company at the time on account of his injuries, was awarded the Iron Cross, First Class. Also presented the Iron Cross, First Class was Tiger commander SS- Unterscharführer Heinz Werner. The Iron Cross, Second Class was awarded to SS-Sturmmänner Johann Schütz, Erich Tille, Alfred Bernhard (loader) and Adolf Frank. Frank was a member of the maintenance echelon and had several times distinguished himself in the front lines during the recovery and repair of disabled Tigers.

On 25 December 1943 the Leibstandarte marched south through the jam-packed city of Zhitomir. The Tigers were moved to Ivankovo, southeast of Zhitomir. On 26 December the IInd Battalion of the 2nd SS Panzer-Grenadier Regiment took Woliza Sarubinezkaja and the Ist Battalion Stepok, gaining ground to the east. Farther to the south, at Gardyschewka, was the 1st SS Panzer-Grenadier Regiment. Then the enemy counterattacked and Stepok was lost. A new order issued by the corps had the Leib-standarte capture and hold the line Minkovtsy-Andrushovka-Staroselje. During the night of 27 December the Ist Battalion of the 1st SS Panzer Regiment was unable to take Andrushovka, which was strongly defended. Meanwhile, in the rear the enemy reoccupied Gardyschewka.

The 27th and 28th of December 1943 were to be big days for SS-Untersturmführer Helmut Wendorff: "In the early morning hours of 27 December 1943 SS-Untersturmführer Wendorff, who was in Ivankovo with his platoon (four Tigers), was instructed to intercept and destroy the Russian armored spearheads advancing out of the forest north of the highway, in order to safeguard the division's withdrawal into the area south of Gujwa during the night. In the course of a series of attacks against these armored spearheads, SS-Untersturmführer Wendorff distinguished himself through exceptional daring and outstanding bravery. He positioned himself in an ambush position at the crossroads north of Ivankovo. After destroying two T 34s, which he allowed to approach before opening fire,

Wendorff was instructed to carry out an attack on a strong armored group in Chubarovka. Making a daring approach along the railway line, he drove into the village from the northeast and destroyed eleven T 34s there. Following his return, he was sent against enemy armor that had broken out of Jusefowka and destroyed three more tanks. In the afternoon the enemy broke into Staroselje and seized the bridges in the area. The only avenue of retreat for the division's heavy weapons was through Ivankovo. Attacking with several armored spearheads, the Ivans attempted to seize these crossings as well, thus threatening the withdrawal of the elements of the division deployed in the Wolossowo-Staraya Kotelnya area. SS-Untersturmführer Wendorff and his three remaining Tigers withstood these Soviet assaults, enabling an artillery battalion and the Armored Troop Carrier Battalion to retreat and allowing some of our damaged tanks to be recovered from the main line of resistance. He was the last to retire—at about midnight—and brought his three panzers safely to the south bank of the Gujwa.

On 28 December 1943 strong groups of enemy armor advanced on the screening forces in Antopol-Bojarka and broke into the town. With a force of four Tigers, several of which were barely serviceable, SS-Untersturmführer Wendorff threw himself against the enemy tanks. Eleven T 34s were destroyed in the ensuing firefight and the enemy was prevented from breaking into the division's flank. Wendorff continued his run of success on the 27th and 28th of December, destroying another ten Soviet T 34s and raising his personal total to 58 enemy tanks destroyed."

The preceding account is taken from Peiper's recommendation for the award of the Knight's Cross to Wendorff. Together with his close friend Michael Wittmann, "Bubi" Wendorff was now among the most successful Tiger commanders. Wendorff, whom Wittmann always called "Axel," had to leave the company soon afterward to take an NCO training course in the area behind the front.

One of the tank commanders who fought with Wendorff at Ivankovo was SS-Unterscharführer Willi Sadzio. His Tiger was knocked out in the fighting; the tank's commander was killed, along with SS-Panzerschützen Helmut Becker and Kurt Cisarz. SS-Panzeroberschütze Johann Graf (radio operator) and SS-Panzerschütze Harald Ramm (ammunition driver) were seriously wounded. SS-Panzeroberschütze Josef Steininger was killed at Turtschinka. All of this took place on 28 December 1943. The day ended with heavy fighting in the Leibstandarte's entire sector. The heavy fighting resulted in a rapid drop in the fighting strengths of the regiments; SS-Obersturmbannführer Frey's 1st SS Panzer-Grenadier Regiment was down to 442 men (14 officers, 49 NCOs, 379 men), while SS-Obersturmbannführer Kraas' 2nd Regiment had 281 soldiers (11 officers, 21 NCOs, 249 men).

The Tiger Company had four operational Tigers, while the Panzer Regiment's strength was down to eight serviceable Panthers and seventeen Panzer IVs.

On 29 December 1943 the enemy attacked the positions at Antopol-Bojarka on a broad front. Defending there were the Ist and IInd Battalions of the 1st SS Panzer-Grenadier Regiment. Approximately forty T 34s rolled toward the grenadiers at about 0900 hours. The assault guns positioned there destroyed twelve enemy tanks. One Tiger was forced to leave its position with barrel damage after knocking out eight enemy tanks.

The Tiger of SS-Unterscharführer Günther Kunze was hit and Kunze seriously wounded. The commander of another Tiger, SS-Unterscharführer Günter Staack, received severe head wounds from shrapnel in the fighting. SS-Panzerschütze Harald Henn was wounded at Anatopol-Bojarka. Also wounded was SS-Panzerschütze Hans-Dieter Sauer, at Chernyakhov, north of Zhitomir. SS-Panzeroberschütze Günter Schade and SS-Panzerschütze Erhard Reeck were killed. Powerful enemy forces crossed the Gujwa during the night of 29 December and threatened the 2nd SS Panzer-Grenadier Regiment at Wolossowo. SS-Obersturmbannführer Kraas led a counterattack by a hastily-assembled force of headquarters personnel, secretaries and medical personnel. Armed with a submachine-gun and a machine-gun, Kraas led his grenadiers as they drove the enemy back. The Soviets attacked fiercely throughout the day. Following orders, with the arrival of darkness the Leibstandarte withdrew to the west toward the line Solotvin-Kodnja.

The division's neighbor on the right was the 1st Panzer Division, positioned northeast of Berdichev. The Leibstandarte's armored group was supposed to destroy the enemy forces on the Zhitomir-Berdichev road and establish contact with the XIIIth Army Corps to the north, south of Zhitomir. Two Tigers had to be blown up during the move: the one in Antopol-Bojarka and another with irreparable running gear damage. The extremely heavy defensive fighting involving the Leibstandarte—which destroyed 59 enemy tanks that day—was mentioned in the Wehrmacht communique.

". . . The 1st SS Panzer Division Leibstandarte SS Adolf Hitler under the command of SS-Oberführer Wisch distinguished itself through its exemplary fighting spirit in the heavy defensive fighting in the Zhitomir area . . ." The 30th of December saw the few available Tigers fighting in a defensive role in the new screening line. The enemy attacked continually with tanks and infantry and the defenders were just able to hold their positions. The division was now firmly on the defensive. There were two Tigers in action. That day the German Cross in Gold was awarded to SS-Hauptsturmführer Kling. The eight points in the award recommendation were repeated in his company's combat reports. Kling was the first member of the company to wear the German Cross in Gold, called the "fried egg" in soldier's jargon. For several days he had commanded the IInd Battalion of the 1st SS Panzer Regiment; Wittmann was now company commander. Kling still kept a firm hand on the company; he was present for all the company's attacks and was fully involved. In contrast to Wittmann and Wendorff, however, he lacked a personal touch with the men of the company. Nevertheless, SS-Hauptsturmführer Heinz Kling was respected by the company as commanding officer.

The last day of the year brought renewed attacks by the enemy. Acting on an order from the corps, beginning at 2200 hours the division began moving to new positions in a line which began at the north end of Berdichev then Kateriniwka-Gwasdawa-Troyanov. The new main line of resistance was occupied on New Years Day 1944. Soviet attacks on a broad front began at 0945 hours. In Troyanov, one of the defensive strongpoints, was SS-Untersturmführer Helmut Wendorff and his Tiger. Wendorff destroyed five T 34s from a group of attacking Soviet tanks. It was on that day that the last Tiger was put out of action. The damaged panzers were taken to Pjatki for repairs. SS-Untersturmführer Fritz Hartel was listed as missing in action near Berdichev in December 1943. There are two versions of his disappearance. One says that Hartel was ordered to Führer Headquarters but his aircraft never arrived. In the other his wife was told that he was to go on leave and nothing was heard of him after that.

The Leibstandarte was moved again on 2 January 1944. The Tiger tanks were in the hands of the panzer repair battalion in Starokonstantinov, which was also the location of the field hospital and the service battalion.

Wittmann still had twelve Tigers under his command, four were lost during the withdrawal. The Leibstandarte successfully fought off every attack on 3 January 1944 but was subjected to artillery fire. The same day the Leibstandarte was placed under the command of the XIIIth Army Corps. The division command was informed of an imminent move to the south. The fuel shortage was making itself felt on the units in the field. When the Leibstandarte asked corps where it should pick up fuel, it received the answer: "Fuel is to be taken from the land." First General Staff Officer Obersturmbannführer Lehmann replied to the Corps Ia: "Our Tigers and Panthers don't eat hay!".

The Leibstandarte fought fiercely in its lines until 5 January 1944. The division command waged a flexible battle and was able to repulse all the Soviet penetrations, some of which were in regiment strength, and inflict heavy losses on the enemy. At this point the Leibstandarte was again placed under the command of the XXXXVIIIth Panzer Corps. The Leibstandarte received new orders to advance to the line Demtschin-East-Ratschki-North and prepare for an attack on Bol. Korowinzy on 6 January 1944.

The enemy struck first, however, on 5 January, and occupied the village; the armored group engaged enemy tanks at Ratschki. By committing the last reserves, Demtschin and Ratschki were held. The withdrawal to a new line Buraki (inclusive)—Selenyy collective farm—Reference Point Dubrovka—Troschtscha began in the afternoon. Serviceable Tigers were sent to Smela.

The mission of the day was an advance on Jassopol with attached groups from the 68th and 208th Infantry Divisions, in which the armored battle group of the Das Reich Division was also to take part. During the night of 8 January those elements of the Armored Troop Carrier Battalion deployed at Reference Point 276.7 heard loud tank noises from Yanushpol. The armored group in Smela was alerted, after which it moved forward to the south end of Stepok. Early in the morning, at 0515 hours, approximately forty tanks of the Soviet 54th Red Guards Tank Brigade with mounted infantry broke through the German main line of resistance at the boundary between the 1st and 2nd SS Panzer-Grenadier Regiments. They reached the gullies north of Stepok (1st SS PGR) and Sherepki (III/2nd SS PGR).

SS-Untersturmführer Wittmann and his Tigers were sent against the enemy incursion into Sherepki. Wittmann led his tanks toward the enemy at maximum speed. Focused as always, he peered through the narrow vision slits in the commander's cupola, scanning the terrain in front of him. He had destroyed 56 enemy tanks in the preceding weeks and with the help of his gunner Balthasar Woll had become the company's most successful tank commander.

Wittmann issued orders to his crew in his usual calm, self-assured way. Woll had already loaded an armor-piercing round. Tensely he watched for the enemy. Now they could hear the sound of fighting; the crack of tank cannon and machine-gun fire told them that the Soviets were nearby. Suddenly Wittmann saw the enemy tanks; using the intercom, he passed the position of the first T 34 to Woll. Woll engaged the turret traverse and swung the long barrel of the 88 in the assigned direction. He targeted the T 34 and fired the first shot into its turret. There was a flash of flame as the turret was blown off the T 34. Direct hit. Now Wittmann had a plethora of targets to choose from. Woll already had the next tank in his sight. The pointed-post target indicator was lined up precisely on the turret. A direct hit finished the enemy tank, which was just about ready to fire itself. Wittmann knocked out three tanks and an assault gun.

The ferocity of the Tigers' attack unnerved the Soviet tank crews, and they halted their attack. The enemy was now caught in a pincer attack by the Leibstandarte's armored group and destroyed. By 0900 hours the dangerous Soviet threat had been neutralized. The panzers had destroyed thirty-three T 34s and seven assault guns. The main line of resistance ran three kilometers north of Sherepki. Further attacks on the German positions were smashed by armored counterattacks as soon as they began. The Leibstandarte Ia's daily report made mention of Wittmann's 60th tank kill. General der Panzertruppe Balck, the commanding general of the XXXXVIIIth Panzer Corps expressed his appreciation to Jochen Peiper for the great defensive success by his panzer regiment.

Wittmann's star had been ascending into the Ukrainian sky for many long weeks. He was now generally considered the best tactician in the company, whose sensitive nose and sure approach guaranteed his success. "Concerning Michael Wittmann, one can only say that he was irrefutably the leading figure in the 13th Company. He sensed this too, and was proud of it," recalled Bobby Warmbrunn of his former company commander. Wittmann spent the evening of 8 January as he usually did, preparing for the next day of operations. He had the Tigers armed and refuelled. Wittmann had the ability to sleep soundly as soon as he was through; in this way he was fresh and rested the next morning. While the others sometimes stayed up late, Wittmann usually "went to bed" early, the "bed" consisting of a few blankets in a primitive sod shack. As well he disapproved of the drinking binges that took place now and then.

A fresh penetration by Soviet tanks was reported on 9 January. Once again Wittmann was first to make contact with the enemy, destroying six tanks in rapid succession. His boldly-executed counterattack brought the dangerous advance to an abrupt halt. Michael Wittmann raised his total of Soviet tanks destroyed to sixty-six that day. In the evening the Leibstandarte began another withdrawal to a line farther south—from Petrikovtsy through Smela and Bespetschna—where it established contact with the Das Reich Division.

The new position was occupied on 10 January 1944. Weak Soviet infantry forces dug in in front of the 2nd SS Panzer-Grenadier Regiment; all was quiet in front of the 1st SS Panzer-Grenadier Regiment. That day a telex was sent from the Leibstandarte division command post in Morosovka recommending Michael Wittmann for the Knight's Cross.

Four Tigers were ready for action on 11 January 1944, as well as eight Panzer IVs and eight Panthers. SS-Sturmmann Warmbrunn knocked out an enemy anti-tank gun. Several tank crews left their vehicles during a pause in the fighting. Then, without warning, a mortar round exploded nearby; SS-

Unterscharführer Eduard Stadler was struck in the temple by shell fragments. Command of his tank passed to SS-Oberscharführer Lötzsch. The day passed quietly for the Leibstandarte. The enemy also seemed to be having difficulty after the constant attacks of the previous day. The following figures are from the strength reports submitted that day.

Combat Strengths   Trench Strengths   Serviceable Weapons

1st SS Panzer Regiment

    15/68/313   7/29/140

                                     4 Panzer VI

                                     8 Panzer V

                                     8 Panzer IV

                                     5 20mm Flak

                                     8 light MG

1st SS Panzer-Grenadier Regiment

    19/71/471   13/40/329

                                   37 light MG, 3 heavy MG

                                   2 hvy mortars, 1-20mm Flak

                                   2 20mm S.P. Flak

                                   1 75mm Pak

                                   3 50mm Pak

                                   2 hvy Inf.gun, 1—lt Inf gun

2nd SS Panzer-Grenadier Regiment

    9/43/330   7/20/174

                                     20 light MG, 1-50mm Pak

                                   2 heavy MG, 2-light MG

                                   5 2-tonne APCs

On 12 January 1944 Soviet tanks broke through the German positions and advanced as far as Ulanov, where they blocked the supply road. Two Tiger tanks just out of the workshop were immediately ordered there. Commanding the two Tigers were Wittmann and "the panzer general," SS-Oberscharführer Lötzsch. They knocked out three Soviet tanks and damaged two; two further Soviet tanks were knocked out by the 473rd Tank-destroyer Battalion.

At 0830 hours on 13 January, the Ivans launched an attack against the center of the 1st SS Panzer-Grenadier Regiment's defensive sector from the Chutorysko collective farm with strong armored forces. The enemy breached the main line of resistance and advanced as far as Chesnovka. In such cases the Tiger Company was ordered to the danger zone at maximum speed. Michael Wittmann and his crew quickly climbed aboard the tank; the commander gave the command "panzer march!" and the Tiger set itself in motion. How often had Wittmann and his well-tried and almost legendary gunner Bobby Woll driven into action together? Both men instinctively understood each other. The small, quick-reacting Saarlander at the 88 mm gun was the perfect complement to master tactician Wittmann. In their actions together, as of 11 January 1944 Rottenführer Woll had destroyed sixty-eight enemy tanks, which made him the most successful gunner in the Leibstandarte's panzer regiment.

It was ice-cold on that January morning; the misty fog banks lying over the fields lifted slowly, resulting in a clear view for the tank crews. Wittmann concentrated on the terrain in front of him, searching for the Soviet anti-tank guns he so respected. Sitting at his feet was Bobby Woll; the gunner slipped on his headset and throat microphone. Conscientiously, he checked the firing switch for the main gun and the handwheels that controlled the elevating and traversing mechanisms. An armor-piercing round already lay in the breech; Woll released the safety in order to be ready to fire immediately. As he knew from countless previous missions, seconds could be decisive. It was quiet inside the tank; the only sound was the rumbling of the Tiger's motor. The tension mounted—they should soon be able to see Chesnovka, where the enemy penetration had been reported earlier that morning.

In staggered positions behind Wittmann were several other Tigers of the 13th Company. Woll was adjusting the range scale, when suddenly he heard Wittmann's voice in his headset: "Attention, tank at two o'clock." Woll immediately trod on the pedal and the Tiger's turret began to rotate in the assigned direction. With his left hand he set the range on his telescopic sight, while with his right he turned the elevation handwheel. Soon the first T 34 was in his sight. As soon as the pointed-post reticle was superimposed on the tank he fired. It was a direct hit which blew off the Soviet tank's turret. Wittmann's driver pulled away immediately and drove on. Wittmann spotted the main body of enemy tanks. He gave the order to fire, but Woll had already targeted the nearest tank. His shot struck it in the side. Woll immediately took aim at the next; the sound of the eighty-eight firing and the impact of the shell were one. Gunner Woll worked with uncanny precision. His forehead was pressed firmly against the telescopic sight's headrest. One tank after another fell victim to Wittmann's Tiger. The tank remained constantly in motion so as not to offer a stationary target to a T 34 or lurking anti-tank gun. Wittmann maneuvered skillfully in front of the Soviet tanks, stopping only briefly to fire. The other Tigers had by now joined the battle, their 88 mm guns barked sharply. Suddenly a fountain of earth rose up in front of Wittmann's Tiger. The driver moved the panzer ahead a distance and halted. Wittmann saw a Soviet heavy assault gun. Two hits were sufficient to disable this new foe. The loader immediately inserted another round and the Tiger moved off.

Then another firing halt and once again an armor-piercing round struck home. There were burning T 34s everywhere in the snow-covered landscape, but several Soviet tanks were still driving about, firing wildly. Wittmann knocked out several more tanks before the furious battle ended. Exhausted and emotionally drained, he set out for home.

Wittmann had destroyed nineteen armored fighting vehicles on the 12th and 13th of January 1944—sixteen T 34s and three assault guns—raising his score to eighty-eight enemy tanks destroyed. SS-Rottenführer Woll's total now stood at eighty.

The remaining enemy tanks were totally wiped out in Chesnovka by SS-Sturmbannführer Peiper's armored group; a total of thirty-seven T 34s and seven assault guns were destroyed. The enemy also launched an attack in the sector held by the 188th Infantry Regiment under Oberst von Künsberg. Tigers also saw action there, at Bespetschna. The officer in command of the battle group, Oberst von Künsberg, wrote: "At that time the good Peiper sent me two Tigers for my sector, where Ustuf. Wittmann destroyed countless tanks and the other about 20 during an attack by the Soviets. The only cost to Wittmann was a front tooth, which he lost in a collision with the front of the turret. At the time I was very impressed by the obliging and selfless cooperation among the commanders."

Wittmann did not in fact lose the tooth in the tank, but during a drive in a Schwimmwagen. Michael Wittmann had scored yet another outstanding success. General Balck sent a radio message addressed to him personally, offering his congratulations. A telex was sent to Berlin the same day, recommending Wittmann for the Oak Leaves and gunner Balthasar Woll for the Knight's Cross.

Tigers of the 13th Company photographed during preparations for an attack. The tank crews are coordinating their advance with that of the accompanying panzer-grenadiers.

Tiger S45, whose right side drive sprocket was destroyed by a direct hit. The tow cables used by the prime mover to tow the Tiger to the workshop are still attached.

An armored group of the IInd Battalion, SS Panzer Regiment Leibstandarte in November 1943; showing a Soviet T-34/76 tank knocked out by the Pz. IV/Hs.

Panzer IV/Hs and assault guns of the Leibstandarte on the advance.

Leibstandarte multiple rocket launcher in firing position.

Two knocked-out T-34s. In the foreground is the turret from one of the Soviet tanks.

Tigers during a brief pause in the fighting. In the foreground is tank commander SS-Unterscharführer Mölly; next to him on the right is medic SS-Unterscharführer Schmidt, who often went along as the sixth man in the tank so that he could more quickly render assistance to the wounded.

A knocked-out Soviet SU85 assault gun.

29 December 1943, a Tiger of the 13th Company in the German newsreel.

Leibstandarte Panther Ausf A in the Ukranian mud.

22 November 1943. The previous day gunner SS-Sturmmann Bobby Warmbrunn knocked out 13 tanks and 7 anti-tank guns, raising his total of enemy tanks destroyed to 42.

A T-34 knocked out near Ivankovo on 27 December 1943.

Loader SS-Sturmmann Paul Sümmich.

30 January 1944. Michael Wittmann receives the news that he has been awarded the Knight's Cross with Oak Leaves.

The commander of the Leibstandarte's panzer regiment, Jochen Peiper (left), congratulates Wittmann and his successful tank crew.

Michael Wittmann
and Balthasar Woll.

The most successful
Tiger crew in the
Leibstandarte:
Wittmann, Woll,
Irrgang, Rößner
and Schmidt.

Wittmann's gunner
Balthasar Woll.

Radio operator
Werner Irrgang.

Michael Wittmann.

Driver Eugen Schmidt   Loader Sepp Rößner.

The crew.

Congratulations from comrades.

Michael Wittmann

Drawing of Michael Wittmann by
Wolfgang Willrich.

Jochen Peiper with Wittmann and Woll.

The division commander, SS-Brigadeführer Wisch and SS-Stormbannführer Peiper.

The division commander, SS-Brigadeführer Wisch (left) congratulates the crew.

Jochen Peiper congratulates Wittmann's crew.

Michael Wittmann and his crew are congratulated by comrades of the panzer regiment.

Another shot of Wittmann and his crew beneath the barrel of their tank's 88.

On 2 February 1944 Michael Wittmann received the Oak Leaves from the hand of Adolf Hitler in the latter's Wolfsschanze headquarters.

Michael Wittmann, photographed in the Führer Headquarters after receiving the Knight's Cross of the Iron Cross with Oak Leaves.

Operation Vatutin and the Relief of the Cherkassy Pocket

MICHAEL WITTMANN RECEIVES THE KNIGHT'S CROSS

The next day, 14 January 1944, Wittmann was awarded the Knight's Cross. That same day the Wehrmacht communique announced: "On 9 January 1944 on the Eastern Front, SS-Untersturmführer Wittmann, a member of an SS panzer division, destroyed his 66th enemy tank with his Tiger tank."

There was no time for a big celebration in those days. SS-Sturmmann Walter Lau remembered the day Wittmann was awarded the Knight's Cross: "We came back from the front that day with four or five Tigers under the command of Untersturmführer Wittmann and parked them on a village street. Suddenly we were ordered to assemble on the village square—it was the usual square found in front of a collective farm. Of the approximately twelve to fourteen men, several had to stay behind to guard the panzers. We were standing in a loose semi-circle when an all-wheel-drive car flying the division standard pulled up on the other side of the square. It was our division commander, Oberführer Teddy Wisch. I was at the edge of the semi-circle and Wittmann instructed me to go fetch the regimental commander, Sturmbannführer Peiper, whose command post was in a Russian house about one hundred meters away. I reported smartly to the Sturmbann-führer that the division commander had arrived and that he might drive to the village square in his VW all-terrain car. Afterward Wittmann informed Wisch that the Tiger crews, who were drawn up in a semi-circle, were all present. Wisch then spoke some words of praise for the Tiger crews in general and for Untersturmführer Wittmann in particular. Then Teddy Wisch placed the Knight's Cross, which was on a long band, around Michel's neck. Warm handshakes from Oberführer Wisch, Sturmbannführer Peiper and all of us. That was it. It was all over in a few minutes. The situation was critical and the war went on pitilessly,—no time for a big celebration."

Wittmann's outstanding success that winter was the product of his superior skill, which made people sit up and take notice. His infinite caution and his precision during operational briefings were well known. Wittmann had been leading the company for several weeks now; his responsibilities were even greater than before and he sensed it. No one prepared for a mission more conscientiously than he. Sometimes in the evening he sat for hours alone in front of the map, evaluating all the possibilities in order to discover the most promising course of action. He listened to the opinions of other experienced commanders. Then, after much consideration and weighing of the options, he made his decision. Never did he allow a matter to be decided by chance.

Those who encountered Wittmann on such evenings in one of the small Ukrainian sod huts were frequently left with the impression that he appeared to be absent-minded, sitting there as he did, so still and reflective, somewhat withdrawn. Such an impression was entirely accurate. His thoughts turned to what was to come, always weighing the options and working out all the possibilities. On such evenings he sometimes went out to the tanks again, checked on the guards and took a short walk in the dark to work off the terrific stress that built up during the day. On such winter nights he could often be seen tramping through the cold alone, smoking.

Michael Wittmann's success wasn't by chance, it wasn't merely luck that allowed him to end an engagement successfully, rather it was his diligence, his conscientious preparation for the coming mission and his brilliant talent in the field of tank tactics. His tactics contained the sum of the abilities he had acquired and the lessons he had learned in the past months. The sum of his experiences, the conditioning as a result of having experienced every situation in tank combat with its many dangers and pitfalls, made Wittmann's decisions and orders so unmistakable that many perceived them as given with a natural ease. Most remained ignorant of the work that lay behind them and of Wittmann's constant evaluation and weighing of the possibilities. Wittmann's natural abilities certainly played a large part in his successes, but his diligence and conscientious concentration and preparation played an equally large part. It was not only his talent that enabled him to master every situation, and an observer wrote: "When I sat in his tank, I had the feeling that he could not be deceived, as if it was impossible for him to walk into a trap. But in truth this was the sum of much hard work on his part, the result of the hours Michel spent in thought even when he was with us in the evening, or when he walked about between the Tiger workshops at night as if he was taking a stroll."

Wittmann embodied a surely unique combination of natural ability in the field of tank tactics and unsurpassed diligence and conscientiousness. The use of all his senses to the full and total concentration on the enemy allowed him to carry on in combat almost to the limit of his strength. His trained instinct enabled Wittmann to smell danger and the ensuing decisions proved to be correct. Michael Wittmann was a virtuosic master, whose successes in a short period of time were unique and unmatchable.

A conversation with Michael Wittmann revealed that this masterful tank commander had no desire to hear about his accomplishments and successes. Talk of him as a hero, which he undeniably was, was met by disbelief and even denial. Wittmann was an easy-going man, yet somewhat self-conscious, which in itself was not necessarily a contradiction. The occasional evening drinking sessions were not his world; when one took place he usually retired early to the sod hut in which he had his quarters. For all that, he was definitely not an anti-social man, but in a conversation he tended to listen more than talk.

Michael Wittmann was 1.76 meters tall, had dark blonde hair and rather pale eyes. His voice was melodious with just a trace of a Bavarian accent. Now and then he emphasized the second syllable of verbs. Wittmann's words were well-considered, he knew what he was saying. Any sort of a cult of personality was foreign to him—it simply wouldn't fit the nature of the young officer from the Upper Pfalz. Nor was their anything extravagant or out of the ordinary about his external appearance. He wore a grey-brown jacket with a fur collar or else the standard black panzer tunic, but without any piping around the collar and the collar patches—in the style of the enlisted men. Wittmann's character was marked by his fairness and objectivity. His men sensed this and they all revered him. To them he was also a good company commander, an assessment based largely on his all-encompassing feeling of responsibility.

Wittmann had no tolerance for carelessness in action; he demanded total concentration and readiness. When he did not sense this, he too could become unpleasant. He was extremely precise about these things, downright fussy. Everything had to be one hundred percent with him, for that was one of the conditions of his success.

After battle the Tiger had to be made ready for action again. In addition to refuelling, ammunition had to be procured for the main gun and the machine-guns and stowed in the fighting compartment. All spent shell casings were removed from the tank. Even a wearer of the Knight's Cross like Wittmann lent a helping hand in this necessary work. He pounded in track bolts with the sledgehammer and helped clean the gun tube. Wittmann became both an example and a model to the company in every situation. The Wittmann legend was born in those winter weeks in 1943–44.

Toward noon on 14 January, the Tigers and the armored group under SS-Sturmbannführer Peiper made preparations to begin an advance to the northeast from the area west of Smela. Objective: to destroy the enemy at the Chutorysko collective farm and take Krasnopol. Near the Chutorysko collective farm the panzers drove into the midst of the enemy withdrawal and destroyed two regiments. By 1400 hours the armored group was in Krasnopol and had reached Molotschki. The Soviets were in full flight, leaving their heavy weapons behind. Wittmann was again successful, destroying several enemy tanks.

On 15 January 1944 Leibstandarte pickets at Krasnopol made contact with the armored group of Kampfgruppe Das Reich. Both armored groups (Leibstandarte and Das Reich) were ordered to drive further northwest in the direction of Ljubar. This armored advance was stopped, principally by heavy fire from anti-tank guns and mortars. Those two days saw the destruction of six enemy tanks, twenty anti-tank guns, sixty guns, thirty-two trucks and countless other vehicles. Five Tigers fought beside nine Panthers and five Panzer IVs in the Leibstandarte armored group. On 16 January 1944 SS-Rottenführer Balthasar Woll received the Knight's Cross. The twenty-one-year-old native of the Saar was the first Waffen-SS gunner to be awarded the high decoration. He was also the only one in the entire panzer arm. There were now two wearers of the Knight's Cross in Wittmann's Tiger, an unprecedented situation. Balthasar Woll—simply "Balthy" or "Bobby" to his friends—was born on 1 September 1922 in Wemmetsweiler, in the Saarland. The son of a worker, he became an electrician and on 15 August 1941 joined the Waffen-SS as a volunteer. As a member of a machine-gun team in the 3rd Company, 1st Infantry Regiment of the Totenkopf Division, Woll fought in the Demyansk Pocket. He was wounded there and evacuated to a hospital in Germany. On 23 July 1942 SS-Oberschütze Woll received the Iron Cross, Second Class and three days later the Wound Badge in Black. After his wounds had healed he became a tank gunner and in late 1942 was assigned to the Tiger company of the Leibstandarte SS Adolf Hitler. SS-Sturmmann Woll took part in all the actions in which the Leibstandarte was involved, and by the time of Operation Zitadelle he was considered one of the best Tiger gunners. On 16 September 1943 he received the Iron Cross, First Class and on 9 November was promoted to the rank of SS-Rottenführer.

As a member of Wittmann's crew, Woll's success surpassed that of every other gunner in the winter battles that began in November of 1943. By 13 January he had destroyed eighty tanks and 107 anti-tank guns. "Bobby" Woll played an important part in the success of Michael Wittmann. With his quick reactions and good eye, he was a master behind the "eighty-eight." Sure of his gunner's ability, Wittmann was able to take on superior numbers of enemy tanks with confidence. The two made a fine team and Woll knew Wittmann's ways to the letter. While a crew's driver, radio operator and loader often changed, the commander and gunner stayed together whenever possible. The commander of a Tiger was closely tied to his gunner, and their actions had to be well-coordinated. In many cases Woll was known to have fired before his commander assigned a target. Making up the rest of Wittmann's crew in January 1944 were SS-Panzeroberschütze Werner Irrgang (radio operator), SS-Sturmmann Eugen Schmidt (driver) and SS-Panzerschütze Sepp Rößner (loader). His original crew from May 1943 included SS-Sturmmann Siegfried Fuß and Bobby Woll, as well as SS-Sturmmänner Karl Lieber (radio operator) and Max Gaube (loader). Each member of a Tiger's crew had a clearly-defined role. The gunner was of decisive importance; the enemy's next shot could mean the end if his aim was poor. The loader, who was responsible for ensuring that the main gun was loaded with the correct ammunition, also observed the surrounding terrain through his vision slit next to the turret number. He could also observe through an episcope which offered him a view to the front. The loader had to do hard physical work in combat; later he was responsible for restocking the tank's ammunition supply and removing the empty shell casings from the fighting compartment.

The radio operator was responsible for maintaining contact with the superior unit, as well as informing the commander of new orders and transmitting messages. The radio operator also operated the Tiger's bow machine-gun. Two episcopes built into their respective access hatches provided the driver and radio operator with an outside view. The radio operator also had a sighting port for use with the machine-gun. In addition to the episcope, the driver could observe the battlefield through his own vision slit. His skill could decide the fate of the tank and its crew.

The commander controlled the operation of the tank, assigned targets to the gunner, directed the driver and kept an eye on accompanying tanks. The crew's success depended on him. It was he who had to pick out the well-camouflaged anti-tank gun and make out the dug-in T 34. If he was also a platoon or company commander, he was responsible for the other tanks under his command as well. These tanks listened to his orders. Tank crews had to be able to adapt extremely quickly to the constantly changing situation and react accordingly. This demanded a high degree of concentration and responsibility from each member of the crew in their life and death struggle. Constantly seeking the enemy, and success, they were in action every day, in the forty-degree heat of summer and the icy cold and morass of the Russian winter.

The Tigers were feared by the Soviets and the heavy German tanks often drew heavy anti-tank and tank fire in their attacks. They smashed gaps in enemy positions for the grenadiers in countless attacks, breached anti-tank fronts and destroyed enemy artillery positions. With their high rate of fire, many commanders achieved an extremely high firepower which was unsurpassed at the time. They performed outstanding feats in the offensive and defensive roles. Constantly under a hail of fire from anti-tank rifles, anti-tank guns and rocket launchers, the Tigers did not get off unscathed; however, thanks to their strong frontal armor they were difficult to knock out. Often shells fired—by enemy tanks and anti-tank guns simply bounced off their frontal armor; nevertheless, the Tiger was not invulnerable.

Hitherto the men of the 13th Company had been singularly successful in destroying enemy tanks and already enjoyed an almost legendary reputation within the division. In the period from 5 December 1943 to 17 January 1944 the handful of serviceable Tiger tanks—sadly many were out of action as a result of mechanical breakdowns—had destroyed 146 tanks and 125 anti-tank guns.

The award of the Knight's Cross to Wittmann and Woll aroused great joy in the Leibstandarte's Tiger company. On the other hand there wasn't much time to celebrate. The armored group was soon sent back to the division.

The days passed quietly in the Leibstandarte's sector. The 17th of January was also uneventful. Jochen Peiper found time to submit a recommendation for the award of the Knight's Cross to SS-Untersturmführer Helmut Wendorff for his successes on 27 and 28 December 1943. SS-Brigadeführer Wisch, the division commander, wrote in his endorsement of the recommendation: "SS-Untersturmführer Wendorff distinguished himself in every day of combat through singular daring and extraordinary bravery. He demonstrated outstanding courage and great initiative on 28 December 1943 in particular, when, after the remaining three Tigers of his platoon were put out of action, he drove alone into a large group of enemy tanks that had entered Antopol-Bojarka and repulsed their attack by destroying eleven of their number. Because of his oft-demonstrated exceptional bravery and the outstanding command of his platoon, I consider SS-Untersturmführer Wendorff worthy of the Knight's Cross of the Iron Cross and request that this high decoration be awarded to SS-Untersturmführer Wendorff."

SS-Hauptsturmführer Heinz Kling was also put up for the Knight's Cross. When the numbers were tallied it was found that 343 tanks, 8 assault guns, 255 heavy anti-tank guns and 20 guns had been destroyed by the Tiger Company in the actions at Kharkov, in Operation Zitadelle and in the fighting near Zhitomir and Berdichev, a total of fourteen weeks of combat. As well, the Tigers had accounted for countless artillery pieces, armored vehicles, trucks and other enemy weapons. The following is the original of the Knight's Cross submission for SS-Hauptsturmführer Kling.

A breathtaking accomplishment for a single company. The numbers underline emphatically the significance and impact the Tiger had on the Eastern Front. Twenty-four Tigers were lost in these actions. The 18th of January 1944 was uneventful. Relief by the 371st Infantry Division began the next day. The Leibstandarte was moved into the Khmelnik area. One Tiger was operational; two more were undergoing short-term and six long-term repairs. Meanwhile, the Panzer Regiment had thirty-six Panthers and thirty-three Panzer IVs, which, in contrast to the previous days, was an acceptable number.

Deployed in the XXXXVIIIth Panzer Corps' sector, during the Battle of Berdichev the Leibstandarte had shown that success could be achieved against the far-superior enemy through use of offensive tactics. Thanks to the steadfastness of the troops, it had proved possible to close the gap between the XXXXVIIIth Panzer Corps and the LIXth Army Corps while inflicting heavy losses on the enemy. Nevertheless, the corps rightly deduced that the enemy would attack again at the same points of main effort after regrouping his forces.

In conclusion, here is another extract from a propaganda company report from that period: "The Soviet winter offensive began after the Christmas season of 1943. The heavy company, which was now under Wittmann's command, put the enemy to a severe test. As in the winter battles, in these days it was a problem reaching Oak Leaves wearer Obersturmbannführer Peiper's battle group, of which Wittmann and his Tigers were an important part. The story was the same at every command post: 'Without tanks we can't get through. Peiper is surrounded, but he'll fight his way out.' And fight his way out he did—even though the battle-weary Leibstandarte was faced with a Soviet Guards tank corps of three Guards tank brigades, a motorized rifle brigade, and a Guards rifle corps with three rifle divisions. Wittmann's Tigers found their way home in spite of the whistling anti-tank shells that seemed to saw shrilly through the armor plate from front to back, dark enemy-occupied woods, burning villages, and slippery ice-covered hills."

Here is a quote from SS-Sturmmann Günther Braubach, a member of Wittmann's platoon since 21 March 1943, which may help understand Wittmann's place in the company: "I can scarcely put into words the respect and love I felt for him. His strict but correct leadership had made soldiers of us, soldiers ready to walk through fire for him at any time. We could take all our problems to him; he had helpful advice, or if appropriate a consoling word, for everyone. He knew all of his 'old' men and appreciated their daily concerns. In action he always drove in the lead, a shining example. If a tank failed to return his greatest concern was for his men. Near him we were sure of refuge and salvation if something happened to us. I never loved an officer more than I did our Michel Wittmann."

OPERATION VATUTIN: THE LEIBSTANDARTE'S ATTACK EAST OF VINNITSA, 22 JANUARY–1 FEBRUARY 1944

The 13th Panzer Company lost three Tigers during the move. On 22 January 1944 the Leibstandarte came under the command of the XXXXVIth Panzer Corps, led by General der Infanterie Gollnick. The Leibstandarte was transferred into the area northeast of Vinnitsa on 24 January. The weather made the move extremely difficult; a thaw had set in and everything sank into the Ukrainian mud. The divisions of the XXXXVIth Panzer Corps attacked on 24 January 1944, achieved a breakthrough, and drove the Soviets back across the Bila River line. The objective was the encirclement of the approximately eight Red divisions and the destruction of the Soviet 1st Tank Army facing the German IIIrd Panzer Corps.

On 24 January 1944, SS-Untersturmführer Walter Hahn of the Tiger Company was decorated with the Iron Cross, Second Class. In contrast to Wittmann or Wendorff he was no great tank-killer, but he was well liked and generally respected within the company. SS-Sturmmann Walter Lau remembered "Papa" Hahn: "True he wasn't the dashing 'lieutenant type' like Michel (Wittmann) and "Bubi" (Wendorff, the author), but he was a fine man with a Rhenish dialect and a sense of humor that we liked. He was an SS-Untersturmführer of the Reserve, at what was for our situation an advanced age. Nevertheless, he was always up front with his panzer and often led the combat echelon—even when there were rather safer security duties to perform. We affectionately called him 'Papa' Hahn.

One day in early February 1944, I was a member of his crew then, the gunner, several of us were sitting around cleaning the weapons. I don't know how it happened; we were sitting in a Russian shack with a thatched roof when suddenly the flare pistol went off and hit the roof. The shack burned so quickly that we barely managed to save ourselves and our few things. Then 'Papa' Hahn said in his Cologne dialect, 'But boys, you can't burn the house down over my head.' That was Papa Hahn. Another day we were up front with three Tigers on guard duty—it was in the sector manned by SS-Sturmbannführer Sandig's battalion. His grenadier companies, which were on a level with us, had a trench strength of approximately fifteen men and were led by an Ober- or Hauptscharführer. It was raining terribly and the rain was mixed with wet snow flurries. We had to leave the hatches open and keep an eye on enemy territory. His humorous cursing in his Cologne dialect—about the weather, about Peter, about the Reds, and the war in general—helped us through this miserable situation caused by the weather. He didn't wear an 'iron collar', as we called the Knight's Cross, but he was a fine fellow."

The Leibstandarte joined the battle on 25 January 1944. The Tigers under SS-Untersturmführer Wittmann drove point and attacked west of the Kalinovka-Uman railway line. Although the panzers were attacked by low-flying enemy aircraft several times, there were no losses. The Tigers reached Reference Point 316.6 west of Ocheretnya. Wittmann destroyed several enemy tanks, something that had long since ceased to be out of the ordinary.

On 26 January the Leibstandarte SS Adolf Hitler attacked again, to the southeast. Once again leading the way, the Tigers crossed an anti-tank trench and advanced in the direction of Ganovka. By noon Napadovka had been taken. At 2350 hours Rossosh was in our hands and had been cleared of the enemy. It was there that the urgently needed deliveries of fuel and ammunition finally took place.

Vehicles belonging to the ammunition and fuel transport columns were constantly on the road, transporting vital supplies to the Tigers up front. Even the supply NCO, SS-Unterscharführer Jarosch, shuttled back and forth in his American Studebaker; the chocolate he kept in his tool box was in great demand.

The accomplishments of the supply units, the workshop platoon and the maintenance echelon rarely enjoyed the limelight, but they were an indispensable part of the long chain which ultimately led to the combat echelon up front. The company's drivers struggled forward through snow storms and icy cold to deliver supplies, fuel or spare parts. The efforts of these men are deserving of acknowledgement; they, too, suffered losses during their often lonely drives.

On 27 January 1944, the Tigers, now part of Kampfgruppe Kuhlmann, set out toward Lipovets. They reached Lipovets Station and the crossroad to the north at 0530 hours. Since the panzers could not refuel during the night, they had to assume an all-round defensive position. The Ivans soon began probing with tanks, after which they launched repeated attacks against the German forces at Lipovets Station. The Tigers knocked out several enemy tanks; the entire armored group accounted for a total of twenty-six Soviet tanks destroyed.

Sturmmann Lau described the problems he encountered while standing guard in the turret of Wittmann's Tiger: "At this time I had been serving as Wittmann's gunner for a few days and I fell asleep in the turret in the magnificent sunshine. Wittmann caught me and cuffed me about the ears several times. That was all there was to it, no shouting, no carrying of a grudge."

The 28th of January 1944 saw the four Tigers in action at Lipovets Station. Untersturmführer Wittmann destroyed several enemy tanks each day. On 29 January Kampfgruppe Kuhlmann took Babin. As the Soviets were breaking out of the Gaissin pocket, the Leibstandarte was immediately sent south toward the Morosovka-Neminka-Parijewka-Krynivka-Shabelnaya-Zurkowzy-Jakubiwka area in order to head off the Soviets and clear the enemy from the forests.

SS-Untersturmführer Michael Wittmann destroyed several more enemy tanks on 29 January, raising his total to 117. It was an accomplishment unique on the Eastern Front and in the entire Wehrmacht. On 30 January Michael Wittmann was awarded the Knight's Cross with Oak Leaves. Only two weeks earlier he had received the Knight's Cross and now the Oak Leaves—the news spread through the company like wildfire. On 7 January 1944 his total of enemy tanks destroyed had stood at 56. In the twenty-two days that followed he accounted for another 61, increasing his total to the unbelievable figure of 117 enemy tanks destroyed. Wittmann now headed the list of the most successful tank commanders. Effective 30 January 1944 he was promoted to Obersturmführer.

The Führer sent him the following telegram: "In grateful appreciation of your heroic actions in the struggle for the future of our people, I award you the Knight's Cross with Oak Leaves as the 380th soldier of the German Armed Forces.—Adolf Hitler."

An article in the "Black Corps" in 1944 came to grips with the unique personality of Michael Wittmann. Several extracts from the article are presented here. A facsimile of the entire article, titled "117 Tanks", is also reproduced in this book.

"Untersturmführer Wittmann of the Waffen-SS destroyed his 117th enemy tank. Why did such news fail to produce the usual exclamations of admiration? The feat was extraordinary, it gave cause for astonishment, but the expression of astonishment was restrained. One suddenly felt oneself transported into an unknown dimension where very dangerous energies overturned the previously accepted notions of bravery. One sensed the need to come to terms with the new type of soldiery which became the master of iron and fire with the precision of a cool and business-like technician. The romantic ideal of the hero has no place in this imaginary world . . .

The destruction of 117 tanks is much more than 117 encounters with the immediate reality of the war, it represents 117 combats to the ultimate consequence—death. It was a psychology which, left to the healthy nerves of a farmer's son, could only lead to a disparaging and unintelligible devaluation . . . but the fiftieth and sixtieth tanks, like all those before them, were not destroyed on a practice range. Within the field of fire of circling and firing tanks they seemed to be mobile, lethally-armed instruments of the enemy's will to destroy, equal in dynamic will to be the first to get in the killing shot—each of these 117 tanks carried it the memories of those destroyed before . . .

The outward appearance of such men, into whose small, select circle we see Wittmann enter, is revealing for those who know how to read the fine, almost hidden scars which mark their faces. If they were superhuman, the result of mutations, beings with gifts not bestowed on the rest of us, placed in our midst by a whim of nature, then their feats would no longer be astonishing, for the abilities and talents, the switching off and on of organs with which the normal man overcomes the danger zone, would offer an explanation for the astonishing.

But these men are beings like us, who share the same passions; their decisions are animated by the same driving forces that determine ours. What distinguishes them and elevates them above others is not so much the sum of their accomplishments and the numbers that express their success—though given the difficulty of comprehending the actual conditions of their success, we need a number, some tangible expression, in order to understand—; it is much more revealing to learn of the abilities that enabled them to survive for so long . . .

The triumph one must keep in mind here is one of the great human victories from which a new world is born. Its birth is prepared in men like Wittmann and his kind. This triumph is enjoyed and revered quietly; it cannot possibly have anything in common with our existing ideas . . ."

The division commander, Brigadeführer Wisch, and Jochen Peiper visited the most successful tank commanders to congratulate them on their most recent decorations. SS correspondent Büschel captured this historic moment on film. War correspondent Joachim Fernau had already spent some time at Wittmann's side. Büschel is responsible for other important photographs; the one taken of the entire crew in front of Tiger S 04, with the 88 victory rings on its gun barrel, is world famous. The white rings were applied especially for the photographer. This occasion also witnessed the awarding of decorations to members of Wittmann's crew: radio operator SS-Panzeroberschütze Werner Irrgang, loader SS-Panzerschütze Sepp Roßler, and driver SS-Sturmmann Eugen Schmidt received both Iron Cross, First and Second Classes. Siegfried Fuß had earlier been sent to the Junkerschule. Wittmann saw to it that he received the Iron Cross, First

Class there. SS-Rottenführer Woll was now the most successful gunner in the Leibstandarte's panzer regiment. Bobby Woll had destroyed a total of 81 Soviet tanks, as well as 107 anti-tank guns, four 172 mm and 125 mm artillery pieces, five flamethrowers, an armored car, and a heavy mortar position. Woll was given home leave on 30 January 1944 and left the company immediately afterward. He received a retroactive promotion to the rank of SS-Unterscharführer effective 30 January 1944. SS-Untersturmführer Helmut Wendorff, who had not yet returned to the company,— "Your dusty contemporary sent me into exile at just the right time!" he wrote to his friend Wittmann—was also promoted, to SS-Obersturmführer. At the same time Michael Wittmann received orders to go to Führer Headquarters to receive the Oak Leaves.

SS-Obersturmführer Wendorff was named company commander. The tank commanders SS-Unterscharführer Eduard Stadler, Ewald Mölly and Herbert Stief were also decorated with the Iron Cross, First Class that day, as were SS-Panzerschützen Harry Teubner, Ewald Zajons and Gustav Brettschneider and SS-Sturmmann Walter Lau. The latter wrote: "We received the Iron Cross, Second Class from Untersturmführer Hahn. He was leading the combat echelon at the time. Because of the heavy casualties among the officers, at that time only one officer was allowed up front with a certain number of tanks, five I believe."

The composition of the Tiger crews never remained the same for a long period. In those weeks of uninterrupted combat the crews changed almost daily. SS-Sturmmann Lau described his own experience: "In case of losses to battle damage or mechanical breakdown the officers always moved to an operational tank and as a rule took their gunner and driver with them. In this way the crews changed every few days. For example, in November-December 1943 I was SS-Unterscharführer Stadler's loader and in January 1944 SS-Unterscharführer Kleber's gunner. In between I served for a time as Wendorff's loader and also as Wittmann's gunner for a few days. I also filled both positions with Hauptsturmführer Kling, Obersturmführer Michalski, Untersturmführer Hahn, Oberscharführer Lötzsch, Oberscharführer Krohn and Unterscharführer Sowa."

The company's chief cook, SS-Unterscharführer Jakob Mohrs, was also awarded the Iron Cross, Second Class. Ignoring the obvious danger, on numerous occasions he and his driver, SS-Sturmmann Fritz Jäger, had delivered food to the exhausted tank crews in the front lines. There was little action on 31 January. One-thousand Red Army troops voluntarily surrendered in the forests south of Morosovka. The Leibstandarte was about to be transferred again and thrown into another sector of the front.

The men of the Tiger Company were exhausted, dead tired. The struggle in the biting cold and bottomless morass demanded that they summon all their physical and psychological strength. The good and thorough training given the tank crews, the solid, unbreakable bonds of comradeship, and the inner willingness—they were after all volunteers—enabled the young soldiers to endure the unspeakable hardships of the winter war. Added to the inclement weather was a foe who was superior in materiel and numbers, as well as a stubborn fighter. No one wanted to be taken prisoner by the Soviets; too often the men had been forced to witness the unspeakable atrocities committed against German prisoners and the wounded by soldiers of the Red Army.

There had never been any difficulties with the Ukrainian civilian population; in their small, straw-roofed houses the men found rest and relaxation after combat missions. A lively barter system, with food the main commodity, sprang up, with advantages for both sides. An eighteen-year-old radio operator, SS-Panzerschütze Hubert Heil, wrote of this time in Russia: "The enemy's tanks were not our only target, his obstinate anti-tank fronts also gave us a hard time. Even their wounded continued to fight us, and the enemy's infantry was also usually superior in numbers to ours. The cold winter with its great masses of snow was also a dangerous foe; hunger also had a weakening effect, of course."

Black leather suits—originating from the navy—provided protection from the cold. As well the thick leather pants and jackets offered good protection against fire in the tank. A large quantity of Tiger ammunition was sent to theIstSS Flak Battalion where, after the threaded primers were changed, it was fired by the 88 mm batteries, whose own stocks of ammunition had dwindled to a dangerous level.

SS-Sturmmann Lau, gunner in SS-Unterscharführer Kleber's tank, described the art of improvisation: "As was usually the case when we stopped in a village, we immediately began looking around for something edible and found a pig standing all alone in a stall. A ladder was found in no time and the pig, which we had killed in the meantime, was placed on it to be cut up. Someone ignited a blowtorch and singed off the hide. At that very moment we heard tank cannon firing nearby. The Ivans were attacking the village with T 34s. Wittmann was immediately ready for battle and raced out of the village to engage the T 34s. Several tanks were destroyed by him there.

We rolled the pig up in a tent square, secured it with rope and tied it to the side of the turret as we drove out of the village. We took up station to Wittmann's right, but we knew that there was little we could do, for our gun's electrical firing mechanism was damaged. At that moment our commander, SS-Unterscharführer Kleber, spotted a Soviet assault gun on a slope about 1,500 meters away. It was an SU 152, a type that was feared by us. What now?

Our 'Quax' came up with an idea which we had already discussed in theory several times. He removed the cover over the batteries in the compartment at the rear of the fighting compartment; using two long wrenches, he made contact between the batteries and the turret traverse mechanism, and thus the electrical firing system. As gunner, I aimed at the assault gun and pulled the firing lever on the elevation mechanism, and by means of the wrenches Kleber fired the shot. Though the shell ricocheted off the assault gun in a shower of sparks, it had obviously crippled the enemy vehicle. Kurt Kleber was one of the former Luftwaffe soldiers; recently he had developed into a capable tank commander. On one occasion the blast wave from an exploding artillery shell hurled him from the turret; he escaped unhurt. He was called 'Quax the hard-luck pilot' on account of his resemblance to Heinz Rühmann, who appeared in the film of the same name. 'Quax' looked very warlike. His outward appearance was pitiful. He wore the standard parka of the panzer-grenadiers, canvas on the outside and fur on the inside, with a fur hood. But the material was completely in tatters and the fur hung down his body, and he had turned the hood into a fur shawl. His fur-lined boots were ruined and he had to bind the soles to the shanks with wire. On his head was a Russian shapka with a death's head on the front. Wittmann couldn't help but run into him: 'Quax, man, dress more sensibly! Everyone must take you for a Russian and you're going to be shot by our own people.' However Quax didn't let such things bother him. He kept running around in the same costume. His only concession was to pull the flaps of the shapka up off of his ears and tie them over his head properly."

In the course of this fighting individual Tigers serving with small battle groups were surrounded by the enemy for brief periods. The 13th Company reported: "That we were encircled was also confirmed by the fact that several rocket launchers that were with us were firing single rockets instead of salvoes. They were short of ammunition and we of fuel. Our morale naturally sank to the zero point. By now it had become afternoon and it began to get dark. As well, it was quite cold. What were we to do for the night?

Wittmann ordered the four or five Tigers parked around the nearest Russian shack with their guns pointing in different directions. Sentries stayed with the tanks while the rest warmed themselves inside the shack. Sleep was obviously out of the question, the situation was too precarious. The night passed quietly, apart from several skirmishes involving the panzer-grenadiers, who had set up a hedgehog position around the small village. Meanwhile, we were now so short on fuel that Wittmann had the Tigers positioned at the edge of the village with their guns facing out. We were exceedingly glad when, on the afternoon of the following day, the rumor began circulating that the tanks of our neighbor unit, the 16th Panzer Division, were on their way to us with the necessary supplies. There was great joy therefore when the first Panzer IVs appeared in our village with several trucks in tow. After refuelling and rearming we continued on our way in the direction of Cherkassy."

Loading of the tanks on to transport trains began on 1 February 1944 in Monastyrishche. Three damaged Tigers could not be towed away prior to departure for the loading station and had to be blown up. This left six operational Tigers. The panzer-grenadiers began a laborious march over muddy roads into the Kishentsy-Kharkovka-Dsengelowka-Nesterovka area; only the armored elements were transported by train.

RELIEF OF THE CHERKASSY POCKET, 2–28 FEBRUARY 1944
On 5 January 1944, powerful elements of the Red Army attacked the Eighth Army's Dniepr position, which extended far to the east. The objective of the Soviet attack was to encircle and destroy the XIth and XXXXI-Ind Army Corps. Two spearheads broke through, with points of main effort at Kirovograd and to the north at Kanev. The Soviet spearheads met at Svenigorodka, thus closing the Cherkassy Pocket. Trapped inside were:

XIth Army Corps	General Stemmermann
XXXXIInd Army Corps	Generalleutnant Lieb
57th Infantry Division	Generalmajor Trowitz
72nd Infantry Division	Oberst Dr. Hohn
88th Infantry Division	Oberst Bährmann
112th Infantry Division	Oberst Fouquet
389th Infantry Division	Generalleutnant Kruse
5th SS Panzer Division Wiking	SS-Gruppenführer Gille
SS Sturmbrigade Wallonien	SS-Sturmbannführer Lippert
167th Infantry Division	
168th Infantry Division	
332nd Infantry Division	
213th security Division	

A potent force was assembled under the IIIrd Panzer Corps to free the approximately 50,000 trapped soldiers. It included the 1st Panzer Division under Generalmajor Koll, the 16th Panzer Division under Generalmajor

Back and the 198th Infantry Division under General von Hoven, as well as the 17th Panzer Division and "Panzer Regiment Bäke." These units were placed under the 1st Panzer Army commanded by General Hube.

There was an abrupt change in the weather beginning on 2 February 1944. A thaw turned the roads into bottomless deserts of slush and mud. SS-Obersturmführer Wendorff had meanwhile rejoined the panzer regiment; on his arrival the regimental adjutant, SS-Hauptsturmführer Nüske, handed him a telegram from Wittmann. Soon afterward he described the state of the company in a letter to Wittmann: "Nüske read me your telegram as soon as I arrived from the rear. I am now leading the proud 13th until you return. But to my great dismay I found it little more than a pile of junk."

Three Tigers of the Wendorff Company also arrived in Krasny on 5 February 1944. The next day the armored group launched an attack on Tinovka under the command of SS-Sturmbannführer Kuhlmann. His force consisted of two Tigers and nine Panthers carrying panzer-grenadiers of the 2nd SS Panzer-Grenadier Regiment. The eastward drive by the Leibstandarte screened the flank and rear of the IIIrd Panzer Corps in a line Kosyakovka-Tinovka. 7 February found Wendorff and his Tigers at Tinovka and Wotylewka, their front facing west. At 1500 ten Soviet tanks broke through and headed down the road south of Fedjukowka. One Tiger destroyed two enemy tanks, other German tanks knocked out five more T 34s. German reconnaissance located a strong anti-tank front south of Tinovka. Four Tigers were in action on that winter day.

The relief attack by the IIIrd Panzer Corps had to battle mud and strong enemy forces. The front before Kampfgruppe Kuhlmann was quiet on 8 February 1944 apart from probing Soviet patrols. The Tigers remained in their positions. Kampfgruppen Kuhlmann and Weidenhaupt repulsed several attacks on the 9th, in the course of which the Tigers destroyed some enemy tanks north of Tatjanowka. 10 February saw the division in the Tatjanowka-Wotylewka-Tinovka sector. The Soviets dug in in front of Repki, where theIstSS Armored Reconnaissance Battalion under SS-Sturmbannführer Knittel took up positions in the evening. The Tigers remained in the defensive front at Tatjanowka until 15 February. The great distances and poor road conditions prevented the units from being properly supplied. Panye vehicles were used to deliver fuel to the front, rations consisted mainly of tinned meat. The Tigers were short of ammunition. SS-Rottenführer Warmbrunn shot down a Soviet Il 2 with his machine-gun. The IIIrd Panzer Corps advanced further to the north and the 16th Panzer Division reached Daschukowka. From there it was twenty kilometers to the edge of the pocket.

The 12th of February brought a further honor to the Tiger Company when SS-Obersturmführer Helmut Wendorff received the Knight's Cross. Popular "Bubi" Wendorff was known as a daring, courageous platoon commander who by then had destroyed 58 tanks. Wendorff was among the most successful of the Leibstandarte tank commanders and at this time was leading the company with skill and aplomb. Helmut Max Ernst Wendorff was born on 20 October 1920 in Grauwinkel in the Schweinitz district of Saxony, the son of a farmer. He had a brother and two sisters. In 1931 his parents moved to Damme in Uckermark, where his father leased a farm. Helmut went to the middle school in Prenzlau until October 1936, after which he transferred to the National-Political Borstel in Naumberg an der Saale. He graduated in the autumn of 1939 then volunteered for the Waffen-SS.

Wendorff's training began on 6 November 1939 with the Replacement Battalion of the Leibstandarte. On November 6 he was sent to the 11th Company which, like the entire Standarte, was located in Prague at the time. Wendorff was a founding member of the Leibstandarte Assault Gun Battery, created in February 1940. There he met Michael Wittmann and Hannes Philipsen, with whom he was to see much action later in the war. In 1941 Wendorff saw combat with the Assault Gun Battery in the Balkans and in Russia, where he received the Iron Cross, Second Class and the Tank Battle Badge in Silver. On 1 November 1941 the intelligent young SS-Unterscharführer was assigned to the Junkerschule at Bad Tölz, together with Hannes Philipsen. Wendorff left the officer school as an SS-Standartenoberjunker on 20 April 1942 and rejoined the Assault Gun Battalion, where he was promoted to SS-Untersturmführer on 21 June 1942. In December he was transferred to the Tiger Company in Fallingbostel.

The move to the southeast began on 14 February 1944, destination Frankovka. The few serviceable panzers spent 15 February towing away the damaged tanks on the catastrophic roads; one Tiger, one Panther, one Panzer IV and an assault gun were involved. Strong elements of the division moved up to Schubenny Staw during the night of 16 February. SS-Sturbannführer Sanding, the commanding officer of the 2nd SS Panzer-Grenadier Regiment, was ordered to advance to Oktyabr and there create the conditions for the link-up with the surrounded elements inside the pocket.

The Soviets produced a leaflet addressed to the troops inside the pocket, which among other things said: " . . . You are spending your last days here . . . In recent days your pocket has been reduced to an infinitely tiny area. Your defeat is near! Your command has long since given up hope of a breakout on your own. With the failure of the breakout attempts you are deluding yourselves into believing that help is coming from outside.

Listen to reason: every attempt to break through to you is an absolute failure and only costs the German Armed Forces tremendous sacrifices. It is not the first time that your pocket has become a grave, both for the encircled and for the 'relief troops.' Just remember Stalingrad and Kirovograd! Don't believe that the Adolf Hitler' SS Division will save you. The Red Army is strong enough to destroy it and you . . ." Propaganda of this sort failed to impress the soldiers, they knew the Soviet lies and promises all too well.

During the night of 17 February 1944, Kampfgruppe Heimann, which included the panzers, was moved forward to Oktyabr. Sanding was on the road to Lisyanka, south of Oktyabr. Snow and severe cold hampered movement, however the drop in temperature did firm up the roads again. Knittel also reached Lisyanka with his reconnaissance battalion. Inside the pocket the units destroyed their superfluous equipment. The pocket's diameter had now shrunk to three to five kilometers. The objective of the units breaking out to the west was Reference Point 239 near Oktyabr. There were also several Tigers there. The surrounded troops began their difficult trek to the west at 2300 hours on 16 February 1944; the watchword was "freedom." One of the leading groups was the reconnaissance battalion of the Wiking Division under Obersturmführer Debus. At 0430 hours elements of the Wiking were pinned down by heavy Soviet fire in front of Hill 239. They veered east and had to cross the Gniloy Tikich. Many lost their lives in the raging torrent, the rest reached the positions of the Leibstandarte Division. On the morning of 17 February Leibstandarte tanks attacked east of Oktyabr and ran into fierce resistance from Soviet tanks and anti-tank guns. The Tigers destroyed several tanks and anti-tank guns and tied up considerable Soviet forces. Harried by the Soviets and pursued by cavalry, the first members of the Wiking Division reached the German positions in the late morning of 17 February. The commander of the Wallonien Assault Brigade, SS-Hauptsturmführer Léon Degrelle, waited in the dark with his assault group in a wood near Oktyabr. "Without food and drink we had survived since morning on nothing but a few handfuls of snow. We squeezed ourselves together as best we could in our holes in the snow, in order to keep warm. But most of all we awaited the end of this frightful day, consumed with fear. Not until after dark, when the tanks on the hill could no longer observe our movements, did we dare leave our foxholes.

We set off in strict order at half past five in the evening . . . Led by scouts, we walked two kilometers along a path that led deep into the swamp. Even there we were up to our knees in mud. None of the Red Army troops had seen us. We climbed a snow-covered slope. On the other side a stream gleamed in the moonlight; one after another we crossed over a heavy, slippery beam. We walked fifty meters farther, then there was a wild commotion. Three shadows wearing steel helmets suddenly appeared before us. After the entire burden and all the pain fell away, we hugged one another, laughed, cried, and leapt about." The following army divisions were also able to reach friendly forces and freedom, though at a cost.

SS-Untersturmführer Günther Zaag of the Ist Battalion of the 1st SS Panzer-Grenadier Regiment, which was positioned near Oktyabr, described the breakout as experienced by the relief force: "Then there was a mighty crash as something came through the roof. Clay fell into our food. 'Good thing the rockets have such sensitive fuses, or else we'd have had it,' someone said drily.

There were suspicious track noises outside and then the beast drove past. The T 34 sprayed shells all over the place without aiming properly. However, our guns had spotted him. The first shot was a hit and the monster blew up immediately afterward. Our situation was ticklish for the enemy could outflank us behind a hill; it was therefore time to move. We came under rifle fire from a long distance away as we crossed a slippery, open slope and we were able to reach our departure position without suffering any losses. The last obstacle for the surrounded to cross was a river (the Gniloy Tikich). Our attack, which struck the enemy flank, created some breathing space for those in the breakout. We were confronted with chaos, mainly totally exhausted, panicky, desperate soldiers, who no longer listened to anyone, who just wanted to escape the grim, weeks-long hell. Everyone had to cross the icy, swift-flowing stream and some drowned from exhaustion or died of heart attack or were forced under the water by wildly- flailing horses. The uniforms froze to the bodies of those soldiers who did make it across. But they had made it, and there was a trace of a smile in the emaciated faces with their ghostly, sunken, wide eyes, which still contained the images of the bestialities they had seen the Ivans commit against exhausted or wounded comrades lying in the snow. We helped our comrades with warm things as best we could."

The breakout from the Cherkassy Pocket saved the lives of 34,000 soldiers; approximately 20,000 were left behind—dead, wounded, and prisoners of war. In the final days until 20 February, the enemy attacked from the forest east of Oktyabr but was beaten back by armored counterattacks. In spite of the atrocious conditions the Tiger Company's supply vehicles managed to reach the tanks at the front, delivering supplies of food and ammunition. The actions of these men were acknowledged by everyone. SS-Sturmmann Lau said of the men of the rear-echelon units: what would have become of us without the boys of the train? Of course, names and details of the members of the train units are not as well remembered as those who took the tanks into combat. They should not be forgotten, however—the medics, the drivers and co-drivers of the munitions and fuel transport columns, the men of the maintenance echelon in their VW Kübelwagens, our comrades of the workshop platoon, especially the tank recovery unit, and last but not least the men of the field kitchens and the rations trucks. Even in the heaviest artillery fire, in the heat of summer and the cold of winter, they came to within a few hundred meters of us in the front lines. As well, I remember two Hiwis who were with us at the time of Zitadelle; together with their German driver they strayed across the Soviet lines and were killed. Two more Hiwis joined us at Cherkassy. They were part of the crew of a T 34 we knocked out. A few days later, during the relief of Cherkassy, one of them was shot by one of our 13th Company sentries as he was going to get coffee for members of the train from the Opel Blitz field kitchen truck. When challenged by the sentry he answered in Russian, and sadly that cost him his life. His companion was still working in our field kitchen in Normandy.

Always on hand were SS-Oberscharführer Sepp Hafner and SS-Sturmmann Adolf Frank. They were among the elite engine specialists. They stayed close to the panzers and could often spot trouble just from the sound of the engine. Oberscharführer Hafner was with us on one occasion in the Zhitomir area; we had been on the retreat for many kilometers. The engine was defective; one of the cylinder head seals was leaking. Hafner gathered up all the cigarette packets and used them to seal up the cylinder heads. All this took place within firing range of the Russian tanks and infantry. He received the Iron Cross, First Class for this and similar actions. In Normandy SS-Unterscharführer Adolf Frank was in charge of the 2nd Company's maintenance echelon and a very important and highly respected personality.

Another unforgettable person is SDG Adolf Schmidt. On my birthday in February 1944, during the retreat after Cherkassy, we were being towed by Obersturmführer Wendorff, who at the time was our acting company commander. It was inhumanly cold and there had been nothing to eat for days. Adolf Schmidt managed to somehow scrounge up a handful of potatoes and each member of the two crews received a hot baked potato with salt, something that could be found in every Russian house. It was a wonderful birthday present. Adolf Schmidt was seriously wounded beside our tank—under which lay Panzermeyer and his aide Ustuf. Puls—in the Laize Valley in Normandy in early August. In Normandy, as he had often done in the east, Schmidt went along as the sixth member of the Tiger's crew; he provided first-aid to many comrades and saved their lives.

I remember the leaders of the ammunition and fuel transport columns in the Zitadelle period and the winter of 1943–44, SS-Unterscharführer Mollenhauer and, from January 1944, SS-Oberscharführer Konradt. They delivered fuel and ammunition with heavy 5-tonne MAN trucks and Italian Spa vehicles. Light Opel Blitz 3-tonne trucks then drove to the front, enabling us to refuel and rearm a few hundred meters behind the main line of resistance. As a relief crew, we sometimes had to go along with the ammunition and fuel transport columns as co-drivers and as a result these men had our greatest respect.

Of course the most welcome were Unterscharführer Mohrs and Unterscharführer Jarosch of the field kitchen and the rations truck. They always brought enough food to last three to seven days, which was then usually eaten in two. The sweets went to the non-smokers and the cigarettes to the smokers. I usually had the luck to be among non-smokers and my headset box to the left of the gunner's seat was usually filled with cigarettes and other tobacco products.

I remember one episode from the period when Untersturmführer Wittmann took over the company. Spieß Habermann was in the habit of giving the combat echelon tobacco and papers for rolling their own cigarettes, while the train received cigarettes for the most part. There was said to have been a terrific blow-up between Wittmann and Spieß Habermann, and from then on the tank crews received cigarettes. For a time the ammunition and fuel echelon under Oberscharführer Konradt also brought the rations to the front and moreover they did it solicitously; this probably led to Spieß Habermann being replaced by Oberscharführer Konradt several weeks later."

On 20 February 1944 the division reported that four Tigers, four Panthers, and three Panzer IVs would have to be towed out of the Rosskoschewka-Pavlovka area as part of the planned transfer, and that the division lacked the resources to move them itself. At least one Tiger was lost in the Cherkassy relief operation. The Tiger of SS-Unterscharführer Kleber was damaged by enemy fire and subsequently had to be blown up when the German forces withdrew (Driver SS-Sturmmann Hepe, loader SS-Sturmmann Lau.) On 23 February Wendorff wrote to his friend Wittmann: "The majority of the trucks got stuck in the mud during the move into the Uman area and still lie along the road today with every kind of defect. None of the cars is running . . . But don't go growing any grey hair over your proud bunch . . . In the most recent days our small force helped extricate the men encircled west of Cherkassy. Most of them were freed, in spite of the mud. I was most pleased over the behavior of the Wiking Division, without whom the whole affair could easily have become a disaster."

A close-knit team. *From left:* SS-Panzerschütz Werner Irrgang (radio operator), SS-Rottenführer Bobby Woll (gunner), SS-Untersturmführer Michael Wittmann, SS-Panzerschütz Sepp Rößner (loader), and SS-Sturmmann Eugen Schmidt (driver). In the background is Wittmann's Tiger S04 displaying a total of 88 victory rings on the barrel of its eighty-eight.

28 January 1944. Four Tigers are involved in the fighting near Lipovets.

Rocket launchers provide supporting fire.

Weather conditions were extremely poor. In the background a Tiger with its engine access panel open.

The Tigers sink into the mud. Here S45 and behind it a vehicle of the panzer regiment headquarters.

A member of the Workshop Platoon with the Ukrainian occupants of the house in which he was billeted.

Road conditions became catastrophic in December 1943. Even tracked vehicles like the ones seen in the above photo had difficulties.

A vehicle column transports rations to the front.

Captured Soviet Stalin Organ multiple rocket launcher.

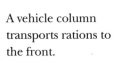

On 19 February 1944 Oak Leave's wearer Michael Wittmann returned to his birthplace of Vogelthal, where he received a warm welcome from the residents.

Michael Wittmann
in February 1944.

Michael Wittmann
in his home village of
Vogelthal in February
1944.

SS-Obersturmführer Helmut Wendorff received the Knight's Cross on 12 February 1944.

The company commander, SS-Hauptsturmführer Heinz Kling, was decorated with the Knight's Cross on 23 February 1944.

Michael Wittmann, 1935, in the 19th Infantry Regiment of the Army.

1934, Michael Wittmann
in the voluntary Labor
Service.

Michael photographed in Benediktbeuren in summer 1934 during his period
of voluntary service with the Arbeitsdienst (Labor Service). Wittmann is on the
far left.

Wittmann as a Gefreiter (3rd from left) in the 19th Infantry Regiment (Army) in Freising.

Siegfried Fuss was Wittmann's tank driver until January 1944. Here he is seen as an SS-Untersturmführer in autumn 1944.

Michael Wittmann as an SS-Unterscharführer in the 5th (Armored Scout) Company of the Leibstandarte's replacement battalion at Berlin-Lichterfelde in October 1939. Wittmann is fourth from the left, standing.

SS-Unterscharführer Alfred Günther served as gunner in Michael Wittmann's assault gun in September 1941 on the Eastern Front. In March 1943 Günther became the first member of the Leibstandarte's assault gun battalion to receive the Knight's Cross.

An assault gun of the Leibstandarte's assault gun battery, which was formed in Jüterbog in spring 1940. Wittmann was placed in command of one of the six StuG. III assault guns assigned to the battery.

Michael Wittmann and His Secret of Success

WITTMANN AND THE FÜHRER

On 2 February 1944, in Wolfsschanze Führer Headquarters, Michael Wittmann received the Knight's Cross with Oak Leaves from the hand of Adolf Hitler. The Führer had a long talk with him, asking for his impressions of the front and his assessment of the situation. Hitler promised Wittmann that the 13th Company would receive as many Tigers as it had personnel for. He also enquired about Wittmann's personal situation; he asked whether Wittmann was married and learned that a wedding was planned. In the course of his conversation with Wittmann, Hitler noticed that he was missing a front tooth. He subsequently sent him to his dentist to have the tooth replaced.

How was it possible for one man to destroy 117 tanks? Was it luck? Certainly luck played a part in it, but for the most part it was the way he led his Tiger in action—his masterful precision, his conscientious preparation for every mission, and his ability to concentrate fully. The success which Wittmann achieved in such a short time was unprecedented.

In early 1944 war correspondent Joachim Fernau, who spent some time with Wittmann, wrote: " . . . We ate together often. He, a little preoccupied, quiet and reflective, often seemingly absent-minded, but in truth always anxious and preoccupied with the coming day and with his responsibility, happy to be among men who in a quiet way were both happy and cheerful. He was seldom so himself but was usually very self-absorbed. He had been leading the Tiger Company, which was in fact a battalion, for some time then. He himself was a very young Untersturmführer. He took this burden seriously.

He sat in front of the maps all evening, he listened to every word, to all the suggestions from other experienced commanders. Then when he led the panzers against the enemy and drove at the head of the company, he possessed a certainty that easily deceived an observer into believing that it all came easily to him, a God-given talent, much in the same way that men

265

mistakenly believe that Mozart really wrote his Don Juan overture in a single night. When I sat in his tank, I had the feeling that he simply couldn't err, as if it was impossible for him to drive into a trap. But in reality this was the sum of laborious work, it was the result of the hours when Michael sat with us deep in thought, not hearing when we spoke to him, or when he crawled around the Tiger workshops at night as if he was taking a walk.

He is the example who corrects all the young hotshots who believe that they need only wait for the moment of one daring act to become a great soldier. Every hour, every minute, he was conscious of his responsibility for the lives of his men, for the valuable material under his command, and often the outcome of a battle; he acquired his great soldierly qualities and paid for his Knight's Cross with a diligence which probably went unnoticed by his superiors and a sense for the endless spade work.

In this war much has been written in praise of obstinacy. We have all experienced it, in the best sense if the long war years have brought us to it, eliminating sentimentality and alertness before the most difficult missions and acquiring the habit of waiting, with which one passes the time almost without consciousness and tension. Wittmann is exactly the opposite. Everything comes to him, which is as he desires it. To the very last second he wants to see everything, hear everything, know everything. This doesn't encumber him as perhaps it does others, instead it gives him clarity. This constant activity has sharpened his senses. He has an unfailing sense of what is going on around him in combat. He sees precisely and hears without error. To those at home this may sound somewhat simple and profane, but in hundreds of cases life depends on these qualities. I have never seen Wittmann display a fear of the dark, which is a common and natural phenomenon. Added to the sum of these qualities is something which in the final sense is decisive: no fear of death.

Hundreds of Knight's Cross winners have been written about. They were all brave, skilled, daring or performed an act that decided a battle. For some it was really just the opportunity of a single moment, for others their all-surpassing physical and spiritual ability, for the rest their inspiring leadership. Closest to us all, however, are those who rise up from the nameless masses, with just as much or as little in their hands as the others, men who acquire at the front what I like to call a 'warrior's heart,' who prepare seriously for each battle as if in prayer, who know that endless diligence and a quiet, smiling calmness are required in the face of death. Knowing this and recording it is therefore important, because we all will have forgotten the individual acts after the war, just as we have already forgotten much today. And because when we see a Knight's Cross we are no longer supposed to ask what precisely the man did to earn it, we should know only one thing:

he is one of those who became great in the most sublime and manly qualities because of the war and in the war. That is what the word hero means in the German language.

I still recall how selfless he was. He never gave a thought for himself when he jumped out of the Tiger to save a wounded man. At such times he undoubtedly possessed an unfailing ability to sense imminent danger; but in battle the word 'I' was totally absent from his vocabulary. I also recall that he loved life. While we talked he would suddenly ask why this or that book was supposed to be so good. And never did I hear him speak a frivolous word about women. I realize that this is not a statement of accounts, the 'debits and credits,' of a wearer of the Knight's Cross; rather it is a monologue about a comrade who was the same even without the Knight's Cross."

WITTMANN AND HIS SECRET OF SUCCESS

Siegfried Fuss, Wittmann's driver through the months of 1943 up to January 1944, described the tank missions in which he participated during his one year association with Michael Wittmann: "There was basically nothing special about it, only that Wittmann and Woll were outstanding experts in their field. There was never a hint of arrogance in spite of their extraordinary success. In every combat situation extreme concentration reigned in the tank and the enemy was never underestimated, even when large numbers of tanks were destroyed.

Our relationship was altogether the best, and Wittmann's skill and his ability to pass this on to others made for ideal coordination. Wittmann's target information was always extremely quick, calm, and concise; Woll put it to use just as quickly and often fired even quicker. We all often asked ourselves—afterwards—how it could all happen so quickly. Our vehicle's success lay in the independence of each individual; that meant that I, as driver, was sometimes jointly responsible for target identification and designation—as was radio operator Karl Lieber—because sometimes multiple targets appeared, especially during combat in villages. For example, the cannon might be turned to the two o'clock position, while the next target was at eleven o'clock; in such a case the entire tank had to be turned in order to place the cannon in the eleven o'clock position, as the turret traverse was incapable of doing so in time.

Here is an example from the 'post-Kharkov battles,' as we always referred to them: an attack against a large town guarded strongly by tanks and anti-tank guns. We cleared the way rather quickly by destroying several tanks and anti-tank guns and reached the town. Our targets were all to the right of our direction of travel, from our twelve to approximately three o'clock positions. Suddenly, to our left, behind a haystack, we sighted a

Josef Stalin I with its gun trained on us. Wittmann: 'Turn left, target one hundred meters, go!' And that was it. This and similar actions resulted in the destruction of fifteen enemy tanks that day, because Wittmann maneuvered the Tiger based on his experience in assault guns. This called for extreme caution with the Tiger, however, because of the great danger of shedding a track while turning in place. This was accomplished by one track turning forward and the other in reverse. The tracks turning in opposite directions caused soil to accumulate under the idler wheels and the tracks snapped. Situations such as this often resulted in the tank being abandoned or destroyed.

The gunner often fired without target designation, for as Wittmann frequently put it, there was no time for a conversation, and Bobby Woll acquired the target just as quickly as the commander or we two in the hull, the driver and radio operator.

Wittmann was no friend of the conventional tank battle; he had seen too many losses while serving in assault guns. He often discussed his tactical concepts with us; Wittmann favored stealth over huge battles and was ultimately vindicated by his success. Thirty-five of the fifty-five successful engagements I participated in with him were not open-field kills but the result of outflanking the enemy and then waiting, followed by a sudden approach. Our conversations revealed him to be a strong advocate of the radio-controlled tank developed by Borgward of Bremen and the explosives carrier likewise developed by Borgward and built by Zünndapp. Wittmann predicted that they would achieve the maximum possible success with a minimum of human casualties. He probably also had the right idea where the massed employment of tanks was concerned, namely that there were also good, large-scale methods of engaging large targets.

The scissors telescope was a standard item of our combat kit, for we destroyed more than a few targets at 3,000 meters, even moving targets using high-explosive shells with delayed-action fuses. This was not a special tactic on Wittmann's part, it was instead a means of conserving armor-piercing ammunition. Firing from 3,000 meters was more in keeping with conventional 88 mm artillery, but the KwK version was also capable of it.

During officer training courses in Fallingbostel and Braunschweig, instructors sometimes made light of Bobby Woll's method of setting his sight at 800 meters and leaving it there. The arguments by the experts there belied the method; obviously experts like Woll did not follow standard practice.

Michel Wittmann said: 'A hunter tracking wild game doesn't reset the sights of his rifle for every range or he'd have nothing to shoot at. The game is gone if preparations to fire take too long.' Wittmann and Woll were past masters of the very simple rules of conventional hunting and shooting: allow lead, aim high, aim low. There were few who could emulate them, except sometimes Heinz Buchner—he was another sly dog! As for Wittmann's qualities: they were all positive, I never saw any negative ones. He was a very normal, reserved, extremely correct, and always proper-thinking superior, and he had the ability to pass on his expertise to the tank men and help them master it. He was extremely knowledgeable in every area of the tank field, there was no one who could hold a candle to him when it came to general technique and practice. This was the guarantee of his success, because he was completely knowledgeable."

In subsequent reports Joachim Fernau wrote the following about Wittmann:

The Black Corps: Michel Wittmann

Born in Vogelthal, not far from Beilngries (Bayreuth District), and a resident of Ingolstadt, Untersturmführer Michel Wittmann, 29 years old, is one of the 'old men' of the Leibstandarte SS Adolf Hitler. The young farmer joined the Waffen-SS in 1937 and served at Berlin-Lichterfelde as an infantry instructor. But in 1940, when the Leibstandarte was given its first six assault guns, Wittmann devoted himself to the armored forces. After a brief action in Greece these assault guns, one of which Wittmann commanded, rolled into the vastness of the east. At the very start of the eastern campaign he engaged a group of 18 enemy tanks. When the assault gun had destroyed six Soviet tanks the enemy fled. The victor was decorated with the Iron Cross, Second Class and soon afterward the Iron Cross, First Class. Twice he returned home wounded. Then he took part in an officer training course at the SS-Junkerschule Bad Tölz. In early 1943 he stood in the turret of a Tiger for the first time. He destroyed eight enemy tanks and seven anti-aircraft guns on the first day of the summer battle near Belgorod. Five days later the list of his success read: 30 T 34s, 28 anti-tank guns and two batteries of Soviet artillery destroyed. On the Kiev highway he disposed of 13 T 34s and seven heavy anti-tank guns in a single day. On 6 December a heavy anti-tank front collapsed under his fire and he destroyed three Soviet tanks as well. Three Tigers which he led against an enemy tank assembly area on 9 January suddenly found themselves facing 20 Soviet tanks. Wittmann single-handedly disposed of six of the enemy. Two days later he raised his total of enemy tanks destroyed to 66. In recognition of his courageous personal action the Führer awarded him the Knight's Cross of the Iron Cross.

How strange it is. I see him quite clearly before me, I remember the hours we spent together, I know how it all was, how it happened and how he himself is. It all seems to stand quite clearly before me. But suddenly one notices that already he can't answer the first question. Suddenly one no longer knows how old he is, where he comes from, what he is, what sort of people his parents are, whether he has brothers and sisters; one has forgotten everything. On a long rail journey with the company from the central Eastern Front to Italy he spent an entire evening describing his quite adventurous experiences during the Battle of Mariupol. Hazardous Mariupol is no more than a silhouette in the memory, no more than a sum. I know that he commanded an assault gun, that he was with Tanzer-Meyer', that Wittmann became lost alone, that he dodged back and forth after encountering superior numbers of the enemy, that those were frightful hours in which everything stood on its head. I know nothing from the time of the French Campaign, though we very often spoke of it, of the battles, the country, of Paris. A few weeks ago I found a photo of him in the archive from that time. An Unterscharführer, he is standing with several comrades who have since been killed.

It is perhaps good that these things are not so clear any more. For then one must recall what actually first makes up the man, a few conversations, a sit together, an act that one has witnessed, things that one has observed and which can soonest answer the question: what sort of men are these and what happens inside them that the war should suddenly raise them up so far from the mass of others; that something inexplicable to the great mass has enabled them to perform acts for which they receive the Knight's Cross?

We sat together often. He a little withdrawn, quiet and reflective, often seeming absent-minded, in truth always concerned and busy with the next day and with his responsibility among men, who in a quiet way were at the same time happy and cheerful. He himself was seldom that way, usually very inwardly directed. By then he had been leading the Tiger company, actually a battalion, for a long time. He had only recently become an Untersturmführer but he took the responsibility seriously. He sat in front of the maps all evening long, he listened to every word, every piece of advice from other experienced commanders. Then when he climbed into his tank and set out against the enemy at the head of his company, he possessed the certainty, which was so deceptive, which looked as if it were done just like that, like a natural gift; it is the same way men are mistaken if they believe that Mozart really wrote his Don Juan Overture in a single night. When I sat in his tank I had the impression that there was nothing that could trick him, as if it were impossible for him to fall into a trap in the field. But in reality that was the sum of his hard work, it was the result of hours when Michel seemed oblivious when someone spoke to him as we sat together in the evening, or when he roamed among the Tigers in the workshops as if he were taking a walk.

He is the example who gives lie to all the young daredevils who believe that they need only wait for the one moment of a daring act to become a great soldier. Always foremost in his mind was his responsibility for human life, for expensive material and often for the outcome of a battle, and with a diligence and sense for the endless detail work that probably went unnoticed by the master, he acquired the great soldierly qualities and thus paid for his Knight's Cross.

In this war much has been written in praise of stubbornness. We have all seen, in the best sense, if the long war years have brought us to it, sensitivity and alertness eliminated before a major action and have become used to waiting, when one passes the time almost without consciousness or nervous tension. Wittmann is exactly the opposite. Everything came to him and was supposed to come to him. To the last second he wanted to see everything, hear every-thing, know everything. Unlike others, perhaps, it did not burden him, instead it produced clarity. This constant activity sharpened his senses. He had an unfailing feeling for what was going around him in battle. He saw and heard precisely, without erring. That may sound simple and profane to those at home, but his life depended on these qualities a hundred times. I have also never seen Michel Wittmann exhibit fear of the dark, which is common and actually quite natural.

Added to this sum is one more thing, which in the final sense is decisive: overcoming the fear of death.

Hundreds of Knight's Cross wearers have already been written about. They were all courageous, daring, reckless or decided a bat-tle with an act. For some it really was perhaps only the opportunity and the recklessness of a single moment, for others all-surpassing physical and mental ability, for yet others the inspiring leadership

Michael Wittmann.

of men. The men that are closest to us, however, are those who like us come from the nameless masses, have as little or as much in their hands as the others, and who acquired at the front what I like to call a 'warrior's heart,' who always prepare themselves for a battle with the utmost seriousness as if in a prayer, who know that an unending diligence and a quiet, smiling composure is needed in the face of death.

To know this and to remember it is therefore important, because after the war we will all have forgotten the individual acts, just as much has already escaped our memory today. And because we should no longer ask the details of what a man has done when we see the Knight's Cross but just know that: here is one of those who became great in the most exalted and manliest qualities through the war and in the war. That is what the word hero means in the German language.

I still remember how selfless he was. He never gave a thought to himself when he jumped out of the Tiger in order to save a wounded man. In doing so he very likely had an infallible sense of deadly danger, but in battle the word 'I' was completely absent from his vocabulary.

I also remember that he loved life. Sometimes he would ask out of the blue why this or that book was supposed to be so good. And I never heard him speak a frivolous word about women.

I have taken care that this has not become a statement of accounts of a Knight's Cross wearer based on 'debits and credits,' rather a monologue about a comrade who was the same even without the Knight's Cross.

The Black Corps: 117 Tanks—A Changed Life

Untersturmführer of the Waffen-SS Wittmann has destroyed his 117th tank. How is it that such a report scarcely draws the usual expressions of admiration? The feat is extraordinary, astonishing, but the expression of astonishment is restrained. One suddenly feels himself transferred into an unfamiliar zone, in which very dangerous energies suspend all previous assessments of bravery. One senses the need to deal with a new type of soldier, one who, like a cool and matter-of-fact technician, becomes the master of iron and fire.

There is no place for the romantic ideal of the hero in this mind. It probably still applies to the outstanding soldier who chooses to make the battlefield, on which all do their duty, the showplace of his great feat. His fearlessness, the only possible condition of victory, triumphs there at the boundary between destruction and victory. But this more or less intuitive ability, to draw the arc which leads from the jump-off point to the point of success, is removed from the mechanics of war, is even in opposition to them, and between departure and arrival the man of action appears to us in the illuminating light of the exceptional; the greatness of the decision enters our consciousness like a flash. We also watch with greatest human interest the emotions of such warriors, we animate the rigid strain, which wants to hide the excitement from us, with the feelings that they had or should have had, because our fantasy is sufficient to emulate the type of conscious effort that precedes success.

The extraordinary steps before us, and the admiration to which it compels us applies above all to the fact that the limits of human strength appear elastic, that the man, even if only for a moment, can through enormous concentration of all the senses dart forward to horizons of our consciousness, which normally appear to us to be sunk in the twilight of distant dreams. We reach them sometime, even if with a few selected representatives of our race, and so as these break the force of gravity, propelled by the lightning of a special inspiration, they remain examples worthy of astonishment of what a man is capable of.

Associated with the exceptional and extraordinary is the further notion that there is, purely from the point of view of time, also a limit of exhaustion during the utmost concentration of mental and physical forces, before which point the decisive must take place. Decision, courage, circumstances and time are like interacting gear wheels of the event, thus a daring operation appears as a unified whole. The highest degree of strain must collapse with success; if the character steps back from this peak of concentration, he takes victory or defeat with him. It seems impossible to us that he should immediately take on a similar stress in order to turn the success into an even greater one, to surpass and crown it, just as impossible as the immediate repetition of the proceedings if the result was defeat. We comprehend the necessity of rest, into which the character retires after very great strain, release of stress is necessary, mentally as well as physically, our abilities do not allow us to set rules for the extraordinary.

But a phenomenon such as that of SS-Untersturmführer Wittmann invites reflection as to whether he, who seems to surpass all the normal rules in achieving his military feats, owes his success to a chain of coincidences, or whether we must wake up to a new concept of the essence of bravery and victory in our century. Let us not forget what is involved. Destroying 117 enemy tanks is very much more than 117 encounters with the harsh reality of war, which demands just as many confrontations with its ultimate consequence, death. A psychology which is based on the sound nerves of a young farmer could only lead to an incomprehensible and disparaging devaluation. Since he had nerves, possessed a healthy, unspent life force, the effects of the horror that swirled up in every combat were less noticeable: that would ultimately be the literary consequence of a way of thinking which in the end would bestow a kind of high bravery on the broken and nerveless men who led an operation to the end with success and distinction.

The calm and confidence of a heart that nourishes itself from the sheltered regions of youth and inexhaustibly mobilizes the strength of existence and stability against the danger posed by the war, is undoubtedly a protection which surrounds his life like a suit of armor and gives good aim to his decisions.

He may also spend much time with young people to achieve that light-heartedness, which laughing dares and thus guarantees

an invincibility that enables him to break through that fiery zone
of the war. Even after the twentieth and thirtieth tank one can
speak of that unthreatened substantial force, for which the thirtieth knocked-out is proof of its unbrokenness.

But the fiftieth and sixtieth tanks, which like those before them
were not destroyed on a firing range, which appeared as mobile,
well-armed instruments in the firing zone of one's own circling
and firing tanks, guided by the enemy's desire to destroy, equal in
the dynamic will to get in the first fiery death blow, each of those
tanks right up to the 117th brought with it the memories of those
destroyed before it. Perhaps Wittmann met the 117th tank with
greater outward composure than the first, he might note the latest
kill total with greater equanimity. One thing has become apparent
with the 117th tank: the intensity with which a man like Wittmann
deals with the will to his own destruction and himself becomes the
destroyer, is different than that of the brief upswing, the sharp
concentration of a unique objective, is a talent of the mastery of
technical life, for which a heavy price was paid.

The appearance of such men, into whose small, select circle we
see Wittmann enter, is revealing to those who know how to read
the fine, almost hidden scars which mark their faces. If they were
supermen, meaning the result of mutations, beings placed in our
midst by a caprice of nature with gifts not given to us, their feats
would no longer appear amazing, for the abilities and facilities
given them, the switching on and off of organs with which the
normal man overcomes the danger zone, would offer an explanation for the astonishing.

But they are men of the same nature, enjoying the same passions as we, their decisions are inspired by the same driving forces
that determine ours. What distinguishes them and raises them up
above the others is not so much the sum of their feats and the success measured in numbers—although given the difficulty of comprehending the actual conditions of their success, a number, a
materially graspable size, must appear on the test-bench of their
life for us to understand; it is much more revealing to learn of the
ability that allows them to endure over such long periods.

We know of a report on the fallen flier Marseille, who wore the
Knight's Cross of the Iron Cross with Diamonds, Germany's highest decoration for bravery. The Berliner describes his face, whose
shining strength strangely seized him before it practically froze and
directed itself with intense concentration on the instrument panel

of his machine, how all his senses felt their way forward, listening, to the engine of the machine, which literally seemed to result in a union with the technical instrument. Writers described Marseille's intuitive security in air combat. A technical body surrounded the man, all the elements of the machine seemed to glow from the will of the man who controlled them. Marseille drove to the center of the highest necessity and thus to the decision with uncanny sureness, but which was the sign of highest intensity, a complete oneness with the technical creations that surrounded him. Reporters describe how he climbed out of the cockpit after an air battle, his face deathly pale, grimacing, beads of sweat on his forehead.

This was repeated ten, twenty, a hundred times and more—an ongoing divesting of human emotions, a difficult return to the areas of normal human life, an imperceptibly growing foreignness to formerly loved and trusted things. Then, finally, life only seems to be complete and to have success if the fusion with the technical conditions for success remains unbroken.

That the development of this new sense of life, a sense for highly intensive life fulfillment, is only possible on the foundation of extremely painful confrontations, is not just proved by Marseille's example. The face of the man who lives in a series of great triumphs provides an insight. When we say triumphs, it is not the acknowledgement of human fame which offers itself with this word. The triumph to think of here belongs in the ranks of the great human victories from which a new world is born. Its birth is prepared in men like Wittmann and his kind. This triumph is enjoyed and honored silently; it has no possible relationship to our common conceptions.

It can be felt sprouting everywhere, and where it appears it is marked by a strange coolness, indeed even a distance from the concepts we still hold of bravery. Perhaps we can call it the total identification of the man with his mission. We have examples of this among armaments workers, among engineers, among chemists. They appear to us at first as an obsession and we approach them with a shiver as if they were something supernatural. In reality what is taking place is the most difficult opening battles for mastery of the reality of our new century, and in this respect men like Wittmann are models of a way of life in which each of us will be put to the acid test.

Many painful confrontations with ways of life that were formerly a part of us, which were once the expression of our determination to live, cannot be avoided. We will sometimes 'be lifted exhausted from our seats, our faces deathly pale, grimacing, beads of sweat on our foreheads.' We will turn to books and with bitterness ascertain that the old trusted comrades have nothing more to say to us. We will hear a phrase and fall silent. But then in our silence the sparks will flare up, which seize every element of our being and transform into feats of arms, in which men like Wittmann stand before us in their quiet, courageous determination.

"One Can Do No More Than His Duty!"

Oak Leaves wearer Michael Wittmann honored in his hometown of Vogelthal Beilngries. Situated on the southern boundary of the Beilngries District Office, the small Village of Vogelthal, with its approximately 140 inhabitants, recently held a day of honor for a local hero, the like of which has never been seen in human memory. Recently promoted Oak Leaves wearer SS-Obersturmführer Michael Wittmann, whose feats of arms have made the name of this modest municipality known beyond the district and province, returned to his home, which prepared for him a warm welcome. It was here, where Wittmann grew up in difficult rural conditions and where he spent his youth, that the foundations of his manly character were laid.

When the Oak Leaves wearer was picked up by representatives of the party (Kreisleiter Reinhardt Neumarkt), of the state (District Administrator Dr. Burger) and the Armed Forces, and was taken to a party in the village inn, the entire village and friends from the surrounding area were already there waiting to greet the

Wittmann and his crew.

courageous son of the municipality with shouts of heil. The series of speeches, in which the Oak Leaves wearer was congratulated on his high decoration, was begun by District Organisation leader Haas, who reverently recalled the fallen Knight's Cross wearer Mosandl von Uschbuch.

Then the mayor of the town, Bg. Wittmann—also an uncle of the hero—spoke and to the applause of the crowd presented him with a document making him an honorary citizen of Vogelthal. In his speech District Administrator Burger suggested that the name of Oak Leaves wearer

Wittmann would go down in the history of the municipality, would be an example to the residents there and to his fellow soldiers, and a role model to our youth, for whose future this terrible struggle was being waged.

As an outward sign of respect the district administrator presented Obersturmführer Wittmann with the ten-volume work "Military History." After a representative of the Armed Forces passed on the congratulations of the senior officer at the base in Neumarkt, the top official of the Neumarkt District and Beilngries-Riedenburg Kreisleiter Neidhardt spoke. He presented congratulations and a memorial gift from the Gauleiter, Fritz Wächtler, and expressed his joy that Oak Leaves wearer Wittmann was one of their own, whose offensive spirit and aggressiveness embodied the best of German soldiery. He said that it is heart that decides battles, and it takes the heart of a warrior to tackle a superior enemy force in a tank, gain the upper hand and defeat him.

The homeland appreciates the courageous actions of our brave panzer men and by doing its duty, especially in the armaments facilities, seeks to prove itself worthy to the front and to provide it with everything needed to achieve the final victory. That victory will be ours there can be no doubt. And when the Oak Leaves wearer is honored wherever he goes while on leave, it is a demonstration of the homeland's love for him. An expression of this love was the presentation to Wittmann by the Kreisleiter of an oil painting by our local artist Lindl, a gift which brought an expression of joy.

Oak Leaves wearer Wittmann expressed his thanks for the honor showed him in the terse words of a soldier and the simple language of the Upper Pfalz. "One can do no more than his duty," said the brave soldier and then continued: "One doesn't think of the danger in combat, one seeks to engage and destroy the enemy and really feels joy when this is accomplished. The German soldier experiences not just hard and difficult hours, but also the finest in his life through the close comradeship that binds everyone out there." In his subsequent remarks SS-Obersturmführer Wittmann spoke out against the murderous terror of the Anglo-American air gangsters, who have carried the war with all its horror into the German homeland, without, however, being able to weaken the German ability to resist. His comrades at the front are firmly convinced that all is in order at home and that someday, with firm faith in the Führer, we will celebrate the most glorious victory in German history.

Then the official part of the social evening ended with the Führer salute and the national anthem. 'The following hours of socializing were filled with singing and dancing, with the choir of the Beilngries BDM base under the direction of its leader Lusta Müller playing an especially prominent role. Oak Leaves wearer Wittmann was constantly surrounded by youths seeking his autograph and never tiring of hearing about his exploits. Everyone who had close contact with the brave Oak Leaves wearer and tremendous man Wittmann this evening wish him all soldier's luck in the future and a victorious return home.

Wilhelm Pfaffer

The Danube Messenger

Oak Leaves winner Wittmann lives here. We have learned: Wearer of the Knight's Cross of the Iron Cross with Oak Leaves and most successful Tiger tank commander of the German Armed Forces, SS-Ustf. Michael Wittmann, was born on 22/4/1914 in Vogelthal, B.A. Beilngries, the son of farmer Johann Wittmann. Wittmann is now a resident here, at Casellastraße 34, and worked as a milling machine operator. In 1936 and 1937 SS-Ustf. Wittmann was an active SS-Mann with the local SS-Sturm. Then on 1/4/1937 he joined the SS-Leibstandarte Adolf Hitler in Berlin-Lichterfelde.— To Oak Leaves wearer Wittmann a very happy homecoming and an enjoyable leave.

Oak Leaves Wearer SS-Obersturmführer Wittmann in Ingolstadt

Oak Leaves wearer SS-Obersturmführer Wittmann, who is a native of Ingolstadt and who worked here, has arrived here on leave. We have already reported on the awarding of his high decorations by the Führer.

The day before yesterday SS-Obersturmführer Wittmann was welcomed by the Kreisleiter, Oberbereichsleiter Pg. Sponsel, in the name of the party. The Kreisleiter wished him an excellent rest during his leave. A reception by the city was held yesterday in the town hall, at which the Oberbürgermeister Dr. Listl presented the Oak Leaves wearer a gift with best wishes.

Roll of Honor: Ingolstadt's Knight's Cross Wearer: 88 Tanks Destroyed—An SS-Untersturmführer Decorated

Ingolstadt, 19 January. It is reported from Berlin: On 14 January 1944, SS-Untersturmführer Mich. Wittmann, a platoon commander in a panzer regiment of the SS Panzer Division Leibstandarte SS "Adolf Hitler" from Ingolstadt a.D., who was named in the Wehrmacht communique on 13 January 1944, was decorated with the Knight's Cross by the Führer in recognition of his outstanding performance.

In the period from July 1943 until the beginning of January 1944 Wittmann and his Tiger tank destroyed 58 enemy tanks, including Soviet T 34 and super-heavy assault guns as well as English and American tanks. On 8 and 9 January 1944 he and his platoon were able to halt a foray by a Soviet tank brigade, smashing the latter, in the course of which he knocked out another ten tanks. In the fighting of 13 January Wittmann engaged a strong armored force and from it knocked out 19 T 34s and three assault guns. Wittmann thus raised his personal number of victories to 88 enemy tanks and assault guns. This tremendous feat is attributable to his aggressive spirit and zeal and to the outstanding effectiveness of the German Tiger tank.

Wittmann was born on 22 April 1914 in Vogelthal (Upper Pfalz).

Oak Leaves for SS-Untersturmführer Wittmann: A Son of the Bayreuth District destroys 117 tanks within 7 months

On 30 January SS-Untersturmführer Michael Wittmann, company commander in a panzer regiment of the SS Panzer Division "Leibstandarte SS Adolf Hitler," who received the Knight's Cross on 14 January 1944 after being named in the Wehrmacht communique, became the 380th soldier of the German Armed Forces to be

Wittmann.

awarded the Knight's Cross of the Iron Cross with Oak Leaves, receiving the decoration from the hand of the Führer.

With his Tiger tank Wittmann destroyed 117 tanks in a very short time during the large-scale offensive and defensive battles in the southern sector of Eastern Front. This outstanding feat is attributable to his daring offensive impetus, his aggressiveness and the skillful tactical employment of his proven battle tank. Wittmann began his record-setting series of tank kills in July 1943. He achieved 56 kills by the beginning of January and in the course of a few weeks, during which he was continually engaged in heavy fighting, raised this figure to 117.

Michael Wittmann was born on 22 April 1914 in Vogelthal, near Beilngries (Upper Pfalz), the son of a farmer and factory worker. After attending school and then working for a time as a farmer, in April 1937 he joined the Leibstandarte. He very soon joined the Armed Forces, served with the 1st Armored Scout Company and following the Balkans Campaign went into the war in the east as an Unterscharführer and commander of an assault gun. Wittmann was twice wounded in the east. After taking part in an officer training course at the SS school in Bad Tölz, on 21 December 1942 he received his promotion to SS-Untersturmführer. Since the beginning of 1943 he has taken part in all the heavy offensive and defensive battles at all the hot spots of the Eastern Front, first as the commander of a tiger and then commander of a Tiger company.

After the awarding of the Oak Leaves, Wittmann began his leave and drove to Ebstorf, near Lüneburg, the home of his future wife, Hildegard Burmester. Together they travelled to Ingolstadt, where Wittmann had lived before joining the Leibstandarte, and visited his father. On 17 February 1944 the city of Ingolstadt, which was represented by the Lord Mayor, Doctor Listl, held a reception for Wittmann in the town hall. He received a gift from the city and his name was entered in the Golden Book of Ingolstadt. Wittmann's entry read: "Wearer of the Oak Leaves (30/1/1944) SS-Obersturmführer Michael Wittmann from Ingolstadt visits his home town. 17/2/44. Signed Michael Wittmann, SS-Obersturmführer."

On 19 February 1944, he drove to his birthplace, Vogelthal, where they were understandably proud to see the municipality's best-known son again. He was picked up at his parent's house and taken through the snow-covered valley to the village gasthaus. Wittmann was there at the invitation of the municipality, which had prepared a triumphal reception, the like of which was never seen before or after. More people attended the reception than the village had residents. Michael Wittmann spoke of his experiences on the Eastern Front, and the engaging modesty with which the Oak Leaves wearer spoke to his listeners captivated everyone. His declaration that, "one can do no more than his duty," met with general approval, for that was how Wittmann saw his mission as a soldier.

SS-Obersturmführer
Wendorff.

For the small village the presence of its most famous son was—as the regional newspaper described the event—a "great day, the like of which has not been recorded in the history of the village in living memory." This assessment reflected the opinion of all the participants. Wittmann, who was accompanied by his future bride Hilde, received numerous honors and gifts, and the village where he was born named him an honorary citizen. Subsequently there was a communal supper for everyone, which in the fifth year of the war was naturally very welcome. Long afterward young and old gathered round the successful tank commander to hear about his experiences in the east. Wittmann was forced to describe his tank duels again and again. The rest of his leave he spent in Ebstorf. The citizens of the small village of Wemmetsweiler in the Saarland also gave their local hero—Knight's Cross wearer Balthasar Woll—a warm welcome.

Proskurov and Ternopol: The Company in Action under Wendorff, 29 February–9 April, 1944

But now back to the desert of snow of the Soviet Union. The units of the Leibstandarte were engaged in a defensive role until 28 February 1944. On 23 February, SS-Hauptsturmführer Heinz Kling, who had not been with the company for some time, was awarded the Knight's Cross. The recommendation—the second—met with some difficulty; the justification described no independent decisions or outstanding successes by Kling. Nevertheless, the award recommendation was accepted on account of the outstanding overall success of the Tiger Company while under his command.

The Tiger Company had produced five winners of the Knight's Cross and one of the Oak Leaves—SS-Unterscharführer Staudegger, SS-Untersturmführer Wittmann, SS-Rottenführer Woll, SS-Untersturmführer Wendorff and SS Hauptsturmführer Kling. It was thus not only the most successful panzer company of the Leibstandarte, but of the entire Waffen-SS as well. Kling had also received the German Cross in Gold. The 13th Company was unique in the Wehrmacht where high decorations within a single company were concerned.

On 22 February 1944 SS-Obersturmführer took his company to Schubenyj in the role of a reserve; four Tigers had to be towed there. Entraining of the Tigers and the tracked elements of the division began in Talnoye on 28 February; once again the wheeled elements had to go by road. Approximately fifty NCOs and men of the Tiger Company were able to go on leave after months of constant action. When their recovery period was over they did not return to the 13th Company, however; instead they were transferred to the 101st SS Panzer Battalion.

Led by the Leibstandarte's Ia (1st General Staff Officer), SS-Obersturmbannführer Lehmann, the division arrived in its new area, Proskurov, between 29 February and 2 March 1944. For the bulk of the

Tiger Company's personnel, however, the end came somewhat sooner. All crews without tanks were routed to Debica via Leibstandarte advance message centers. There approximately thirty men boarded trains and headed west; in the second week of March they arrived in Mons, Belgium, site of the formation of the 101st SS Panzer Battalion.

To this group belonged SS-Oberscharführer Lötzsch and Behrens, SS-Unterscharführer Cap, and SS-Sturmmänner Gaube, Lau, Kammer and Hepe. The group was led by the Senior NCO, SS-Oberscharführer Konradt. The bulk of the NCOs and men still with the company loaded their material aboard trains in Christinovka in the first days of March and soon after began the rail journey to the west. Once again they had left the Eastern Front alive. However, one small group from the company under the command of Obersturmführer Wendorff remained in action. There is little information available concerning this remnant group's actions, which lasted more than a month. Ten new Tigers were delivered to the company on 5 March 1944, fallout from Wittmann's discussion with the Führer. Veteran gunners, men like SS-Rottenführer Warmbrunn and Aumann, but also serving NCOs, were made Tiger commanders, as were SS-Oberscharführer Karl Müller and SS-Unterscharführer Kleber, Seifert and Wilhelmi. For them and the entire Leibstandarte the weeks that followed were a sequence of attacks and counterattacks which decimated the units. Nineteen-year-old SS-Rottenführer Bobby Warmbrunn was especially successful in the fighting in this period.

His diary notes give an approximate idea of the company's role at that time: "6 March: entrained—9 March: detrained Proskurov—10 March: highway cleared." On 10 March 1944 Warmbrunn destroyed an anti-tank gun, on 12 March he was placed under the command of the Leibstandarte's reconnaissance battalion: "14 March: attack made with engine hatches open. One tank and four anti-tank guns knocked out (two 76.2 mm and two 50 mm anti-tank guns)."

On the following day Warmbrunn received chocolate for his crew from Obersturmführer Wendorff. The Tigers were able to break out of the pocket on 18 March 1944; Warmbrunn destroyed two T 34s, one 150 mm gun and two anti-tank guns.

On 21 March Warmbrunn destroyed a 92 mm anti-tank/anti-aircraft gun. He noted: "24 March: Broke out of the second pocket. One 76.2 mm anti-tank gun destroyed. Cut off, airdrop of supplies. Heavy Russian attacks from all sides.—28 March: Division pushed through Russians under sustained fire. Snowstorm, broken track, engine fire. Four hours spent in repairs. Another 39 kilometers through the pocket.—6 April: Broken track.—7 April: At the Seret. Took eleven hits, two 76.2 mm anti-tank guns destroyed. Concealed anti-tank guns, thus the large number of hits. Makeshift repairs of damage caused by hits. The track links hung around the tank prevented and limited serious damage."

On 6 April 1944 the decimated remnants of the Leibstandarte reached Ulaszkowcze on the Seret. In spite of fierce resistance by the enemy, the IInd SS Panzer Corps (the Hohenstaufen and Frundsberg Divisions), which had set out to relieve the pocket, was able to link up with the spearheads of the First Panzer Army attacking west. The next day several divisions crossed the Seret through the bridgeheads held by the Leibstandarte. The Leibstandarte rear guards followed them across the river by 9 April 1944. That day Warmbrunn destroyed two 92 mm anti-tank guns. During the fighting in the pocket Warmbrunn knocked out eight enemy tanks.

The Tiger Company, too, had suffered losses. Tank commander SS-Unterscharführer Hans Rosenberger had been missing since March. His last report came from Skalat. While the division moved to Lvov (Lemberg) after the breakout from the Hube Pocket, the rest of the Tiger Company entrained for transport to Belgium. A single commander, SS-Rottenführer Warmbrunn, took his Tiger to the 10th SS Division Frundsberg, where he was supposed to train a new crew.

On 16 April 1944 Warmbrunn and elements of the Frundsberg Division, which also included Tigers of the 506th (Army) Panzer Battalion, supported an attack east and west of Strypa, which crushed the Soviet bridgehead at Bobulince. Warmbrunn destroyed a T 34 and a Sherman. The latter was his 51st tank kill. SS-Oberscharführer Georg Konradt, SS-Oberscharführer Karl Müller, SS-Unterscharführer Kurt Kleber, Hans Seifert, Hans Rosenberger, Joachim Wilhelmi, and Ernst Wohlleben, SS-Rottenführer Willy Wils and Werner Licht, SS-Sturmmänner Paul Bender, Friedhelm (Fred) Zimmermann, Fritz Höneise, Max Gaube, Hermann Grosse, and Christel Diemens, and SS-Panzerschützen Kurt Kämmer and Johannes Kotzold were awarded the Iron Cross, Second Class on 3 June 1944 in recognition of their efforts in the most recent battles on the Eastern Front.

The 101st SS Panzer Battalion

THE FORMATION OF THE 101ST SS PANZER BATTALION OF THE IST SS PANZER CORPS LEIBSTANDARTE SS ADOLF HITLER, 19 JULY, 1943–5 JUNE, 1944

In Germany an increased effort to exploit to the utmost every possibility in the fields of economics and armaments began—in general much too late— as an after-effect of the German defeat at Stalingrad on 2 February 1943. These and other measures involved in "total war" should have been implemented in a concentrated way much sooner, in order to expand the armaments industry to the extent necessary to meet the demands of the expanded war. In 1943 German forces were manning huge fronts, from the Finnish Northern Front, to the occupied nations—France, Italy and the Scandinavian Countries—, the Soviet Union, and Crete to Africa.

As was the case with the army and the other elements of the German Armed Forces, the Waffen-SS also formed numerous new units in the fourth year of the war, 1943. The Leibstandarte was to be joined by a new division whose corps of enlisted men was to consist exclusively of volunteers from the Hitler Youth and whose NCOs and officers were—if possible—to also be former members of the Hitler Youth organization. Formation of this unique division was discussed at the Führer Headquarters as early as February 1943.

The new division, which was given the name Hitlerjugend, and the battle-tested Leibstandarte were to form a panzer corps: the Ist SS Panzer Corps Leibstandarte SS Adolf Hitler.

Following on the heels of a Führer Order, on 24 June 1943 the SS-Führungshauptamt (Operational Headquarters) issued the initial organization order for the SS Panzer-Grenadier Division Hitlerjugend. During the formation process the division was organized and equipped as a panzer division. On 27 July 1943 the SS-Führungshauptamt ordered the formation of the corps units for Headquarters, Ist SS Panzer Corps Leibstandarte SS Adolf Hitler. SS-Obergruppenführer and Panzer General der Waffen-SS Sepp Dietrich was named corps commanding general. Prior to this Dietrich had commanded the Leibstandarte Division. The Ist SS Panzer Corps consisted of the corps units plus the Leibstandarte SS Adolf Hitler and Hitlerjugend Divisions. In order to better distinguish it from the division of the same name, the corps was later referred to only as the Ist SS Panzer Corps Leibstandarte and this title was used in all correspondence with other units.

The order for the formation of a heavy panzer battalion for the Ist SS Panzer Corps was issued on 19 July 1943. The site specified for the formation of the panzer battalion was Mailly-le-Camp training grounds in France, which was also where the panzer regiment for the Hitlerjugend Division was formed. Initial organization of all other corps units was to take place at Beneschau, near Prague, and that of the corps headquarters at Berlin-Lichterfelde.

In addition to the panzer battalion, the corps units included a heavy artillery battalion, rocket battalion, signals battalion, medical battalion, corps supply units, flak battery, escort company, and eight further corps units of limited strength. The Corps Chief-of-Staff was Fritz Kraemer, a wearer of the Knight's Cross. Kraemer, who had held the rank of General Staff Oberst in the army, transferred to the Waffen-SS and held the rank of SS-Oberführer as of October 1943. He was also the disciplinary superior for all corps units. As early as late May 1943, the Panzer-Grenadier Division Leibstandarte SS Adolf Hitler, which was then refitting in Kharkov, dispatched several NCOs and men who seemed suitable for the heavy panzer battalion to Paderborn-Sennelager. There they joined the 500th Heavy Panzer Training and Replacement Battalion, an army unit, which was responsible for providing all Tigers units with replacement personnel.

This was the first action that had to do with the formation of the heavy panzer battalion for the Ist SS Panzer Corps. The battalion was assigned the number 101, which was used by all corps units of the Ist SS Panzer Corps. The number consisted of the corps headquarters designation (1) plus 100.

At no time were there personnel for the yet-to-be-formed 101st SS Panzer Battalion at the Mailly-le-Camp training grounds; at this time the first contingent was based exclusively at Sennelager. The site of the initial organization was therefore soon changed to the Sennelager Troop Training Ground. Driver training was already well under way there in late May 1943. The first radio operators arrived at the same time; SS-Untersturmführer Helmut Dolinger, a Leibstandarte signals officer, took the new arrivals under his wing. Many NCOs and men came from the Leibstandarte Assault Gun Battalion, including SS-Hauptscharführer Alfred Günther, who had been decorated with the Knight's Cross on 3 March 1943.

The Leibstandarte Panzer Regiment's 13th Tiger Company also sent a limited number of personnel to Sennelager.

The large proportion of assault gun personnel was due to the person of the future battalion commander. SS-Sturmbannführer Heinz von Westernhagen, who had commanded the Leibstandarte Assault Gun Battalion since June 1942, was the officer chosen to command the 101st SS Panzer Battalion. Westernhagen had suffered serious head injuries on 6 July 1943 during the Zitadelle summer offensive.

Additional NCOs and men began arriving in Paderborn-Sennelager on 19 July 1943. Among those coming from the Leibstandarte Assault Gun Battalion were NCOs Traue, Richter, Otterbein, Rolf von Westernhagen (a brother of the CO) and Heinz Belbe. At that time the Leibstandarte was withdrawn from the front after the cancellation of Operation Zitadelle and was transferred to Italy. SS-Sturmbannführer Heinz von Westernhagen formally became commander of the 101st SS Heavy Panzer Battalion on 5 August 1943; however, because of his wounds he was not yet able to return to duty. He therefore only visited his men in Sennelager once, very briefly.

The organization of the 101st SS Heavy Panzer Battalion was established as follows: the battalion headquarters, a headquarters company, three panzer companies (Tiger), and a workshop company. The Tiger company—the 13th (Heavy) Company, SS Panzer Regiment Leibstandarte SS Adolf Hitler—was to join the battalion as its 3rd Company. As well, the 13th Company's workshop platoon was to be incorporated into the battalion's Panzer Workshop Company as its IInd Platoon. Therefore, in addition to battalion headquarters and the headquarters company, the formation order called for the creation of only two Tiger companies and the Panzer Workshop Company less the IInd Platoon. Officers, NCOs and men were provided for the battalion ". . . from existing cadres and by the SS-Führungshauptamt." The assignment of weapons and equipment was likewise regulated by the SS-Führungshauptamt by special order."

It was anticipated that, in addition to reconnaissance, pioneer and signals platoons, the headquarters company would also include a flak platoon. Initially, it was intended to transfer to the 101st SS Heavy Panzer Battalion one of the flak platoons formed for the SS Panzer Battalion Hermann von Salza (SS Panzer-Grenadier Division Nordland). This proved impracticable, and in the end personnel were taken from the SS Flak Replacement Battalion and brought together in Munchen-Freimann under the command of SS-Oberscharführer Hein Swoboda. The resulting unit was transferred to Paderborn-Sennelager—still without weapons—on 18 August 1943.

One gun commander, SS-Unterscharführer Kurt Fickert, recalled his stay in Paderborn: "Everything for the 101st SS Panzer Battalion was gathered in Paderborn under the command of Untersturmführer Dollinger. Our Senior Sergeant was Hauptscharführer Höflinger, a Bavarian. At first we were little more than a collection of NCOs and men. To some degree Höflinger kept the new arrivals together. Vogt, Hahn, Iriohn, Lukasius and Kalinowsky arrived one evening in a rather drunken state; they demanded that I, as duty NCO, send several men to fetch their luggage from the station. I then informed Höflinger, who gave the young whippersnappers a frightful bawling out, leaving them in no doubt as to whom they were dealing with. He was rather more courteous to Vogt, who sported the Iron Cross, First Class on his breast. Soon after that we left for Italy."

The group that got the disrespectful welcome consisted of SS-Oberscharführer and Reserve Officer Candidates Walter Hahn, Wilhelm Iriohn, Paul Vogt, Eduard Kalinowsky, Winfried Lukasius and Sepp Stich. They had all been transferred to the 101st SS Panzer Battalion effective 30 July 1943 after completing reserve officer training courses at the Junkerschule and subsequent weapons courses.

The following was noted in the war diary of the Ist SS Panzer Corps on 17 August 1943: "The SS-Führungshauptamt ordered the heavy panzer battalion (Tiger) transferred from the Sennelager training grounds to the Verona area. Transport movements will begin on 23/8/1943." On 28 August 1943 the battalion's entire personnel complement was transported from Sennelager to Italy by rail. The Leibstandarte's Tiger Company, and with it the entire division, had already arrived there at the beginning of the month. The 13th Panzer Company had fought in the Kursk salient as part of Operation Zitadelle in July 1943 and after being withdrawn from the front had handed its tanks over to the Das Reich and Totenkopf Divisions.

On 29 July 1943 the company left by Blitz-Pfeil train for Innsbruck, taking only wheeled vehicles only. From Innsbruck the company drove overland through South Tirol, where the troops received an enthusiastic reception, into Italy. As of 8 August the men camped in a vineyard on the outskirts of Reggio Emilia. Having recovered from his wounds, the commander of the Tiger Company, SS-Hauptsturmführer Heinz Kling, was now placed in charge of the formation of the 101st SS Panzer Battalion, as SS-Sturmbannführer Heinz von Westernhagen was not yet fit to return to duty, due to his serious head injury.

Twenty-seven new Tigers, including two command vehicles, arrived at the railway station in Reggio Emilia in mid-August 1943. Their arrival was followed by the first division of the 13th Tiger Company. SS-Hauptsturmführer Kling took over the 1st Company, while SS-Untersturmführer Helmut Wendorff led the 2nd Company. SS-Untersturmführer Helmut Dollinger assumed the duties of adjutant and signals officer. New arrivals included the administration officer, SS-Obersturmführer Alfred Veller, and two officers transferred from the LAH Anti-Tank Battalion, SS-Untersturmführer Georg Bartel, Battalion Technical Officer Motor Vehicles (TKF), and SS-Untersturmführer Herbert Walther. Platoon commanders in the panzer companies included SS-Untersturmführer Wittmann, SS-Hauptscharführer Höflinger, Günther and Hartel, and SS-Oberscharführer Brandt, Lukasius and Iriohn. Hahn, Stich, Kalinowsky and Vogt were all assigned to the battalion headquarters staff.

All existing elements of the battalion were fully engaged in training; this included both panzer companies as well as the headquarters and workshop companies. At this time all of the units were far from complete. Classes, training on the Tiger and unit inspections made up the standard routine in those weeks and ensured that the men were kept busy. However, they also had free time with which to enjoy the amenities of Italy. Many went swimming in an artificial lake near Reggio or drove to Modena to the public swimming pool. Officers, NCOs and men alike played plenty of sports. Rations were first-class with plenty of variety.

On 1 September 1943 SS-Oberscharführer and Reserve Officer Candidates Hahn, Vogt, Iriohn, Kalinowsky, Lukasius and Stich were promoted to the rank of SS-Untersturmführer. SS-Untersturmführer Hannes Philipsen, who had been wounded at Kharkov while serving with the Tiger Company, joined the battalion but was unable to carry out normal duties on account of his injured leg. A training company was established, in which all arriving enlisted men were trained. SS-Untersturmführer Dollinger set up a radio platoon for continued, intensive training of tank radio operators.

The Americans landed at Salerno on 10 September 1943; the Allies had earlier set foot on Sicily on 10 July. None of the units of the 101st SS Panzer Battalion were sent there. On 8 September 1943 the Italians surrendered to the Allies, contrary to their obligations to their ally Germany. At 0100 hours on 9 September German forces began disarming Italian troops in their garrisons and occupied a number of Italian cities. The Tiger battalion was not called upon to participate in these actions. By 1300 hours the elements of the Italian Army stationed in Reggio had been disarmed and the military airfields at La Villa and San Ilario occupied.

The men of the battalion took advantage of the situation to supply themselves with footwear and leather belts from the stores of their former Italian allies. Especially popular were the black shirts, which looked very smart when worn under the black panzer jacket. A number of Italian military vehicles were also added to the motor pool, the headquarters staff, for example, drove a large number of Fiat automobiles.

Some Italians joined the battalion as volunteer auxiliaries, or "Hiwis," and several as volunteers. On 16 September 1943 those men originating from the 13th Company were awarded decorations for their efforts in the Kursk offensive.

On 21 September there was a sumptuous party in a Dopolavoro house in Reggio. Two days later the battalion was transferred to Correggio, northeast of Reggio. The men were quartered in a party building and a school. Motor vehicles and tanks were camouflaged to prevent them being seen from the air and were parked near the sports field. At that time SS-Untersturmführer Paul Vogt commanded the headquarters company, which still had very few of the vehicles and equipment allocated to it.

The anti-aircraft platoon had no guns; the reconnaissance platoon was in Meran, which was also the location of the headquarters staff of the Ist SS Panzer Corps. In October 1943 members of the flak platoon escorted a POW train bound for Ostmark (formerly Austria). The train's destination was Villach in Carinthia. SS-Untersturmführer Herbert Walther, whose most recent command had been the 3rd Company of the SS Anti-Tank Battalion of the Leibstandarte, was placed in charge of forming the workshop company. In addition to the daily training routine the men played plenty of sports, with the officers also taking part. A non-commissioned officer training course, held in Correggio under SS-Untersturmführer Wendorff, gave deserving enlisted men the chance to make Unterscharführer (sergeant). In an effort to speed the process of bringing the Tiger Battalion to operational readiness, beginning on 1 October 1943 the Leibstandarte Panzer Regiment provided training personnel. Consequently, the battalion was subordinate to the panzer regiment for training purposes, but tactically it remained under the command of the division.

On 10 October 1943 the battalion was transferred to Pontecurone, southwest of Voghera, where the Tigers were hidden in a brickworks and the men housed in a large school.

Just prior to the move, on 5 October, there was another division of the company, based on the current state of training. Formation of the 3rd Company was officially begun the next day. Transferred to the new company was SS-Untersturmführer Philipsen, as well as Knight's Cross wearer SS-Hauptscharführer Alfred Günther. On 7 October SS-Rottenführer Herbert Stewig of the 3rd Company lost his life in an accident in Reggio Emilia. An honor guard of his comrades escorted him to his final resting place.

In October twelve NCOs from the Führer Escort Detachment and the Reich Chancellery driver pool were transferred to the battalion, where they were trained as tank commanders and drivers. The group included Hauptscharführer Helmut Fritzsche, Max Görgens and Hermann Barkhausen, Oberscharführer Grosser and Unterscharführer Heinrich Ernst, Walter Stuhrhahn and Hein Bode. The battalion had meanwhile received its own postal numbers; number 48165, formerly used by the 13th Company, was struck off. The new postal numbers: 101st SS Heavy Panzer Battalion—Headquarters and Headquarters Company 59450 A—1st Company, 101st SS Panzer Battalion 59450 B—2nd Company, 101st SS Panzer Battalion 59450 C—3rd Company, 101st SS Panzer Battalion 59450 D—Workshop Company 59450 E.

Further reorganizations of the companies took place on 18 and 24 October 1943. On 21 October it was announced that a deployment to the Eastern Front was imminent and the advance order for entraining arrived on the 27th. In order to bring the battalion up to its full authorized strength, ten more Tiger tanks were to be picked up in Germany. This would raise the battalion's strength to thirty-seven tanks, with which it could equip two companies, one of four and the other of three platoons, each with five tanks, as well as one tank each for the battalion commander and his adjutant.

Tank commanders SS-Hauptscharführer Spranz and SS-Unterscharführer Wendt, together with ten tank drivers, including SS-Unterscharführer Sturhahn and Röpstorff, SS-Rottenführer Ludwig Hofmann and Paul Rohweder, and SS-Sturmmann Theo Janekzek, drove to Burg, near Magdeburg, to pick up ten new Tigers at the army ordnance depot there. The men first had to finish equipping the tanks, install machine-guns and radios, and take on ammunition. The process took several days and when it was complete the Tigers were loaded aboard two transport trains which set off across Germany to Lvov. On 2 November 1943, the trains were halted in Lvov on senior orders and sent back, finally arriving in Paderborn several days later. Because of the threat of air attack, the trains were shunted to the rail stations in Geseke and Salzkotten. These tanks never reached the battalion in Italy.

In Italy, meanwhile, preparations were in full swing. On account of the continuing personnel shortages, varying levels of training of the new men, and the insufficient numbers of tanks and vehicles on hand, one over strength company was formed from the combat-ready personnel and the available twenty-seven Tiger tanks.

Five platoons were formed, each with five Tigers, to which were added the tanks of the company commander and company headquarters squad leader. This company—which possessed an imposing strength—was assigned the designation used by the old Tiger Company—the 13th (Heavy) Company, 1st SS Panzer Regiment Leibstandarte SS Adolf Hitler—and was placed under the command of the division's panzer regiment. Internally, it was the 1st and 2nd Companies of the 101st SS Panzer Battalion. One platoon was removed from the workshop and rejoined the company.

SS-Hauptsturmführer Kling took command of the company, platoon commanders were SS-Untersturmführer Wendorff, Wittmann, Hahn, Kalinowsky and Hartel. SS-Obersturmführer Michalski commanded Ist Platoon in the first action. On 29 October 1943 SS-Untersturmführer Stich was killed during the loading of the Tigers in Voghera when he made contact with an overhead power line. The battalion provided a guard of honor when the twenty-three-year-old SS-Untersturmführer was buried in Pavia cemetery.

The pleasant Italian interlude now ended for the men of the Tiger Company; they rolled toward the Eastern Front and a return to action. While part of the battalion left by rail for the Eastern Front beginning on 27 October 1943, the remaining elements transferred to Paderborn, this time to Sennelager-South, Augustdorf. The Tiger Company's tour of duty in Russia has been described in detail elsewhere in the book.

Personnel of the Leibstandarte's assault gun battery, which was formed in Jüterbog in March 1940 under SS-Hauptsturmführer Schönberger. Michael Wittmann is seventh from the left, standing.

Eastern Front, summer 1941. A StuG III/B assault gun of the Leibstandarte.

Wittmann in front of his assault gun.

November 1941, before the attack on Rostov. *Standing, third from right:* SS-Unterscharführer Wittmann, next to him on the left SS-Untersturmführer Stübing and SS-Oberscharführer Fischer.

Early 1942 in a courtyard in Taganrog. SS-Oberscharführer Wittmann with four senior non-commissioned officers of the Assault Gun Battalion. *From left:* Ernst Walter, Michael Wittmann, Richard Heinz, Walter Koch and Siegfried Pohnert.

Two assault gun commanders in the east in the late summer of 1941. Michael Wittmann and Hannes Fischer.

Left to right: SS-Unterscharführer Wittmann and Fischer, SS-Oberscharführer Walter, two unidentified men and SS-Unterscharführer Pohl in Dieditz in June 1941 shortly before the attack on the USSR.

In February 1944 Woll was given a special reception in his home town of
Wemmetsweiler.

On 16 January 1944 SS-Rottenführer Balthasar Woll became the first tank gunner in the Waffen-SS to be decorated with the Knight's Cross in recognition of his dauntless readiness for action and his 88 tank kills.

The 17th Armored Scout Company of the Leibstandarte in 1937 in the Berlin-Lichterfelde barracks. SS-Sturmmann Michael Wittmann is seated in the front row, second from the right. In the middle are the platoon commanders Bahls and Pfeiffer, the company commander Schönberger and Max Wünsche.

The head table, dignitaries and friends at Woll's special reception in his home town of Wemmetsweiler.

In February 1944 the Leibstandarte's few operational Tigers were fighting at the edge of the Cherkassy Pocket. Here several men prepare a meal in a Russian cottage. From left: Max Gaube, Kurt Kleber, Walter Lau, behind left an army soldier, then Pollak and on right Werner Hepe.

Sitting on this Tiger is its driver, SS-Unterscharführer Pollak. Standing are SS-Sturmmann Werner Hepe (driver), SS- Unterscharführer Kurt "Quax" Kleber (commander), SS-Sturmmann Walter Lau (gunner), SS-Sturmmann Max Gaube (loader) and an army soldier, February 1944.

At the same time the
elements of the 101st
SS Panzer Battalion in
Mons, Belgium were in
training. Here a tank
crew of the 3rd with
gunner SS-Sturmmann
Alfred Lünser on the
left.

SS-Rottenführer
Bobby Warmbrunn
after destroying his
51st enemy tank on
16 April 1944 with his
gunner SS-Sturmmann
Fritz Höneisen (right).
On the barrel of the
Tiger's gun are five
thick and one thin rings,
which symbolize the
fifty-one kills.

Warmbrunn in front
of his Tiger. Just
discernable in front of
the victory rings is a
small tank painted on
the barrel. The tank
exhibits numerous hits,
none of which was able
to penetrate the armor
of the Tiger, for example
on the left side of the
bow plate.

Men of the 3rd Company, 101st SS Panzer Battalion in Mons, Belgium in early 1944.

Siegfried Walther and Wilhelm Weishaupt of the maintenance echelon of the 3rd Company, 101st SS Panzer Battalion, in Mons.

SS-Sturmmann
Alfred Lünser.

February 1944, tank
driver school in Mons.
The turret has been
removed from the Tiger
used for driver training.

Siegfried Walther.

THE 101ST SS PANZER BATTALION IN AUGUSTDORF, 5 NOVEMBER, 1943–9 JANUARY, 1944

In November 1943 all elements of the battalion not involved in the Eastern Front deployment were transported by rail to Sennelager-South, Augustdorf. SS-Obersturmbannführer Leiner had assumed command of the battalion a short time before. The thirty-eight-year-old Leiner had commanded the anti-tank battalion of the Totenkopf Division in the Western Campaign of 1940, and in 1943 had led the same division's panzer regiment in the Battle of Kharkov. Leiner was married to one of SS-Obergruppenführer Eicke's daughters, and he was a long-serving member of Eicke's division, where he was sure of the division commander's good will. Leiner did not enjoy much popularity among the members of the 101st SS Panzer Battalion. His cold, unfriendly manner and his lack of understanding prevented any bonds from being established with the enlisted men, NCOs and officers.

The ten Tigers from Burg, which ended up sitting at the stations of Salzkotten and Geseke, were sent to Augustdorf, where they were taken charge of by the battalion. The soldiers who had picked up the tanks in Burg likewise joined the battalion. As the unit's 1st and 2nd Companies were currently fighting in the Soviet Union as one company—13th Company, 1st SS Panzer Regiment Leibstandarte SS Adolf Hitler—all remaining personnel were concentrated in the 3rd Company in Augustdorf. After their wounds received on the Eastern Front had healed, convalescents also proceeded directly to the 3rd Company, which for the time being was the battalion's sole panzer company. Ten Tiger tanks represented the battalion's entire strength. Also in Augustdorf were the headquarters company and the workshop company (less one platoon).

SS-Hauptsturmführer Schweimer was transferred to the 3rd Company of the 101st SS Panzer Battalion as company commander. The thirty-year-old Günther Schweimer came to the Leibstandarte as an SS-Untersturmführer from the Junkerschule in 1938. Soon afterward he was assigned to the Foreign Office and on 25 August 1938 was promoted to Hauptsturmführer. As legation secretary he became the Foreign Minister's adjutant. Schweimer later returned to the Leibstandarte and from May 1943 belonged to the headquarters staff of the panzer regiment.

On 19 November 1943 SS-Untersturmführer Hannes Philipsen arrived in Augustdorf. He had sustained serious injuries in March 1943 when his Tiger was knocked out at the outskirts of Kharkov. Complications from a fractured knee-cap prevented him from carrying out normal duties and at first he was employed by 3rd Company as an instructor and special duties officer. Acting platoon commanders were SS-Untersturmführer

Lukasius and SS-Hauptscharführer Gunther and Spranz. A number of NCOs and men from the Leibstandarte's assault gun battalion also came to Augustdorf.

The battalion was housed in brick buildings, the tanks and vehicles were parked in open hangars on the training grounds. The gloomy surroundings had no effect on the high morale of the men in the fall of 1943. The camp had a movie theater, which attracted many off-duty soldiers. Many also made the three-kilometer walk to the outskirts of Detmold, where they could catch a streetcar into the city.

Two more officers were transferred to the battalion, SS-Obersturmführer Hanno Raasch and SS-Untersturmführer Jürgen Wessel. For the newly-arrived officers, NCOs and men there began an extensive training program on the Tiger directed by Leutnant Felkel of the army's 500th Tiger Training and Replacement Battalion.

Initial trials with an infra-red night vision device were carried out at Augustdorf. This innovative piece of equipment, which was still in the experimental stage, was installed in a Tiger not belonging to the 101st Battalion. Test firing at night yielded good results. The Gauleiter of Hanover, Hartmann Lauterbacher, was invited to watch another firing trial by a Tiger. Lauterbacher had adopted the Leibstandarte's Tiger Company when it was formed in November 1942.

SS-Sturmmann Alfred Lünser, a veteran Tiger crewman from the old 13th Company, remembered Augustdorf: "Training was done by the army's Tiger instruction company. I became Leutnant Felkel's batman. We of the old unit—there were fifteen of us—took part in almost none of the training, therefore we had to take on other functions. The Wehrmacht officers all lived in one barracks; the chief, SS-Hauptsturmführer Schweimer, also had his room there.

One day we were joined by Obersturmführer Hanno Raasch. His batman, like Schweimer's, was one of the old fifteen. Hanno Raasch knew nothing about the Tiger, but he didn't want to look like a 'Wehrmacht man' so I had to help out. Each afternoon he had one of the training Tigers driven in front of the hangar, after which we drove there in his Kübelwagen. We both climbed in and I had to explain, demonstrate and show everything, and he learned quickly. Naturally I also got to know him somewhat better; he was an excellent type and never played the officer. He could draw very well and had three girlfriends; he placed the appropriate portrait in the frame whenever one of them was about to visit. One day one of them arrived unexpectedly and asked to wait in his room until he went off duty. His batman saved the situation and only allowed her in after he had placed the proper picture in the frame. The batman received an extra weekend pass."

Further personnel arrived in Augustdorf in the form of a trained replacement company—120 men strong—of the Leibstandarte's SS Panzer-Grenadier Training and Replacement Battalion. In November SS-Hauptsturmführer Rolf Möbius arrived. Thirty-one years old, in 1941 the Carinthian had taken part in the Balkans Campaign as a platoon commander in the Leibstandarte's 7th Company. When the Eastern Campaign began he was the commander of a 37 mm flak battery; in June 1942 he assumed command of an 88 mm flak battery. Möbius led both units with great success. He was decorated with the German Cross in Gold on 28 March 1943 following the recapture of Kharkov. Möbius subsequently participated in the 12th general staff training course held at the army war college in Hirschberg. Unfortunately he failed to achieve the necessary qualifications and was then transferred to theIstSS Panzer Corps. He joined the Tiger battalion on 16 November 1943. Möbius at first assumed command of the headquarters company. The same month the company's anti-aircraft platoon received three quadruple flak mounted on eight-tonne prime movers. The platoon commander was Hein Swoboda, who had been an SS-Oberscharführer since the battalion's formation. The armored reconnaissance platoon, whose armored troop carriers had not yet arrived, was taken over by SS-Untersturmführer Jürgen Wessel, whose most recent post had been that of operations officer with the IIIrd Battalion of the Leibstandarte's 1st SS Panzer-Grenadier Regiment.

For unexplained reasons, SS-Hauptsturmführer Schweimer's batman was suddenly infested with lice. The entire unit had to be deloused, which all the participants naturally found extremely amusing. In preparation for the transfer of the battalion, at the beginning of December 1943 an advance party of fifteen NCOs and men under the command of SS-Untersturmführer Philipsen was sent to Mons, Belgium. Philipsen arranged a modest celebration in the soldiers' hostel in Mons on Christmas Day 1943. No one would have been better suited to deliver the Christmas message than this great idealist. He knew how sensible even long-serving front-line soldiers could be on such a day. The men of the battalion and the German nurses sat together in the stylishly-decorated hall of the soldiers' hostel.

All those present listened expectantly to the words spoken by the young Untersturmführer: "Comrades! It is Christmas again. For the fourth time in this war. For many of you it is your first Christmas as soldiers. Peace settles upon our hearts, dreams of childhood awaken in them, deep longing and quiet happiness grow in them. For nowhere do we experience this most beautiful of all celebrations—Christmas—than in the unshakable community of soldiers. There is no need for a program or lengthy preparations, nor is the decoration of the room a problem. Many nice greetings and packages have arrived from home. Do you see the lights glowing on the Christmas tree? At this moment we are in fact at home, we stand in the intimate circle of our family and see the tree with the clear, trusting eyes of childhood. There our hearts are warm and we find the true peace of Christmas. For Christmas is a German celebration. Only we enlightened people know the deep significance of the holy night. We know that ages and ages ago our ancestors celebrated the feast of the rebirth of light and life as their most important festival. For:

"Much grain grows in the winter night, because the seeds flourish beneath the snow. Not until the sun laughs in spring, do you sense what good winter has done. And if the world finds you deserted and bare, and your days are raw and hard; Be still and heed life! Much corn grows in the winter night!"

And new life in the womb of the eternal mother is tender and loving like the seed in the womb of the ancient earth. It bears the future well-protected beneath a loving heart. That is the secret of Christmas. It is the eternal truth, which is clear to us in these hours and which claims its right from the moment. For it is children's or father's love which softens the otherwise hard warrior's heart. The father sees his children playing happily beneath the Christmas tree. He sees the tears in the eyes of his beloved wife, who, happy over her children, nevertheless feels a sharp pain in her heart for those warriors far away watching over the homeland. And the son looks into the care-furrowed faces of his parents, whose thoughts and wishes are with us.

Our tongues loosen imperceptibly. Each tells of his home, of wife and children, of parents and siblings. Memories from long-gone childhood days come alive as they are retold with feelings that many years ago fired the youthful soul. Then photos are brought out, faded and tattered, for many times in difficult hours they have been taken out and gazed at and that is how we wish to keep it for the rest of the evening. Songs spring up or poems we know from childhood. While sitting together this way, telling stories, singing, eating and exchanging photographs, we all feel that our comradeship is somehow becoming deeper. We will need this more than ever in the struggle to come. There in our midst are all the comrades whom death in battle has taken from us. They have suddenly come alive in our stories and a special salute goes out to the broken-hearted mothers who mourn proudly for their sons. Thus the magnificent community of a great people suddenly becomes clear. Your heart joins the great longing, which flows home in a mighty stream from mIIIions of soldiers' hearts, opening into many mIIIions of parents' and children's hearts."

Several days later Hannes Philipsen wrote to his parents. In the letter were reflected the front-line soldier's wishes for the new year just beginning.

"Loved ones at home!   Belgium, 31/12/1943

It has been three weeks now since I was home with you, and as is now the lot of us young front-line officers, we are constantly on the move. So it is now. I hope that you received my two letters. I had a very lovely Christmas with my men and with German sisters in a local soldiers' hostel. The day before we cut down a Christmas tree in the still autumnal forest, then put it up in the big lobby of the hostel and gave it a simple, festive coat, Mother, just like the Christmas trees at home which I remember so fondly. Then the candles were put on, and afterward we and the sisters decorated the entire hostel for Christmas, and you can't imagine what joy it gave me. We were all in a cheerful mood and it seemed to me as if there was deepest peace on earth. But the world struggle is raging more fiercely than ever, and I am actually sorry that I'm not there. Yes, you will say, you should grant yourself some rest, you have already survived many battles. No, dear ones, I will not rest until victory is ours and I will always endeavour, as long as my health permits, to be in the front rank of fighters for Germany. 'And if the world were full of the devil, we would still succeed.' This is just what I shouted to my men in the clear, pure light of the candles and swore anew never to grow weary.

On Christmas Eve of this fifth year of the war the glowing candles on the Christmas tree told me that those of good will must someday triumph over everything wrong, false and dark. On that night of shining stars I thought a lot about my beautiful youth, which you, my parents, allowed me to shape as I desired and which also bore good fruit. How proud I am of my boys. Today we are all front-line soldiers and can now prove that what we preached and hammered into the hearts of the young men was not lip service, rather something that we uncompromisingly put into action. Our best march silently in the great army of our dead heroes; they will remind us of our obligation until the end of our lives. All you loved ones at home were with us by the Christmas tree. Even my uncle Johannes, who lies not so far from here. Please write me as soon as you can and tell me the exact location of his grave and how I can best get there from Brussels. Then when the battalion arrives I will ask my commanding officer for permission to drive there some day. Also tell me the exact place where Hans Braun is buried. I will also see if I can drive there sometime. I can't go anywhere for the time being, as there is still a great deal of work to be done. It would be nice if it should work out. This thought came to me by the Christmas tree too.

Today marks the end of another year of exertion and sacrifice for our people. It has demanded much of all of us, however the coming year shall find us even more ready in unshakable faith in our Führer. He will lead us into a happier future. Let us therefore remain true to the war, for then we are serving peace! We wish to continue on our path exactly as before. May our Lord God keep our people and our Führer in the coming year and bring us peace and give us all strength to hold out in spite of terror and privations!

To you at home I wish the very best and especially good health. I wish to thank you from the bottom of my heart for all the love you gave me while I was in hospital, especially you, my Peter, who stayed with me in my most painful hours. Through your presence you gave me so much relief and set me on this path to Gudrun, to whom now belongs all my love forever.

That time was lovely in spite of everything. My dear parents, never forget the day when you visited me in Meiningen. It was too nice, mother, how I clung to your arm like a little child and walked, so laboriously but yet so happily, on my plaster leg. Then came the long, wonderful days on leave with you at home and my Gudrun; I was probably the happiest man alive. I don't know if you felt it, for it was probably more of a silent joy! In the midst of the splendid harvest time and we seven Philipps all together, and I could once again pedal through our Angelland. Yes, dear ones, at the year's end I wish to thank you for all that and for much more. Please write to me diligently in the coming year so that we can always stay together. If I should write less frequently sometimes, then know that your Hannes has something more important to do and that I am always in good spirits!

And now my most heartfelt greetings to you all and a happy New Year! Heil! Your Hannes."

In Augustdorf many men went home on leave for Christmas. Knight's Cross wearer SS-Hauptscharführer Alfred Günther led the 3rd Company in those days. Hauptscharführer Heinz Belbe was taken to hospital on Christmas Day with a severe case of tonsillitis and suspected diphtheria. He was later transferred to a hospital in Templin. The threat of an outbreak of diphtheria in the battalion was averted. Intensive training resumed immediately after the quiet Christmas holidays, in the platoons of the 3rd Company and of the headquarters and workshop companies. Platoon commanders in the 3rd Company now were SS-Obersturmführer Raasch, SS-Untersturmführer Lukasius and SS-Hauptscharführer Günther.

The authorized strength of the 101st SS Panzer Battalion was laid down precisely in the table of organization. The situation report submitted by the battalion on 1 January 1944 revealed the following picture:

	Officers	NCOs	Men	Total
Authorized Strength:	27	153	419	599
Actual Strength:	18	83	365	466
Shortfall:	9	70	54	133

On 3 January 1944 SS-Hauptscharführer Spranz and SS-Unterscharführer Wendt were again given the task of picking up new Tigers from the army ordnance depot in Burg. Together with the tank drivers, in Burg they completely outfitted seven battle and two command tanks and loaded the nine Tigers aboard two trains. The transports arrived in Mons, Belgium on 9 January 1944. Spranz and Wendt were amazed to find no one from the battalion in Mons. The battalion began entraining in Sennelager that day, and all the trains arrived in the battalion's new quartering area by 13 January 1944.

THE 101ST SS PANZER BATTALION IN MONS, BELGIUM, 10 JANUARY–3 APRIL 1944

The Mons-Maisières training grounds became the 101st SS Panzer Battalion's new home. The large troop training ground was located three kilometers northeast of Mons, directly on the Mons-Soignies road. Beyond the main road entrance stood rows of closely-spaced, one-story houses in which the men lived. The officers lived in a large house situated in a wood opposite the road. Several soon had their wives join them. The tanks and vehicles, camouflaged against discovery by aerial reconnaissance, were also parked in this wood. The seven new Tigers were incorporated into the 3rd Company, while the two command tanks were assigned to the battalion headquarters. One was allocated to the battalion commander, the other to the signals officer.

The 3rd Company now had at its disposal seventeen Tigers, which were organized into four platoons, each with four tanks. Platoon commanders Raasch, Lukasius and Günther were now joined by SS-Hauptscharführer Spranz. SS-Untersturmführer Walter Hahn, who had been wounded in Russia, arrived at the battalion. Hahn was one of those officers who had joined the battalion in Paderborn in 1943. Born in Cologne on 9 June 1913, Hahn was a government worker when he volunteered for military service. He was assigned to the 9th SS Infantry Regiment and later to the Das Reich Division. After a reserve officer training course and weapons course he joined the 101st SS Panzer Battalion on 30 July 1943 and was promoted to SS-Untersturmführer in Italy on 1 September. He accompanied the 13th Company to the Eastern Front, where he saw action from November 1943 and was decorated with the Iron Cross, Second Class.

Extensive training for all elements of the Tiger Battalion resumed in Maisières. On 23 December 1943 SS-Obersturmführer Gottfried Klein took over command of the workshop company which SS-Obersturmführer Herbert Walther had formed in Italy. Walther was transferred to the headquarters company as an infantry instructor and for special duties. SS-Hauptscharführer Reinhold Wichert arrived from the Vienna Automotive Training Institute on 7 January 1944 to command the workshop company's recovery platoon. On 1 February 1944 he was promoted to SS-Standartenoberjunker. The workshop platoon was commanded by SS-Hauptscharführer Oskar Glaeser. On 28 January 1944 the 101st Corps Signal Battalion sent a teletype communications section to the Tiger Battalion.

The 3rd Company's first tank exercise took place on 12 February 1944. Among the observers was the Commanding General of the Ist SS Panzer Corps, SS-Obergruppenführer and Panzergeneral der Waffen-SS Sepp Dietrich. SS-Sturmbannführer von Westernhagen had overcome some of the effects of his serious head injury in the past months, and he took part in a training course for battalion commanders at the Armored Forces School in Paris. He joined the battalion in Mons on 23 February 1944. The commander who gave the battalion a special profile and made it an extraordinarily potent force was undoubtedly Heinz von Westernhagen, simply Hein to his men.

Von Westernhagen described his early life: "I was born in Riga, Latvia, on 29 August 1911, the fourth son of dentist Karl Friedrich Max von Westernhagen and his wife Hedwig Angelica von Westernhagen, nee Bertels. I was baptized a protestant with the Christian names Heinz Otto Alexander.

In the winter of 1914/15, when my father returned from Siberia, we escaped through Finland and Sweden to Germany. When Riga was taken by German forces in 1917, we returned at once with a shipment of troops. Then came the Russian Revolution and for a second time we lost everything we had, this time to the bolsheviks. We left our home for good in the summer of 1919 and travelled to Hamburg as part of a shipment of 3,000 German refugees. In October 1921 we moved to Berlinchen in the Neumark. There I went to middle school, having attended secondary school in Riga and elementary school in Hamburg. I left school on 25 March 1927 and went to Hamburg, signed aboard a sailing ship and served aboard it until summer 1929. Then I tried to change horses to farming. During this period I joined the NSDAP, but in early 1930 I turned once again to the sea. I was let go in April 1932 and was unemployed until February 1933. At this time I applied to join the newly-formed SS in Harburg.

On 15 February 1933 I signed on as a sailor again, aboard a steamer out of Hamburg. I remained there until 20 November 1933, when I was let go on account of complaints about bad food. I applied to the Reich Water Guard in Stettin and was accepted. Expecting to be let go, I sought work on land and from 13 December 1933 until 1 October 1934 I worked at the Phoenix AG rubber factory in Harburg. I was supposed to be laid off in Stettin, but several days before that I was called up by the Verfügungstruppe in Hamburg and forgot about the police."

Heinz von Westernhagen became a member of the Allgemeine-SS on 1 April 1932 and was assigned to the 1st Sturm of the 17th SS-Standarte. After going back to sea from February to November 1933, he subsequently returned to Germany. Heinz had seen much of the world, including Australia, and had enjoyed a rich variety of experiences. He composed several articles in which he described his adventures on the seven seas. As well, he wrote interesting and exciting articles about life at sea, some of which were picked up by newspapers. He was promoted to the rank of Sturmmann on 1 November 1933 and to Rottenführer on 1 May 1934. The former sailor was then leading the modest life of a worker at the Phoenix Works in Harburg. On 20 August 1934 he received his promotion to Unterscharführer; at this time he could only serve during his off hours.

Von Westernhagen joined the SS-Verfügungstruppe on 1 October 1934 and was taken on strength by the 1st Company of the Germania Regiment in Hamburg-Veddel. On account of his wide range of experiences and resulting maturity, von Westernhagen was sent to Bad Tölz after only six months. There he successfully passed the second officer training course, and on 1 February 1936 he became a Standartenoberjunker. He subsequently took part in the obligatory platoon commander training course (10 February to 4 April 1936). Because of his time spent abroad and his maturity, after leaving Bad Tölz, von Westernhagen was transferred to the security service (Sicherheitsdienst) instead of to the SS-Verfügungstruppe. He passed through another course, in Berlin-Grunewald, from April to May 1936, and on 20 April 1936 he was promoted to SS-Untersturmführer. Von Westernhagen and other SS-Untersturmführer were introduced to Adolf Hitler as part of the events marking Reich Party Day 1936.

The young SS-Untersturmführer wrote: "It was a great day today. We were presented, or to put it better 'awarded,' our swords of honor by Reichsführer-SS Heinrich Himmler. This morning we young Sturmführer were received by the Führer in the hall of the Hohenzollernburg, where he shook hands with each of us. The Führer subsequently gave a speech. There was just us in the hall." Von Westernhagen worked in the foreign service of Amt III, which frequently took him abroad. He was assigned to Mussolini's chief of police Bochini as liaison officer during the Duce's visit to Berlin in September 1937. Von Westernhagen was promoted to Obersturmführer on 13 September 1937.

In the following month, on 13 October 1937, Heinz married his fiancee, the twenty-four-year-old Elisabeth Zwick. His wife came from Berlinchen, where he had met her in the twenties. 1938 saw von Westernhagen in Austria, followed by an extended period in Rome. On 10 September 1938 he was transferred to the 1st Company of the SS Regiment Deutschland in Munich; from there he was assigned to the army. From 23 September until 21 December 1938 he was a platoon commander in the 16th Company of the 94th Infantry Regiment. Von Westernhagen returned to the main office of the Security Service on 1 January 1939 and on 30 January was promoted to SS-Hauptsturmführer. As criminal investigation work no longer appealed to him in the long run, he pressed for a return to the Verfügungstruppe, especially after the war broke out. Von Westernhagen was assigned to the headquarters staff of the Leibstandarte, and he took part in the fighting in Holland, Belgium and France in 1940 as an acting company commander. Though he wanted to stay with the troops, he was subsequently transferred back to the Security Service and in September 1940 took part in a course on Africa in Rome. He vigorously renewed his efforts to obtain a transfer to a front-line unit, ". . . so I will not have to feel ashamed to myself and to the world later on."

He was assisted in his efforts by his roommate from Bad Tölz, SS-Hauptsturmführer Richard Schulze, who was serving as a company commander with the Leibstandarte, and on 14 March 1941 Heinz von Westernhagen returned to the unit. The campaign in the Balkans began soon afterward and he served for the duration in the staff of the Leibstandarte's Ist Battalion commanded by Fritz Witt. He described his first post: "That didn't suit me at all, as there was no shooting there and I had to do all my fighting with a fountain pen." This was soon to change during the fighting in Greece, however, as he later described in a letter: "The Tommies harried us with bombs and strafing attacks in the first days of fighting in Greece. Many times we were forced to run for cover when a Spitfire dove and raked us with its machine-guns from a height of from twenty to fifty meters; however, we took satisfaction in the fact that our flak was able to bring down just as many of the birds.

I learned a great deal in this campaign; one's thoughts are quite extraordinary while under fire and one determines by the whine of the approaching shells whether the beast will explode in front of or behind the foxhole, so that he can press himself against the correct wall to avoid getting iron in the back. I understand what the Führer means when he says that war is madness." On 13 May 1941 Heinz von Westernhagen received the Iron Cross, Second Class. Following the conclusion of the campaign in Greece, in June 1941 the Leibstandarte was transferred into the Wischau-Brünn area in the Protectorate; many of the unit's officers brought their wives to join them. Von Westernhagen spent several carefree days with his wife Elisabeth in Habrovan.

At the beginning of the Russian Campaign, von Westernhagen took over the duties of First Special Missions Staff Officer of the Leibstandarte SS Adolf Hitler. As for all German soldiers, the war in Soviet Russia set completely new dimensions for him. The pace of the advance into Southern Russia in the first months was breathtaking and soon the Leibstandarte SS Adolf Hitler was advancing east along the Sea of Azov. The immeasurable vastness of the country and the previously unknown fighting methods of the Soviets brought to the men of the Leibstandarte a sense of foreboding about the future course of the war. The Soviets had suffered unprecedented losses in men and materiel in the greatest battles of encirclement history had ever seen, yet their reserves seemed inexhaustible.

But there were other things that shocked the German soldiers: "Repeated cases of brutally massacred German soldiers, who had become separated from their units or were captured, were enough to make one lose his composure."

In November 1941 the Leibstandarte attacked Rostov. It took the city but was compelled to withdraw again on orders from above. Von Westernhagen wrote on 25 November: "Rostov is ours, our guns roar without pause, and the shells howl through the night . . . There can be nothing more desolate than the area in which we have been stuck for weeks now, and still the 'Red madness' continues to fight with all doggedness . . . Yet, what luck that we struck before the Russians. Poor Germany, what would have become of us if these masses had rolled first."

The Leibstandarte subsequently occupied a winter position on the Sambek River. After six months of uninterrupted fighting the unit's strength had shrunk to a dangerous level. On 1 June 1942 SS-Hauptsturmführer Max Wünsche was assigned to the military academy in Berlin; Heinz von Westernhagen succeeded him as commander of the Assault Gun Battalion. He had already spent some time in the battalion staff, where he had been able to amass some experience with this type of weapon.

In July 1942 the Leibstandarte was transferred to France to rest and refit, while at the same time being reorganized as a panzer-grenadier division. The Assault Gun Battalion was organized into three batteries and a headquarters battery. On 10 July 1942, SS-Hauptsturmführer von Westernhagen was awarded the Royal Bulgarian Medal of Bravery IVth Class, 2nd Grade, which was followed on 3 September by the Romanian Crown with Swords without Ribbon Vth Class and on 4 September the Eastern Front Medal. As commander of the Assault Gun Battalion, on 9 November 1942 he was promoted to SS-Sturmbannführer. His battalion trained intensively in Verneuil, for its next deployment was imminent. His brother Rolf was also serving in the battalion as an assault gun commander. The period of quiet in France quickly came to an end. In January the division was transferred back to the Soviet Union. Von Westernhagen and his battalion went into action immediately in the Kharkov area, engaging Soviet assault forces which until then had been advancing almost unopposed. The batteries of his battalion were assigned to the Leibstandarte's panzer—grenadier units; rarely did von Westernhagen lead his entire battalion into action.

On 25 February he gave a vivid description of his experiences at the front: "All of us just hope that now the entire world understands what is at stake here and that it is a worthy cause! Out here the men do not ask for their portion from the field kitchen but for ammunition. The infantry goes without hot food for fourteen days and more and their fighting spirit is unbroken. Our youngest soldier understands that everything is at stake here . . . All the customary and minor things have fallen away from us, I never thought that one could adapt so. Nothing can scare us—and you must adapt yourselves too, so that we can calmly do our duty out here. I'm sitting in a stinking sod hut, at least ten persons are squatting by the stove, with them a pig and a goat, hens and doves sit on shelves. The air is thick enough to cut. Four weeks ago I had a tiled bathroom and a bed with white sheets, and now my feet are frozen, I'm infested with lice, my face is seared from the cold, and I recently had my first good, long sleep in a haystack, only because all their efforts to wake me failed. That is our war.—I'm not writing to complain—none of us want to complain, we only want to let those at home know what is being done here so that the homeland will remember. No one can rob us of our humor! If the homeland is as strong as our young men out here, then even the entire world can't overrun us."

Soon afterward, with the unspeakable hardships of the war in the Russian winter and the cruelties he had seen inflicted on prisoners and the wounded fresh in his mind, he wrote: "Our soldiers fight with an unimag-

inable hardness—sixteen-year-olds have become men in three weeks—
apparently the scum of the entire world is being hurled against us—no
quarter is given by either side . . . All hell seems to have risen up against us.
But we will prevail, and if one of us should fall out here, dear parents, it is
a small sacrifice to protect our home and family from this flood."

The attack on Kharkov began on 6 March 1943; the Leibstandarte was
now on the offensive. Von Westernhagen was decorated with the Iron
Cross, First Class and the Tank Battle Badge in Silver. His assault guns took
part in numerous attacks. Often the battalion commander accompanied
his batteries. He was always on the move, talking to the commanders of the
panzer-grenadiers, his company commanders and gun commanders.
There was no rest for him or any of the others.

On 24 March 1943, ten days after the capture of the city, he wrote:
"What lies behind us is frightful. There can scarcely be a repetition and it
can never be worse. You wouldn't recognize Kharkov if you returned to it
now. There is scarcely a house intact and no one will ever forget the street
battles. No one can describe what took place here in the winter battles.
Every single man deserves the Knight's Cross. In Kharkov itself we drove
our assault guns to within thirty meters of fortified houses and fired into
them; our enemies tossed hand grenade clusters down on us and as soon
as the brick dust and powder smoke had cleared they opened fire again."

After this fierce and costly fighting the Leibstandarte went into rest
positions in Kharkov. Replacements came from home and slowly the units
reached their authorized strengths again. There was much training activity; but the quiet was deceptive, for the preparations for a fresh offensive
were already in high gear. Heinz von Westernhagen's thoughts turned to
his future after the war: "In our area the fields are under full cultivation—
wheat, root crops and sunflowers all look promising. I am just amazed how
the few remaining old, bent people till these huge areas with spades and
subsequently work the fields. I am beginning to get used to Russia and find
things that appeal to me. The vastness of the land seizes a man and
enthralls him. I can imagine staying in Russia at some time in the future. I
won't always remain a soldier, rather I consider myself a wartime soldier.
I'll fight, as long as my bones are whole, where there is something to fight
and then I too will have my rest. Well, it will be a little while before that
happens."

The long-planned Operation Zitadelle, which was to cut off the Soviet
salient around Kursk, began on 5 July 1943. On the very first day of the
attack Heinz was badly wounded in the head. In spite of the severity of the
wound, on 17 July he wrote his brother Harald from hospital: "You will

have learned from mother that I got hit. I am doing very well in spite of the seriousness of the wound. The care I am receiving from German nurses in an SS hospital in Kharkov is exemplary, and in ten to twelve days they will be flying me back to the Reich . . . I don't know where they usually set the boundary between pain and discomfort, but I don't think I have one. They operated on my skull while I was conscious and I didn't go mad, so I'm doing great and I'm cheerful and in good spirits . . . Yes, Harald, we soldiers are a merry lot and hard to kill."

Heinz von Westernhagen arrived in Germany and at the end of July he was reunited with his wife in Hamburg. In an advanced stage of pregnancy, after the British bombing raids she went to a clinic in the Johnsallee. But the hospital had been hit too and there was no electricity or water. They were unable to admit Frau Westernhagen for the birth of her child. Heinz, his head swathed in a thick bandage, drove her out of Hamburg into the Mark Brandenburg. Their first daughter came into the world in Perleberg on 5 August 1943. Being wounded only strengthened von Westernhagen's resolve to leave the service after the war. "If I survive this war I'll hang my soldier's coat on a nail and become a farmer in the Baltic States. Or else let the devil take me."

When he had regained his health, von Westernhagen learned that a new mission awaited him: he was to help build up the heavy panzer battalion for the new 1st SS Panzer Corps. As of 5 August 1943 he was the official commander of the 101st SS Heavy Panzer Battalion. Further treatment of his head wound and subsequent participation in a training course for battalion commanders at the Armored Forces School in Paris delayed his arrival, and he was unable to begin his duties with the battalion until 23 February 1944. The new commander introduced himself to his men with an impressive inaugural address. He referred to the difficulty of the tasks facing the battalion in the future and appealed to the sense of responsibility in each man. In his speech he made reference to his style of command, which was based on personal, mutual trust between officers, non-commissioned officer and enlisted men: "Here stands no baron before you." As soon as the battalion passed into von Westernhagen's hands the atmosphere changed abruptly. In his humane way, the much-travelled commander established an almost chummy relationship with his men. He was calm and understanding, yet he was the embodiment of the fresh, willing, aggressive front-line soldier. His sometimes downright casual behavior while maintaining his full authority soon won him the affection of his men.

In any case, to the many members of the battalion who had come from the assault gun battalion he was not an unknown quantity. An all-round program of training was begun. Exercises were carried out in the surrounding area, combat in towns was practiced in Mons. The tank crews were made familiar with the unpopular, but necessary task of performing maintenance on the Tiger and they soon mastered the complicated inner workings of this highly sophisticated tank. The reconnaissance platoon, which was commanded by SS-Hauptsturmführer Wessel, was also trained on the tank. The battalion medical officer, SS-Hauptsturmführer Dr. Wolfgang Rabe, arrived on 18 January 1944. Rabe was born in Vienna on 27 February 1917 and received his degree there in 1940. After basic infantry training he joined the Leibstandarte's medical battalion in 1940. In early 1942 hebecame battalion medical officer of the Assault Gun Battalion and during the fighting at Kharkov in 1943 participated in attacks in an assault gun. He received the Iron Cross, First Class on 13 April 1943 and was promoted to SS-Hauptsturmführer on 21 June. Von Westernhagen had him transferred from the Medical Replacement Battalion to the 101st SS Panzer Battalion. The mens' feeling of belonging was reinforced by platoon and company parties. The troops went together to the movie theater and soldiers' hostel in Mons, attended cabaret shows, and used their free time for other forms of entertainment. On the occasion of an non-commissioned officers' party, the 3rd Company produced a humorously written and Illustrated rag magazine.

The members of the battalion serving with the 13th Company in the Soviet Union were very successful in spite of the extremely difficult conditions there. SS-Untersturmführer Michael Wittmann was decorated with the Knight's Cross and the Oak Leaves within two weeks; on 14 and 30 January 1944. On 16 January 1944 his gunner, SS-Rottenführer Balthasar Woll, also received the Knight's Cross. SS-Untersturmführer Helmut Wendorff was decorated with the Knight's Cross on 12 February 1944 and SS-Hauptsturmführer Heinz Kling on 23 February.

The 13th Company returned from the Eastern Front at the beginning of March 1944, without tanks and with only a few wheeled vehicles. The battalion gave a tremendous welcoming party for the men of this extraordinarily-successful company in Mons. Numerous delicacies from the kitchen were arranged on tables in a decorated hall, there was sandwiches and beer. The festive mood reached its high point at around midnight. Led by Heinz von Westernhagen, the men marched and jumped over the tables which had been arranged in the shape of a horseshoe. Understandably, the next day all was quiet until noon.

SS-Hauptsturmführer Kling was no longer commander of the 13th Company. He had already handed the company over to Wittmann in

December 1943 and assumed command of the IInd Battalion, 1st SS Panzer Regiment Leibstandarte. In addition to his adjutant, Obersturm-führer Wendorff, he took several members of the 13th Company with him, including Spieß Habermann and SS-Hauptscharführer "Bimbo" Porupski, the commander of the workshop platoon. As an SS-Hauptscharführer, in the IInd Battalion Habermann commanded the headquarters company and for a time the motor transport company. Porupski was promoted to SS-Obersturmführer and before the invasion was made foreman in the Panzer Workshop Company of the Leibstandarte SS Adolf Hitler Panzer Regiment.

The 101st SS Panzer Battalion held an NCO training course in March 1944 under the direction of SS-Untersturmführer Wessel. As Wessel also wanted to offer the participants something cultural, he took them to Brussels, where they took in a theater presentation of Goethe's "Faust." Later, in Mons, Wessel had the men write an essay about what they had seen. Several jokers instead composed satirical revues of "Faust." At the end of the course Wessel and the commander of the Flak Platoon, SS-Oberscharführer Swoboda, moved over to the panzer companies. The battalion was reorganized after the return of the Eastern Front fighters, and it was finally able to begin establishing the 1st and 2nd Companies. The personnel of the old 13th Company formed the bulk of the 2nd Company. Oak Leaves wearer Obersturmführer Wittmann became its company commander. It was to the battalion's 2nd Company that SS-Untersturmführer Wessel was assigned.

The 3rd Company's IVth Platoon under SS-Hauptscharführer Spranz was transferred complete to the 1st Company and there formed its IIIrd Platoon. The personnel for the other two platoons of the 1st Company came in part from the 13th Company and from the steady flow of replacements. The IIIrd Platoon also brought its tanks with it from the 3rd Company. SS-Hauptsturmführer Möbius assumed command of the 1st Company. SS-Untersturmführer Philipsen became commander of Ist Platoon. Placed in command of the IInd Platoon was SS-Untersturmführer Lukasius. The Viennese SS-Hauptscharführer Leo Spranz had been with the troops since the outbreak of war and had joined the battalion in Italy.

Following the departure of Möbius, SS-Untersturmführer Vogt took over the Headquarters and Supply Companies, which he had commanded since September 1943 in Italy. Paul Vogt was born in Pirmasens on 20 October 1907. He worked as a shipping clerk, office clerk and bookkeeper. Vogt was an Alte Kämpfer and soon joined the Allgemeine-SS, on 1 May 1929. In 1935, as an SS-Hauptscharführer, he commanded the Pirmasens Motor Squad, which belonged to the 9th Sturm of the 10th SS Standarte.

He was promoted to SS-Untersturmführer on 9 November 1935 and to Obersturmführer two years later. On 20 April 1939 he became an SS-Hauptsturmführer of the Allgemeine-SS. He volunteered for service in the Waffen-SS on 6 March 1940 and served as an infantryman on the Eastern Front, where he was decorated with the Iron Cross, First and Second Classes, the Infantry Assault Badge, the Eastern Front Medal and the Wound Badge in Black. In early 1943 he was assigned to the SS-Junker-schule in Bad Tölz, subsequently to the SS Panzer-Grenadier School in Prosetschnitz (Kienschlag) and on 30 July 1943 to the 101st SS Panzer Battalion. In Italy he was a close friend of Sepp Dietrich and on 1 September 1943 was promoted to SS-Untersturmführer. SS-Untersturmführer Herbert Walther, instructor in the Headquarters Company, left the battalion and was transferred to the 12th SS Panzer Regiment Hitlerjugend.

Two veteran SS-Hauptscharführer, Heinz Belbe and Thomas Amsel-gruber, were promoted to SS-Standartenoberjunker for bravery in the face of the enemy. Belbe was transferred from the 3rd Company to the 2nd. Technical Officer Ordnance (TFW) was SS-Untersturmführer Berger, who was assisted by the ordnance technical sergeant, SS-Oberscharführer Heinz Niesler. The battalion administration officer since Italy was SS-Obersturm-führer Alfred Veller, who together with the finance officer was in charge of pay. Alfred Veller was born in Spreitgen, near Gummersbach, on 19 August 1908. He worked as a manager in several commercial enterprises. A member of the Allgemeine-SS since 1 May 1932, he joined the Leibstandarte on 10 May 1933. On 1 October 1934 he was promoted to SS-Scharführer while serving with the Ist Battalion and went on to serve as staff sergeant. He attended Administrative Officer School from 29 April to 10 July 1940 and on 30 January 1941 was promoted to SS-Untersturmführer. On 4 June 1942 he was posted from the SS Administration Office to the command staff of the Reichsführer-SS as mess officer. From there Veller was assigned to the Leibstandarte's Guard Battalion in Berlin on 20 July 1942. On 20 April 1942 he was promoted to Obersturmführer. He was later transferred to the Leibstandarte's artillery regiment and on 20 August 1943 to the Ist SS Panzer Corps. On 24 September 1943 he took over the duties of the administration officer of the 101st SS Panzer Battalion in Italy.

The Technical Officer Motor Vehicles was SS-Untersturmführer Georg Bartel, who had also been with the battalion since Italy. He came from the Leibstandarte's anti-tank battalion. The 1st Company was transferred closer to Mons in mid-March 1944 and occupied the Château Niemes. The companies were still far from being up to strength in tanks; only the 3rd Company and the 1st Company's IIIrd Platoon were fully equipped.

At this time Michael Wittmann was present with the 2nd Company only sporadically. He did not return to the 13th Company in Russia after receiving the Oak Leaves from Hitler in the Wolfsschanze Führer Headquarters on 2 February 1944, instead Wittmann was transferred to the 101st SS Panzer Battalion. First, however, he went on leave and drove directly from Führer Headquarters to Erbstorf, near Lüneburg, to see his fiancee Hilde Burmester. He had known the nineteen-year-old since late 1942. Soon afterward the pair drove to Ingolstadt, where he visited his father and on 15 and 16 February 1944 was hosted by city officials. Michael and Hilde subsequently visited Vogelthal, Wittmann's birthplace, where the inhabitants prepared a splendid reception. They then returned to Erbstorf, from where Michael drove to Berlin for a few days. On 1 March 1944 Michael Wittmann married his Hilde in the chapel of the Lüneburg town hall. His best man was his gunner Bobby Woll. As a personal gift from the Führer the young couple received a crate with 50 bottles of various sorts of wine. The same day Michael Wittmann signed his name in the Golden Book of the city of Lüneburg. The local Lüneburg press gave extensive coverage to Wittmann's marriage; the articles reflected the pride felt at having such a highly-decorated soldier as a new resident of the district.

"Wedding vows of an Oak Leaves wearer. The wedding of Oak Leaves wearer SS-Obersturmführer Michael Wittmann and his bride Hildegard, nee Burmester, of Erbstorf (Lüneburg District), took place yesterday in the chapel of the town hall. SS comrades and boys and girls of the Hitler Youth made the wedding a dignified ceremony. When selected music by the band had accompanied the bride and bridegroom to their places, the girls of the BdM choir began to sing the well-balanced songs in their clear voices, offering the couple words for their life together. After the wedding ceremony by the civil magistrate, who delivered the best wishes of the city council and the gift copy of Mein Kampf, a speech was given by SS-Sturmbannführer Pein. He declared that the philosophy of life of the Teutons still has meaning in our lives. The substance of their existence was struggle, struggle against the errors in their own breast and against the external enemy. Their high fighting morale, which carried in itself it the concept of honor, loyalty and honesty toward friend and foe, has been handed down to us as their descendants. These virtues are not just valid on the battlefield, they apply equally to the husband and wife in marriage. The SS-Sturmbannführer went on to speak of the sense of family and of the bride and groom's responsibility to their forbearers and descendants. Following the exchange of rings, which was accompanied by solemn words spoken by a BdM officer and soft music, SS-Sturmbannführer Pein adopted the young bride into the SS family and offered the congratulations of the SS-Gruppenführer. At the conclusion of the ceremony Teutonic virtues, without which no marriage becomes a true life partnership, were once again praised in verse and song.

Oak Leaves wearer SS-Obersturmführer Michael Wittmann, who hails from Bavaria, will now make his home in Erbstorf. Yesterday he entered his name in the Golden Book of the city of Lüneburg."

Michael Wittmann was now one of the best-known German soldiers, all the papers carried stories about him. If he and his wife went about town they were mobbed by youths requesting autographs and photos. If they entered a cafe it wasn't long before they were recognized. Their quiet time was then quickly over, for the cheerful mob grew rapidly. Soon the extent of his popularity became too great for him and he took to buttoning up his collar to hide his Knight's Cross with Oak Leaves. Letters from all over Germany, from people asking for signed photographs, piled up in his apartment.

In April 1944 Wittmann spoke to the staff at the Henschel Works in Kassel, where the Tiger was built. He passed on to the workers the thanks and appreciation felt by the front-line soldiers for their outstanding work. On 8 March 1944, Wittmann visited the 2nd SS-Panzerjunker special training course at Fallingbostel, in which four members of the 13th Company—Staudegger, Schamp, Knöss and Söffker—were taking part. SS-Junker Rolf Schamp, who had served in the same company as Wittmann from November 1942 to December 1943, recalled his visit: "The last time I saw him was in Fallingbostel; in March 1944 he visited members of his former company who were on the 2nd Panzerjunker special course. That's how he was! There was a solemn, simple lunch in the mess with a speech by the school commander in the presence of the training officers. Of course we cadets were dizzy with excitement and almost forgot the meal!" Wittmann made a note in his pocket diary to request soon-to-be Untersturmführer Schamp, Knight's Cross wearer Staudegger, Knöss and Söffker for the Tiger Battalion.

Also on Wittmann's list of names was SS-Oberscharführer Jürgen Brandt. He was also in Fallingbostel, but sinus problems and an abscessed jaw prevented him from taking part in the course. He had already asked Wittmann to take him into his unit again. From his letter to him one can sense the closeness that bound Wittmann to his men:

"Dear Michel   Fallingbostel, 8 February 1944

You will not have received my letter and my congratulations on your Knight's Cross in the east. Today I must write you for the third time in such a short time. You know that I'm lazy in writing to you, but your breathtaking pace simply forces me to. From Knight's Cross to Oak Leaves in fourteen days, that may be unprecedented! So, dear Michel, I heartily congratulate you on your new, terrific successes and the Oak Leaves. I called Walsrode and learned that you will probably be spending part of your well-deserved leave in Erbstorf. Perhaps we might see each other after the first 'wild' weeks of your leave. You must help me again. So far I've not been able to sit in on twenty hours of classes on this course, to say nothing of outside duty. I keep sitting there with my infected sinuses and two abscessed jaws and in six or seven weeks the course is over. Do me one favor, get me out of here and take me with you to your company or to wherever else you can use me. If I have to take part in the next course they'll make me sit around here in the Reich the whole summer. You can believe me when I say that I will slowly but surely go mad.

Well, dear Michel (or shouldn't I write highly-respected Untersturm-führer?), fond greetings to your bride from me and regards to you, enjoy your leave,

Your Captain"

At Mons training went on unabated. The battalion officers gathered in the mess following a combat exercise on the training grounds. Generaloberst Guderian, who had observed the exercise, asked Wittmann to explain how it was possible to successfully engage targets while on the move. Wittmann argued that the Tiger's weight and its high speed made it unnecessary for a good gunner to stop in order to hit his target.

After the meal, Generaloberst Guderian turned to the circle of battalion officers and asked: "Are the young lieutenants full too?" Thereupon the quick-witted SS-Untersturmführer Lukasius jumped to his feet and replied, "Not me, Herr Generaloberst!"—"So, how much did you have to eat?"—"Two helpings, Herr Generaloberst." On hearing this Guderian said, "When I was a lieutenant I always ate three helpings. Come here, we'll eat one more together."

UNIT PARADE BY THE SS-STURMBRIGADE WALLONIE IN BRUSSELS

On 1 April 1944 SS-Obersturmführer Michael Wittmann and other prominent guests witnessed an impressive unit parade. The SS-Sturmbrigade Wallonie had returned home to Belgium from the Eastern Front. Also present in Brussels were the commanding general of the Ist SS Panzer Corps, SS-Obergruppenführer and General der Waffen-SS Sepp Dietrich, the commanding officer of the 12th SS Panzer Division Hitlerjugend,

SS-Brigadeführer and Generalmajor der Waffen-SS Fritz Witt, and the regimental commander of the 12th Panzer Regiment Hitlerjugend, SS-Obersturmbannführer Max Wünsche. SS-Sturmbannführer Degrelle, commander of the SS Sturmbrigade Wallonie, wrote: "The march column was seventeen kilometers long. Our young Belgian soldiers of the Waffen-SS, in their field-gray uniforms, their newly-won decorations on their breasts, looked down proudly at the jubilant masses from their tank turrets. The Iron Crosses were well-earned. On the other hand the tanks with which we were able to shine in this parade were not as real. We had had to borrow them for this purpose, for we had in fact come out of the Cherkassy Pocket on foot without a single vehicle and were still in the process of reorganization.

It was a fortunate coincidence that the 12th SS Panzer Division Hitlerjugend was quartered at the same Beverloo Training Grounds to which we had been transferred from Wildflecken, home of our replacement unit, on 28 March 1944. Together with the Leibstandarte SS Adolf Hitler, it made up the Ist SS Panzer Corps under the legendary Sepp Dietrich. This elite of the elite loaned us Burgundian volunteers their panzers. I was able to review the parade by my Wallonie Legion from an armored car parked in front of the stock exchange. I was proud and happy like never before in my life when the tracked and other vehicles loaned me by Sepp Dietrich, but manned by our Belgian soldiers, rattled past with a deafening noise. I saluted every single vehicle with my right arm raised high, steel helmet on my head and the newly-won Knight's Cross at my throat. With the other I took turns holding the hands of my four children, who had climbed on to the steel giant and who were allowed to stand beside me. The crowd, estimated at one-hundred-thousand, cheered us and showered us with flowers."

That evening Wittmann attended an official reception which Léon Degrelle gave for invited guests in his apartment in the Drève de Lorraine in Brussels. Also present was Sepp Dietrich.

In February 1944 SS-Sturmbannführer Heinz von Westernhagen became the
commanding officer of the 101st SS Panzer Battalion. Taganrog, 20 April 1942.
SS-Hauptsturmführer von Westernhagen (center), SS-Hauptsturmführer
Wünsche (left) and SS-Oberscharführer Günther (2nd from right).

Von Westernhagen on
13 May 1941 in Greece
after receiving the Iron
Cross, Second Class.

In May 1942 Max Wünsche (right) handed over the Assault Gun Battalion to Heinz von Westernhagen.

Hrabovan, near Brünn, June 1941, before the start of the war with Russia. Von Westernhagen with his wife Elisabeth.

On 12 February 1944 an exercise was held in Mons observed by SS-Obergruppenführer Dietrich. *From left:* Jäsche, SS-Unterscharführer Diefenbach, Schenk and Rößner.

The same Tiger with gunner SS-Sturmmann Alfred Lünser standing in the commander's cupola. On the far right is the tank commander, SS-Unterscharführer Kurt Diefenbach.

A Tiger of the 3rd Company, 101st SS Panzer Battalion in Mons, Belgium.

Tiger 313 in Mons.

Tiger 314 in Mons.

SS-Unterscharführer
Otto Blase in front of his
Tiger 314 of the 3rd
Company.

SS-Sturmbannführer
Heinz von Westernhagen
in the spring of 1944.

Von Westernhagen
and Peiper in March
1943 during the
Kharkov action.

Wedding photo of
Michael and Hilde
Wittmann, 1 March
1944.

The happy couple with
members of their
families. Above right is
Wittmann's sister Anna,
far right brother Hans,
an Oberleutnant in the
army. In the middle of
the second row is the
witness to the wedding,
Bobby Woll.

Michael Wittmann
with his wife, Hilde,
in March 1944.

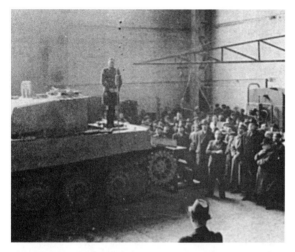

April 1944. Wittmann speaks to workers involved in production of the Tiger. Henschel works, Kassel.

View of the production hall. Those present listen attentively to the experiences of the Oak Leaves wearer.

Wittmann in conversation with Robert Pertuss, head of Tiger production, and Erwin Aders, the designer of the Tiger.

Wittmann with SS-
Obersturmführer Oskar
Röntgen, left, Technical
Officer in Charge of
Ordnance in the 2nd SS
Panzer Grenadier
Regiment Leibstandarte.

On 8 March 1944 Wittmann visited the second SS Panzerjunker special training
course in Fallingbostel, in which several of his men were taking part. Here
souvenir photos are taken. Right SS-Untersturmführer Girg, who later received
the Knight's Cross and the Oak Leaves while serving in Skorzeny's commando
units.

Tiger 314 of the 3rd Company, 101st SS Panzer Battalion. On the left is the tank's commander, SS-Unterscharführer Otto Blase.

SS-Sturmmann Willibald Schenk, gunner, in front of Tiger 314.

Tiger of platoon commander SS-Obersturmführer Hanno Raasch.

SS-Unterscharführer
Kurt Diefenbach (right)
and Rottenführer
Ludwig Hoffmann,
Raasch's gunner and
driver.

THE 101ST SS PANZER BATTALION IN THE GOURNAY AREA, 20 APRIL, 1944–5 JUNE, 1944

Meanwhile, Michael Wittmann was home again. Together with his driver, SS-Oberscharführer Lange, on 21 April 1944 he and his wife drove from Erbstorf to the battalion in Belgium. They spent the night in the soldiers' hostel in Brussels. The next morning Wittmann learned by telephone that the remaining element of his 13th Company would be arriving at the station in Mons that day. This element had fought in the Kamenets-Podolsk pocket under his friend SS-Obersturmführer Wendorff and had now come straight from the Eastern Front by rail.

Wittmann and his wife drove to the railway station in Mons, and soon afterward the train carrying the 13th Company arrived. The men were beside themselves with joy to see their Michel waiting for them at the station and they gave him a tumultuous reception. Then Wittmann had hot food brought to the platform, pea soup, which he ate with his wife and comrades while they sat on simple wooden crates. The noisy reception by his men came on just the right day for Wittmann; it was 22 April, his thirtieth birthday.

The battalion was to be moved from Mons to a site nearer the area of operations of the expected Allied invasion of Northern France. Gournay-en-Bray, between Rouen and Beauvais, had been selected as the battalion's new quartering area. On the afternoon of 23 April 1944, Michael Wittmann and his wife set out by car for France, in order to find suitable accommodations for the company. Several villages offered acceptable quarters, but there was nowhere to hide the tanks from enemy aircraft. After visiting several villages, Wittmann spoke to one mayor and asked him for his help. Four kilometers from Gournay-en-Bray they found the Château Elbeuf, whose large wood offered the necessary cover for the Tigers. The château itself was unoccupied apart from a caretaker who also served as gardener. Wittmann decided to stay there; his wife also found the idyllic château very much to her liking. A major clean-up operation began the next day; the first members of a small advance party from the company had also arrived and they pitched in to help make the rooms liveable. Frau Wittmann, her husband's batman Sturmmann Alfred Bernhard, Bobby Woll, Senior NCO Konradt, and two Ukrainian Hiwis had their hands full preparing the quarters for their new occupants.

The other companies also found suitable accommodations and moved into their new quarters, all of which were situated near Gournay-en-Bray. The battalion's tanks and wheeled vehicles entrained in Mons and arrived in Gournay unmolested. From there the units drove to their nearby billets.

The battalion occupied the following quarters: Headquarters and Signals Platoons: Crillon, northeast of Gournay. Reconnaissance, Flak and Pioneer Platoons: Cremeville. 1st Company: St.-Germer-de-Fly, southeast of Gournay. 2nd Company: Elbeuf-en-Bray, four kilometers west of Gournay. 3rd Company: Songeons, 13 kilometers northeast of Gournay. The heavy rail transport was carried out without loss. The Flak Platoon provided air cover during entraining and detraining and during the journey to France.

In April 1944 several NCOs and enlisted men were given leave, the first for some time. As well, the battalion finally received its twenty-six remaining Tigers. The headquarters was issued one tank with the new running gear. Its two existing Tigers were equipped with the old running gear, which was equipped with twenty-four road wheels with rubber tires on each side. The new running gear used steel road wheels or steel tires. In addition to the four tanks of the Bird Platoon, all of which had the old running gear, the 1st Company had another with the old running gear and nine with the new running gear. One Tiger still had the early bolted-on commander's cupola, the "Knight's Cross cupola" in soldiers' jargon. This Tiger also lacked the now standard periscope. All the 3rd Company's tanks had the old running gear, as this company had been equipped with Tigers for some time.

All the Tiger companies were now at authorized strength, each with fourteen Tigers. According to the table of organization still valid at that time, each of the panzer companies were supposed to consist of 4 officers, 58 non-commissioned officers and 107 enlisted men. All platoon commander positions were to be held by officers. All units moved into quarters in the above-mentioned villages around Gournay-en-Bray in the third week of April. Accommodations in the new quarters were good. As the companies were to spend the next weeks there, their quarters will now be described in greater detail.

1st Company: directly opposite St.-Gerner-de-Fly's marketplace were two huge cathedrals, one behind the other. Access to the inner courtyard of the former monastery, which was bounded by several buildings, was through a gate-shaped entrance in a nearby house. To the right was the house in which the officers lived, with the orderly room located on the ground floor. Right beside this house was the first church and its entrance. The company was billeted in the building opposite it. By crossing the paved courtyard, which opened at the rear, and proceeding through the gate, one reached the park in which the Tigers were hidden from enemy reconnaissance aircraft. The entrance for the tanks lay on the other side, to the right of the two churches. The former monastery in the small village was now home to SS-Hauptsturmführer Möbius and his men.

2nd Company: Four kilometers west of Gournay at a crossroads one came upon the entrance to the enchanted area of Château Elbeuf. On the right beyond the entrance gate was a small house, which housed the guard. The three-story château was overgrown with ivy up to the roof; adjoining it to the right there was a conservatory with numerous windows. Behind the buildings there was a small lake, magnificent to look at, surrounded by tall, full trees. A small island projected from the middle of the lake. The château grounds were bordered by a large wood; the Tigers were parked out of sight in its dark interior.

The expansive château grounds were bordered by long, high stone walls. All the officers, NCOs and enlisted men of the combat echelon lived in the château proper. Obersturmführer Wittmann and his wife had their refuge on the second floor. The remaining elements of the company, such as the maintenance echelon and the train, were quartered in buildings behind the château. Elbeuf was certainly the loveliest of the battalion's billets. The picturesque château was situated fairy-tale-like in the pleasant park with its lush trees; the lake and the wood behind it gave Elbeuf a dreamlike, romantic atmosphere. It was difficult to understand why this jewel was unoccupied, with only a caretaker to look after the estate.

3rd Company: At the eastern exit from the large town of Songeons was Château Songeons. The history of the château had been dominated by higher French nobility for many years. It was built in the year 1720 by Diane Gabrielle de Jussac, dame d'honneur de la Duchesse de Berry, wife of Michel de Conflans, Viscount d'Oulchy, Marquis d'Armentières. The family of Conflans de St. Rémy d'Armentières were masters of the Château Songeons for a long time, until the estate was sold in 1778. After that it changed owners several times. During the First World War the château was used to billet Senegalese troops. It subsequently returned to private hands until, at the beginning of the Second World War, a hospital for French troops was set up there.

The estate and its magnificent park were in good condition, but completely empty. In front of the free-standing building there were gardens and outside the grounds, opposite the main entrance, there was a fruit orchard, where the Tigers were parked and camouflaged. Behind the château was the estate park. The château housed the combat echelon and the orderly room; the company commander, the platoon commanders and the senior NCO, as well as the medics, were quartered in the town, near the war memorial. As the château lacked beds, these had to be obtained in the town in exchange for vouchers.

In the early days of April 1944 three young Untersturmführer were transferred to the battalion after spending several months in training: Hantusch, Stamm, and Henniges. All three had taken the same courses and had trained as tank platoon commanders. Hantusch was assigned to Wittmann's 2nd Company. Georg Hantusch was born on 7 October 1921 in Eichgraben, St. Pölten District, Austria, the son of a professor. After leaving school he worked in an auto repair business. After completing his labor service duty, on 15 December 1939 he volunteered for the Waffen-SS. He took part in all the battles in the Western Campaign with the 2nd Company of the Leibstandarte, first as a mortarman and later as company mechanic and maintenance sergeant. In this period the young man from Ostmark was decorated with the General Assault Badge, the Eastern Front Medal and the Romanian Medal of Bravery with Swords.

Chosen for a maintenance technical sergeant training course, at the beginning of 1942 he began studying mechanical engineering at the SS School of Engineering. After two semesters, in spring 1943 he joined the SS Panzer Training and Replacement Regiment in Bitsch. Hantusch became a tank commander and took part in a training course for officer candidates. He subsequently went to Putlos, where he attended an SS-Panzerjunker Special Course from 17 August to 6 November 1943. He made SS-Standartenjunker there on 1 October 1943 and a month later SS-Standartenoberjunker. Hantusch subsequently joined the armored command officer candidate course in Alt-Gleinicke and took part in a special course at the gunnery school at the Putlos Troop Training Grounds. On 1 March 1944 he was promoted to the rank of SS-Untersturmführer. Effective 1 March 1944 Hantusch was transferred to the 101st SS Panzer Battalion, but first he took part in a "Tiger tank course" at Paderborn from 6 March 1944 to 1 April 1944.

Fritz Stamm was born in Wevelinghoven, near Grevenbroich, on 11 December 1922. He left school prior to graduation and at the beginning of 1941 joined the Leibstandarte as a volunteer. As a member of the Leibstandarte's 16th Company, he took part in the campaign in the east which began on 22 June 1941 and on 31 October was decorated with the Iron Cross, Second Class. In 1943 he served as an SS-Unterscharführer in the 11th (Armored) Company of the 2nd SS Panzer-Grenadier Regiment on the Eastern Front. Following the capture of Kharkov, on 20 April 1943 he received the Iron Cross, First Class and on 1 September 1943—by which time he had left for Germany—the Close Combat Clasp in Bronze. In Bitsch Stamm, too, became a tank commander and attended the various courses with Hantusch and Henniges. On joining the battalion Stamm took over the armored reconnaissance platoon and then in June 1944 a platoon of the 1st Company.

Like Fritz Stamm, SS-Untersturmführer Rolf Henniges was assigned to the Headquarters Company and led the reconnaissance platoon. Born in Berlin on 21 August 1921, Stamm was preparing to write his final exams when he joined the Waffen-SS on 1 March 1940. He served with the Der Führer Regiment in France and was wounded in action. In the Balkan and Eastern Campaigns Henniges served as a driver and then a squad leader in the 18th Company of the Leibstandarte SS Adolf Hitler. In August 1941 he was wounded again, at Nikolayev. Later he reported to the SS School of Engineering from the replacement battalion. There he studied mechanical engineering like Georg Hantusch.

Henniges later described how he ended up in the armored command instead of becoming an engineer: "After I was forced to leave the SS School of Engineering in Vienna after two semesters on account of the order calling for total war, I took part in a tank commander training course with the SS Panzer Replacement Regiment in Bitsch. I was then assigned to a senior officer candidate course for the armored command. From there I was sent to the SS-Panzerjunker special course in Putlos in Holstein. Now I'm on the armored command's officer candidate course in Groß- Gleinicke." After taking the same courses as Stamm and Hantusch, Henniges joined the Tiger battalion. Henniges wore the Infantry Assault Badge in Bronze and the Wound Badge. Another Technical Officer Motor Vehicles had been transferred to the battalion at the beginning of 1944. He was SS-Obersturmführer Franz Heurich. Born on 16 April 1914 in Dortmund, and a baker by trade, he joined the Leibstandarte on 12 September 1934 and was assigned to the 3rd Company. From the time of the Polish Campaign he served in the headquarters staff of the Ist Battalion and took part in the campaign in Western Europe in 1940 as an SS-Hauptscharführer and Oberschirrmeister (master technical sergeant). Heurich received the Iron Cross, Second Class. He was wounded, and as a result of his injuries was left with one leg shorter than the other. He was then sent to the Automotive School in Vienna. After completing a technical officer (motor vehicle) training course, Heurich was promoted to the rank of SS-Untersturmführer. Later he was assigned to the Leibstandarte's division engineer and repair battalion. On 1 December 1943 he was transferred to the 1st SS Panzer Corps and joined the Tiger battalion in January 1944. The former Technical Officer Motor Vehicles, SS-Untersturmführer Georg Bartel, now became Technical Officer Motor Vehicles II; the two men divided their area of responsibility. SS-Sturmbannführer Heinz von Westernhagen's adjutant was SS-Untersturmführer Helmut Dollinger, who was also his signals officer.

Born on 8 June 1922, Dollinger was a member of the 2nd Radio Company of the Leibstandarte's signals battalion; he received the Iron Cross, Second Class on 30 December 1941 while at the rank of SS-Sturmmann. In 1942 he was sent to the Junkerschule in Braunschweig. In May 1943, SS-Untersturmführer Dollinger became one of the first members of the Tiger Battalion at Sennelager. The battalion's operations officer was SS-Untersturmführer Willi Iriohn. The twenty-seven-year-old Iriohn was an ethnic German from Groß-Scham in Romania. He was one of the Junkerschule graduates assigned to the battalion on 30 July 1943.

There were promotions in all units of the battalion on 20 April 1944. In the 1st Company the commander of the Ist Platoon, Hannes Philipsen, was promoted to SS-Obersturmführer, as was the commander of the 2nd Company's Ist Platoon, Jürgen Wessel. Shortly before, the commanding officer of the 3rd Company, SS-Hauptsturmführer Schweimer, fell ill with jaundice and had to leave the battalion. SS-Obersturmführer Hanno Raasch took over the company and became a popular and capable company commander. SS-Standartenoberjunker Thomas Amselgruber of the 3rd Company was promoted to SS-Untersturmführer. The battalion's Technical Officer Motor Vehicles I, Franz Heurich, became an SS-Hauptsturmführer. In the battalion workshop company, SS-Hauptscharführer Oskar Glaeser and SS-Standartenoberjunker Reinhold Wichert were also promoted to the rank of SS-Untersturmführer.

Among the soldiers who came directly from Russia to the battalion with the old 13th Company was SS-Rottenführer Walter Lau: "The 101st SS Heavy Panzer Battalion was transferred from Mons into the Beauvais area at the beginning of April 1944. As we know today, this was because the Supreme Command expected an Allied landing in the Calais area. Obersturmführer Wittmann's 2nd Company was in a château in Elbeuf, the 3rd Company about fifteen kilometers away, and between them the workshop company and the headquarters. I was one of the forty to fifty men of the former 13th Company who joined the newly-formed Corps Tiger Battalion of the 1st SS Panzer Corps in Belgium following five months of heavy fighting in the areas of Kiev, Zhitomir and Cherkassy.

The battalion's commanding officer, Sturmbannführer von Westernhagen, was probably acting in his unit's best military interests when he split up the personnel of the old 13th Company. The majority went to the 2nd Company, the rest to the 1st and 3rd Companies. I had the bad luck—as I perceived it—to be assigned to the 3rd Company, while most of my old buddies went to Wittmann's 2nd Company. But as chance would have it, following his 'Oak Leaves leave' and marriage leave Obersturmführer Wittmann visited the workshop company, where I happened to be with my tank (3rd Company, Ist Platoon) which had transmission trouble. I spoke to Wittmann and asked for a transfer to his company. The very next day a VW Schwimmwagen came and took me to the 2nd Company. As the company had already established crews, I was at first assigned to the so-called alternate crew—that was at about thebeginning of May—and later became a loader in the company headquarters panzer with Unterscharführer Seifert. There were no formal alternate crews, not even complete ones, just a dozen or so gunners, loaders, radio operators and drivers who went along as passengers assigned by the Senior NCO. When it was quiet they were attached to the Ist to IIIrd Platoons for training purposes."

The group to which Walter Lau belonged was followed by one final group from the 13th Company, which arrived in Mons from the Soviet Union on 22 April 1944. It was met in Mons by Wittmann. The bulk of the group was from Wittmann's 2nd Company; SS-Rottenführer Bobby Warmbrunn, arrived even later, the last member of the 13th Company to return from the Soviet Union. Now that the three panzer companies were up to strength and all the platoon commanders had been permanently assigned, individual training on the Tiger and platoon and company exercises in the field could go ahead.

The platoon commanders in Wittmann's 2nd Company were SS-Obersturmführer Wessel, SS-Untersturmführer Hantusch and SS-Standartenoberjunker Belbe. The platoons of the 3rd Company under Hanno Raasch were commanded by Knight's Cross wearer SS-Untersturmführer Günther, SS-Hauptscharführer Görgens and SS-Untersturmführer Amselgruber. SS-Hauptscharführer Spranz had been transferred to 12th SS Panzer Regiment of the Hitlerjugend Division, where he was promoted to SS-Untersturmführer on 20 April 1944 as a member of the IInd Battalion. The companies had settled into their billets, the 2nd and 3rd Companies both occupied small châteaus. SS-Obersturmführer Raasch, who was extremely gifted artistically, showed a sense for the beautiful. SS-Sturmmann Alfred Lünser recalled of Songeons: "From Mons we moved to Château Songeons in France, it was spring 1944. There they brought us numerous cans of green paint, and all the walls and ceilings were painted using paintbrushes and shoe brushes. Afterward Oberscharführer Rolf von Westernhagen painted great caricatures on the walls; it made everything somewhat more homey.

We had many lessons, including some at the sand table. During one of these Obersturmführer Hanno Raasch asked me: 'Here is a church steeple, you miss the steeple with your first shot, how do you adjust the range setting?' (on the telescopic sight). My answer: 'If I don't hit this steeple with the first shot you can put me on the retired list, Obersturmführer!' My commander, Unterscharführer Otto Blase was sitting behind me. He nudged me in the back and hissed, 'Don't blame us.' But before Hanno Raasch reacted, as senior gunner present I gave the justification for my saucy answer: 'Assuming that the steeple is twelve meters high and between one-thousand and three-thousand meters away, and I aim at the center of it with a range setting of two-thousand meters, given the Vo (descent of the shot per thousand meters) of this 88 mm tank cannon, I'll always hit the steeple! I know what you want to hear, Obersturmführer. Up to two-thousand meters I must elevate two-hundred meters and from two-thousand meters I must elevate four-hundred meters.' Hanno Raasch was satisfied."

The relationship of the men to the French population was correct in every town. Many established good personal relationships, and some of the French girls were very taken with the young panzer soldiers. There was no activity of any sort by the underground movement in the battalion's area. On the basis of a report, in April the 3rd Company had to strengthen the guard on its Tigers, which were parked in the orchard in front of the château. At this time the guard was increased in size to five soldiers: two men with carbines, backed up by a man carrying a machine-gun, and then by two men with submachine-guns. However, as there was no sign of the expected hostilities, things soon returned to normal in Songeons. There never was an indication of activity by the resistance even on the drives between the individual companies, some of which led through extended areas of forest, such as between Elbeuf and Songeons.

Members of 3rd Company set up a radio in a room of the Château Songeons. Now and then they listened to Radio Calais, an enemy transmitter, which was forbidden. One day SS-Obersturmführer Raasch walked into the room unexpectedly. All was still except for an announcer on the radio. 'What are you listening to?' asked the company commander. Sturmmann Lünser was first to regain his composure: 'Obersturmführer, if you really believe that we would allow ourselves to be influenced by this propaganda in any way, then we are in bad shape.'—At this Hanno Raasch replied, 'Then at least turn it down a little.' This ended the matter for him. After the alert before our departure for the invasion front the radio was taken back to its owner in Songeons.

Twenty-two-year-old Hanno Raasch was the battalion's youngest company commander. Günther Hanno Oswald Johannes Raasch was born on 14 March 1921 in Ratzdorf, near Schönebeck. He was a longtime member of the 5th Company of the Germania Regiment. He had won the Iron Cross, First and Second Classes, the Infantry Assault Badge in Bronze and the Eastern Front Medal in Russia. On 21 June 1943 he was promoted to SS-Obersturmführer. Raasch had two experienced platoon commanders in Günther and Amselgruber, both of who served as a model for SS-Hauptscharführer Görgens.

Alfred Günther was born on 25 April 1917 in Magdeburg. His father was killed in the First World War. A qualified typesetter, in April 1937 he joined the SS-Verfügungstruppe and in 1940 came to the Leibstandarte via the Germania Regiment. He became one of the original members of the Assault Gun Battery. In 1941 he served in Russia as Wittmann's gunner and later as a gun commander. SS-Unterscharführer Günther was successful in both roles and in 1941 he received both Iron Crosses. On 3 March 1943 Günther, now an SS-Oberscharführer, became the first member of the Assault Gun Battalion to receive the Knight's Cross. In May 1943 he left his 1st Battery and went to Sennelager for the formation of the 101st SS Panzer Battalion. He did not go to the Eastern Front from Italy in November 1943 but instead went to Augustdorf with the rest of the battalion. Freddi Günther was promoted to SS-Untersturmführer on 30 January 1944.

SS-Hauptscharführer Max Görgens, born in Hamborn on 7 November 1914, joined the 1st Company of the Leibstandarte SS Adolf Hitler on 1 August 1934. He later moved to the 2nd Company, with which he took part in the campaigns in Poland and Western Europe. After being wounded in front of Dunkirk in Northern France, he was transferred to the Führer Escort Detachment and served in Führer Headquarters. In 1943 Görgens became the driver of SS-Obergruppenführer Sepp Dietrich, the commander of the Leibstandarte SS Adolf Hitler. In autumn 1943 he happened to run into Hein von Westernhagen in Innsbruck; the latter asked if he would like to join him, as he was forming a Tiger battalion. Görgens wasn't the only one to join the battalion that way; von Westernhagen was always on the lookout for qualified men he knew from the past to serve in his battalion. He acquired the driver of the commander of the Corps Headquarters, SS-Rottenführer Waldemar Warnecke, for the battalion in the same way.

Görgens was trained as a tank commander in Augustdorf and served as section leader in the IInd Platoon of the 3rd Company. When his platoon commander, SS-Untersturmführer Philipsen, was transferred to the 1st Company, Görgens assumed command of the IInd Platoon. SS-Hauptscharführer Barkhausen, also from the Führer Escort Detachment, became his section leader.

Thomas Amselgruber was born on 18 December 1905 in Kirchweidach in Upper Bavaria. He joined the Allgemeine-SS in Munich in July 1931 and came to Berlin via the Eher Verlag, where he was placed in charge of the garage of the Reichsführer-SS. Amselgruber was promoted to SS-Untersturmführer on 20 April 1938. In 1940 he joined the Leibstandarte's assault gun battery and took part in all its actions, first as a driver, then as an assault gun driver. On 2 July 1943, Amselgruber, now an SS-Hauptscharführer, received the Iron Cross, First Class. He destroyed eighteen enemy anti-tank guns and eight T 34s during Operation Zitadelle. On 12 July 1943 he was badly wounded in the left hand, losing four fingers. After convalescing, Amselgruber, who had also been decorated with the Tank Battle Badge, the Wound Badge in Silver and the Royal Bulgarian Soldiers' Cross of the Order of Bravery IInd Class, reported to his former commanding officer Heinz von Westernhagen, who in December 1943 had him transferred to the Tiger Battalion. There Thomas Amselgruber was promoted to SS-Standartenoberjunker for bravery in the face of the enemy and then to SS-Untersturmführer on 20 April 1944.

In spite of being only nineteen years old, "Amsel," as he was called, was an uncommonly brave and tireless platoon commander, who was generally well known even beyond the confines of his company. He belonged to the core of former assault gun personnel, men like Wittmann, Philipsen, Günther, Brandt, Dr. Rabe, Belbe, Traue, Zahner, Heinz and Rolf von Westernhagen, Otterbein, Renfordt and others. The scout, pioneer, reconnaissance and flak companies, which until now had been part of the Headquarters Company, were to be completely removed and concentrated in a company of their own. Once finally established in July 1944, this 4th Company, which was also designated as a light company, was placed under the command of SS-Obersturmführer Wilhelm Spitz, who had previously served for a time as operations officer in the battalion staff.

Wilhelm Spitz was born in Munich on 6 May 1915. After finishing his apprenticeship as a draftsman with a glass painter and attending arts and crafts school for two semesters, on 8 January 1934 he joined the Deutschland SS-Regiment in Munich, after having been a member of the Allgemeine-SS since July 1933. Spitz later became chief records officer in the Hauptamt SS Court and on 30 January 1941 was promoted to Untersturmführer. With interruptions for active service—during which he earned the Tank Battle Badge in Silver, the War Merit Cross Second Class with Swords, and the Wound Badge in Black, and was promoted to the rank of SS-Obersturmführer on 30 January 1942—on 7 July 1943 Spitz moved from the

Hauptamt SS Court to the Ist SS Panzer Corps. Then on 21 February 1944 he was transferred to the 101st SS Panzer Battalion.

This 4th Company was supernumerary and existed only in the 101st SS Panzer Battalion; a heavy panzer battalion did not normally have a fourth company.

After SS-Untersturmführer Wessel's departure from the reconnaissance platoon, the unit was led by Untersturmführer Fritz Stamm and from June 1944 by SS-Hauptscharführer Benno Poetschlak. In 1942 Poetschlak became one of the first tank commanders in the Leibstandarte's Tiger Company and among the decorations he earned on the Eastern Front was the Iron Cross, First Class. The reconnaissance and pioneer platoons were supposed to be equipped with armored troop carriers. The pioneer platoon was commanded by SS Standartenoberjunker Walter Brauer.

Brauer was born in Angermünde on 6 October 1921 and came to the Leibstandarte's pioneer battalion in 1940 via the pioneer battalion of the SS-Verfügungstruppe. While serving with the 2nd Company as an SS-Rottenführer, he was decorated with the Iron Cross, Second Class on 15 August 1942; on 7 April 1943, by then an SS-Unterscharführer, he received the Tank Battle Badge in Bronze and the Wound Badge in Black. In autumn 1943 Brauer was sent to the SS Pioneer School for officer training, after which, in spring 1944, he was transferred to the 101st SS Panzer Battalion.

The scout platoon consisted of three scout squads each with three VW Schwimmwagen amphibious vehicles. Commanding the platoon was SS-Untersturmführer Henniges; his three squad leaders were SS-Unterscharführer Heidemann, Mankewitz and Krebs. SS-Oberscharführer Swoboda was succeeded as commander of the flak platoon by SS-Unterscharführer Fickert, who had previously served as one of the platoon's gun commanders.

Kurt Wolfgang Fickert was born in Plauen in the Vogtland on 4 October 1921. Prior to the outbreak of war he studied for three years at the music school in Zahna, where his main instrument was the oboe. He took part in the landing in Oslo with the 6th SS Infantry Regiment and subsequently fought on the northern front with the SS Mountain Infantry Division North until wounded. He received the Infantry Assault Badge and the Wound Badge. After recovering from his injuries, Fickert went to a military training camp as an instructor and in March 1943 completed an NCO training course in Wildflecken. He became an SS-Unterscharführer on 1 June 1943 and subsequently went to Munich-Freiman for the formation of the 101st SS Panzer Battalion's flak platoon.

After the division the headquarters company—the fuel and ammunition transport columns, vehicle maintenance echelon, combat trains I and II, medical squad, echelon for administration and supply, ration supply train (for the entire battalion), baggage train, and the technical officers responsible for motor vehicles and ordnance—was a pure supply company. The signals platoon was the sole exception; it remained with the headquarters and supply company, as its new designation read.

The signals platoon was equipped with three Tigers, the staff tanks for the battalion commander, adjutant and signals officer. These tanks were fitted with an extensive radio system and were equipped with an additional umbrella antenna. The distribution of duties among the crews was therefore somewhat different, for two of the loaders were also radio operators. The platoon also included a signals vehicle (Kfz. 15 Horch) with equipment for the field telephone squad as well as a "trunk" which housed the radio station. Platoon personnel consisted of one officer, twelve NCOs and six men. The commander of the signals platoon and signals officer was SS-Untersturmführer Helmut Dollinger, who had previously served in the radio company of the Leibstandarte's signals battalion.

The fuel transport column had twenty-two vehicles, ten of which had trailers, while the munitions transport column had a complement of twenty vehicles, all twin-axle types. The commander of the medical echelon was the battalion medical officer, Hauptsturmführer Dr. Rabe; the dentist was SS-Untersturmführer Dr. Hausamm, called "Doctor Grausam" (cruel). The battalion medical officer had one medical armored troop carrier, an ambulance and an equipment truck.

The men discovered old friends, and not just from the assault gun battalion and the old 13th Company. In February 1944, the signals officer, SS-Untersturmführer Dollinger, discovered SS-Oberscharführer Johann Schott, whom he had as a student during his time as an instructor at the Braunschweig Junkerschule in 1942. He had him transferred to his signals platoon in the capacity of technical sergeant. Training was hard in those weeks and the officers attempted to make it as realistic as possible in order to prepare their men for the coming actions.

The 1st Company included in its ranks two tank commanders from the old Tiger Company of 1942, Obersturmführer Philipsen and SS-Unterscharführer Wendt. SS-Unterscharführer Cap, together with SS-Oberscharführer Zahner and SS-Unterscharführer Otterbein, both former members of the assault gun battalion, all had Eastern Front experience. The rest were new arrivals, including former members of the Führer Escort Detachment SS-Hauptscharführer Kurt Michaelis (gunner), Fritz

Hibbeler, SS-Oberscharführer Heinrich Ernst (tank commander), Hein Bode and SS Unterscharführer Walter Sturhahn.

SS-Obersturmführer Michael Wittmann had been able to keep the majority of crews from the old 13th Company in his 2nd Company. Michael Wittmann was one of Germany's most successful tank commanders, having destroyed 117 enemy tanks on the Eastern Front. His almost equally famous gunner, Bobby Woll, who had received the Knight's Cross shortly after Wittmann, had meanwhile been promoted to SS-Unterscharführer and was now a tank commander. As a gunner, Bobby Woll had destroyed eighty-one Soviet tanks as well as 107 anti-tank guns and four each of 172 mm and 125 mm artillery pieces, five flamethrowers, one armored car and a heavy mortar position.

The 2nd Company possessed experienced section leaders in SS-Oberscharführer "Captain" Brandt and Schorsch Lötzsch as well as SS-Hauptscharführer Hans Höflinger. Platoon commanders SS-Obersturmführer Wessel and SS-Untersturmführer Hantusch were new to the panzer arm, but SS-Oberjunker Belbe had seen action with the assault gun battalion.

Jürgen Wessel was born in Tessin, Rostock District, on 19 July 1920; the son of a teacher, he grew up in Parchim. After leaving school he did his stint in the labor service; he and his Reich Labor Service Battalion were employed within the 3rd Construction Battalion during the Polish Campaign. On 13 November 1939 he joined the Leibstandarte as a volunteer and served with the 18th Company of the Guard Battalion in Berlin. Following an NCO training course, on 1 July 1940 he was promoted to SS-Sturmmann. At the end of 1940 the company was transferred to Metz to join the field regiment, becoming the Leibstandarte's 13th Company. In the east Wessel was promoted to SS-Unterscharführer on 1 July 1941 and was decorated with the Iron Cross, Second Class, the Infantry Assault Badge in Bronze, the Wound Badge in Black and the Royal Bulgarian Soldiers' Cross of the Order of Bravery IVth Class.

He attended the Braunschweig Junkerschule from 1 November 1941 until 30 April 1942 and was subsequently assigned to the Leibstandarte's VIth Battalion in Sennelager. There Wessel became operations officer with SS-Sturmbannführer Weidenhaupt and on 21 June 1942 was promoted to the rank of SS-Untersturmführer. When incorporated into the division in June 1942, the VIth Battalion became the IIIrd Battalion of the 1st SS Infantry Regiment. Wessel remained in his position of operations officer until May 1943 and subsequently served with the replacement battalion of the Leibstandarte until December 1943. After joining the Tiger Battalion Wessel initially led the reconnaissance platoon. The IInd Platoon commander, SS-Untersturmführer Hantusch, had already been chosen. The IIIrd Platoon was commanded by SS-Standartenoberjunker Belbe, an old friend of Michael Wittmann's from their time together in the Leibstandarte's armored car replacement company.

Heinz Belbe, called "Balbo," was born in Hindenburg, Templin District, Uckermark, on 20 April 1916. He had seven sisters. A trained agriculture official, he worked on his parents' farm and in the thirties did his compulsory military service with the SS-Verfügungstruppe. He joined the Allgemeine-SS in 1934. Belbe returned to the service on 27 August 1939, serving with the Leibstandarte's armored car company and from 1940 the assault gun battery. He won both Iron Crosses and other decorations while serving as a gun commander on the Eastern Front. SS-Hauptscharführer Belbe joined the Tiger Battalion in 1943 and in Mons was promoted to SS-Standartenoberjunker for bravery in the face of the enemy.

The bespectacled Belbe was one of Wittmann's old comrades from the Leibstandarte Assault Gun Battery formed in 1940. Others included Philipsen, Günther, Amselgruber and Brandt. He also had two brothers serving in the Tiger Battalion, August-Wilhelm, called Büding, a loader in the 3rd Company, and SS-Unterscharführer Fritz Belbe, a radio operator in the 1st Company.

The tank commanders SS-Unterscharführer Augst, Stief, Mölly and Kleber had all served on the Eastern Front with the 2nd Company. The same applied to a number of gunners and loaders, men such as SS-Rottenführer Lechner and Lau, as well as radio operators and drivers like SS-Sturmmann Heil and SS-Rottenführer Elmer. At nineteen years of age, SS-Rottenführer Bobby Warmbrunn, a former gunner, was the youngest tank commander in the company. As a gunner he destroyed forty-four tanks, sixty-two anti-tank guns, two 122 mm guns, seven bunkers, ten flamethrowers and one armored car. As a commander he had destroyed six more tanks and six anti-tank guns. He became an SS-Unterscharführer on 1 June 1944. Compared to the personnel of the other companies, the men of Wittmann's 2nd Company were more skilled on account of their greater Tiger experience. This did not apply to Wessel and Hantusch, however. Hantusch in particular worked hard to establish a good relationship with the men of the company; he often sat and talked with the NCOs and other men late into the evening.

Michael Wittmann trained the company hard and conscientiously in Elbeuf, drawing on his great skill and rich store of experience. His men revered him, he was their idol. Wittmann was also generally well known and popular in the Reich. His home district, Bavarian Ostmark, invited Wittmann to come and speak in Bayreuth; however, preparing his men for the coming struggle, training them carefully, seemed more important than making speeches. He subsequently wrote to the local Kreisleiter (District Leader), Neidhardt, 'Kreisleiter, I ask that you withdraw your invitation to Bayreuth as long as the war is on. I cannot justify going away, for some of my men have not had any leave for over a year. I love my men and want to be a tough, but nevertheless a good leader.'

Wittmann knew exactly where he was needed and his entire behavior oriented itself on his feeling of responsibility toward the men of his company. In Château Elbeuf, where Wittmann lived with his young wife Hilde, the men of his company wanted to do something for the young couple. Once they offered to bake cakes, then they wanted to brew real bean coffee. Wittmann asked if the same was available to all the men of the company. When they answered in the negative he turned down their well-meaning offer. This simple example shows what kind of man Michael Wittmann was. The high decorations hadn't changed him, he remained a man and a comrade and as such stayed true to himself and to his philosophy of life. Beyond question Wittmann was the example to the tank men, young and old; but more than that, he was a role model in every way, in his personality and his being.

For Frau Wittmann, being with her husband in Château Elbeuf went some way toward making up for the honeymoon which they could not have. She automatically became caught up in the company's routine. She had been with her husband and his unit since the transfer from Mons to France. Of the search for quarters in France and the time in Château Elbeuf, she wrote in her diary: " 23 April 1944: Slept late, in the afternoon with Hstuf. Heurich and wife to the workshop company, then searched for quarters for the company. Convent being cleared. Wonderful herb gardens and orchards (rows). Continued on. By chance we discovered Château Elbeuf-en-Bray, immediately determined to stay there. Large park, big old trees. 24 April 1944: Frau Heurich and I visited all the companies with Dr. Rabe, also saw the dentist Dr. Hausamm; fixed my wisdom tooth. Michel to Elbeuf to set up, everything in barns, what a mess! Decided to move here on Wednesday. Thursday Paris? 25 April 1944: Nothing special, another tour of the companies. 26 April 1944: Move. Everything set up reasonably well with the help of Bernhard, Bobby, Spieß and two Hiwis, Ukrainians. Turned out very nice. 27 April 1944: Heurichs to Paris. I have terrible cold, fever of 39 degrees. 28 April 1944: Hauptmann of the military administration headquarters here this morning, very surprised to meet a German woman. Returned in the evening from Brussels with the woman who runs the soldiers' hostel, brought flowers and a home-made cake. Invited for Sunday. 29 April 1944: Feeling better, inspected the park, met the gardener. Vases for flowers. Very quiet today, wrote letters. Michel has almost no time, gone all day. 30 April 1944: Found some flowers. In afternoon to soldiers' hostel, very nice; stayed there till evening. 1 May 1944: Meeting with CO, I went too. Frau Heurich came by in afternoon to say goodbye, leaving tomorrow, pity. Evening everyone invited to eat with the CO. Frau Schwemmer's 'self-trained' dog, flower vase gone! Not home until 4 A.M., three aircraft crashed at about 3 A.M., horrible. Our two month's anniversary, didn't celebrate alone but very, very lovely! 2 May 1944: Absolutely no cats, odd. Frau Heurich left this morning at five, shame to see her go. Did some washing, wrote letters. Rain. 3 May 1944: Magnificent weather today. Michel and I lay in the sun by the water at noon. Feeling rather lazy, did some reading. Table tennis with Wessel and Hantusch. 4 May 1944: Belbe (called Balbo) arrived. Drove with him to Gournay to hairdresser's. Hairdresser was awful. Bought writing paper, not expensive. Michel went to see CO (afternoon), evening to Beauvais, picked up Heurich, took him to the CO. Returned at 1 A.M. 5 May 1944: Michel and the commander to see Peiper, plan to be back tomorrow night. Rain. Read, wrote letters. Wessel provided company now and then. 6 May 1944: Saw the film The Big Number in the morning, afternoon table tennis with Hantusch. Picked more lilacs, played chess. Michael not back. Woke up during the night, often, aircraft. Wessel brought books in morning. 7 May 1944: Read, Michael returned at about 3 P.M., ate, slept. He hadn't slept all the past night. Hantusch to battalion. Aircraft. Michael slept anyway. 8 May 1944: Michael to battalion. I made preparations for Paris. Plan to drive there tomorrow, with Frau Schweimer and Dr. Rabe. Evening visit; Klein, 'Amsel,' Hafner ate with us. Drank brandy flips, homemade. Tried out a Schwimmwagen, marvelous! Invitation for Wednesday. Left at 10 P.M. Michael still making up duty schedules, will surely be late."

Château Elbeuf stood alone in an extraordinarily beautiful setting; nevertheless, the men preferred to spend their free time in the small city of Gournay, four kilometers away. They were happy to make the journey there on foot. One day there was a great fuss in Elbeuf: a camera had disappeared. Obersturmführer Wittmann took the matter seriously. He assembled the company and gave a short speech about the sanctity and inviolability of the property of others and emphatically reminded them of the code of the Waffen-SS. Then he gave the unknown criminal one more chance. Within the next hour the camera was to be on the table in front of Wittmann's room. He promised to keep the company changing clothes until then. In a few minutes the company was standing in formation wearing camouflage uniforms, followed by fatigues, sports wear, black panzer uniform, and so on. This was no joking matter with Wittmann. After half an hour Spieß Konradt assembled the company again and informed Wittmann that the camera had been returned.

Wittmann followed with concern the development of the military situation on all fronts. Night after night the English and Americans carried out their terror raids against German cities; their targets were no longer limited exclusively to armaments production. They brought death and destruction to Germany's residential areas, which were methodically razed to the ground. In the Tiger battalion, too, there were men who had lost family members and their parents' homes and belongings through this bombing terror. They were gripped by an understandable feeling of bitterness and rage. In one of his letters Wittmann described the inner feelings of his men, now in their fifth year of war. They were feelings that he shared, for after all they were all members of a close-knit team.

"We soldiers know that the homeland has to make great sacrifices, especially our beautiful German cities. The sight of such senseless destruction is enough to make one's heart bleed, but don't they know that the resulting distress has created a true sense of community. And the most important thing: the Anglo-Americans have taught us to hate. But those gentlemen shall find this hate transformed into energy and fighting strength. District leader! My company and I are now in the west. My soldiers desire only one thing: to at last get the Tommies and the Americans in front of their guns. We have only one watchword and that is 'revenge!'

We will not throw ourselves blindly upon the enemy, however. You may believe me, we know our job. We intend to and will demonstrate this to our enemies until they are crushed by our fighting morale, our fighting spirit and our fighting strength. Even harder and more difficult times may lay before us, but we have learned to believe and to fight."

Each of the three Tiger companies now consisted of three platoons each with four tanks, as well as the company commander's and headquarters squad leader's Tigers, for a total of fourteen tanks. According to the current table of organization, a Tiger company in an independent battalion consisted of four officers, fifty-six NCOs and eighty-seven men.

In the combat echelon, each of the three platoons was supposed to have one officer, eleven NCOs and eight men, however in practice the situation was often different. The table of organization also specified the number of enlisted men per platoon, for example. Of the four tank commanders one was an officer (platoon commander) and the other three NCOs. Three of the four gunners were NCOs and one an enlisted man. All four drivers were NCOs. Of the radio operators one was an NCO and three enlisted men; all of the loaders were enlisted men. The company's command group consisted of one officer (company commander), six

NCOs and seven enlisted men. This number included the crews of the company commander's and headquarters squad leaders' tanks as well as three motorcycle dispatch riders (350 cc, one with sidecar) and a driver (one medium car and one bicycle).

In addition to a combat echelon, each panzer company included a maintenance echelon, which carried out battlefield repairs to tanks disabled in combat. The I-Staffel officially consisted of twenty-six men who worked from eight vehicles equipped according to their respective missions. They included specialists for engines and transmissions and final drives. The maintenance echelon also included tank mechanics (18), tank radio technicians (2), welders, electricians (1 each), armorer-artificer assistants (2), and drivers. The echelon's vehicle complement consisted of three Volkswagens (Kfz. 1), one small maintenance truck (Kfz. 2/40), one medium, open 3-tonne truck for workshop equipment, a heavy, open 4.5-tonne truck for replacement parts, and two light 1-tonne prime movers (Sd.Kfz. 10).

Commanded by the Senior NCO (Stabsscharführer), the Ist Combat Train (Gefechtstroß I) was comprised of a motor transport sergeant, technical sergeant radio, armor-artificer official, quartermaster sergeant, field cook, and medics, as well as armorer-artificer assistants, drivers and clerks. The train had at its disposal the following vehicles: five 4.5-tonne trucks for transporting fuel and special equipment, one 3-tonne truck for the large field range (cooker), and two Volkswagens. The Ist Combat Train had a strength of eight NCOs and eighteen men.

The IInd Combat Train (Gefechtstroß II) consisted of replacement truck drivers and volunteer auxiliaries, as well as the men of the alternate tank crews. It had one 4.5-tonne truck for transporting personnel (five NCOs and eleven men) and equipment. Both combat trains also included a machine-gun, a bicycle and Soviet and Italian volunteer auxiliaries, or Hiwis. The baggage train was led by the Accountant and Pay NCO and also included the tailor and shoemaker (Hiwis) and the driver. The four men of the train had one 3-tonne truck at their disposal. The combat echelon thus consisted of four officers, thirty-nine NCOs and thirty-two enlisted men, a total of seventy-five soldiers. The support units including the Maintenance Echelon consisted of seventeen NCOs and fifty-five enlisted men, altogether seventy-two soldiers. The total strength of a Tiger company was therefore 147 soldiers. This description is based on authorized strengths—the real situation was often quite different.

The 4th Company's armored reconnaissance platoon had meanwhile received seven armored troop carriers. The vehicles were C-Versions of the Sd. Kfz. 251, armed with the MG 42 machine-gun. One carrier belonged to the platoon commander, the other six to the three squads. According to the table of organization, the Armored Reconnaissance Platoon consisted of one officer, seven NCOs and thirty-three men, for a total of forty-one soldiers. The Pioneer Platoon, commanded by SS-Standartenoberjunker Brauer consisted of three armored troop carriers (Sd.Kfz. 251) and three Maultier (Sd.Kfz. 3) half-tracked vehicles. Each of the three pioneer squads had one troop carrier and a Maultier. The Flak Platoon under SS-Unterscharführer Fickert had received its three quadruple flak on eight-tonne prime movers in November 1943. Protection of important objects, like bridges, but also general air cover during movement by road and rail required an anti-aircraft weapon with a very high rate of fire. The 20 mm Vierlingsflak 38 had proved to be an outstanding weapon, especially against low-flying aircraft. Mobility was provided by the eight-tonne prime movers (Sd.Kfz. 7/1), a half-tracked vehicle produced by Krauss-Maffai (KM 11).

The technique of target acquisition was based on the stereoscopic range-finder. The range-finder operator had to be able to see stereoscopically, or three-dimensionally. In the stereoscopic range-finding method a stereoscopic picture of the target was compared with a second stereoscopic picture of a range-marking system. The numbers appeared three-dimensionally and showed the range in hectometers. The range-finder operator had to locate the range value for the selected target, read it off, and call it out to the gun crew. Hits were scored only if the aircraft did not change its direction of flight, height or speed during the time of flight of the projectiles. The difficulty lay in calculating the aiming point, which had to lie ahead of the aircraft on its flight path and be reached by the aircraft during the time of flight of the projectiles. Other components also came into play, windspeed, barrel wear, air resistance, air density, and the mass of the projectile. Behavior of the target during the time of flight of the projectile could only be estimated based on the aircraft's mode of flight. As a rule of thumb target speed multiplied by the time of flight of the projectile equalled the linear travel of the target.

It required eleven men to operate a 20 mm quadruple flak mounted on the eight-tonne prime mover: gun commander, six gunners, three ammunition carriers and two drivers. Absent from the crew was a range-finder operator. Aiming was by ring sight or tracer. The Vierlingsflak had a range of 4.8 kilometers and a ceiling of 3.7 kilometers. Normal rate of fire was 800 rounds per minute, maximum rate 1800 rounds per minute, which represented a great deal of concentrated firepower.

Fickert's three gun commanders were SS-Unterscharführer Gottlob Braun, Heinrich Hölscher and Werner Müller. According to the table of organization, the Flak Platoon consisted of five NCOs and forty-one enlisted men. The principal disadvantage of the Vierlingsflak 38 was the limited protection given the gun crew. An armored shield offered some protection from in front, but otherwise the crew were exposed to cannon and machine-gun fire from enemy fighter-bombers. The half-tracked prime movers and the anti-aircraft guns were given a camouflage finish of dark ocher-yellow oversprayed with a pattern of dark green and brown.

The Workshop Company under SS-Obersturmführer Klein was now also adequately equipped to carry out its role. Gottfried Klein was born on 15 April 1915 in Immekoppel, near Cologne. In 1936 the trained mechanic joined the 5th Company, Leibstandarte. In 1940 he was transferred to the Assault Gun Battery, where he stayed until the latter part of 1941. SS-Hauptscharführer Klein next took part in a course for motor vehicle technical officers at the Waffen-SS Automotive School in Vienna. Klein returned to his old unit and was promoted to SS-Untersturmführer on 30 January 1942. He remained with the Leibstandarte as the Assault Gun Battalion's Technical Officer Motor Vehicles until autumn 1943, when he returned to the Automotive School. Klein had received a promotion to SS-Obersturmführer on 20 April 1942 and was decorated with the Iron Cross, Second Class, the War Merit Cross, First and Second Class with Swords and the Royal Bulgarian Soldier's Cross of the Order of Bravery Second Class. He joined the Tiger Company shortly before Christmas 1943.

The Workshop Company's recovery platoon was commanded by SS-Untersturmführer Reinhold Wichert, the workshop platoon by SS-Untersturmführer Oskar Glaeser and the weapons workshop platoon by SS-Standartenoberjunker Hartmann at first, then SS-Oberscharführer Reichert. Reinhold Wichert was born on 21 June 1911 in Groß Maulen, Braunsberg District, East Prussia. On 25 July 1933 Wichert, then a salesman, joined the Leibstandarte, where he initially served with a machine-gun company and later became a technical NCO. In 1943 he was sent from the 3rd Panzer Workshop Company to the Automotive School in Vienna. On 7 January 1944, SS-Hauptscharführer Wichert, now an armored vehicle specialist, was assigned to the 101st SS Panzer Battalion as commander of the recovery platoon and Technical Officer Motor Vehicles. On 1 February 1944 Wichert became an SS-Standartenoberjunker; this was followed on 20 April 1944 by his promotion to SS-Untersturmführer.

Oskar Glaeser was born in Trier-Quint on 11 November 1913 and after leaving school worked in an iron works. From December 1930 until May 1934 he worked as an enameler in a machine factory and iron foundry in Hungary. After returning to Germany, Glaeser voluntarily served with the Labor Service from June 1934 until April 1935. He joined the Leibstandarte SS Adolf Hitler on 1 April 1935 and was assigned to the 11th Company. At the beginning of 1942, Glaeser, an SS-Unterscharführer in the 20th Company, was sent to the Automotive School in Vienna to take the motor transport sergeant training course. He was subsequently assigned to the Leibstandarte's 2nd SS Panzer-Grenadier Regiment. Promotion to SS-Oberscharführer followed on 1 September 1942 and to SS-Hauptscharführer on 1 June 1943. Glaeser had been decorated with the War Merit Cross Second Class with Swords, the Motor Vehicle Driver's Badge of Merit in Gold and the Eastern Front Medal. He was promoted to SS-Untersturmführer on 20 April 1944 while serving with the 101st SS Panzer Battalion.

According to the table of organization, the Workshop Company was to consist of two platoons each with three tank engine mechanics, three transmission mechanics (of which two were electro-mechanics), two motor vehicle mechanics, and a stock keeper for administering spare parts (all of whom were supposed to be NCOs). Some of these specialists were from the enlisted ranks, however, as were the electro-mechanics, arc welders, lathe operators, blacksmiths, harnessmakers and carpenters. Among the sixteen vehicles of the two platoons were fourteen 4.5-tonne trucks and two trucks with rotary cranes, one with a lifting power of 3 tonnes (Sd.Kfz. 100) and one with a lifting power of 10 tonnes (Sd.Kfz. 9/2). Each platoon consisted of one officer, five NCOs and twenty-five men.

The IIIrd Platoon was the recovery platoon. Equipped with four 18-tonne prime movers (Sd.Kfz. 9), a Bergepanther—a recovery vehicle based on the Panther chassis without a turret (not included in the table of organization)—, three tractors (Sd.Kfz. 360) with tank recovery powered trailers, and two trucks with rotary cranes (3- and 10-tonne lifting power), its mission was to recover Tigers which had been disabled. For major repairs requiring removal of the Tiger's turret, the platoon had a gantry crane (not included in the table of organization). One officer, five NCOs and twenty-five men belonged to the recovery Platoon.

The Workshop Company also included the armorer-artificer's staff, which was comprised of six armorer-artificer assistants and two electro-mechanics (panzer). The staff's four vehicles included a Kfz. 1 (VW), a Kfz. 15 with tool boxes, and two 4.5-tonne trucks. The signals equipment workshop, which was commanded by the Technical Sergeant Radio, repaired unserviceable radio equipment. Under the command of the senior non-commissioned officer, the train was organized in a similar fashion to the panzer companies. Also a member of the company was SS-Oberscharführer Sepp Hafner, engine and transmission specialist and an employee of the Maybach Company. By May 1944 the battalion was at its authorized strength in personnel. There were also transfers within the battalion. For example, SS-Rottenführer Ernst Weller was transferred from the 101st SS

Signals Battalion to the Tiger Battalion, where he was employed as a tank driver.

The company trained with elan and enthusiasm. There was a high degree of comradeship and harmony in all units. The officers had developed a good relationship with the NCOs and men, one they could depend on in action. A battalion exercise was planned for May. At the time some men were on leave—for many their first in over two years. They were sent telegrams ordering them to return so that the crews might be complete. The one and only battalion-size exercise then took place from the 10th to the 17th of May 1944. Not all of the battalion's tanks could be used, however.

SS-Rottenführer Walter Lau of the 2nd Company recalled the exercise. As SS-Sturmmann Henn of Höflinger's crew was absent, Lau joined Höflinger as gunner, radio operator was SS-Sturmmann Hubert Heil: "Sometime in May there was an exercise by the now complete 101st SS Panzer Battalion in the area between Beauvais and the coast. Thanks to Wittmann's influence, I had just been transferred from the 3rd to the 2nd Company and was back with most of my chums from the old 13th Company. For one reason or other, whether sickness or leave, during the exercise I was assigned to SS-Hauptscharführer Höflinger, section leader in SS-Oberscharführer Wessel's Ist Platoon, as gunner. The area of the exercise had been chosen, as we know today, because that is where the Supreme Command expected the Allied invasion. I remember that days before the exercise the platoon commanders and section leaders carried out practice night marches to the coast with Schwimmwagen amphibious vehicles in battalion formation, to become familiar with the localities. SS-Untersturmführer Hantusch, who occupied the room next to us in quarters, often came by for a chat and told us of the results of the practice marches.

Although it was a battalion maneuver, not once did I see the 1st and 3rd Companies during the exercise, which included security while on the march. The emphasis was 'practice in company formation.' Our company commander, SS-Obersturmführer Wittmann, watched the progress of the exercise very closely. The three platoons had to carry out an attack in inverted wedge formation involving every possible wrinkle in a large, open area. After each individual exercise the participants gathered for a critique of the maneuver. The company or combat echelon was first formed into a semicircle by SS-Obersturmführer Wessel, and I recall the smart way he reported several times a day: 'Obersturmführer, I respectfully report the combat echelon assembled as ordered.' ('Respectfully' was a typical figure of speech for Wessel, no one else in the battalion reported that way. The author.) Then Wittmann gave the platoon commanders, tank commanders and the other participants his pointed, insightful critique, which spoke of his wealth of operational experience.

The conclusion of the exercise was a company attack from the march in inverted wedge formation, and I can still hear Wittmann's command in the last phase of the attack: 'Carbide, carbide!'

I remember particularly well a bivouac in a low wood. It was in the area of a fork in the road. Near the fork sat Wittmann's tank and his tent. Parked on the main road were the four tanks of the Ist Platoon (Wessel, Woll, Höflinger, Warmbrunn) and on the other two sections of road the tanks of the IInd (Hantusch) and IIIrd (Belbe) Platoons. This night outdoors was a planned part of the exercise. Tents were pitched and there was only the food we had with us. There was an alert during the night. The crews checked all the required technical functions in the dark, without Illumination, and reported battle readiness. We practiced camouflaging the tanks against being seen from the air and eliminating the track marks left by the tanks until we were ready to drop.

Not all the units in the coastal region were prepared as carefully and conscientiously as our 101st SS Panzer Battalion. With his vast experience, Michael Wittmann was in his element there. Strict, razor-sharp training regulations were enforced, from SS-Obersturmführer Wessel down to the youngest trooper. Every error committed under combat conditions was substantiated with examples from Zitadelle or the winter battles at Zhitomir and Cherkassy and was sharply criticized."

SS-Sturmbannführer Heinz von Westernhagen was satisfied with the course of the exercise. Following the conclusion of the maneuvers the men of the 3rd Company made use a children's carousel in a nearby village to blow off steam, boisterously and in cheerful high spirits. Afterward the company set out to return to its billets led by the company commander. Along the way the 3rd Company passed through a village on foot, and von Westernhagen had the men do the "Dr. Goebbels march." To do this they walked with the right foot on the sidewalk and the left on the street. It was an example of the sense of sarcasm occasionally displayed by the commander of the battalion (Dr. Goebbels had a crippled foot and a permanent limp). The discipline of the troops was outstanding. The commander was indulgent in punishing minor offenses. He showed understanding and thoughtfulness in dealing with the wishes of the men, who thanked him with their sincere admiration.

The men spent most of their free time together. In any case there were few opportunities for social gatherings, for apart from the usual village pubs the French villages had little to offer. With the battalion since its time in Italy were approximately five Italian volunteer auxiliaries and several volunteers, while the headquarters company even had an Italian Rottenführer. The Ukrainian Kiwis also did good work.

The battalion was now solidly established and fully operational. The men were carefully trained and had faith in their arms. They harbored no illusions as to the difficulty of the mission that lay before them, nevertheless they were optimistic that they could hold their own against their English and American foes.

On 1 June 1944 the battalion had thirty-seven operational Tigers and eight more were in the workshop. All forty-five Tigers had been coated with Zimmerit, for this cement-like coating prevented tank-killing squads from affixing magnetic hollow charges. The Tigers were finished in an ocher-yellow base coat, over which a pattern of green and brown was sprayed to match the local terrain. The identification numbers on the sides and rear of the turret were applied in red with a white outline.

The battalion insignia of two crossed skeleton keys was interesting in that, unlike the Leibstandarte, the bits pointed upward. The emblem was applied in several places on the tank, on the glacis on the front and above the track fenders on the side. The companies applied the emblems as follows: 1st Company: right front, left side—2nd Company: left front, left side—3rd Company: right front, left side. Only the Tigers of the 1st Company wore the tactical symbol for a panzer company, on theleft side of the glacis. Inside the parallelogram was a "S" for heavy company and beside it on the right a "1" as company number. This combination of emblems was also found on the right rear of the tank.

The 1st Company was also joined by Knight's Cross wearer SS-Standartenjunker Franz Staudegger, who had been forced to leave the 2nd SS-Panzerjunker Special Course in Fallingbostel early on account of Illness.

A brief summary of the civilian and military careers of the battalion's officers has been provided in the description of the unit's formation and training period. As the SS officers had an educating influence on the men under their command and were supposed to be an example to them, especially in action, special significance should be allotted to them and their soldier's trade.

The following list of the officer corps of the 101st SS Panzer Battalion is based solely on military qualifications. Criteria were as follows: general front-line experience—operational experience with the armored forces—special training at the tank schools.

As former commander of the Leibstandarte Assault Gun Battalion, SS-Sturmbannführer Heinz von Westernhagen possessed the necessary operational experience. A number of the battalion's officers and NCOs came from the assault guns and their operational experience was rated at least similar to that of the armored forces. The commanding officer had also taken a battalion commander training course at the Armored Command School in Paris and could be considered fully qualified for his position. The signals officer, SS-Untersturmführer Dollinger, and Adjutant Iriohn both had the required training. Dollinger was a good signals man, with an impulsive desire for front-line action. Iriohn had not yet seen action with the armored forces.

The commander of the 1st Company, SS-Hauptsturmführer Möbius, was an infantryman and then battery commander of an 88 mm anti-aircraft battery before he came to the battalion after a general staff training course. His tank training was of a purely theoretical nature. The commander of his Ist Platoon, SS-Obersturmführer Philipsen, was a Tiger commander with frontline experience. SS-Untersturmführer Lukasius was an infantryman when he went to the Junkerschule in 1943 and he was subsequently retrained for the panzer arm. He, too, had yet to see his first combat in the Tiger. SS-Untersturmführer Hahn joined the battalion in Italy after a reserve officer training course and commanded a platoon during the Eastern Front deployment in the winter of 1943/44.

In the 2nd Company SS-Obersturmführer Michael Wittmann was the undisputed authority in all things. His unequalled score in the east served as inspiration and example to his company. Commanding his Ist Platoon was SS-Obersturmführer Wessel, a former infantryman with no armor experience. SS-Untersturmführer Hantusch had not seen front-line action since December 1941. After studying mechanical engineering for two semesters at the SS Automotive School in Vienna, he took a series of training courses before joining the battalion. SS-Standartenoberjunker Belbe was a veteran assault gun commander with the Leibstandarte SS Adolf Hitler and had distinguished himself in the east. An experienced Hauptscharführer (equivalent to a master sergeant) he was made an Oberjunker (officer candidate) for bravery in the face of the enemy.

The commander of the 3rd Company, SS-Obersturmführer Raasch, was new to the panzer arm and his experience with the Tiger was limited to training. Commanding his Ist Platoon was Knight's Cross wearer SS-Untersturmführer Alfred Günther. He became the first member of the Assault Gun Battalion to win the Knight's Cross on 3 March 1943 and could look back on a wealth of operational experience. SS-Hauptscharführer Görgens, commander of the IInd Platoon, had come from the Führer Escort Detachment and was retrained on tanks. SS-Untersturmführer Amselgruber commanded the IIIrd Platoon. He was a veteran assault gun commander with plenty of operational experience. He was made an Oberjunker while an Hauptscharführer for bravery in the face of the enemy.

The commanders of the 4th (Light) Company and the Headquarters Company, SS-Obersturmführer Spitz and Vogt, were reserve officers. Neither unit had seen action as a company. With the exception of the signals platoon, the Headquarters Company was organized purely as a supply company. The platoon commanders of the 4th Company, SS-Untersturmführer Stamm, SS-Hauptscharführer Poetschlak, SS-Standartenoberjunker Brauer and SS-Unterscharführer Fickert all had combat experience. Poetschlak was a veteran Tiger man and Brauer had seen action as a trained pioneer. Only Fickert, a former infantryman, was new to the flak. Both of the battalion's Technical Officers Motor Vehicles, SS-Hauptscharführer Heurich and SS-Untersturmführer Bartel, were fully qualified for their positions. Both were in their tenth year of service. The same could be said of SS-Obersturmführer Klein and the platoon commanders of his Workshop Company.

As well as experienced tank officers, all three panzer companies had young, eager officers who had only recently completed their training courses. The ratio of officers who had gained their experience in the long battles in the Soviet Union to those just out of the schools was one to one, with six experienced officers and six with no tank experience in the three panzer companies.

None of the young officers who came from the training courses had any experience in the armored forces. During the course of their training all tried to become adequate platoon commanders. The task facing them was to put their doubtless good theoretical foundation into practice in action. One can say of them all, that they built a good relationship with the NCOs and enlisted men of their company and created a close-knit team.

"WATCH ON THE CHANNEL": 2 JUNE, 1944
Six Tiger Commanders Destroy Nearly Three Armored Brigades:
An Illustrated Report by War Correspondent Scheck

His comrades call him the "panzer general." However as it turns out there's nothing about the Tiger that Oberscharführer Georg Lötzsch doesn't know. He transferred from the Allgemeine-SS to the Waffen-SS in 1933, however the trained auto mechanic wasn't really happy until he got his hands on a Tiger. That was the stuff! He also participated in the entire development of the Tiger, worked for a long time in the workshops, and took part in the initial test drives and trials, until it was finally ready. Lötzsch is from Dresden and is now 30 years old.

Hauptscharführer Hans Höflinger, his name betrays him as a Bavarian, has not been with the armored forces as long. Until 1942 he was an infantryman in the east with the SS Division "Reich," was then retrained,

Lötzsch.

Höflinger.

Woll.

Warmbrunn.

Kleber.

Wittmann.

came just in time for the new development, the Tiger, and acted as godfather to the "newborn." And then it was right back to Russia, in the fall his battalion was deployed to Italy, and a few months later it reappeared in Russia. The 26-year-old is presently a Tiger commander and section leader.

Unterscharführer Balthasar Woll earned the Knight's Cross while a gunner. Several numbers show best what this not yet 22 year old Saarlander has done. He destroyed: 81 tanks, 107 anti-tank guns, one complete battery each of 172 mm and 125 mm artillery (a battery equals 4 guns), 7 bunkers, 5 flamethrowers, 1 armored car, 2 prime movers and a heavy mortar position. Yes, it certainly takes a lot of doing.

Nineteen years old, heavy set, 1.87 meters tall, that is Rottenführer Karlheinz Warmbrunn of Nuremberg. He is the youngest tank commander in the company. While a gunner, he destroyed 13 enemy tanks in one day. Meanwhile he has raised his kill total to 51 tanks, 68 anti-tank guns, 7 bunkers, 2 122 mm guns and 10 flamethrowers.

Unterscharführer Kurt Kleber from Bütow is called "Quax" for short by his comrades. "Quax" comes from the Luftwaffe, has just come of age and is always cheerful. He is never grouchy. Even today there is laughter when someone talks about how "Quax" was thrown from the commander's cupola by the blast wave from a direct artillery hit and in spite of everything escaped unhurt. He calls that getting out!

With his 117 tank kills, Obersturmführer Michael Wittmann stands not only at the apex of his company but is also the most successful tank commander of all. In addition to him, his company has produced five tank commanders who were decorated with the Knight's Cross for conspicuous bravery in the face of the enemy. That alone speaks for the spirit that prevails in this company. Within the fourteen days Obersturmführer Wittmann was decorated with the Knight's Cross and the Oak leaves, however in this period he destroyed a further 28 Russian tanks, the majority of them T 34s. When one sees the company commander from Vogelthal in the Upper Pfalz, who at 30 years of age is scarcely older than the majority of his tank commanders, in conversation with his men, one instinctively senses the comradeship born of many battles, which is necessary to create a successful whole from lone warriors.

SS-Hauptsturmführer Kling (center) and his adjutant, SS-Obersturmführer Wendorff (right) pay a visit to Wittmann and the 101st SS Panzer Battalion.

Wittmann with his old friends, SS-Untersturmführer Hannes Philipsen (left) and Knight's Cross wearer Alfred Günther.

Philipsen and Günther, both platoon commanders in the 101st SS Panzer Battalion's 3rd Company. Mons, February 1944.

Wittman greets SS-Hauptscharführer Thomas Amselgruber, tank commander in the 3rd Company, in Mons. March 1944.

SS-Untersturmführer Lukasius, Philipsen, Günther and Iriohn.

SS-Hauptsturmführer Rettlinger (left), Wittmann's platoon and battery commander in the assault guns in 1940–42, during a visit to the Tiger Battalion. *Right:* von Westernhagen and Wittmann.

Tigers of the 3rd Company during an exercise in Mons, spring 1944.

The Flak Platoon, standing on the left is the platoon commander, SS-Unterscharführer Kurt Fickert. 20mm four-barrelled flak on the 8-tonne prime mover.

Tiger 312, tank commander SS-Unterscharführer Schöppner, radio operator SS-Sturmmann Gerhard Jäsche (left), loader SS-Sturmmann Willi Schenk (left background).

Tiger 305, the company commander's tank.

SS-Unterscharführer
Kurt Fickert (center
foreground) in front of
one of the Flak Platoon's
three Vierlingsflak.
On far right is SS-
Untersturmführer
Lukasius.

Tiger 312.

Tank commander Schöppner (2nd from right), loader Willi Schenk (left),
radio operator Gerhard Jäsche (2nd from left), on far right the driver.

SS-Obersturmführer Klein, the commander of the Workshop Company, with SS-Untersturmführer Lukasius and Glaeser.

SS-Hauptsturmführer Möbius and SS-Untersturmführer Wessel, Headquarters Company.

SS-Rottenführer Paul Bender, radio Operator in the 2nd Company.

SS-Untersturmführer Georg Bartel, TFK II.

SS-Hauptscharführer Leo Spranz, who transferred to the HJ Division in April 1944.

SS-Untersturmführer Kurt Stamm, who was transferred to the 101st SS Panzer Battalion on 1 March 1944.

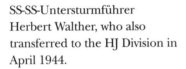

SS-SS-Untersturmführer Herbert Walther, who also transferred to the HJ Division in April 1944.

SS-Untersturmführer Georg Hantusch, who was also transferred to the 101st on 1 March 1944.

SS-Untersturmführer
Rolf Henniges, who was also
transferred to the 101st on
1 March 1944.

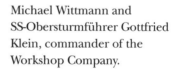

Michael Wittmann and
SS-Obersturmführer Gottfried
Klein, commander of the
Workshop Company.

SS-Obersturmführer
Alfred Veller, administration
off the Tiger Battalion.

In April 1944 the 101st SS Panzer Battalion was transferred from Mons into the Gournay-en-Bray area of Northern Europe.

Beginning of the rail transport in Mons.

Tiger 313 seen en route.

On the train.

Air defense by the four-barrelled flak. SS-Unterscharführer Hölscher (left, standing) watches over the detraining. Standing in front of the gun is platoon commander SS-Unterscharführer Fickert.

The 3rd Company's field kitchen truck.

St.-Germer-de-Fly, where the 101st SS Panzer Battalion's 1st Company was billeted in France before the invasion.

The entry gate to the residential building. On the right is the first of the two churches.

Château Elbeuf, the quarters of Wittmann's 2nd Company, 101st SS Panzer Battalion before the invasion. Standing in the window is Frau Wittmann.

Michael and Hilde Wittmann in front of Château Elbeuf.

The two churches of the former monastery next to which was the building housing the living quarters of the 1st Company.

The picturesque idyll of Elbeuf. Michael and his wife in an amphibious Schwimmwagen on the small, tree lined lake that was on the grounds of the château.

The entrance to Château Elbeuf.

Michael Wittmann in the Château park with a small fellow resident.

ORDER OF BATTLE:
101st SS Panzer Battalion, 6/6/1944

007
Commander
Ostubaf. Heinz von Westernhagen

008
Adjutant
Ustuf. Eduard Kalinowsky

009
Signals Officer
Ustuf. Helmut Dollinger

Headquarters & Supply Company, 101st SS Panzer Battalion, 6/6/1944

Company Commander: Ostuf. Paul Vogt

Fuel Transport Column

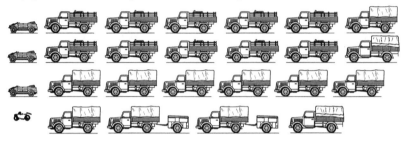

Ammunition Transport Column

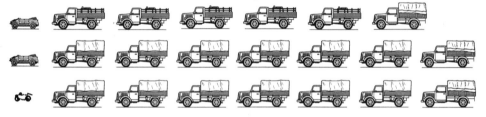

Signals Platoon: Hstuf. Helmut Dollinger   **Medical Echelon:** Hstuf. Dr. Wolfgang Rabe

Strm. Arthur Bergmann	Uscha. Wolfgang Unruh	Pz.Schtz. Johann Müller
Strm. Jochen Borchet	Pz.Schtz. Albert Habenicht	Pz.Schtz. Lothar Krüschel
Rttf. Herbert Debusmann	Strm. Karl-Heinz Heim	Uscha. Hartwig
Strm. Alfred Bahlo	Pz.Schtz. Franz Krippel	Rttf. Otto Hahn
Oscha. Robert Bardo	Strm. Kurt Krötzsch	**Senior NCO:** Hscha. Willi Hamm
Ustuf. Peter Harsche	Uscha. Lothar Kühn	**Technical Sergeant (radio):** Oscha. Johann Schott
Pz.Schtz. H. Rudolf Schneider	Rttf. Edmund Laule	**Motor Transport Sergeant:** Oscha. Alfred Lasar

1st Company, 101st SS Panzer Battalion, 6/6/1944

105
Company Commander
Hstuf. Rolf Möbius

104
Company HQ Squad Leader
Uscha. Sepp Franzl

Ist Platoon

111
Ostuf. Hannes Philipsen

IInd Platoon

121
Ustuf. Fritz Stamm

IIIrd Platoon

131
Ustuf. Walter Hahn

112
Uscha. Cap

122
Uscha. Arno Salamon

132
Uscha. Werner Wendt

113
Oscha. Heinrich Ernst

123
St.Jk. Franz Staudegger

133
Oscha. Fritz Zahner

114
Uscha. Willi Otterbein

124
Jk. Erwin Asbach

134
Uscha. Helmut Dannleitner

GUNNERS:
Uscha. Georg Przybilla
Strm. Friedel Fischer
Rttf. Alfons Ahrens

LOADERS:
Pz.O.Schtz. Alfred Weyel

RADIO OPERATORS:
Strm. Helmut Schrader
Uscha. Fritz Belbe
Rttf. Lorenz Mähner

DRIVERS:
Strm. Theo Janekzek
Oscha. Hein Bode
Rttf. Walter Bingert
Uscha. Gerd Beutel
Oscha. Walter Sturhahn
Uscha. Paul Berendt
Rttf. Kurt Koch
Rttf. Lemaire
Rttf. Anesi

Senior NCO: Hscha. Günter Lueth
Technical Sergeant (radio): Oscha. Quenzer
Clerk: Uscha. Karl Mollenhauer
Account & Pay NCO: Uscha. Peter Schnitzler
Motor Transport Sergeant: Oscha. Seifert
Maintenance Echelon: Uscha. Heinrich Wölfel
Ordnance & Equipment: Uscha. Bernhard Bauer

2nd Company, 101st SS Panzer Battalion, 6/6/1944

205
Company Commander
Ostuf. Michael Wittmann

204
Company HQ Squad Leader
Uscha. Seifert

Ist Platoon

IInd Platoon

IIIrd Platoon

211
Ostuf. Jürgen Wessel

221
Ustuf. Georg Hantusch

231
St.O.Jk. Heinz Belbe

212
Uscha. Balthasar Woll

222
Uscha. Kurt Sowa

232
Uscha. Kurt Kleber

213
Hscha. Hans Höflinger

223
Oscha. Jürgen Brandt

233
Oscha. Georg Lötzsch

214
Uscha. Karl-Heinz Warmbrunn

224
Uscha. Ewald Mölly

234
Uscha. Herbert Stief

GUNNERS:
Strm. Erich Tille
Strm. Werner Knocke
Rttf. Rudi Lechner
Uscha. Karl Wagner
Rttf. Kern (221)
Strm. Max Gaube
Rttf. Walter Lau (234)
Rttf. Kaschlan
Strm. Deutschwitz
Rttf. A. Falkenhausen
Strm. Sepp Rößner

LOADERS:
Strm. Peter Mayer
Strm. Helmut Hauk
Strm. Günther Weber
Strm. Günter Boldt (222)
Strm. Willibald Schenk
Strm. Paul Sümnich

RADIO OPERATORS:
Rttf. Werner
Strm. Fred Zimmermann
Strm. Hubert Heil
Rttf. Gerhard Waltersdorf
Uscha. Wohlgemuth
Strm. Rudolf Hurschel
Strm. Franz Rausch

DRIVERS:
Rttf. Franz Ellmer
Uscha. Jupp Selzer (211)
Rttf. Kurt Kämmerer
Uscha. Heinrich Reimers (205)
Uscha. Walter Müller
Rttf. Herbert Stellmacher
Strm. Piper
Uscha. Ludwig Eser
Rttf. Erlander (221)
Rttf. Fritz Jäger
Strm. Werner Hepe
Strm. Augst
Rttf. Eugen Schmidt

Senior NCO: Hscha. Georg Konrad
Ordnance & Equipment: Uscha. Heib
SDG: Uscha. Adolf Frank
Maintenance Echelon: Uscha. Adolf Frank
Reports: Rttf. Adolf Becker
Rttf. Hans Schmidt
Field Kitchen: Uscha. Günter

3rd Company, 101st SS Panzer Battalion, 6/6/1944

305
Company Commander
Ostuf. Hanno Raasch

304
Company HQ Squad Leader
Uscha. Heinrich Ritter

Ist Platoon

IInd Platoon

IIIrd Platoon

311
Ustuf. Alfred Günther

321
Hstuf. Max Görgens

331
Ustuf. Thomas Amselgruber

312
Oscha. Peter Kisters

322
Uscha. Heimo Traue

332
Uscha. Albert Leinecke

313
Uscha. Schöpper

323
Hscha. Hermann Barkhausen

333
Uscha. Waldemar Warnecke

314
Uscha. Otto Blase

324
Uscha. Jürgen Merker

334
Oscha. Rolf von Westernhagen

GUNNERS:
Strm. Alfred Lünser (314)
Uscha. Kurt Diefenbach (305)
Strm. Wagner (333)
Rttf. Otto Garreis
Strm. Heinz Bannert
Strm. Leopold Aumüller (331)

LOADERS:
Strm. Ewald Graf (331)
Pz.Schtz. August-Wolhelm
Belbe (333)
Pz.Schtz. Lund

RADIO OPERATORS:
Strm. Gerhard Jäsche (313)
Strm. Richard Garber (333)
Strm. Werner Dörr
Strm. Duwecke
Strm. Ernst Kufner (305)
Strm. Hagen
Strm. Mitscherlich
Pz.Schtz. Jonny Heuser (314)

DRIVERS:
Uscha. Ludwig Hofmann
Uscha. Gerhard Noll (333)
Rttf. Paul Rohweder
Strm. Sippel
Uscha. Bernhard Ahlte
Strm. Joseph Heim (311)
Rttf. Herbert Bölkow
Rttf. Konrad Peuckert
Strm. Ulrich Kreis
Rttf. Müntrat (314)

Senior NCO: Hscha. Wilhelm Hack
Technical Sergeant (radio):
Uscha. Maier
Clerk: Uscha. Robert Bofinger
SDG: Rttf. Gerhard Scherbarth
Motor Transport Sergeant:
Oscha. Herbert Tramm
Maintenance Echelon:
Uscha. Foko Ihnen
Account & Pay NCO: Uscha. Martens
Field Kitchen:
Uscha. Hüsken, Rttf. Käse

4th Company (Light), 101st SS Panzer Battalion, 6/6/1944

Company Commander: Ostuf. Wilhelm Spitz

Company HQ Squad Leader: Oscha. Gerhard Klett

Pioneer Platoon: St.O.Jk. Walter Brauer

Uscha. Richard Ackermann   Uscha. Heinz Fiedler   Uscha. Thomsen

Armored Reconnaissance Platoon: Hscha. Benno Poetschlak

Scout Platoon: Ustuf. Rolf Henniges

Uscha. Mankewitz   Uscha. Krebs   Uscha. Richard Heidemann

Anti-Aircraft Platoon: Uscha. Kurt Fichert

Uscha. Gottlob Braun   Uscha. Heinrich Hölscher   Uscha. Werner Müller

Schtz. Willi Gerstner
Schtz. Anton Hriberscheg
Schtz. Horst Kahlfeld
Flakzug. Strm Dörr
Strm. Jakschas
Rttf. Velentin Roth
Rttf. Hans Gaiser
Kan. Rolf Bergmann

Rttf. Hans-Adalbert Gürke
Rttf. Eduard Hofbauer
Rttf. Ewald Mletzko
Rttf. Gustav Look
Uscha. Walter Frisch
Rttf. Viktor Bolduan

Senior NCO:
Hscha. Fritz Müller

Motor Transport Sergeant:
Oscha. Heinz Pfeil

Workshop Company, 101st SS Panzer Battalion, 6/6/1944

Company Commander: Ostuf Gottfried Klein

Workshop Platoon: Ustuf. Oskar Glaser

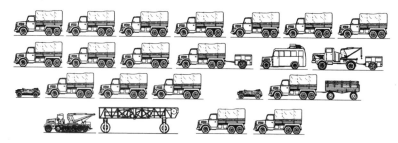

Recovery Platoon: Ustuf. Reinholt Wichert

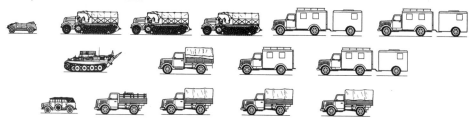

Armorer-Artificer Platoon: Oscha. Reichert

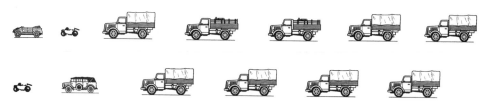

Uscha. Willi Seibert
Rttf.. Oskar Ganz
Uscha. Werner Freytag
Rttf. Franz Gilly
Oscha. Benno Bartel
Uscha. Jupp Schmitz
Uscha. Heinrich Roth
Strm. Otto Büchner
Strm. Heinz Feldstedt
Schtz. Franz Janski

Strm. Willi Kalender
Strm. Robert Oswald
Uscha. Heinz Fiebig
Uscha. Erwin Reisch
Oscha. Lehman
Strm. Fehrmann
Uscha. Schulz
Strm. Pitt Roland
Rttf. Langholz

Rttf. Ludwig Schulz
Rttf. Walter Rudolf
Oscha. Sepp Hafner
Strm. Paul Kleinschmidt
Strm. Paul Müller

Senior NCO: Hscha. Seidel
Account & Pay NCO: Oscha. Walter Havemann
Motor Transport Sergeant: Oscha. Michael Heimes

Château Songeons Quarters of the Third Company, 101st SS Panzer Battalion prior to the invasion.

Standing in the second Schwimmwagen is SS-Hauptsturmführer Schweimer; in the foreground is his wife.

The 3rd Company tries out its new Schwimmwagen amphibious cars.

SS-Obersturmführer
Hanno Raasch.

SS-Untersturmführer Alfred
Günther (seen here while still
an SS-Hauptsturmführer).

SS-Untersturmführer Thomas
Amselgruber (as an
Scharführer, 1936).

Conference during
Battalion maneuvers in
May 1944. *From left:*
SS-Untersturmführer
Willi Iriohn, SS-
Sturmbannführer Heinz
von Westernhagen and
SS-Obersturmführer
Hanno Raasch.

The commander of the IInd Platoon of the 3rd Company, 101st SS Panzer
Battalion, SS-Hauptscharführer Max Görgens. Standing in the turret, on the
left is loader Kupp, and below left the radio operator Frahm Görgen's driver
and gunner were Peukert and Ewald.

The battalion commander, SS-Sturmbannführer von Westernhagen, talking to the commander of the 3rd Company, SS-Obersturmführer Raasch (in the coat), left: SS-Untersturmführer Iriohn.

SS-Sturmbannführer von Westernhagen (in camouflage uniform) listens as SS-Obersturmführer Raasch explains how he intends to proceed. Behind the Tiger's gun is SS-Unterscharführer Hofmann, Raasch's driver, and third from the right SS-Unterscharführer Otto Blase, a tank commander in the 3rd Company.

A 3rd Company Tiger during the battalion exercise,

In the field Tigers of the 3rd Company, 101st SS Panzer Battalion practice various attack formation, such as the inverted wedge and the arrowhead.

Tigers during the battalion exercise in the Beauvais area in May 1944.

Tiger 321 of the 3rd Company.

SS-Obersturmführer Raasch and battalion commander Hein von Westernhagen (right).

Tiger 232 of the 2nd Company.

SS-Untersturmführer Amselgruber in Tiger 304.

Tiger crew of the
1st Company, 101st
SS Panzer Battalion
with a tame raven.
Second from left in
the top photo is
tank commander
SS-Junker Erwin Asbach.

Fuelling one of the command panzers.

Moser, Magerle, and Jahn of the 2nd Company's maintenance echelon in front of their 2-tonne prime mover.

Men of the 3rd Company's maintenance echelon. *From left:* Alwin Götz, Wilhelm Weishaupt and Neubrand.

Krüger, Georg Sittek, Neubrand and Götz of the 3rd Company's maintenance echelon.

SS-Hauptsturmführer
Rolf Möbius

SS-Untersturmführer
Fritz Stamm.

SS-Untersturmführer
Walter Hahn.

Tiger commander
SS-Standartenjunker and
Knight's Cross wearer
Franz Staudegger.

SS-Obersturmführer
Hannes Philipsen.

Michael Wittmann.

SS-Unterscharführer Balthasar Woll and Jupp Sälzer, tank driver. Wittmann's gunner from the Eastern front was now a tank commander.

Bobby Woll.

Woll and Sälzer.

Index

Page numbers in italics indicate illustrations.

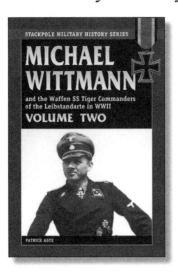

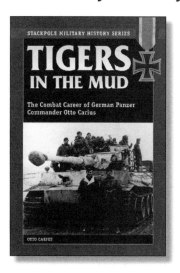

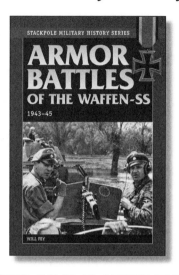